Library of
Davidson College

THE NAVY OF THE

AMERICAN REVOLUTION

The Navy of the American Revolution

Its Administration, its Policy and its Achievements

A DISSERTATION

Submitted to the Faculty of the
Graduate School of Arts and Literature
In Candidacy for the Degree of
Doctor of Philosophy
Department of History

By
CHARLES OSCAR PAULLIN

HASKELL HOUSE PUBLISHERS Ltd.
Publishers of Scarce Scholarly Books
NEW YORK, N. Y. 10012
1971

First Published 1906

HASKELL HOUSE PUBLISHERS LTD.
Publishers of Scarce Scholarly Books
280 LAFAYETTE STREET
NEW YORK, N. Y. 10012

973.3
P329n

Library of Congress Catalog Card Number: 73-122997

Standard Book Number 8383-1130-X

86-3589

Printed in the United States of America

PREFACE

Several narrative accounts of the navy of the American Revolution have been written. These usually form the introductory part of a history of the American Navy since 1789. The earliest of these accounts is that of Thomas Clark, published in 1814, and probably the best that of James Fenimore Cooper, first printed in 1839. Later narratives are rather more popular than Cooper's. Many sources of information, which were not accessible to the earlier writers, and were not much used by the later, were drawn upon in the writing of this book. Moreover, the information that is here presented is of a somewhat different sort from that of previous writers; and the method of treatment is new.

This book is written from the point of view of the naval administrators; hitherto, historians have written from the point of view of the naval officers. Their narratives treat almost exclusively of the doings at sea, the movements of armed vessels, and the details of sea fights. They have the advantage of dealing primarily with picturesque, and sometimes dramatic, events. Their accounts, however, lack unity, since they consist of a series of detached incidents.

In the first place an attempt has been here made to restore the naval administrative machinery of the Revolution. The center of this narrative is the origin, organization, and work of naval committees, secretaries of marine, navy boards, and naval agents. Next, inasmuch as the men who served as naval executives administered the laws relating to naval affairs, and indeed often prepared these laws before their adoption by the legislative authorities, it was thought best to give a fairly complete *resume* of the naval legislation of the Revolution. Those laws with which the naval administrators were chiefly concerned have received most attention. The legislation with reference to prize courts and privateering has been treated more briefly. As the privateers do not, properly speaking, form a part of the Revolutionary navy, no attempt to write their history has been made. In order that the subject may be seen in its true relations, some statistics and other interesting facts concerning this industry have, however, been introduced. An account of the State Navies is now given for the first time.

Since naval committees, navy boards, and naval agents issued written orders to the naval commanders prescribing the time place, and manner of their cruises, it has seemed logical and proper to consider the naval policy of the administrators, and the movements of the armed vessels. So detailed an account of naval movements, as would be given by those writers who proceed from the point of view of the doings of the naval officers, would obviously not be expected in this book. My plan has been to describe the various classes of naval movements, to present the sum total of their results, and to give briefly the details of a few typical cruises and sea fights. The cruises of the American vessels were much alike; they were minor affairs, and many of them scarcely merit individual treatment.

It is evident that one who proposes to write the history of the navy of the American Revolution from the point of view which I have described, will not only avoid excessive detail in respect to individual naval achievements, but will be particularly determined not to allow their brilliancy or their dramatic quality to fix the amount of detail with which each shall be narrated. For instance, several historians have been inclined to dwell at some length upon the brilliant and picturesque achievements of John Paul Jones. Sometimes they have devoted more than one-third of their narratives of the Continental navy to this hero, undoubtedly the greatest naval officer of the Revolution. As a result, the pictures which they have presented are somewhat distorted, and many brave sea officers have had scant justice done their gallant services.

An attempt is made in this book to present a better balanced narrative, and to make a juster estimate of the work of the Revolutionary navy. The scope and method of treatment adopted by the author has compelled a certain economy of phrase, precision of statement, and sharpness of outline.

I am very grateful to the many persons who have assisted me. Space does not permit me to thank each of them by name. I am under special obligations to the librarians and officials of the Library of Congress, the Library of the Department of the Navy, the Bureau of Rolls and Library of the Department of State, the State Library of Massachusetts, the Office of the Massachusetts State Archives, the Boston Public Library, the Boston Athenaeum, the Library of Harvard University, the State Library of Rhode Island, the Rhode Island Historical Society, the State Library of Connecticut, the Connecticut Historical Society, the Pennsylvania Historical Society, the State Library of Virginia, the Virginia Historical Society, the Office of the Secretary of State of South Carolina, the Charleston (South Carolina) Public Library, and the Library of the University of Chicago. Far more than to any one else, I am indebted to Professor John Franklin Jameson, Director of the Department of Historical Research in the Carnegie Institution of Washington. I have had the advantage of Professor Jameson's extensive knowledge of bibliography, his fruitful suggestions as to treatment, and his painstaking care in reading and criticising my manuscript. Parts of the narrative, somewhat popularized, have appeared in the Proceedings of the United States Naval Institute and the Sewanee Review.

C. O. P.

Washington, D. C.
March 1, 1906.

CONTENTS

THE CONTINENTAL NAVY

CHAPTER I.—The Naval Committee.

The need in 1775 for an army and for a navy	31
Agitation for a navy outside of Congress	32
Agitation for a navy in Congress	34
The first naval legislation	35
Appointment of the Naval Committee	38
First work of the Naval Committee	38
Reconstitution of the Naval Committee	38
John Adams's description of the Naval Committee	39
The organization and decline of the Naval Committee	40
Growth in Congress of naval sentiment	41
Naval legislation under the Naval Committee	42
The procuring of a fleet	51
The appointment of officers	52
The first naval expedition	55
Résumé of the work of the Naval Committee	60

Contents

CHAPTER II.—The Fleets of Washington and Arnold.

Fitting out of the "Hannah"	61
Fitting out of Washington's "Boston fleet"	62
Washington's opinion of his commanders	64
Services rendered by Washington's "Boston fleet"	65
Broughton and Selman's raid on Prince Edward island	66
The disposition of Washington's prizes	67
The delay in bringing them to trial	68
History of the fleet after the evacuation of Boston	69
Washington's "New York fleet"	70
Beginning of the fleet on lakes Champlain and George	71
Its increase in the summer of 1776	72
The work of Benedict Arnold	73
The British fleet on the Lakes	76
The battle of Lake Champlain, October 11-13, 1776	77
Results of the naval campaign on the Lakes	77

CHAPTER III.—The Organization of the Marine Committee.

The maritime interests of New England	79
Naval enterprise in Rhode Island	80
The naval situation in Congress, 1775-76	81
The Rhode Island instructions	81

Contents

The debate in Congress thereon.	82
Postponement of action on instructions.	83
Favorable action by Congress, December 11, 1775.	85
Decision of Congress to build thirteen frigates.	85
Appointment of the Marine Committee	86
The Marine Committee absorbs the Naval Committee.	87
The organization and pay of the Marine Committee.	87
Its chairmen.	88
Other valuable members.	90
Naval agents for building the Continental frigates.	90
Prize agents.	93
Continental agents.	95
Aid rendered the Marine Committee.	95
Navy Board at Philadelphia.	96
Navy Board at Boston.	97
Designations of the boards.	99
The organization of the boards.	100
The personnel of the boards.	101
Salaries.	102
Enumeration of the principal agents of the Marine Committee.	103
Minor agents.	103

CHAPTER IV.—The Work of the Navy Boards and the Marine Committee.

Lack of system in the Naval Department of the Revolution.	104
Examples.	105

Work and duties of the navy boards..	107
Men and materials needed in building a ship.	110
Provisions needed in fitting out a ship	112
Division of labor among the naval commissioners.	112
The heavy work of the Boston Board..	113
Two-fold duties of the Marine Committee.	115
Administrative duties of the Marine Committee	116
Naval uniform.	117
Communications of the Marine Committee.	118
Reports of the Marine Committee.	120
Naval legislation under the Marine Committee.	121
Naval increases	121
Naval appointments and promotions..	123
Relative rank.	125
Captures and the sharing of prizes.	126
Privateers.	127
Naval pay.	128
Naval pensions.	129
Courts-martial and courts of enquiry..	131
Important naval trials.	133
The case of Commodore Esek Hopkins	134
Provision for the fleet of Count D'Estaing.	139
The Marine Committee as a consular bureau	139

Contents

CHAPTER V.—The Conditions of the Continental Naval Service.

The recent revolution in navies and naval conditions...... 141
Constancy of the principles of naval strategy...... 143
Maritime conditions in America in 1775, and in 1900...... 144
Difficulties in procuring seamen during the Revolution...... 144
The privateers of the Revolution...... 147
State navies...... 152
The naval defence of America...... 153
Naval stations of the Americans...... 154
Naval stations of the British...... 155
Comparison of the British and American navies...... 156
Weakness of the American navies...... 159
Diffusion of authority in naval administration...... 160

CHAPTER VI.—Movements of the Continental Fleet under the Marine Committee.

Work of the fleet of a non-military character...... 161
Classification of military operations... 162
Primary naval operations...... 163
Enumeration of secondary operations. 164
Defence of American commerce...... 164
Coöperation with the army...... 166
The striking of the enemy's lines of communication...... 167

Commerce-destroying.................. 169
The threatening and attacking of the
  enemy's coasts...................... 173
A naval plan of Robert Morris......... 174
The Marine Committee and its plans... 176
Success and failure of the navy....... 177
The navy of the Revolution and of the
  Spanish-American war............... 179

CHAPTER VII.—The Board of Admiralty.

Defects of the Marine Committee...... 181
Criticism of the administration of Congress.............................. 182
A new system of Executives........... 184
Criticism of the Naval Department by
  Washington and Jay................. 184
Establishment of a Board of Admiralty,
  October, 1779...................... 187
Powers and duties of the Board of Admiralty............................ 188
Salaries.............................. 189
Selection of commissioners of Admiralty 190
Francis Lewis and William Ellery..... 193
Congress and the Board of Admiralty . 194
Work of the Board of Admiralty...... 195
Decrease in naval machinery.......... 195
Reports of the Board of Admiralty.... 196
Naval legislation under the Board of
  Admiralty.......................... 197
The granting of naval commissions by
  the states......................... 201
The American navy and British models 202
Court of appeals for prize cases....... 203

The fleet under the Board of Admiralty 203
Embarrassments of the Board of Admiralty. 204
Success and failure of the fleet........ 205
Discontinuance of the Board of Admiralty. 208
Defects of the Board of Admiralty.... 209

CHAPTER VIII.—The Secretary of Marine and the Agent of Marine.

The two factions during the Revolution 210
Supremacy of the "dispersive school". 211
The "concentrative school" in 1780.... 212
Agitation for administrative reform.... 213
The success of the "concentrative school"............................ 214
Establishment of the office of Secretary of Marine, February, 1781.......... 216
Duties of the Secretary of Marine...... 216
Appointment of McDougall as Secretary of Marine..................... 217
Failure to obtain a Secretary of Marine............................... 218
Robert Morris and the naval business. 218
Reorganization of the Naval Department............................. 220
The Agent of Marine................. 223
Robert Morris as Agent of Marine..... 226
The organization of the Naval Department under Morris................. 227
Reports of the Agent of Marine....... 228
Naval legislation under the Agent of Marine... 228

The court-martialing of three seamen.. 230
Morris and the control of the fleet. ... 234
The strength of the navy............. 235
Success and failure of the fleet........ 235
The cruise of the "Alliance," 1782-1783 236
The capture of the "Trumbull" by the
 "Iris"........................... 238
Attempts of Morris to increase the navy 239
Morris's views after the treaty of peace 244
Congress goes out of the naval business 245
Settling of the naval accounts........ 245
Disposing of the naval vessels......... 247
Retirement of the Agent of Marine.... 250
The end of the naval business......... 250

CHAPTER IX.—Naval Duties of American Representatives in Foreign Countries.

Mutual interests of the United States
 and France...................... 252
Duties of the Naval Office at Paris.... 252
Personnel of the Naval Office......... 254
Communication with the Naval Office.. 255
Agents of the Naval Office............ 256
Appointment and recommendation of
 officers.......................... 257
Privateers........................... 260
The purchase and construction of vessels............................. 261
The fitting out of vessels............. 265
The trial of prize cases............... 266
American prisoners................... 267
Breaches of neutrality................ 273

| Contents | 19 |

Miscellaneous duties.................. 274
The Naval Office a channel of naval intelligence......................... 276
Naval plans of the Naval Office....... 276
Plan of the Committee of Foreign Affairs............................. 278

CHAPTER X.—Naval Duties of American Representatives in Foreign Countries. Continued.

Work of the Naval Office in 1777..... 281
Attempts to obtain the freedom of French ports....................... 282
The first prizes of the "Reprisal".... 283
Difficulties between the English and the French governments................ 284
The American Commissioners and the French government................ 285
The cruise of the "Reprisal," February, 1777.............................. 286
The cruise of Conyngham in the "Surprise"............................. 287
The cruise of the "Reprisal," "Lexington," and "Dolphin".............. 287
Strained relations between the Commissioners and the French Court....... 289
The cruise of Conyngham in the "Revenge"............................. 290
Departure of the "Reprisal" and the "Lexington"....................... 291
Naval movements in 1778............ 292
The cruise of Captain Jones in the "Ranger"........................ 293

The Naval Office at Paris, 1779–1780 .. 294
John Paul Jones and Peter Landais .. 294
Plan for an expedition against England 295
The cruise of Captain Jones in the "Bon
 Homme Richard"................. 295
Dispute between Jones and Landais.... 298
Their departure for America......... 300
The trials of Franklin............... 300
Work of the Naval Office, 1781–1783. 301
Thomas Barclay, consul and commis-
 sioner........................... 302
John Paul Jones, agent for settling ac-
 counts.......................... 303
Naval stations in the West Indies...... 305
Duties and work of the commercial
 agent at Martinique............... 305
Naval affairs on the Mississippi........ 307
Oliver Pollock and Galvez............ 307
Pollock and privateers............... 308
Pollock and the "Rebecca"........... 308
The "West Florida"................. 310

THE STATE NAVIES

CHAPTER XI.—The Navy of Massachusetts.

The state craft..................... 315
Naval administration in the states.... 316
The problems of naval warfare........ 317
Military situation in Massachusetts,
 1775............................ 318
Action of the Provincial Congress...... 318

Massachusetts seaports ask for naval
    aid.............................. 319
Act establishing privateering and prize
    courts, November 1, 1775........... 320
Subsequent naval activities of the General court, 1775.................. 323
The fitting out of a fleet, 1776......... 324
Naval legislation, 1776............... 325
Remodelling of the law of November 1,
    1775.............................. 327
Orders to naval officers—a sample.... 328
Establishment of a Board of War, October, 1776....................... 329
Duties of the Board of War........... 330
A new naval establishment........... 333
Naval rules and regulations........... 334
Naval increases, 1777–1779 335
Launching of the "Protector"......... 336
Naval administration, 1779–1783...... 337
Naval increases, 1780–1783........... 338
Massachusetts privateers............. 339
The cruises of the state fleet.......... 341
Coöperation of state vessels and privateers............................ 344
The engagements of the state vessels—
    a sample........................ 345
The Penobscot expedition............ 347
Losses of the state fleet.............. 352
The end of the navy................. 353

CHAPTER XII.—The Navy of Connecticut.

The Revolutionary government of Connecticut........................ 354

Fitting out of the "Minerva" and the "Spy".............................. 355
Failure and discharge of the "Minerva"................................ 357
The "Defence" and the "Oliver Cromwell"................................ 358
The building of three row-galleys.... 360
Naval duties of the Governor and the Council of Safety................... 360
Naval agents......................... 361
New London and Nathaniel Shaw, jr.. 362
Bushnell's submarine boat............ 363
Privateers and prize courts........... 364
Naval pensions....................... 366
Naval rules and regulations.......... 366
A new naval establishment, 1779..... 366
Cruises of the navy.................. 367
Losses of the navy................... 369
Warfare of whale-boats on Long Island Sound........................... 370

CHAPTER XIII.—The Navy of Pennsylvania.

Objects of naval enterprise in Pennsylvania.............................. 373
The fleet of galleys.................. 373
Rules and regulations................ 375
The "Montgomery".................. 375
Strength of the navy, August, 1776... 376
Naval uniforms and flag.............. 377
Organs of naval administration....... 377
Commodores of the navy............. 378
Naval pay and the sharing of prizes.. 380

The Pennsylvania Navy Board....... 381
Work of the Navy Board............ 382
The navy in 1777................... 383
Services rendered by the fleet......... 383
The campaign on the Delaware, 1777–
 1778............................ 384
Trials for desertion.................. 386
The Navy Board, 1777–1778.......... 387
The fleet, April–July, 1778............ 388
Sale of the fleet and dismissal of the
 Navy Board...................... 388
The "General Greene," 1779.......... 390
Naval legislation.................... 391
Privateers.......................... 392
Commissioners for the defence of the
 Delaware........................ 393
The "Hyder Ally" and "Washington" 394
The end of the navy................. 395

CHAPTER XIV.—The Navy of Virginia.

Lord Dunmore's movements in Virgin-
 ia, 1775.......................... 396
Authorization of a navy, December,
 1775............................ 396
Work of the Committee of Safety...... 397
The "Potomac River fleet".......... 398
The Virginia Navy Board............ 398
Duties of the Navy Board........... 399
The location of shipyards............ 400
Naval manufactories and magazines... 401
James Maxwell, naval agent.......... 401
Naval officers...................... 401
Naval increases, 1776............... 402

Courts of Admiralty.................. 403
Privateers........................... 405
The vessels of the Virginia navy....... 405
Condition and services of the navy, 1775–1779........................ 407
Losses of the navy, 1775–1779........ 408
The Board of War and the Naval Commissioner......................... 408
The Commissioner of the Navy........ 409
Military situation in the South in 1780 410
Naval legislation, 1780................ 411
The raid of Arnold and Phillips, 1781. 413
The navy at Yorktown............... 415
Dismissal of the officers, seamen, and Commissioner..................... 415
Virginia's defence of Chesapeake Bay, 1782–1783........................ 415
The end of the navy................. 416

CHAPTER XV.—The Navy of South Carolina.

First naval enterprises of South Carolina............................. 418
Events of September, 1775........... 419
The "Defence"...................... 420
Work of the Provincial Congress, November, 1775..................... 420
Work of the Committee of Safety, December, 1775..................... 421
The mission of Cochran.............. 421
Naval legislation, February–March, 1776 422
The Constitution of 1776............. 423
Naval legislation, April, 1776......... 423

South Carolina Navy Board............ 424
Work and organization of the Navy
  Board........................... 424
Naval legislation, 1777-1778.......... 427
Naval increases, 1776-1779........... 428
Privateers........................... 429
Services rendered by the South Carolina navy, 1776-1779............... 429
The "Randolph" and the State fleet... 430
The campaign against Charleston, 1779–1780............................. 431
The navy in 1781 and 1783........... 434
Commodore Gillon and the "South Carolina"............................ 435
Gillon in Europe..................... 436
The "South Carolina" in European waters............................ 436
The expedition against the Bahamas.. 438
The "South Carolina" at Philadelphia. 439
Capture of the "South Carolina"...... 439
Settlement of the Luxembourg claims.. 439

CHAPTER XVI.—The Minor Navies of the Southern States.

Organs of naval administration in Maryland.......................... 441
Work of the Maryland Provincial Convention, 1776...................... 441
Work of the Maryland Committee of Safety, 1776...................... 441
Maryland vessels..................... 442
Recruiting of the navy............... 443
Naval officers....................... 443

Court of Admiralty................. 444
Maryland privateers................ 444
Sale of naval vessels, 1779.......... 444
Naval conditions, 1779–1783.......... 445
Acts for the defence of the Chesapeake 445
Transporting of the Continental army. 446
British depredations, 1782–1783...... 446
Commissioners for the defence of the
   Bay............................. 447
Services rendered by the Maryland
   navy............................ 448
The Battle of the Barges............. 449
End of the Maryland navy............ 451
The navy of North Carolina, December,
   1775–May, 1776................. 451
The "Washington," "Pennsylvania
   Farmer," and "King Tammany".... 452
The defence of Ocracoke Inlet......... 454
Services of the "Caswell"............ 456
North Carolina admiralty courts and
   privateers....................... 459
Georgia's first naval enterprise........ 459
Naval preparations.................. 460
Georgia's galleys.................... 460
Georgia's prize court................ 462

CHAPTER XVII.—The Minor Navies of the
Northern States.

British depredations in Rhode Island,
   1775............................ 463
Naval operations.................... 463
The "Katy" and "Washington"....... 464

Contents

The "Washington" and "Spitfire" galleys.............................. 465
Organs of naval administration........ 466
Prize court and privateers............ 467
An attempted naval increase, 1777..... 468
Coöperation of Rhode Island with Congress, 1778-1779.................. 468
The "Pigot" and the "Argo"......... 469
The "Rover"....................... 470
Naval preparations in New York..... 471
New York's naval establishment....... 472
Washington and the New York vessels 473
Services of the New York fleet........ 474
Additional facts about naval affairs in New York......................... 475
New Hampshire and the Penobscot expedition.......................... 476
New Hampshire privateers and prize court............................ 476
Naval suggestions of New Jersey...... 477

APPENDICES

A bibliography....................... 481
A list of commissioned officers in the Continental Navy................. 506
A list of commissioned officers in the Continental Marine Corps.......... 512
A list of armed vessels............... 516

PART I
THE CONTINENTAL NAVY

CHAPTER I

THE NAVAL COMMITTEE

The history of the Continental navy covers a period of ten years, extending from 1775 to 1785. During this time the Continental Congress made many experiments in naval legislation and devised several organs of naval administration. The first of these organs, with whose origin and work this chapter is concerned, was the Naval Committee. It lasted for only a few months. Its lineal successors, each of which will be duly considered, were the Marine Committee, the Board of Admiralty, and the Agent of Marine. These four executive organs, for the most part, administered the Continental navy. Certain odds and ends of the naval business, however, fell to the commander-in-chief of the army and his officers, and to the American representatives in foreign countries. The second chapter will treat of the fleets of the army, and the closing chapters of the narrative of the Continental navy will consider the naval services of our representatives in foreign lands.

In maritime countries the military service is generally ambidextrous. Whether the army or navy is first brought into play at the opening of a war depends upon various circumstances. The presence of a British army at Boston, already on colonial soil, when the American Revolution broke out early in 1775, naturally led to the immediate organization of an army by the colonists. The need of a navy was at this time not quite so insistent. Moreover, the building, or even the purchase, of an armed fleet required more time than did the raising of an army, which was rendered comparatively easy by the previous training of the colonists in the local militia. Nevertheless, since both countries engaged in the war were maritime, the creating of a navy could not long be delayed.

The reader recollects that by the middle of 1775 the battles of Lexington, Concord, and Bunker Hill had been fought, a Continental army had been organized, and Washington had been made commander-in-chief. Outside of Congress the agitation in behalf of a Continental navy had begun. That the first suggestions and advances for a navy should come from New England, where the concrete problems of the defence of her ports and coasts were being faced, was to be expected. One of the first men to make such suggestions was Josiah Quincy of Massachusetts. On July 11, 1775, he wrote to John Adams in Philadelphia that the best method of securing the coastwise navigation of the colonies was by row-galleys. He then continued: "As the whole Continent is so firmly united, why not a Number of Vessels of War be fitted out and judiciously stationed, so as to intercept and prevent any supplies going to our Enemies; and consequently, unless they can make an Impression inland, they must leave the Country or starve."[1] The first formal movement in behalf of a Continental navy came from Rhode Island, which state was during the summer of 1775 suffering serious annoyances from the British ships. On August 26 her legislature instructed the Rhode Island delegates to the Continental Congress to use their influence at the ensuing session of Congress to obtain a fleet for the protection of the colonies.[2] On September 2, 1775, Washington, in order to prevent reinforcements from reaching the enemy at Boston, instructed Nicholson Broughton to proceed in the schooner "Hannah" on a cruise against the British transports.[3]

---
1. Manuscript Letters of John Adams, lodged with the Massachusetts Historical Society by Mr. Charles Francis Adams, who kindly permitted the writer to see them.
2. See Chapter III, The Organization of the Marine Committee.
3. See Chapter II, The Fleets of Washington and Arnold. After a thorough investigation and study of the sources of the early history of the Continental navy, I am compelled to reject many of the statements and conclusions found in Chapter II, Volume I, of Augustus

That the question of providing a Continental navy would come up during the fall session of Congress was certain. The arguments in its behalf, which were made almost unanimously later in the session, must have been on the lips of several of the members when they assembled in Philadelphia in September: an army had been organized, why not a navy? The situation of the combatants, separated by the great Atlantic highway; and their character, one a great naval and commercial power, and the other with maritime interests by no means inconsiderable, would necessarily make the impending struggle in no small part a naval one. America had seacoasts and seaports to be defended, a coastwise navigation to be secured, and above all commercial and diplomatic communications with foreign powers to be kept open. These communications were a jugular vein, whose severing would mean death to the United Colonies. The urgent and specific calls for armed vessels, which were being made, must be met at once. Had not America conveniently at hand materials for ships, and abundant men who had the "habit of the sea"?

In the early months of the session there certainly would arise opposition to the new military project. The inertia and conserv-

---

C. Buell's book, Paul Jones, Founder of the American Navy.

atism of some of the members would set them against so great an innovation. To others the fitting out of a fleet, at a time when the length, seriousness, and meaning of the war with the motherland were but half unveiled, would seem an unwise and hasty action.

The question of procuring a fleet of armed vessels was first brought to the attention of Congress on October 3, 1775, when the Rhode Island members presented their instructions, an account of which will be given in a succeeding chapter.[1] It is sufficient for present purposes to say that until December the Rhode Island instructions had little other result beyond crystallizing and clarifying opinion on naval affairs by means of the debates which they caused in Congress.

On October 5 sundry letters from London were laid before the Congress and read. They conveyed the intelligence of "the sailing of two north country built brigs, of no force, from England, on the 11th of August last, loaded with arms, powder, and other stores, for Quebec, without convoy." Congress at once saw the importance of capturing these two vessels, in order both to deprive the British of these stores and to obtain them for the Continental army around Boston, which sorely needed all the munitions of war it could get. A motion was

---

[1] See Chapter III, The Organization of the Marine Committee.

therefore made that a committee of three be appointed to prepare a plan for intercepting the two brigs, and that it "proceed on this business immediately."[1] John Adams in his autobiography says that the opposition to this motion was "very loud and vehement," and included some of his own colleagues, and also especially Edward Rutledge of South Carolina. It seems to have been recognized that the carrying of the motion would be the initial step in the establishment of a Continental navy. Such an undertaking its opponents declared, with a greater display of rhetoric than judgment, was the "most wild, visionary, mad project that ever had been imagined. It was an infant taking a mad bull by his horns; and what was more profound and remote, it was said it would ruin the character and corrupt the morals of all our seamen. It would make them selfish, piratical, mercenary, bent wholly upon plunder, etc., etc." The friends of the motion, in colors equally glowing, set forth "the great advantages of distressing the enemy, supplying ourselves, and beginning a system of maritime and naval operations." On the taking of the vote the motion passed in the affirmative; and ac-

---

1. Journals of Continental Congress, October 5, 1775. Waite, H. E., Origin of American Navy, 1-5, containing letters of John Adams, Elbridge Gerry, and John Langdon, written in 1813.

cording to John Adams's recollection, he, John Langdon of New Hampshire, and Silas Deane of Connecticut, "three members who had expressed much zeal in favor of the motion," composed the committee.[1]

A little later on the same day this committee reported; and thereupon Congress decided to write a letter to Washington directing him to obtain from the Council of Massachusetts two of that state's cruisers, and to despatch them on the errand of intercepting the two supply ships. It also directed that letters be written to the governors of Connecticut and Rhode Island asking for the loan of some of their armed vessels, which were to be sent on the same mission. "The committee appointed to prepare a plan for intercepting the two vessels bound to Canada" made another report on the 6th, which was ordered to lie on the table "for the perusal of the members."[2] This report was acted upon on October 13, when Congress decided to fit out two armed vessels, one of ten and the other of fourteen guns, to cruise three months to the

---

1. Works of John Adams, III, 7, 8. I have accepted the account of this debate as found in John Adams's autobiography, although it is possible that writing many years after its occurrence Adams may have confused it with the debate of October 7 on the Rhode Island resolutions.—Works of John Adams, I, 187.

2. Journals of Continental Congress, October 6, 1775.

eastward for the purpose of intercepting the enemy's transports laden with warlike stores and other supplies. A committee consisting of Silas Deane, John Langdon, and Christopher Gadsden of South Carolina was appointed to estimate the expense which would be incurred in fitting out the two vessels.[1]

In four days this new committee reported an estimate, which was unsatisfactory and was recommitted.[2] When it again reported on October 30, two more vessels, one to mount not more than twenty and the other not more than thirty-six guns, were ordered to be prepared for sea, and "to be employed in such manner, for the protection and defence of the United Colonies, as the Congress shall direct." It should be noted that the two vessels for which provision was now made were to engage in the defence of the colonies, and not merely in the interception of transports, an indication of an advance in the naval policy of Congress. Four additional members were now added to the committee, Stephen Hopkins of Rhode Island, Joseph Hewes of North Carolina, R. H. Lee of Virginia, and John Adams of Massachusetts.[3] This reconstituted committee

---

1. Journals of Continental Congress, October 13, 1775. The armament of the second vessel was not determined until October 30, 1775.
2. Ibid., October 17, 1775.
3. Ibid., October 30, 1775. John Adams, in his Notes on Debates for October 30, 1775,

composed of seven members was sometimes called "the committee for fitting out armed vessels," occasionally the "Marine Committee," but most frequently the "Naval Committee." It secured for its use a room in a public house in Philadelphia, and in order that there should be no conflict between its meetings and those of Congress, it fixed its hours from six in the evening until the close of its business. Its sessions were sometimes pleasantly continued, even until midnight, by conversational diversions, marked by a rich flow of soul, history, poetry, wine, and Jamaica rum.

John Adams, who always wrote pungently, has left us a lively picture of the Naval Committee. His description makes it clear that the deliberations of this committee were not always marked by that exalted seriousness and impassive dignity, which we too habitually ascribe to the Revolutionary Fathers. "The pleasantest part of my labors for the four years I spent in Congress from 1774 to 1778," he said, "was in this Naval Committee. Mr. Lee, Mr. Gadsden, were sensible men, and very cheerful, but Governor Hopkins of Rhode Island, above

reports George Ross of Pennsylvania as saying: "We can't get seamen to man four vessels. We could not get seamen to man our boats, our galleys." Adams also tells us that three of the Virginia members, Wythe, Nelson, and Lee, were "for fitting out four ships." —Works of John Adams, II, 484.

seventy years of age, kept us all alive. Upon business, his experience and judgment were very useful. But when the business of the evening was over, he kept us in conversation till eleven, and sometimes twelve o'clock. His custom was to drink nothing all day, nor till eight o'clock in the evening, and then his beverage was Jamaica spirit and water. It gave him wit, humor, anecdotes, science, and learning. He had read Greek, Roman, and British history, and was familiar with English poetry, particularly Pope, Thomson, and Milton, and the flow of his soul made all of his reading our own, and seemed to bring to recollection in all of us, all we had ever read. I could neither eat nor drink in these days. The other gentlemen were very temperate. Hopkins never drank to excess, but all he drank was immediately not only converted into wit, sense, knowledge, and good humor, but inspired us with similar qualities."[1]

The active life of the Naval Committee lasted from October, 1775, until January, 1776, during which time it laid the foundations of the navy. Its chairman in January, 1776, was Stephen Hopkins; whether he was the first to fill this position is not known. His knowledge of the business of shipping made him particularly useful to the Committee.[2] The accounts of the Naval Com-

1. Works of John Adams, III, 9, 12.
2. Appleton's Cyclopedia of American Biography, III, 259.

Navy of the American Revolution 41

mittee were kept by Joseph Hewes, who was settling them with the Board of Treasury in September, 1776.[1] Early in December, 1775, John Adams returned home, and by January only four members of the Committee were left to transact its business.

In October Congress ordered the fitting out of four vessels, and appointed the Naval Committee, but did nothing more. By the first of November the sentiment of Congress was setting strongly towards organizing a navy. In its debates on the State of Trade during the latter half of October the necessity of having a navy in order both to defend the colonial commerce and to carry on the war was generally recognized.[2] The members from the South were as a rule now lining up with those of the North in behalf of a naval armament. Events had happened and were daily happening in New England which were convincing the doubtful members of Congress. As a military necessity

---

1. Journals of Continental Congress, September 19, 1776.
2. Works of John Adams, II, 469-83. In one of these debates, according to Adams, George Wythe of Virginia said: "Why should not America have a navy? No maritime power near the seacoast can be safe without it. It is no chimera. The Romans suddenly built one in their Carthaginian war. Why may not we lay a foundation for it? We abound with firs, iron ore, tar, pitch, turpentine; we have all the materials for the construction of a navy."
—Works of John Adams, II, 479.

for conducting the siege of Boston, and with no intention whatever to create a navy, as such, Washington had obtained seven small cruisers, and either had sent or was sending them to sea in pursuit of the enemy's transports. The logic of events had forced him, on his own responsibility, to create a little fleet of his own.[1]

With the passage of each day, the gap between the mother-country and her revolting subjects widened, and the feeling became stronger and more general that an irrepressible war, which must be fought to a just conclusion, had begun. What in October seemed chimerical, might in November appear practicable.

Beginning with November the naval legislation of Congress moved rapidly. The duty of preparing much of it naturally fell to the Naval Committee. Its work in large part may be found in the Journals of the Continental Congress for November and December, 1775, and January, 1776. A brief summary of the most important Congressional resolutions for this period will be here presented.

On November 2, 1775, Congress voted $100,000 for the work of the Naval Committee, and empowered it "to agree with such officers and seamen as are proper to man and command" the four vessels already

---

1. See Chapter II, The Fleets of Washington and Arnold.

ordered to be prepared for sea. Congress also fixed the "encouragement" of the officers and seamen at "one-half of all ships of war made prize of by them, and one-third of all transport vessels."[1]

On November 10 the first legislation relating to the Marine Corps of the United States was passed. Two battalions, which were to be called "the first and second battalions of American Marines," were to be raised, consisting of one colonel, two lieutenant-colonels, two majors, and "other officers as usual in other regiments." There is some doubt whether Congress fully understood the duties of marines, for it provided that "no persons be appointed to office, or inlisted into said Battalions, but such as are good seamen, or so acquainted with maritime affairs as to be able to serve to advantage by sea when required."[2] Such a requirement seems to overlook the fact that the duties of marines are military in character, rather than naval.

The Naval Committee made what probably was its most important report on No-

---

1. Journals of Continental Congress, November 2, 1775.

2. Ibid., November 10. Congress first ordered the marines to be raised from the Continental army, but on the objecting of Washington to such weakening of his forces, they were directed to be raised independent of the army.—Journals, November 10, 30, 1775; Ford, Writings of Washington, III, 225, 274.

vember 23, when it laid before Congress "a draught of rules for the government of the American navy, and articles to be signed by the officers and men employed in that service." On the 25th and 28th of November, these were debated by paragraphs and after slight amendment were adopted.[1] The rules, eight or ten pages in length, are brevity itself as compared with the present rules and regulations of the United States navy, which make a book of some six hundred pages. More than one-half of the navy's first rules are concerned with the feeding, care, rights, duties, and punishments of the ordinary sailor; while the present rules of the American navy in large part apply to officers.

A few of the provisions of these old rules are worthy of notice. The commanders of ships of the thirteen united colonies were "to take care that divine service be performed twice a day on board, and a sermon preached on Sundays, unless bad weather or other extraordinary accidents prevent." Sailors were to be punished for swearing by the wearing of a wooden collar, "or some other shameful badge of distinction." Sailors were to be put in irons for drunkenness; while officers guilty of the same offense forfeited two days' pay. The extreme punishment which an officer might inflict on a seaman was "twelve lashes upon his bare back,

---

1. Journals of Continental Congress, November 23, 25, 28, 1775.

with a cat of nine tails." In case a sailor deserved greater punishment, he must be tried by a court-martial, which should consist of "at least three captains and three first lieutenants, with three captains and three first lieutenants of marines, if there shall be so many of the marines then present, and the eldest captain shall preside." A penal code was established. A court-martial might inflict death for desertion, mutiny, or murder.

Rations for the sailors were fixed by these old rules for each day of the week. Saturday's bill of fare, which consisted of "1 ℔. bread, 1 ℔. pork, half pint peas, and four ounces cheese," may be taken as a sample one. Each seaman was given a half-pint of rum a day, with a "discretionary allowance on extra duty, and in time of engagement." The following provision, for keeping the eatables sweet and palatable, is noted: "The captain is frequently to order the proper officers to inspect the condition of the provisions, and if the bread proves damp, to have it aired upon the quarter deck or poop, and also examine the flesh cask, and if any of the pickle be leaked out, to have new made and put in, and the cask made tight and secure."

The following naval offices were established; the first two only were commissioned: captain, lieutenant, master, master's mate, boatswain, boatswain's first mate, boatswain's second mate, gunner, gunner's mate, surgeon, surgeon's mate, carpenter, carpenter's mate, cooper, captain's clerk, steward, and chaplain. Five marine offices were established; the highest was that of captain. A pay-table was provided, according to which the monthly wage ranged form $32 for captains, to $6.67 for able seamen and marines. According to the form of a contract of enlistment which accompanied the rules, a bounty of $400 was to be deducted from the proceeds of prizes and to be paid to the commander, in all cases where he lost a limb in the engagement, or was incapacitated from earning a livelihood; if the commander was killed, an equal sum was to be paid to his widow. Minor officers under the same circumstances received proportionately smaller sums. The man who first discovered a vessel that was afterwards captured was rewarded with a double share of prize money; he who first boarded a prize was entitled to a treble share. Ten shares of every prize were set aside "to be given to such inferior officers, seamen and marines, as shall be adjudged best to deserve them by the superior officers."

These rules, which were in force throughout the Revolution, and which were re-adopted for the government of the new navy under the Constitution,[1] were drawn up by

---
1. Thomas Clark, Naval History of United States, II, 108.

John Adams, and "examined, discussed, and corrected" by the Naval Committee. They are an abridgment and adaptation of parts of the British naval statutes and regulations in force in 1775. That part of Adams's rules which constitutes the penal code of the navy, he obtained from the Naval Discipline Act passed by the British Parliament in 1749.[1] In adapting the British code, however, he made it less stringent. The British also found it advisable in 1779 to lessen the severity of their code. The rest of Adams's rules are, with verbal changes and omissions, chiefly taken from the King's Regulations and Admiralty Instructions of 1772. An extract from the King's regulations followed by the corresponding one from Adams's rules will illustrate the closeness of the parallelism: "No Commander shall inflict any punishment upon a Seaman, beyond Twelve Lashes upon his bare Back with a Cat of Nine Tails, according to the ancient Practice of the Sea."[2] "No commander shall inflict any punishment upon a seaman beyond twelve lashes upon his bare back, with a cat of nine tails."

1. Pickering's Statutes, 22, George II, chapter 33; title of act, "An act for amending, explaining, and reducing into one Act of Parliament, the laws relating to the government of his Majesty's ships, vessels, and forces by sea."

2. King's Regulations and Admiralty Instructions of 1772.

An additional example of the influence of the British upon the American navy is found in the fact that the naval offices as given above were already established in the navy of the Stuarts, indeed, many of them in the navy of Elizabeth. The Americans were still British at the time of the Revolution, and they intuitively went home, so to speak, for the naval models with which they were familiar.

On November 25, 1775, Congress enacted some very important naval legislation, which in John Adams's opinion was "the true origin and foundation of the American navy," and in producing which he "had at least as great a share . . . . . as any man living."[1] The occasion of this legislation was certain recommendations of Washington. On October 5 he requested the "determination of Congress, as to the property and disposal of such vessels and cargoes, as are designed for the supply of the enemy and may fall into our hands." On November 8 he pointed out the necessity of establishing proper admiralty courts. On November 11

---

1. Works of John Adams, III, 11. Certain words of John Adams in a letter dated, Philadelphia, April 28, 1776, have an interest in this connection: "I have vanity enough to take to myself a share in the merit of the American navy. It was always a measure that my heart was much engaged in, and I pursued it for a long time against the wind and tide, but at last obtained it."—Force, American Archives, 4th, V, 1111.

he recommended to Congress the establishment of an admiralty court for the trial of prize cases arising from Continental captures.[1] A report of a committee of seven members, which had been appointed on the 17th to take Washington's request of November 8 into consideration, was, on the 23rd, laid on the table "for the perusal of the members," and was debated and agreed to by paragraphs on the 24th and 25th.[2] Congress now took the decisive step of authorizing the capture of all British vessels employed against the United Colonies, either as armed vessels of war, transports, or supply ships. Provision for privateering was made in part. It was recommended to the legislatures of the several colonies to establish courts for the trial of prize cases. In all cases appeals to Congress were to be allowed, when made in accordance with certain prescribed rules. Prosecutions in prize cases must commence in the court of that colony in which the capture was made, but if the capture took place on the open sea the captor had the privilege of selecting the most convenient court. Congress fixed the shares of the proceeds of prizes. In the case of

1. Ford, Writings of Washington, III, 165, 203-04, 213-14; Washington to President of Congress, October 5, November 8, 11, 1775. See Chapter II, page 67.
2. Journals of Continental Congress, November 17, 23, 24, and 25. The Journals for November 25 contain the resolutions.

privateers the whole of the proceeds of captures went to the captors. In the case of vessels fitted out by a colony, or by Congress, two-thirds were to go in the first instance to the colony, and in the second, to Congress; and one-third was to go to the captors: provided that, if the prize should be a vessel of war, the captor's share should be increased to one-half, and the government's share correspondingly decreased.

On December 2, 1775, Congress authorized the Naval Committee to employ two additional vessels, and also to "prepare a proper commission for the captains or commanders of the ships of war in the service of the United Colonies."[1] On the report of the committee on recaptures, Congress on December 5 fixed the compensation of recaptors, which varied from one-eighth to the whole of the value of the vessel and cargo, depending on the time which elapsed between the capture and recapture.[2] On December 9 the following new naval offices were established: midshipman, armorer, sailmaker, yeoman, quarter-master, quarter-gunner, cook, and coxswain.[3] On December 13 the wages of able-bodied seamen were raised to $8 a month; and on the 22nd

1. Journals of Continental Congress, December 2, 1775.
2. Ibid., December 5, 1775. This legislation refers to American vessels captured by the British and recaptured by the Americans.
3. Ibid., December 9, 1775.

the salary of the commander-in-chief of the navy was fixed at $125 a month.[1]

In accordance with the direction of Congress, the Naval Committee, on January 6, 1776, reported on the division of the captor's share of prizes, among officers, seamen, and marines; whereupon, Congress divided the captor's share into twenty parts, and allotted them equitably between the officers and men. The commander-in-chief received one-twentieth, and the captains of the fleet making the capture, two-twentieths. After the officers had been provided for, the remaining eight and one-half parts were allotted to the seamen, "share and share alike."[2]

Meanwhile, the Naval Committee had been busy purchasing, fitting for sea, and officering a fleet. About the first of November John Adams was writing from Philadelphia to James Warren in Massachusetts, inquiring whether naval vessels might be purchased or built in Massachusetts, and whether suitable officers could be procured there; and also at the same time to Samuel Chase in Baltimore, in regard to the purchase of certain vessels in that city.[3] On

---

1. Journals of Continental Congress, December 13 and 22, 1775.
2. Ibid., January 6, 1776.
3. Manuscript letters of John Adams, Massachusetts Historical Society; Warren to Adams, November 14, 1775; Chase to Adams, November 16 and 25, 1775.

November 17 the Committee ordered Silas Deane to go to New York and to purchase a 20-gun ship and a 10-gun Bermudan-built sloop.[1] Under the authorizations of Congress of October 13 and October 30, the Naval Committee purchased four vessels, the "Alfred," "Columbus," "Cabot," and "Andrew Doria;" named, respectively, for the founder of the English navy, the discoverer of America, the first English explorer of America, and the great Genoese Admiral.[2] The first vessel to be bought was the "Alfred," a ship of two hundred tons burden. The "Alfred" was originally the "Black Prince," and belonged to John Nixon, the well-known Philadelphia merchant of Revolutionary times.[3]

On November 5 the Naval Committee appointed Esek Hopkins, of Rhode Island, commander-in-chief of the fleet.[4] The Committee may have created this office as analogous to Washington's position in the army. It is more probable that the office was borrowed from the British navy, in which the

1. Collections of New York Historical Society, Deane Papers, I, 91-92.
2. Works of John Adams, III, 12.
3. M. I. J. Griffin, Commodore John Barry, 19; Pennsylvania Archives, 2nd, II, 668. In December, 1774, the "Black Prince" belonged to Thomas Willing, Robert Morris, Thomas Morris, John Wharton, and John Nixon.—Pa. Magazine of History and Biography, October, 1904, 495.
4. Edward Field's Esek Hopkins, 78-9.

commander-in-chief was the chief admiral of a port or station, who held command over all other admirals within his jurisdiction.[1] The first and only commander-in-chief of the American navy was at the time of his appointment fifty-seven years of age. He was a member of an influential Rhode Island family, and a brother of Stephen Hopkins, of the Naval Committee. About 1745 Esek Hopkins was a sea captain and merchant adventurer. In the French and Indian War he had commanded a privateer.[2] At the breaking out of the Revolution he received the appointment of captain and then of brigadier-general in the Rhode Island forces. Deliberate in action and irascible in temper, Hopkins was at the same time industrious, steadfast, and veracious. The following description was written by Henry Knox to his wife, probably in April, 1776: "I have been on board Admiral Hopkins' ship, and in company with his gallant son, who was wounded in the engagement with the 'Glasgow.' The admiral is an antiquated figure. He brought to my mind Van Tromp, the famous Dutch admiral. Though antiquated in figure, he is shrewd and sensible. I, whom you think not a little enthusiastic, should have taken him for an angel, only

---

1. British Marine Encyclopedia, in Hogg's Naval Magazine for 1801.
2. Edward Field, State of Rhode Island and Providence Plantations, II, 422.

he swore now and then."[1] The choice of Hopkins as head of the navy was, at the time, as promising as could have been made. On December 7, 1775, a commission was given to John Paul Jones, an energetic and capable young man, twenty-eight years old, whose brilliant career was still unforeseen.[2] On December 22 the Naval Committee laid before Congress a "list of the officers by them appointed."[3] It included, besides Hopkins and Jones, the names of four captains, four first-lieutenants, five second-lieutenants, and three third-lieutenants. The little roll of captains was headed by Dudley Saltonstall, who owed his appointment to his brother-in-law, Silas Deane, a member of the Committee; and was ended by John Burroughs Hopkins, a son of the commander-in-chief. Immediately above J. B. Hopkins in rank was Nicholas Biddle, a young Philadelphian, twenty-five years old, and very promising material for a naval officer. He had entered the British navy in 1770, and had served as midshipman on board the same vessel with Lord Nelson. In the summer of 1775 he was appointed commander of the "Franklin" galley of the Pennsylvania navy. The fourth captain was Abra-

---

1. Edward Field's Esek Hopkins, 134, quotes from Drake's Life of Knox.
2. Sands, Life and Correspondence of John Paul Jones, 32.
3. Journals of Continental Congress, December 22, 1775.

ham Whipple, the commodore of the Rhode Island navy.

In these first appointments of the Committee it takes no eagle eye to discern the workings of nepotism and sectional influences. Of the five largest naval plums, New England plucked four. This may have been, however, right enough, as the South was credited with the commander-in-chief of the army, and New England greatly exceeded the Middle and Southern states in the number of men who were experienced in maritime affairs.

In December, 1775, the Naval Committee was preparing a fleet for sea, which was to make the first naval essay of the new government. The Pennsylvania Committee of Safety was contributing arms, ammunition, and sailors. Commodore Hopkins enlisted for the service of his fleet more than one hundred seamen in Rhode Island, whom Whipple brought to Philadelphia in the "Katy." On December 3, 1775, John Paul Jones hoisted the Continental flag on board the "Alfred," Hopkins's flagship, the first Continental vessel to fly the colors of the new nation.[1] By the end of January, 1776, the Committee had added four other small vessels to the navy, the sloops "Providence," and "Hornet," and the schooners, "Wasp,"

---
1. Force, American Archives, 4th, IV, 360; letter to Earl of Dartmouth, dated Maryland, Dec. 20, 1775.

and "Fly."[1] The "Providence" had been the "Katy" of the Rhode Island navy. The "Hornet" and the "Wasp" were obtained in Baltimore.

On January 5, 1776, the Naval Committee issued sailing orders to the commander-in-chief. He was ordered, "if Winds and Weather possibly admit of it, to proceed directly for Chesapeake Bay in Virginia." Here he was to strike the enemy's fleet under Lord Dunmore, unless it was found to be greatly superior to his own. If he was so fortunate as to execute this business successfully, he was to continue southward and master the British forces off the coast of the Carolinas, and from thence he was to sail northward directly to Rhode Island and "attack, take, and destroy all the enemy's naval force that you may find there."[2] This program seems rather ambitious, when one considers the motley assemblage of officers, seamen, and cruisers, that composed this fleet of made-over merchantmen.

The ice in the Delaware greatly delayed the expedition. Early in February, 1776,

---

1. Journals of Continental Congress, December 2, 1775, January 9 and 16, 1776. The Naval Committee spent $134,333 on the eight vessels which they fitted out.—Journals of Continental Congress, September 19, 1776.

2. Records and Papers of Continental Congress, 78, III, 239-40, orders of Commodore Hopkins, signed by four members of the Naval Committee.

the fleet was assembling at Cape Henlopen. It then consisted of the flagship "Alfred," 24, Captain Dudley Saltonstall; the ship "Columbus," 20, Captain Abraham Whipple; the brigs "Andrew Doria," 14, Captain Nicholas Biddle, and "Cabot," 14, Captain J. B. Hopkins; the sloop "Providence," 12; and the schooner "Fly," 8. On February 15 the sloop "Hornet," 10, and the schooner "Wasp," 8, joined the fleet from Baltimore.[1] On the 17th the fleet sailed outside the Capes into the broad Atlantic. A new nation in whose veins flowed the blood of a long line of seafaring and sea-fighting ancestors was about to put to the initial test its skill in naval warfare, and under conditions far from auspicious. If the doughty Admiral should get all his queer craft once more into a safe harbor he would be doing well.

Hopkins had apparently concluded that his Armada might prove vincible on the stormy coasts of Virginia. Indeed, the enemy must have heard of his intended coming, and awaited it. Not only discretion, but good military judgment advised him to abandon for the present the visitation to the Chesapeake.[2] Before sailing on Feb-

---

1. Force, American Archives, 4th, V, 823.
2. Ford, Writings of Washington, III, 299-300, 319. Washington wrote on January 4, 1776, to Joseph Reed: "I fear your fleet has been so long in fitting, and the destination of it so well known, that the end will be de-

ruary 17 he had determined to make a descent on Nassau, New Providence, and accordingly he gave orders to his captains and commanders to keep in company, if possible, but if not, to make for the island of Abaco, one of the Bahamas, where the fleet would next rendezvous.[1]

On the 3rd and 4th of March Nassau was taken after a slight resistance and without bloodshed, by a landing party consisting of two hundred marines under one of their officers, Captain Samuel Nichols, and fifty sailors under Lieutenant Weaver of the "Cabot." Eighty-eight cannon, fifteen mortars, a large quantity of shot and shell besides other munitions of war were captured. Since the governor of the island succeeded the night before the landing was effected in removing the gunpowder to a safe hiding place, the expedition failed of its chief object.[2]

On March 17, having loaded his vessels and a borrowed sloop with the warlike stores, Hopkins set sail for Rhode Island,

---

feated, if the vessels escape." In July, 1776, Dunmore's fleet consisted of more than forty vessels, most of which, however, were probably unarmed, being occupied by refugee Tories.—Maryland Archives, XII, 24-25.

1. Edward Field's Esek Hopkins, 101; a copy of Hopkins's orders is given.

2. Papers of Esek Hopkins, Rhode Island Historical Society, an invoice of captured articles.

taking with him as prisoners of war several important officials, including the Governor and Lieutenant-Governor of New Providence. On April 4 the squadron, having reached the eastward end of Long Island, captured the British schooner "Hawk," 6, and the bomb brig "Bolton," 8. At 1 o'clock on the morning of the 6th the "Alfred," "Cabot," "Columbus," "Andrew Doria," and "Providence" engaged His Majesty's ship "Glasgow," 20, Captain Tyringham Howe. After a severe fight of about three hours, the "Glasgow," was permitted to escape, leaving her tender with the Americans.[1] The loss of the enemy was four; that of the Americans, twenty-four, of which number twenty-three were on board the "Alfred" and "Cabot," the two vessels which bore the brunt of the encounter.[2] Each of these vessels had a lieutenant killed.

The American commanders in this engagement exhibited little skill in tactics. A fleet permitted a single vessel of the enemy to escape. Something can be said for them by way of extenuating circumstances. It should also be said that they showed no lack of spirit. As was natural, Commodore

---

1. Force, American Archives, 4th, V, 823, Hopkins to President of Congress, April, 1776, giving an account of the expedition.

2. W. L. Clowes, Royal Navy, IV, 3, 4; Connecticut Gazette, April 12, 1776.

Hopkins was made the target for much adverse criticism. Nations, it is said, are seldom just under disgrace, imaginary or real.

The expedition to New Providence was the sole naval enterprise made by the Continental vessels, while they were under the direction of the Naval Committee. Early in 1776 this Committee, reduced in membership, yielded its control of marine affairs to a new committee with a fuller complement of members. It scarcely needs to be said that the Naval Committee's claim to distinction rests not upon its military achievements, but upon its work of a civil character, whereby it laid the foundations of the Revolutionary navy. It acquired the first American fleet, selected its officers, and fitted it for sea. It drafted the first civil and penal code of the navy, and prepared not a little fundamental naval legislation.

CHAPTER II

THE FLEETS OF WASHINGTON AND ARNOLD[1]

The first armed vessels that sailed under Continental pay and control were those that composed the little fleet fitted out by Washington in the ports of Massachusetts in the fall of 1775. As these vessels were manned by soldiers and were commanded by army officers, and were designed to weaken the army of the enemy by capturing his transports carrying supplies and troops, Washington was able to derive his authority for procuring and fitting out the fleet from his commission as commander-in-chief of the Continental army. The first vessel employed in this service was the schooner "Hannah," commanded by Nicholson Broughton, a captain in the army. According to his instructions, issued September 2, 1775, and signed by Washington,

1. This chapter, which is presented here for chronological reasons, is not closely related to the main narrative, which will be resumed at the beginning of Chapter III.

Broughton was directed to proceed "immediately on a cruise against such vessels as may be found on the high seas, or elsewhere, bound inwards and outwards, to or from Boston, in the service of the Ministerial Army, and to take and seize all such vessels, laden with soldiers, arms, ammunition, or provisions, for or from said Army, or which you shall have good reason to suspect are in such service." One-third of all captured cargoes were to be given to officers and crews as an encouragement. The proportions according to which the captors' share was to be divided were fixed. The captain was to receive six times as much as a private. Prizes were to be sent to the "safest and nearest port to this camp." Prisoners were to be treated with kindness and humanity. Broughton was directed to be exceedingly careful and frugal with his ammunition, and not to waste it in salutes.[1]

Not until a month after the fitting out of the "Hannah" did Washington begin to add to his naval force. On October 4 he appointed Colonel John Glover and Stephen Moylan agents to equip two vessels at Salem, Marblehead, or Newburyport, and they were directed to name suitable men for prize agents in the leading ports of Mas-

---

1. Force, American Archives, 4th, III, 633-34, Instructions to Broughton.

sachusetts.[1] When Washington received the letter of Congress of October 5 directing him to obtain two vessels from Massachusetts and to send them to the St. Lawrence river to intercept two British transports bound from London for Quebec, he ordered on this service, since Massachusetts at this time had no armed vessels, the schooners "Lynch," Captain Nicholson Broughton, and "Franklin," Captain John Selman, which had been or were being fitted out by Glover and Moylan.[2] In October and November four other small vessels, the schooners "Lee," "Harrison," and "Warren," and the brigantine "Washington" were fitted out and sent cruising against the enemy's transports. About the first of January, 1776, the schooner "Hancock" was added. Washington had the entire management of his fleet. Stephen Moylan, who was attached to his staff, conducted most of the correspondence with the captains and naval agents while Washington was at Cambridge.[3] Agents for fitting out the fleet and receiving its prizes were established in Plymouth, Boston, Lynn, Salem, Marblehead, Beverly, Newburyport,

1. Force, American Archives, 4th, III, 946.
2. See Chapter I, The Naval Committee, page 37; Ford, Writings of Washington, III, 174-5.
3. Moylan had been for some months a member of Washington's official household before he was appointed aide-de-camp in March, 1776.

and Portsmouth, N. H. In January, 1776, Washington appointed John Manly commodore of the fleet. The other commanders thereby became subject to Manly's orders.

With the exception of Manly, Washington had a poor opinion of the abilities of his commanders. On January 28 he wrote to Manly: "I wish you could inspire the captains of the other armed schooners under your command with some of your activity and industry."[1] In November, 1775, he had written: "Our rascally privateersmen go on at the old rate, mutinying if they can not do as they please. Those at Plymouth, Beverly, and Portsmouth have done nothing worth mentioning in the prize way, and no account as yet received from those farther eastward," referring to the "Lynch" and "Franklin," whose commanders he feared "would not effect any good purpose."[2] Early in December Washington was still more emphatic: "The plague, trouble, and vexation I have had with the crews of all the armed vessels, are inexpressible. I do believe there is not on earth a more disorderly set. Every time they come into port, we hear of nothing but mutinous complaints. Manly's success has lately, and but lately, quieted his people.

---

1. Ford, Writings of Washington, III, 382-83.
2. Ibid., 231-32, Washington to Joseph Reed, November 20, 1775.

The crews of the Washington and Harrison have actually deserted them; so that I have been under the necessity of ordering the agent to lay the latter up, and get hands for the other on the best terms he could."[1]

Notwithstanding the Commander-in-chief's unfavorable judgment, it must be said that his fleet, upon the whole, was quite as successful as were other fleets of equal size and force during the Revolution. The vessels which composed it were small and lightly armed. Manly's first vessel, the "Lee," with which he rendered effective service, carried fifty men and four 4-pounders. The brigantine "Washington" was somewhat larger, mounting ten guns. Altogether the fleet captured some thirty-five prizes.[2] The first important capture, that of the brigantine "Nancy," was an exceedingly timely one, and was made by Manly in the "Lee" on one of the last days of November, 1775. Among other stores the "Nancy" had on board 2,000 muskets, 100,000 flints, 30,000 round shot, more than 30 tons of musket shot, 11 mortar beds, and a brass mortar weighing 10,000 pounds. It would have taken the

---
1. Ford, Writings of Washington, III, 261-62, Washington to President of Congress, December 4, 1775.
2. This calculation is made chiefly from accounts of the vessels found in Force's American Archives and Ford's Writings of Washington.

Americans eighteen months to have manufactured a like quantity of ordnance.¹ In June, 1776, the fleet, together with the "Defence" of the Connecticut navy, captured four British transports, which had on board besides a quantity of supplies upwards of three hundred and twenty Scottish troops.²

Washington's fleet cruised chiefly off the Massachusetts coast. Broughton and Selman, whom Washington dispatched to the river St. Lawrence to intercept the two British transports, did not enter the river at all. After making several unauthorized captures, they turned their attention to the island of St. Johns, now Prince Edward island. Here they pillaged the defenceless inhabitants, and robbed the houses of the Governor and Acting-Governor of plate, carpets, curtains, mirrors, table linen, and wearing apparel. They made prisoners of the Acting-Governor and two other leading men of the island, whose families were left in great distress. Washington was highly indignant at these unwarranted acts of his captains, and at once on their arrival in Massachusetts he released their three prisoners.³

---

1. Ford, Writings of Washington, III, 252 and note; Letters of John Adams, Massachusetts Historical Society, William Tudor to John Adams, December 3, 1775.
2. Boston Gazette, July 6, 1776.
3. Force, American Archives, 4th, IV, 451-52, Memorial of Philip Callbeck and Thomas

Moved by the need for a proper judicial tribunal to try the prize cases arising from captures made by his vessels, Washington on November 11, 1775, wrote to Congress on the subject. He enclosed in his letter a copy of the Massachusetts law establishing admiralty courts, and explained that this law did not apply to the captures made by Continental vessels. "Should not a court," he asked, "be established by authority of Congress, to take cognizance of prizes made by the Continental vessels? Whatever the mode is, which they are pleased to adopt, there is an absolute necessity of its being speedily determined on, for I can not spare time from military affairs to give proper attention to these matters." As early as October 5 Washington had requested the "determination of Congress, as to the property and disposal of such vessels and cargoes, as are designed for the supply of the enemy, and may fall into our hands." On November 8 he called the attention of Congress to the same subject. On December 4 and December 14 he again urged Congress to establish a Conti-

Wright; Ford, Writings of Washington, III, 175 and note, 261-62 and note. H. E. Waite, Origin of American Navy, 26-28. Report on Canadian Archives, 1895, Prince Edward Island, 15-16. The number of vessels captured by Broughton and Selman on this cruise has been given by Elbridge Gerry as ten and by Selman as seven. Both figures are probably too high.

nental prize court.[1] Finally, on December 20 Congress resolved that the several vessels heretofore carried into Massachusetts by the armed vessels in the service of the United Colonies should be "proceeded against by the rules of the law of nations, and libelled in the courts of admiralty erected in said colony."[2] The method of procedure which Congress here established was followed throughout the Revolution in all prize cases arising from captures made by Continental vessels. Congress permitted the states to exercise original jurisdiction in all Continental prize cases, and reserved to itself appellate jurisdiction, so far as it had power to do so.

It is recalled that Congress, on November 25, 1775, having under consideration the report of a committee on Washington's letter of November 8, determined the kinds of British property which should be subject to capture, fixed the shares of prizes, and established certain forms of procedure in the trial of prize cases.[3] The lack of correspondence

---

1. Ford, Writings of Washington, III, 165, 203-04, 213-214, 251-58, 274.

2. Journals of Continental Congress, December 20, 1775.

3. See Chapter I, The Naval Committee, page 48. It would seem that Congress, by its resolutions of November 25, intended to give colonial courts original jurisdiction in Continental prize cases. Washington did not so understand these resolutions. See his letter

between these resolutions and the Massachusetts law of November 1, establishing admiralty courts, caused long and serious delays in bringing the Continental prizes to trial. Washington, on April 25, 1776, wrote from New York: "I have not yet heard, that there has been any trial of the prizes carried into Massachusetts Bay. This procrastination is attended with very bad consequences. Some of the vessels I had fitted out are now laid up, the crews being dissatisfied that they cannot get their prize money. I have tired the Congress on this subject, but the importance of it makes me again mention, that, if a summary way of proceeding is not resolved on, it will be impossible to get our vessels manned."[1]

On the evacuation of Boston by the British in March, 1776, Washington soon removed his headquarters to New York. He left his fleet in charge of General Artemas Ward, who reported its movements to him. In February, 1777, the Marine Committee of Congress ordered the Continental agent at Boston to pay off and discharge the fleet.[2]

of December 14, 1775, to the President of Congress, and his letter of December 26, 1775, to R. H. Lee.

1. Ford, Writings of Washington, III, 404; IV, 44, 45.
2. Marine Committee Letter Book, Robert Morris, Vice-President of the Marine Committee, to John Bradford, Continental agent at Boston, February 7, 1777. The "Lee," Captain Skimmer, was still in the Continental

In March the Marine Committee appointed three commissioners to settle the accounts of Washington's prize agents.[1] These commissioners had not completed their task in April, 1778.[2]

In April, 1776, immediately upon Washington's arrival in New York, he began to equip a fleet similar to the one at Boston. He requested from the New York Committee of Safety the loan of their state vessels, which he wished to use in suppressing illicit trade with the enemy. Some disagreement arose as to the terms of the loan. Washington insisted that if he manned the "General Schuyler," he would expect to appoint her officers. In the end, the "General Schuyler" was turned over to Washington, and the captain of the "General Putnam" was directed to obey his orders.[3] Washington now obtained from other sources the sloop "General Mifflin." These vessels, which cruised during the summer of 1776 chiefly in the neighborhood of Long Island, and usu-

---

service in November, 1777, when the Navy Board was ordered to discharge Skimmer, and to take the "Lee" into the regular Continental navy, if she was adapted for it.—Marine Committee Letter Book, Committee to Navy Board at Boston, November 22, 1777.
  1. Marine Committee Letter Book, Committee to the three Commissioners, March 21, 1777.
  2. Journals of Continental Congress, April 9, 1778.
  3. Journals of New York Committee of Safety, April 24, May 10, 1776.

ally with the New York state sloop "Montgomery," captured several British vessels.[1] In the summer of 1776 Washington was constructing some "gondolas," row-galleys, and fire-ships, for the defence of the Hudson. The galley "Lady Washington," which was manned and completed by the summer of 1776, was still in service on the Hudson in June, 1777.[2]

In the significance of their results the operations of no other naval armament of the Americans during the Revolution compare with those of Arnold's fleet on Lake Champlain in the fall of 1776. On May 31, 1775, the Continental Congress desired the New York Provincial Congress "to take effectual care that a sufficient number of batteaus be immediately provided for the lakes."[3] Major-General Schuyler commanded the Continental forces in this region, including the naval armaments upon the Lakes. These last, in September, consisted of a sloop, a schooner, two row-galleys, and ten "bat-

---

1. The movements of these vessels may be followed in Force's American Archives, Ford's Writings of Washington, and the Journals of the New York Provincial Congress and Committee of Safety.

2. Journals of Continental Congress, May 30, 1776; Force, American Archives, 5th, I, 1263; Journals of New York Provincial Congress, June 7, 1777.

3. Journals of Continental Congress, May 31, 1775.

teaus."[1] About the first of August the New York Provincial Congress sent James Smith to Schuyler to take command of the sloop "Enterprise."[2] Smith either received or gave to himself the title of "Commodore on the Lakes." He did not long hold this title; for in March, 1776, the Continental Congress appointed Major William Douglass of New York, "Commodore on the Lakes," a place for which General Schuyler had recommended Captain Jacobus Wynkoop, of the same state.[3] In April Wynkoop was enlisting seamen in New York City.[4] In May, since Douglass did not enter upon his appointment, Schuyler, acting under the orders of Congress, put the armed vessels under the command of Wynkoop.[5]

About the first of July, 1776, the American forces were driven out of Canada. They retreated southward as far as the forts on the Lakes. The holding of Lakes Champlain and George, which were a strategic part of the line of communication between Canada and the Hudson, now became a mat-

---

1. Force, American Archives, 4th, III, 738.
2. Ibid., 11, 14.
3. Journals of Continental Congress, March 26, 1776; Journals of New York Committee of Safety, March 18, 1776.
4. Journals of New York Committee of Safety, April 24, 1776.
5. Force, American Archives, 5th, I, 1186. 1277; Journals of New York Provincial Congress, March 16, 1776; Journals of Continental Congress, May 2, 1776.

ter of vital importance. Providing against a possible failure in Canada, Congress, Washington, and Schuyler had, in May and early June, been increasing the effectiveness of the naval armament on the Lakes. On June 17 Congress ordered Schuyler to build "with all expedition, as many galleys and armed vessels as, in the opinion of himself and the general officer to be sent into Canada, shall be sufficient to make us indisputable masters of the lakes Champlain and George." A master carpenter, acquainted with the construction of the galleys used on the Delaware, other carpenters, and models of galleys, if required, were to be sent on from Philadelphia.[1]

Towards the end of June, Brigadier-General Benedict Arnold, recognizing the supreme importance of maintaining a naval superiority on the Lakes, began to exert an influence in naval affairs. Arnold was not without marine experience; as a resident of New Haven, engaged in the West India trade, he had sometimes commanded his own ships. On June 25, 1776, he wrote to Washington: "It now appears to me of the utmost importance that the Lakes be immediately secured by a large number (at least twenty or thirty) of gondolas, row-galleys, and floating batteries. . . . . I think

---

1. Journals of Continental Congress, May 22, May 25, June 17, 1776; Ford, Writings of Washington, IV, 101.

it absolutely necessary that three hundred carpenters be immediately employed."[1] Towards the end of July, General Gates appointed Arnold to command the naval forces on the Lakes. Wynkoop, who held a similar command by virtue of an appointment from Congress and Schuyler, refused to yield to Arnold. He was thereupon arrested by Gates and sent as a prisoner to Schuyler.[2]

During July and August, 1776, Skenesborough, at the head of Lake Champlain, was the scene of the greatest naval activity. Requisitions were made upon Pennsylvania, New York, Connecticut, Rhode Island, and Massachusetts for carpenters. Naval stores and munitions of war of all sorts, sail-cloth, cordage, anchors, cannon, and ammunition were sent to the Lakes from the seaboard, especially from New York and Connecticut. Seamen were hurried forward. On August 13 the Governor and Council of Safety of Connecticut voted £180 to Captain Seth Warner of Saybrook to enable him to raise a crew of forty seamen for the naval service on the Lakes. These men were "to receive a bounty of £6 for inlisting; and for finding themselves blankets, 12s; guns, 6s; and cartouch-box and belt and knapsack, 2s; and one month's wages

---
1. Force, American Archives, 4th, VI, 1107-08.
2. Ibid., 5th, I, 1186-87.

being 48s advanced, according to proclamation." On August 16 the Governor and Council of Safety authorized two other companies to be raised.[1] In September Gates understood that two hundred seamen had been enlisted in New York city.[2]

On July 24, 1776, Arnold wrote from Skenesborough to Gates: "I arrived here last evening, and found three gondolas on the stocks; two will be completed in five or six days, the row galley in eight or ten days. Three other gondolas will be set up immediately, and may be completed in ten days. A company of twenty-seven carpenters from Middletown are cutting timber for a row-galley, on the Spanish construction, to mount six heavy pieces of cannon. One hundred carpenters from Pennsylvania and Massachusetts will be here this evening. I shall employ them on another row-galley. In two or three weeks, I think we shall have a formidable fleet. No canvass or cordage is yet arrived, though much wanted."[3] Through strenuous exertions the American fleet on the Lakes was greatly increased and strengthened. By October it consisted of one sloop, three schooners, eight "gondolas,"

---

1. Colonial Records of Connecticut, XV, 500, 503. The rolls of these three Connecticut companies, containing eighty-five names, will be found in the Connecticut Historical Society Collections, VIII, 235-37.
2. Force, American Archives, 5th, II, 186.
3. Ibid., I, 563.

and four galleys, mounting a total of 94 cannon, 2-pounders to 18-pounders. With a full complement, the fleet would have carried 856 men. It probably numbered about 700 officers and men, such as they were.[1] Arnold said that he had a "wretched motley crew in the fleet; the marines the refuse of every regiment, and the seamen few of them ever wet with salt water." Many of his seamen and marines were almost naked.[2]

During the first days of October the naval superiority on the Lakes shifted to the British. General Sir Guy Carleton, the British commander, drawing upon superior naval resources, had outbuilt Arnold. Early in October Carleton's fleet consisted of one ship, two schooners, one "radeau," one large "gondola," twenty gunboats, and four armed tenders. Some of these vessels and the material for others he had brought from the St. Lawrence up the Richelieu. The ship "Enterprise," eighteen 12-pounders, 180 tons burden, whose construction had been begun at Quebec, he thus transported in pieces. She was set up at St. Johns, on the Richelieu, where the British shipyard was situated. This vessel in size and armament greatly exceeding any one craft of the

---

[1] Force, American Archives, 5th, II, 1039. One galley which was fitting at Ticonderoga is not included in the above list. The exact number of men in Arnold's fleet is uncertain.

[2] Ibid., 481, 834.

Americans. A fleet of transports and ships of war in the St. Lawrence furnished Carleton with seven hundred experienced officers and seamen.[1]

The two fleets engaged each other on Lake Champlain on October 11, 12, and 13, 1776. Ten of the American vessels were captured or destroyed. General Waterbury, second in command, and 110 prisoners, were captured. In killed and wounded Arnold lost about eighty men; and the British forty. The British were left in command of the Lake; the Americans retreated to Ticonderoga.[2]

Although most decisively defeated in the battle upon the Lake, Arnold had delayed the advance of the British some two or three months, while they were obtaining a naval superiority. This delay had far-reaching consequences. Carleton now found the season too late to pursue his advantage, and to make, or attempt to make, a juncture with Howe to the southward. He therefore soon returned to winter quarters at Montreal. When Burgoyne, in 1777, repeated the attempt to penetrate to the Hudson, Howe's removal of his army to the Chesapeake in his movement against Philadelphia, deprived Burgoyne's army of the support on

-----
1. Force, American Archives, 5th, II, 1178-79; Clowes, Royal Navy, III, 353-370, Chapter XXXI, written by Captain A. T. Mahan.
2. Force, American Archives, 5th, II, 1079-80; Almon's Remembrancer, 1777, 356.

the Hudson, which it might have had in the fall of 1776. It has been strikingly said, by Captain Mahan, that Arnold's and Carleton's naval campaign on Lake Champlain was a "strife of pigmies for the prize of a continent." Although the American flotilla was wiped out, "never had any force, big or small, lived to better purpose, or died more gloriously; for it had saved the Lake for that year."[1]

1. Clowes, Royal Navy, III, 363, 368. In the campaign of Burgoyne, in July, 1777, the British destroyed or captured a small American flotilla at Skenesborough.—Winsor, Narrative and Critical History, VI, 297.

CHAPTER III

THE ORGANIZATION OF THE MARINE COMMITTEE

In the years immediately preceding the Revolution the four New England colonies were largely engaged in shipbuilding, fishing, whaling, and commerce. The forests of Maine and New Hampshire afforded incomparable oaks and white pines for ships. Indeed, not a few of these trees were sealed for the use of the Royal Navy, and their high quality authenticated, by the mark of the "King's broad arrow." New England's hardy dwellers on the seacoast had long engaged in fishing on the Newfoundland banks, or in whaling in many seas, and had bred a race of sailors. The Atlantic withheld few secrets from the bold Yankee skippers. They were equally at home in the coastwise navigation, reaching from Nova Scotia to Florida, in deep-sea voyages to the motherland or the Continent, in skirting the Guinea coast in quest of its dark-skinned trade, or in slipping down the trade winds with canvas set for the sunny sugar islands of the

West Indies or the Spanish Main. In no other section of the revolting colonies was the first formal movement for the building of a Continental navy so likely to be made as in New England. Here were ships, sailors, and a knowledge of the sea.

Certainly not a whit behind the other three New England states in nautical interests was little sea-cleft Rhode Island. In the establishing of state navies she had moved first, and on June 15, 1775, had put two vessels in commission. On the same day her Commodore Whipple captured an armed tender of the British frigate "Rose"— the first authorized capture made by the Americans at sea during the Revolution.[1] Already her coasts and her trade were being annoyed by the enemy. It was then in keeping with her maritime character, with her forwardness in naval enterprise, and with her needs for defence, that her Assembly should have instructed her two delegates to the Continental Congress, on August 26, 1775, "to use their whole influence, at the ensuing Congress, for building at the Continental expense, a Fleet of sufficient force for the protection of these Colonies, and for employing them in such manner and places as will most effectually annoy our enemies, and contribute to the common defence of these Colonies." The Assembly was per-

---

1. See Chapter XVII, The Minor Navies of the Northern States.

suaded that an American fleet "would greatly and essentially conduce to the preservation of the lives, liberty, and property of the good people of these Colonies."[1]

The naval situation in Congress during the fall of 1775 and the winter of 1775-76 should be clearly understood. The debates and legislation of Congress concerning naval affairs are attached, as it were, to two threads. One thread, beginning with the appointment of a committee, on October 5, 1775, to prepare a plan for intercepting two British transports, has already been unraveled. The other, which had its origin in the introduction in Congress of the Rhode Island instructions, will now be followed.

The delegates of Rhode Island to the Congress in the fall of 1775 were two sterling patriots, Samuel Ward and Stephen Hopkins. Each had been governor of Rhode Island, and each had grown old in the public service. Once bitter political rivals, they were now yoked together in the common cause of their state and country. On October 3, 1775, one of the Rhode Island delegates, presumably Samuel Ward, laid before Congress the instructions of his state in behalf of a Continental fleet. On this day the consideration of the instructions went over until the 6th, and on the 6th until the 7th.[2]

---

1. Force, American Archives, 4th, III, 231; Sparks, American Biography, 2nd, IX, 314-15.
2. Journals of Continental Congress, Octo-

When the Rhode Island instructions came up on October 7, a debate ensued, a synopsis of which has been left us by John Adams.[1] The discussion was participated in by Robert Treat Paine, Samuel Adams, and John Adams of Massachusetts, John Rutledge and Christopher Gadsden of South Carolina, Samuel Chase of Maryland, Stephen Hopkins of Rhode Island, Dr. John J. Zubly of Georgia, Eliphalet Dyer and Silas Deane of Connecticut, and Peyton Randolph of Virginia. When the debate took place, the consideration of the Rhode Island instructions had been postponed until the 16th, and the motion before the Congress was to appoint a committee "to consider the whole subject."

The establishing of a navy naturally found least favor among the members coming from the agricultural South, and most support from those of maritime New England. Chase, of Maryland, declared, "It is the maddest idea in the world to think of building an American fleet; its latitude is wonderful; we should mortgage the whole continent." He added, however: "We should provide, for gaining intelligence, two swift sailing vessels." Zubly, of Georgia, said: "If the plans of some gentlemen are to take place, an American fleet must be a part of it, ex-

---

ber 3, 1775; Force, American Archives 4th, III, 1888-91; Works of John Adams, II, 462.
1. Works of John Adams, II, 463-4.

travagant as it is." Gadsden, of South Carolina, temperately favored the procuring of armed vessels, thinking that it was "absolutely necessary that some plan of defence, by sea, should be adopted." He was opposed to the "extensiveness of the Rhode Island plan," although he thought that it should be considered. The friends of the navy acted on the defensive. They probably realized that their cause might well bide its time. Its opponents, to use John Adams's phrase, were "lightly skirmishing." In the end the motion was lost, and consideration of the instructions was deferred until the 16th.

On October 16, and again on November 16, the Rhode Island instructions were postponed.[1] Samuel Ward had hopes for a favorable action on the latter day. On November 16 he wrote from Philadelphia to his brother in Rhode Island: "Our instruction for an American fleet has been long upon the table. When it was first presented, it was looked upon as perfectly chimerical; but gentlemen now consider it in a very different light. It is this day to be taken into consideration, and I have great hopes of carrying it. Dr. Franklin, Colonel Lee, the two Adamses, and many others, will support it. If it succeeds, I shall remember

---

1. Journals of Continental Congress, October 16, November 16, 1775.

your ideas of our building two of the ships."[1]

The several postponements of the Rhode Island instructions make it clear that Congress was slow to reach the conclusion that the "building of a fleet" was desirable or feasible. It was one thing to fit out a few small vessels for intercepting British transports, and quite another to build a fleet of frigates. It is not surprising that under the circumstances Congress hesitated to embark on the larger undertaking. The difference in the presentation to Congress of the two propositions, both of which involved the procuring of a naval armament, is worthy of note, for it had its influence on legislation. The appointment of a committee to prepare a plan for intercepting transports, put the question in a softened, more veiled, and less direct form. It pointed the wedge of naval legislation by a tactful presentation, and drove it home with an exigency.

In Chapter I the increase of sentiment in favor of a naval armament during the latter part of October and during November has been shown, and the important naval legislation of November has been presented. It was now only a question of time until Congress would heed the recommendations of Rhode Island. On December 9, 1775, the Rhode Island instructions once more

---

1. Gammell, Life of Samuel Ward, in Sparks's American Biography, 2nd, IX, 316

came up, and a day for their consideration was fixed, Monday, December 11.[1] On the 11th, "agreeable to the order of the day, the Congress took into consideration the instructions given to the delegates of Rhode Island;" whereupon a committee of twelve was appointed to devise ways and means for furnishing these colonies with a naval armament.[2] This committee performed its work with commendable celerity, and brought in, on December 13, one of the most important reports in the history of the naval affairs under the Revolution, for by its acceptance Congress committed itself to the establishment of a considerable naval force. Congress determined to build thirteen frigates, five of 32, five of 28, and three of 24 guns, to be distributed, as regards the place of their construction, among the states as follows: New Hampshire, one; Massachusetts, two; Rhode Island, two; Connecticut, one; New York, two; Pennsylvania, four; and Maryland, one. It was estimated that these ships would cost on the average $66,666.67 each, and that their whole cost would amount to $866,666.67. All the materials for fitting them for sea could be procured in America except canvas and gunpowder.[3]

1. Journals of Continental Congress, December 9, 1775.
2. Ibid., December 11, 1775.
3. Ibid., December 13, 1775.

On December 14 a committee consisting of one member from each colony was chosen by ballot to take charge of the building and fitting out of these vessels. The members chosen with their states were as follows: Josiah Bartlett, New Hampshire; John Hancock, Massachusetts; Stephen Hopkins, Rhode Island; Silas Deane, Connecticut; Francis Lewis, New York; Stephen Crane, New Jersey; Robert Morris, Pennsylvania; George Read, Delaware; Samuel Chase, Maryland; R. H. Lee, Virginia; Joseph Hewes, North Carolina; Christopher Gadsden, South Carolina; John Houston, Georgia.[1] This committee was substantially the same as that which reported the naval increase on the 13th; the only changes were in the members from Massachusetts and Maryland, and in the addition of a member from Georgia. The committee was a very able one, comprising several of the foremost men of the Revolution. Hancock, Morris, Hopkins, and Hewes were especially interested in naval and maritime affairs. The absence of the name of John Adams is probably accounted for by his return home early in December.

This new committee was soon designated as the Marine Committee, by which name it was referred to throughout the Revolution. Larger, and, with its engrossing work

1. Journals of Continental Congress, December 14, 1775.

of building and fitting out the thirteen frigates, more active than the Naval Committee, it soon overshadowed and finally absorbed its colleague. This absorbtion was facilitated no doubt by the fact that the four members of the Naval Committee remaining in January, 1776, also belonged to the new committee. With the exception of the rendering of its accounts, the duties of the Naval Committee came to an end with the sailing of Hopkins's fleet in February, 1776.[1] The Marine Committee now acquired a firm grasp of the naval business of the colonies, and from this time until December, 1779, it was the recognized and responsible head of the Naval Department, and as such, during the period that saw the rise and partial decline of the Continental navy, its history is of prime importance.

The Marine Committee like the Naval Committee had at Philadelphia an office of its own, and held its sessions in the evening. Its officers consisted of a chairman or president, a vice-president, and a secretary.[2] Its clerical force comprised one or more clerks. On June 6, 1777, Congress resolved that five of its members—which number thereafter constituted a quorum—should

---

1. Journals of Continental Congress. January 25, September 19. 1776. See Ford's new edition of the Jouruals.
2. The Secretary of the Marine Committee was John Brown.

form a "board" for the transaction of business.[1] Each of the thirteen states had one member on the Committee. Rarely did more than one-half of the Committee's members attend its sessions. Its personnel was continually changing. This was necessitated in part by a similar change in the membership of Congress; as the old members retired, the new ones filled their places. The members of the Marine Committee received no pay for their naval services as such. Each state of course paid its member of the Committee for his services as a delegate to the Continental Congress. The wages of the secretary of the Committee and of its clerical force varied. On June 16, 1778, the Committee was permitted to raise the wages of its clerks to $100 a month.[2] The secretary was paid at the rate of $8,000 a year after November 2, 1778.[3] During 1778 and 1779 Congress was raising the salaries of its executive employees because of the depreciation of the currency.

The most responsible duties of the Committee naturally fell to the four or five members oldest in its service. From this class it drew its chairmen. Three out of the five men who are known to have filled this office were on the first list of the Com-

1. Journals of Continental Congress, June 6, 1777.
2. Ibid., June 16, 1778.
3. Ibid., January 27, 1780.

mittee's members. During possibly all of 1776, and for a part of 1777, courtly John Hancock presided over the Marine Committee, while at the same time he dignified the chair of the President of Congress. In December, 1777, Henry Laurens of South Carolina had succeeded to both of Hancock's positions.[1] In 1778 and 1779 the mantles of the first leaders in naval administration, whether they exactly fitted or not, were worn by Richard Henry Lee, "one of the fine fellows from Virginia"; Samuel Adams of Massachusetts; and William Whipple of New Hampshire. Lee was chairman in the summer of 1778. Probably before December of that year, certainly by that time, Adams had succeeded him.[2] Adams

[1]. Journals of Continental Congress, December 27, 1777.

[2]. Lee, however, signed a letter as chairman in March, 1779. Relative to Samuel Adams's work in the Marine Committee, these words of his biographer possess interest: "Upon his arrival in Congress [May 21, 1778], he was added to the Marine Committee, of which important Board he was made chairman, and continued to direct its duties, for the next two years. In this arduous position, judged from the great number of reports and the multiplicity of business submitted to it, Adams might fairly have claimed exemption from all other employments."—Wells, Life and Public Services of Samuel Adams, III, 13. Mr. Wells exaggerates the length of the naval services of Adams, who left Philadelphia about June 20, 1779; whereupon William Whipple succeeded him as chairman of the Marine Committee.

in turn yielded in June, 1779, to Whipple, who continued to fill the office until the Committee was superseded by a Board of Admiralty in December, 1779.

There were other members besides the chairmen upon whose shoulders rested the burden of the naval business. Morris, Hewes, and Hopkins have been previously mentioned as members who were deeply interested in naval affairs. Morris was for a time vice-president of the Committee. During the winter of 1776-77, while Congress was at Baltimore, he remained in Philadelphia, and, for a time, practically without assistance from the Committee, administered the naval affairs of the colonies. William Ellery of Rhode Island, who on October 13, 1776, succeeded Hopkins, showed zeal in the business of the navy. The work of Francis Lewis of New York deserves mention. No doubt there were other members whose naval services were considerable. Unfortunately, time has been careless with many of the records of the Marine Committee.

In carrying out the resolutions of Congress of December 13, 1775, authorizing the building of thirteen frigates, the Marine Committee employed agents to superintend the work. These agents, who were variously designated, were residents of the colonies in which they were employed, and their selection was usually determined by local advice and influence. The New Hampshire frigate, the "Raleigh," 32, was built at Portsmouth under the direction of John Langdon, formerly a member of the Naval Committee, but now Continental agent at Portsmouth. He employed three masterbuilders, who completed the frigate within less than sixty days after raising it.[1] The Massachusetts frigates, the "Hancock," 32, and the "Boston," 24, were built at Salisbury and Newburyport, under the direction of an agent.[2]

The Rhode Island vessels, the "Warren," 32, and the "Providence," 28, were constructed at Providence, under the superintendence of a committee of twelve influential men of that city, who were appointed by Stephen Hopkins, the Rhode Island member of the Marine Committee. Certain complaints were lodged with the Marine Committee against the committee at Providence. One of these was made by Commodore Hopkins, who charged that the "Providence" and the "Warren" had cost twice as much as their contract price, "owing to some of the very committee that built the ships taking the workmen and the stock agreed for off to work and fit their privateers, and even threatening the workmen

---

1. New Hampshire Gazette, June 1, 1776.
2. Probably put upon the stocks at Salisbury and completed at Newburyport.

if they did not work for them."[1] When in the fall of 1776 the Marine Committee wrote to the committee, blaming its members for some of their proceedings, they relinquished their authority over the two vessels to Stephen Hopkins.[2]

The "Trumbull" was built under the direction of agents at Chatham on the Connecticut river.[3] Two other frigates were begun in Connecticut in 1777, the "Confederacy," 36, on the Thames river between Norwich and New London, and the "Bourbon," 28, at Chatham on the Connecticut. Each of these two frigates was constructed under a superintendent responsible to Governor Jonathan Trumbull and the Connecticut Council of Safety.[4] Two Commissioners at Poughkeepsie, New York, had charge of the work on the "Montgomery," 28, and "Congress," 24. The Marine Committee kept fairly well in its own hands the direction of the building at Philadelphia of the Pennsylvania frigates, the "Randolph," 32, the "Washington," 32, the "Effingham,"

1. Edward Field, State of Rhode Island and Providence Plantations, II, 423.
2. Staples, Annals of Providence, 267-8; Marine Committee Letter Book, Marine Committee to Stephen Hopkins, and Marine Committee to Committee for Building the Continental Frigates at Providence, October 9, 1776.
3. Colonial Records of Connecticut, XV, 526.
4. Records of State of Connecticut, I, 177.

28, and the "Delaware," 24. The "Virginia," 28, was built at Baltimore, Maryland, with the assistance of the Baltimore Committee of Observation.[1] When under the resolves of Congress of November 20, 1776, two frigates were begun at the Gosport navy-yard in Virginia, the work was placed in charge of two commissioners and a master-builder. Richard Henry Lee, the Virginia member of the Marine Committee, made the contract with the master-builder.[2]

The need of some one to receive and dispose of prizes soon led to the appointment of "agents for prizes" in the leading seaports of the colonies. On April 23, 1776, Congress, on the recommendation of the Marine Committee, appointed prize agents as follows: One at Boston; one at Providence; one at New London, Connecticut; one at New York; two at Philadelphia; one at Baltimore; one at Williamsburg, Virginia; and one each at Wilmington, Newbern, and Edenton, North Carolina.[3] On June 25, 1776, Congress appointed an agent at Portsmouth, New Hampshire.[4] In November,

---

1. Force, American Archives, 5th, II, 350, 636, 989; III, 827.
2. Marine Committee Letter Book, Marine Committee to David Stodder, master-builder, April 11, 1778.
3. Journals of Continental Congress, April 23, 1776.
4. Ibid., June 25, 1776.

1776, the Marine Committee selected two prize agents for South Carolina and one for Georgia.[1] This list was not completed until September 1, 1779, when Congress appointed a prize agent for New Jersey.[2] These agents had charge of all Continental prizes sent into their respective states. By far the most important agency was that of John Bradford at Boston. It may be estimated that one-half of all the prizes captured by the Continental vessels in American waters were ordered to Boston. The naval port second in importance was Philadelphia.

The duties of the prize agents were to libel all of the Continental prizes sent into their jurisdiction, see that the prizes were tried by the proper admiralty court; and after they had been legally condemned, to sell them, and make an equitable distribu-

---

1. Force, American Archives, 5th, III, 671, 739-40. The first prize agents to be appointed, many of whom held their offices throughout the greater part of the Revolution, were as follows: John Langdon, Portsmouth; John Bradford, Boston; Daniel Tillinghast, Providence; Nathaniel Shaw, jr., New London; Jacobus Vanzant, New York; John Nixon and John Maxwell Nesbit, Philadelphia; William Lux, Baltimore; John Tazewell, Williamsburg; Robert Smith, Edenton; Richard Ellis, Newbern; Cornelius Harnet, Wilmington; Livinus Clarkson and John Dorsius, Charleston; John Wereat, Savannah; and Okey Hoaglandt, New Jersey.

2. Journals of Continental Congress, September 1, 1779.

tion of the proceeds, in accordance with the resolutions of Congress governing the sharing of prizes. The prize agents were directed by the Marine Committee to render to it a quarterly statement showing the prizes received, sales effected, and distributions of the proceeds made.[1]

The same men who were prize agents were also as a rule "Continental agents," in which latter capacity they served the various administrative organs of Congress, including the Marine Committee. They assisted the Committee and commander-in-chief of the fleet in purchasing, refitting, provisioning, and manning the armed vessels. The naval services of some of these men, both as prize agents and as Continental agents, were so considerable as to render their names worthy of mention. Most conspicuous among the several naval agents were John Bradford of Boston, John Nixon and John Maxwell Nesbit of Philadelphia, John Langdon of Portsmouth, New Hampshire, Nathaniel Shaw, jr., of New London, and Daniel Tillinghast of Providence.

The governors and legislatures of the colonies and other local governmental authorities often aided the Committee in its work. The work of Governor Trumbull and the Connecticut Council of Safety in the building of the Continental frigates in that state

---

1. Force, American Archives, 5th, II, 1113-14.

has already been noted. In the latter part of 1776 the New York Convention attempted in behalf of the Marine Committee to secure the two Continental frigates at Poughkeepsie from the British when they occupied the lower Hudson. Such illustrations could be multiplied. In two services so closely connected as the navy and the army, the officers and agents of one were naturally now and then called upon to serve the other. They borrowed from and lent to each other cannon, ammunition, and military stores. The Commissaries of one and the Navy Boards of the other had mutual dealings. The Commissary-General of Prisoners of the Army had much to do with the care of the marine prisoners.

Towards the close of 1776 the unsatisfactory state of the naval business, together with its increase and its growing complexity, forced home upon the Committee the necessity of providing some permanent force to take charge of the details of naval administration. Accordingly, on November 6, 1776, Congress at the instance of the Marine Committee resolved "that three persons, well skilled in maritime affairs, be immediately appointed to execute the business of the navy, under the direction of the marine committee."[1] Later in the same month John Nixon, John Wharton, and Francis

---

1. Journals of Continental Congress, October 28, November 6, 1776.

Hopkinson were selected as suitable persons for this work, all three living within or near Philadelphia.

Nixon with his experience as a shipping merchant was probably best fitted for his task. Fancy may discern a poetic fitness in his choice, since he had been the owner of the "Alfred," the first vessel of the American navy. Nixon also had the distinction of being the first man to read publicly the Declaration of Independence. Wharton belonged to the distinguished Philadelphia family of that name. Of the three men, Hopkinson probably had the widest culture. At the outbreak of the Revolution he was practicing law at Bordentown, New Jersey. He was one of the Signers of the Declaration of Independence. From 1779 to 1789 he was judge of the Admiralty Court of Pennsylvania. He is best known, however, not for his substantial services, but as the author of the humorous ballad, the "Battle of the Kegs."

On April 19, 1777, Congress on the motion of John Adams decided to form a similar board for the New England states, the members of which were to "reside at or in the neighborhood of Boston, in the state of Massachusetts Bay, with a power to adjourn to any part of New England; who shall have the superintendence of all naval and marine affairs of these United States within the four eastern states, under the direction of the marine committee."[1] Adams secured the filling of this board with some difficulty owing to the indifference of Congress to its establishment. Finally, nine men were nominated, and on May 6 three of these were chosen commissioners, James Warren of Plymouth, Massachusetts; William Vernon of Providence, Rhode Island; and John Deshon of New London, Connecticut.[2]

Foremost of the three Commissioners was Warren, an eminent patriot, who had been President of the Massachusetts Provincial Congress and also of the Massachusetts Board of War. He was an intimate friend of John and Samuel Adams, and, it is said, much resembled the latter in character.

---

1. Journals of Continental Congress, April 19, 1777.
2. On May 6, 1777, John Adams wrote to James Warren notifying him of his appointment. He added a few words explaining the character of the position: "You will have the building and fitting of all ships, the appointment of officers, the establishment of arsenals and magazines, which will take up your whole time; but it will be honorable to be so capitally concerned in laying a foundation of a great navy. The profit to you will be nothing; but the honor and the virtue the greater. I almost envy you this employment."—Works of John Adams, IX, 465. On May 9, the Rhode Island member of the Marine Committee notified William Vernon of his appointment.—Publications of the Rhode Island Historical Society, VIII, 206. See also Massachusetts Historical Society Collections, 7th, II, 45.

Vernon, who served as President of the Navy Board, was a most distinguished Newport merchant and one of the most self-sacrificing of patriots. During the Revolution he advanced large sums of money to the government, which were only in part repaid. Before the war his trade extended to all the maritime nations of Europe and to the West Indies and Africa.[1] Deshon was of Huguenot descent. He was conspicuous in the Revolutionary party of New London, and was a captain in his state's military forces. He rendered much assistance in fitting out the Connecticut navy.

These two boards were variously designated in the official documents of the time. The one was most frequently called the Navy Board of the Middle Department or District, or the Navy Board at Philadelphia, Bordentown, or Baltimore, according to its location; and the other, the Navy Board of the Eastern Department or District, or the Navy Board at Boston. The Navy Board at Philadelphia was at first referred to as the Continental Navy Board, or the Board of Assistants. These two names indicate that when the board at Philadelphia was formed, the establishing of a second board was not in contemplation. The Navy Board at Philadelphia seems to have taken little or no part in the naval affairs in New Eng-

---

1. New England Historical and Genealogical Register, XXX, 316-18.

land. It was hardly settled in its work before the Navy Board at Boston was created. Attention should be called to the fact that the offices of Navy Board and of Commissioner of the Navy had long been established in the British navy. The British offices served in some degree as models to Congress and the Marine Committee.[1]

Each board had a secretary, treasurer, and paymaster; but one person sometimes served in two, or even the three, capacities. Each board had one, and sometimes two clerks. A clerkship was at times joined with one of the other offices. The boards as a rule selected their own employees. Any

---

1. When the Navy Board at Philadelphia was being established and its commissioners appointed, William Ellery wrote to William Vernon as follows: "I should be glad to know what is the Office of Commissioners of the Navy, and that you would point it out particularly; unless you can refer me to some Author who particularly describes. The Conduct of the Affairs of a Navy as well as those of an Army, We are yet to learn. We are still unacquainted with the systematical management of them, although We have made considerable Progress in the latter. It is the Duty of every Friend to his Country to throw his Knowledge into the common Stock. I know you are well skilled in Commerce and I believe you are acquainted with the System of the British Navy, and I am sure of your Disposition to do every Service to the Cause of Liberty in your Power."—Publications of Rhode Island Historical Society, VIII, 201, Papers of William Vernon and the Navy Board.

two members of the Navy Board at Boston were empowered by Congress on October 23, 1777, to form a quorum.[1]

With the exception of the resignation of Deshon in May, 1781, the Navy Board at Boston did not change in personnel. Its headquarters remained continually at Boston. On the other hand, the membership of the Navy Board at Philadelphia made several changes. On May 9, 1778, William Smith of Baltimore was elected in the place of John Nixon, who had resigned.[2] On August 19, Hopkinson and Smith having resigned, Captain Nathaniel Falconer and James Searle, both of Pennsylvania, were appointed.[3] Falconer declined the appointment; Searle accepted, but resigned on September 26.[4] Meanwhile, Wharton had resigned, and the three commissionerships were vacant. On November 4, 1778, the vacancies were filled by the reappointment of Wharton, and the selection of James Read of Delaware, the clerk and paymaster of the Board, and William Winder,[5] a captain in the military forces of Maryland and a judge of the court of appeals of Somerset county in that state. When in

---

1. Journals of Continental Congress, October 23, 1777.
2. Ibid., May 9, 1778.
3. Ibid., August 19, 1778.
4. Ibid., September 28, 1778.
5. Ibid., November 4, 1778.

December, 1776, Philadelphia seemed to be in danger from the enemy, Congress and the Board retreated to Baltimore, where they spent the winter of 1776-1777. The fortunes of war compelled the Board in the fall of 1777 to retreat to Bordentown, New Jersey; and after the American fleet in the Delaware was destroyed, the Marine Committee early in 1778 ordered it to Baltimore,[1] where it was situated for a few months. In the summer of 1778 it returned permanently to Philadelphia.

The salary of a commissioner of the navy was first fixed at $1,500 a year. On October 31, 1778, "in consideration of the extensive business of their departments," this salary was raised to $3,000, and on November 12, 1779, on the depreciation of the currency, to $12,000. It was reduced on September 25, 1780, to $1,500, and was now paid quarterly in specie or its equivalent. The salaries of the employees of the Navy Boards underwent like variations. Beginning with $500, they advanced in some instances as high as $2,000 a year. On August 4, 1778, the clerk of the Navy Board at Boston was made a special allowance of $500, "in consid-

---

1. Marine Committee Letter Book, Marine Committee to Navy Board of Middle Department, January 22, 1778. The Philadelphia Board was ordered on January 22 to remove to Baltimore, but it appears that it did not go until April.

eration of the great and constant business," in which he had been engaged.[1]

To recapitulate, the chief agents of the Marine Committee were these: the Navy Boards, the prize agents, the Continental agents, and the agents for building vessels. After the creation of the Navy Boards, the latter three classes served in part as their sub-agents; but by no means entirely so, for the Marine Committee gave many orders over the heads of the Boards.

The Marine Committee and its principal agents employed many minor agents. One illustration, taken from the work of the Navy Boards as purveyors of the navy, will suffice to show the subordinate character of the services which these minor agents rendered. It is recorded that the Navy Board at Boston had in its employ in New Hampshire "a contractor of beef for the navy," who in turn had in his employ a single drover, that by September, 1779, had purchased more than one thousand head of cattle for the use of the Navy Board at Boston.[2]

---

1. For salaries of the Commissioners of the Navy and their employees, see Journals of Continental Congress, November 7, 1776; April 19, 1777; October 23, 1777; October 10, 1778; October 31, 1778; November 12, 1779; January 28, 1780; and September 25, 1780.

2. Miscellaneous Manuscripts, Division of Manuscripts, Library of Congress.

CHAPTER IV

THE WORK OF THE NAVY BOARDS AND THE MARINE COMMITTEE

There was a painful lack of system about the business methods of the Naval Department of the Revolution. Then, official routine was not settled as at present. Usage had had no opportunity to establish fixed and orderly forms of procedure; and amid the distractions of war, when some real or supposed emergency was continually inviting one authority or another to disregard regularity and order, usage could obtain but scant permission to begin its work. Wars are famous for breaking through, not for forming a crust of official precedent. The administrative machinery of armies and navies tends to adapt itself to the conditions of peace—now the normal state of nations. During long periods of partial stagnation this machinery becomes complicated; its tension is weakened; and many of its axles grow rusty from disuse. When war breaks out, the conditions of administration are greatly changed. A thousand extra calls for work to be done at once are loud and inexorable. Expedition must be had at all hazards and costs. Rapid action of the administrative machinery must be obtained, its tension screwed down, extra cog wheels discarded, and efficient machinists substituted for the dotards of peace. It is obvious that with this sort of difficulty those who managed the naval affairs during the Revolution did not have to contend, for the organ of naval administration was then created from its foundation. Their difficulties sprang not from the age, but from the newness of this organ. It lacked a nice correlation of parts, the smooth action that comes from long service, and the system that immemorial routine establishes.

The absence of system in the Naval Department was most conspicuous in the appointment of naval officers, from the captain to the coxswain. This work was shared by Congress, the Marine Committee, the Navy Boards, the Continental agents, the Commander-in-chief of the navy, the commanders of vessels, recruiting agents, the Commissioners at Paris, and the commercial agents residing in foreign countries. Appointments were sometimes actually determined by the governors of states, "conspicuous citizens," and local governmental bodies. A good illustration of the way in which convenience was sometimes consulted is found in the resolution of Congress of June 14, 1777, which designated **William**

Whipple, the New Hampshire member of the Marine Committee, John Langdon, Continental agent at Portsmouth, and John Paul Jones, the commander of the ship "Ranger," to select the commissioned and warrant officers of the "Ranger," then at Portsmouth.[1] In a new navy without *esprit de corps*, to permit a commander to have a voice in choosing his own officers often made for proper subordination.

It was a source of annoyance and confusion to the Navy Boards to find through accidental sources of information, as they sometimes did, that the Marine Committee had given orders to naval agents to transact business, the immediate control of which was vested in the Boards. Naval agents sometimes discovered that they were serving in a single task two or three naval masters. Irregularities were chargeable not alone to the Naval Department. The governor of a state was known on his own authority, to the vexation of the rightful executive, to take part in the direction of the cruises of Continental vessels. Naval commanders were now and then guilty of breaches of their orders. Congress had its share in the confusing of business. On one occasion, making a display of its ignorance, it suspended Captain John Roach from a command to which he had not been appointed;

1. Journals of Continental Congress, June 14, 1777.

Roach in fact was not an officer in the Continental navy.[1] It sometimes made impracticable details of the armed vessels. It also exercised its privilege of referring to special committees bits of business that logically belonged to the Marine Committee.

These irregularities, notwithstanding their number, were after all exceptions. The very nature of business forces it to follow some system, however imperfectly. Where there is a number of agents there must be a division of labor. Without such arrangements chaos would exist. It is therefore possible to set forth with some detail the respective duties of the Marine Committee, the Navy Boards, and the various naval agents. The work and duties of the naval agents have already been treated with sufficient particularity. The work of the Navy Boards and the Marine Committee will be considered in this chapter.

The duties of the Navy Boards were of a varied character. Each Board superintended the building, manning, fitting, provisioning, and repairing of the armed vessels in its district. It kept a register of the vessels which it built, showing the name, dimensions, burden, number of guns, tackle, apparel, and furniture of each vessel. Each

---

1. Journals of Continental Congress, June 14, 1777. Marine Committee Letter Book, Committee to Navy Board at Boston, March 6, 1778.

Board had records of all the officers, sailors, and marines in its district, and required the commanders to make returns of these items upon the termination of their cruises. It was the duty of the Boards to notify the Marine Committee of the arrivals and departures of the Continental vessels. They were required to settle the naval accounts and "to keep fair Books of all expenditures of Publick Moneys." The records of their transactions were to be open to the inspection of Congress and the Marine Committee. They rendered to the Committee annually, or oftener when required, an account of their disbursements. The Boards paid the salaries of officers and seamen, and audited the accounts of the prize agents.[1]

In the appointment of officers the Navy Board at Boston was given a freer rein than was its colleague at Philadelphia. The share of the Navy Boards in selecting officers and in enlisting seamen was about as follows. The Boards superintended the appointing of petty officers and the enlisting of seamen, both of which duties were chiefly performed by the commanders of vessels and by recruiting agents. The Boards generally selected the warrant officers, very frequently on the recommendation of the commanders. If the one appoint-

---

1. Publications of Rhode Island Historical Society, VIII, 208, Instructions of Marine Committee to the Eastern Navy Board, July 10, 1777.

ment to the office of Commander-in-chief be disregarded, there existed but two classes of commissioned officers in the Revolutionary navy, captains and lieutenants. The Boards often chose the lieutenants; and they generally recommended the captains to the Marine Committee. The Committee furnished the Boards with blank warrants and commissions, signed by the President of Congress. When one of these forms was properly filled out by a navy board for an officer, the validity of his title to his position and rank could not be questioned.

The Boards were empowered under certain circumstances, and in accordance with the rules and regulations of the navy and the resolutions of Congress, to order the holding of courts of enquiry and courts-martial. They could administer oaths to the judges and officials of these courts. A Board might suspend an officer of the navy who treated it with "indecency and disrespect."[1] On October 23, 1777, the Navy Board at Boston was given power to suspend a naval officer, "until the pleasure of Congress shall be known."[2] Not always

---

1. Journals of Continental Congress, December 30, 1777. The occasion of this grant of power by Congress was a letter complaining of "disrespect and ill treatment" which a member of the Navy Board of the Middle Department had received at the hands of John Barry, commander of the frigate "Effingham."

2. Journals of Continental Congress, October 23, 1777.

did the kindliest relations exist between the Navy Boards and the commanders of the vessels. Officers who but yesterday tramped the decks of their own merchantmen, giving commands but not receiving them, chafed under the subordination that their position in the navy exacted.

The Navy Boards made public the resolutions of Congress on naval affairs, copies of which they lodged with the prize agents, the commanders of vessels, and all interested persons. They distributed among the naval captains the rules and regulations of the navy, the sea-books, and the naval signals. The Boards acted in an advisory capacity to the Marine Committee, which frequently called upon them for information or opinions; when a revision of the rules and regulations of the navy was under consideration their assistance in the work was requested. Sometimes they volunteered important suggestions looking to the betterment of the navy. They communicated frequently with the Committee, giving in detail the state of the naval business in their respective districts.

In the hiring, purchase, and building of vessels the Boards had to do with craft of all sorts, freight-boats, fire-ships, galleys, packets, brigs, schooners, sloops, ships, frigates, and men-of-war. Measured by the standards of the time, the building of one of the larger vessels was a work of some magnitude. A notion of the men and materials requisite for such an undertaking may be gained from an estimate, made early in 1780, of the sundries needed to complete the 74-gun ship "America," the largest of the Continental vessels constructed during the Revolution. The construction of this ship had been begun at Portsmouth, New Hampshire, in 1777. It was computed that one hundred and fifty workmen for an average period of eight months would be required. Fifty carpenters, twenty ordinary laborers, twenty caulkers, ten riggers, ten sailors, two master-builders, and an uncertain number of blacksmiths, sail-makers, coopers, plumbers, painters, glaziers, carvers, boat-builders, ship-copperers, tinners, cabinet-makers, and tanners were demanded. Materials and provisions were needed as follows: Seven hundred tons of timbers, one hundred casks of naval stores, forty tons of iron, one thousand water-casks, masts and spars of all sorts, sheets of lead, train oil, and oakum; provisions for most of the above workmen, and lastly, an indispensable lubricant for all naval services at this time, "rum, one half pint per day, including extra hands, say for 150 hands, 8 months, 12 hhds, 1310 gallons."[1] In building the armed vessels, the Boards were greatly hampered by the difficulty of ob-

1. Records and papers of Continental Congress, 37, p. 217.

taining artisans, owing to their being called out for military service, or to their engaging in privateering. In providing armament and equipment, they were embarrassed by the inexperience of the colonists in casting cannon, and by the obstacles which they encountered in importing canvas, cables, arms, and ammunition.

For the future use of the fleet the Navy Boards collected in due season provisions and naval stores. In their work as purveyors for the navy a knowledge of the baking of bread and the curing of meats might not prove amiss. The kinds and quantities of provisions which they bought may be judged from an estimate of the supplies that were requisite to equip for sea and for a single cruise the 36-gun frigate "Confederacy." The names and quantities of the articles needed were as follows: bread, 35,700 lbs.; beef, 15,300 lbs.; pork, 15,300 lbs.; flour, 5,100 lbs.; potatoes, 10,000 lbs.; peas, 80 bus.; mutton, 2,500 lbs.; butter, 637 lbs.; rice, 2,550 lbs.; vinegar, 160 gals.; and rum, 2,791 gals.[1] The Boards' supplies of naval stores consisted chiefly of canvas, sails, cordage, cables, tar, turpentine, and ship chandlery.

The commissioners of each district made some division of their work among themselves. For instance, the special task of

---

1. Records and papers of Continental Congress, 37, p. 273.

Wharton of the Philadelphia Board was the superintending of the accounting and the naval finances of the Middle District. During 1778 Deshon of the Boston Board spent much time in Connecticut attending to the naval business in that state. This had to do chiefly with freeing the "Trumbull" frigate from a sandbar upon which she had grounded. During the same year Vernon was for a time at Providence endeavoring to get to sea the Continental vessels which the British had blockaded in that port. For a part of the year Warren alone attended to the business of the Board at its headquarters at Boston. On August 4, 1778, Congress appropriated $365 to each of the commissioners of the Navy Board at Boston to pay their traveling expenses during the past year, since in the right discharge of their office they were obliged "frequently to visit the different parts of their extensive district."[1]

In the extent of its powers and in the amount of its business the Boston Board exceeded the one at Philadelphia.[2] This was largely owing to the centering of naval affairs in New England after the occupation of Philadelphia in September, 1777;

1. Journals of Continental Congress, August 4, 1778.
2. In the transmission of foreign mail the Navy Board at Boston acted as the agent of the Committee of Foreign Affairs. It both purchased and hired packet boats.

and to the capture or destruction in that year of a large part of the fleet to the southward of New England. After 1776 all the new vessels added in America to the navy, with the exception of two or three, were either purchased or built in New England. The long distance of the Marine Committee from Boston, with the consequent difficulties and delays in communication, made it necessary for the Committee to grant to the Boston Board larger powers than to the Philadelphia Board.

The most important work of a Naval Office is the directing of the movements of the fleet, or in other words, the determining of the cruises of the armed vessels. This power the Marine Committee jealously guarded, and was loathe to yield any part of it. The Committee was forced at times, however, to give to the Boston Board a considerable discretion. In July, 1777, it ordered the Board to send out the cruisers as fast as they could be got ready, "directing the Commanders to such Latitudes as you shall think there will be the greatest chance of success in intercepting the enemy's Transports and Merchant Ships"; and in November, 1778, to send the vessels out, "either collectively, or singly, as you shall judge proper, using your discretion as to the time for which their Cruises shall continue, and your best judgment in directing the commanders to such places and on such stations as you shall think will be for the general benefit of the United States, and to annoy and distress the Enemy."[1] Such general orders were always subject to the particular plans and directions of the Committee, which were by no means few. The Committee itself determined the service of all vessels that refitted at Philadelphia. As a consequence the duties of the Navy Board of the Middle Department had to do chiefly with the minor details of administration.

Turning now from the work of the Navy Boards to that of the Marine Committee, one finds the significant fact to be the twofold relation that the Committee bore to the Continental Congress. By reason of the union in Congress of both legislative and executive functions, the Committee was at one and the same time an administrative organ of Congress charged with executing the business of its Naval Department, and its legislative committee on naval affairs. Naturally, there were at points no lines of demarkation between these two functions; and it is therefore not always easy, or even possible, to determine in which capacity the Committee is acting. The Committee's administrative duties, *par excellence*, were the enforcing and the carrying out by means of its agents of the various

---

[1] Marine Committee Letter Book Committee to Navy Board at Boston, July 11, 1777; November 16, 1778.

resolutions of Congress upon naval affairs. Already much light has been thrown upon this phase of the Committee's work in the treatment of the Navy Boards and the naval agents.

It was the duty of the Marine Committee to see that the resolutions on naval affairs were brought to the attention of the proper persons, officers, agents, and authorities. As the head of the Naval Department, it issued its commands and orders to the Navy Boards, the naval agents, and the commanders of vessels. This was done both verbally and by letters. The Navy Board of the Middle Department, the naval agents at Philadelphia, and often the naval officers in that port, conferred with the Committee and received orders by word of mouth. In the prosecution of its work outside of Philadelphia the Committee conducted a large correspondence, chiefly with the Navy Board at Boston, the naval agents at Portsmouth, Boston, New London, and Baltimore, and the leading captains of the navy. It addressed letters to the governors of most of the states and to many of the local governmental authorities; to the Commander-in-chief of the navy, Washington, General Heath, General Schuyler, the Commissary-General of Prisoners, Commissary-General of Purchases of the army, the merchants of Baltimore, Count D'Estaing, the Commissioners in Paris, and most of the captains of the navy. This list of correspondents well represents the range of the business of the Committee.

Through its recommendations to Congress the Marine Committee virtually selected almost all the captains of the navy and of the marine corps, many lieutenants of both services, as a rule the commissioners of the navy, the prize agents, and the advocates for the trying of maritime causes. Appointments to these offices were rarely made by Congress contrary to the recommendations of the Committee, or on its own initiative independent of the Committee. A few captains and lieutenants of the navy were appointed by representatives of the United States residing abroad.

As is well known, all executive offices are called upon to establish certain forms, rules, and regulations for the guidance and government of their agents. Of this character was the fixing by the Marine Committee of the naval signals, the forms for sea-books, and the proper uniforms for the naval officers. The Committee's regulations on uniforms were dated September 5, 1776. For captains they prescribed a blue coat "with red lappels, slash cuff, stand-up collar, flat yellow buttons, blue britches, red waistcoat with narrow lace." The uniform of the officers of the marines was equally resplendent in colors. It included a green coat, with white cuffs, a silver epaulet on the shoulder, white waistcoat and breeches edged with green, and black gaiters and garters. Green was the distinctive color of the marines. The privates were to display this badge in the form of green shirts, "if they can be procured."[1] Not enough information is accessible to the writer to determine what influence the regulations prescribing the uniform of British officers had on those adopted by the Marine Committee. Both required in the uniform of captains, blue coats, standing-up collars, and flat buttons; neither required epaulets, the wearing of which, as is well known, originated in France.[2] It is probable that the prescribed uniform was little worn by the Continental naval officers. Grim necessity forced each officer to ransack whatever wardrobe Providence offered, and it is somewhat inaccurate to call their miscellaneous garbs "uniforms."

As the Naval Office at Philadelphia developed, letters, memorials, and petitions poured in upon it in increasing numbers. Many of these communications were addressed to the President of Congress, were read in Congress, and were formally referred to the Marine Committee to be acted or reported upon. It was only infrequently that Congress offered any suggestions as to

1. Sherburne, Life of John Paul Jones, ed. 1851, 30. Copies of the regulations on uniforms will be found in John Paul Jones manuscripts, Library of Congress.
2. Clowes, Royal Navy, III, 347-50; IV, 182.

their proper disposition. These complaints and requests were of a varied character, and came from many sources; not a few originated with that obsequious crowd, with axes to grind, that always attends upon official bodies. The wide range of these communications may be judged from the following subjects selected at random:

New Hampshire and Massachusetts request that the frigates building in those states be ordered to defend the New England coast.[1] Governor Livingston of New Jersey asks for a naval office for a relative, Musco Livingston.[2] Gerard, the minister of France to the United States, wishes to know "the opinion of Congress respecting his offering a premium to the owners of privateers that shall intercept masts and spars belonging to the enemy, coming from Halifax to New York and Rhode Island."[3] John Macpherson asserts that the position of commander-in-chief in the navy was promised to him by Messrs. Randolph, Hopkins, and Rutledge, to whom he communicated an important secret.[4] An affront has been offered several French captains in Boston by the commander of the Continental frigate "Warren."[5] Twelve lieutenants,

1. Force, American Archives, 5th, II, 315.
2. Journals of Continental Congress, September, 17, 1779.
3. Ibid., December 7, 1778.
4. Ibid., July 11, 1776.
5. Ibid., June 16, 1778.

who had been dismissed from the navy for combining in order to extort an increase of pay, ask to be reinstated.[1] The ambassador of Naples at the Court of France, whose king has opened his ports to the American vessels, wishes "to know the colours of the flag, and form of the sea-papers of the United States."[2] Captain Biddle writes concerning the cruel treatment inflicted by Lord Howe upon Lieutenant Josiah of the Continental navy.[3] Captain Skimmer has been killed in an action with the "Montague," and has left eleven children, nine of whom are unable to earn a livelihood. His widow asks for a pension.[4]

The Marine Committee made frequent reports to Congress, both in response to previous orders therefrom, and of its own accord in the course of its business. Occasionally parts of its reports were recommitted by Congress to a limited number of the Committee's members, doubtless for the

---

1. Journals of Continental Congress, July 23, 24, 1777.
2. Ibid., February 24, 1779.
3. Ibid., August 7, 1776.
4. Ibid., September 14, 23, 1778. The Marine Committee reported and Congress agreed that "the eastern navy board be directed to supply 400 dollars annually, in quarterly payments, for the support of Captain Skimmer's widow and nine youngest children, and that this provision be continued three years." This is the first instance of the granting by the United States of a pension to the family of a naval officer upon his death.

purpose of obtaining prompt and expert action. The Committee sometimes assigned special business to sub-committees, or to single members. The subjects which the Committee considered, discussed, and reported upon ran the whole gamut of naval activities and interests. The substance of many of its reports may be found in the Journals of the Continental Congress for the years 1776, 1777, 1778, and 1779. During this period the Marine Committee prepared and reported the larger part of the naval legislation of Congress. It is true that special committees contributed something to this work, but these were composed in part of members of the Marine Committee. Congress, as a body, originated little, although occasionally it was moved to the passage of resolutions on naval affairs by some real or supposed emergency, the importunities of the self-seeking, or the whims of individual members. It of course amended the reports of its committees.

The principal legislation of Congress relating to the navy which was passed during the incumbency of the Marine Committee will now be noted. No attempt will be made to separate those provisions that were the special work of the Marine Committee from the whole legislative output.

During 1776 and 1777 Congress authorized important naval increases. It directed the Marine Committee in March and April,

1776, to purchase "the armed vessel now in the river Delaware" and the ship "Molly," to fit out two armed cutters, and to build two galleys "capable of carrying two 36 or 42 pounders."[1] On November 20, 1776, Congress resolved to build immediately, one ship, 74, in New Hampshire; two ships, 74 and 36, in Massachusetts; one ship, 74, a brig, 18, and a packet boat, in Pennsylvania; two frigates, 36 each, in Virginia; and two frigates, 36 each, in Maryland.[2] Later, the size and armament of some of these vessels were reduced by the Marine Committee, and some of them were never completed. Only three of these ten vessels were armed, manned, and sent to sea as a part of the forces of the Continental navy. They were the "Alliance," 36, the "General Gates," 18, both built in Massachusetts, and the "Saratoga," 16, built in Pennsylvania. The 74-gun ship "America," constructed at Portsmouth, New Hampshire, was not launched until shortly before the Revolution ended. On January 23, 1777, Congress ordered the construction of two frigates, 36 and 28, in Connecticut. These two ships were named respectively the "Confederacy" and "Bourbon." On March 15, 1777, the Marine Committee was ordered to purchase

---

1. Journals of Continental Congress, March 13, March 28, April 3, April 14, 1776.
2. Ibid., November 20, 1776.

three ships.[1] Congress gave directions for other naval increases, but they were not fully carried out. In July, 1777, owing to the "extravagant prices now demanded for all kinds of materials used in ship-building, and the enormous wages required by tradesmen and labourers," Congress empowered the Committee to stop the building of such of the Continental vessels as they should judge proper.[2]

During 1776 many important appointments and promotions in the navy and the marine corps were made by the Marine Committee, and confirmed by Congress. Samuel Nichols was placed at the head of the marines, with the rank of major. Twenty captains of the navy were appointed. Four of these had been appointed lieutenants on December 22, 1775, and were promoted, but the remaining sixteen were new appointees. John Manly was taken from Washington's fleet. Nicholas Biddle, Thomas Read, Charles Alexander, and James Josiah had seen service in the Pennsylvania navy; and James Nicholson in the Maryland navy. During this year there was a great scramble to obtain offices on board the thirteen frigates, and amid the rivalries of politics, it is not surprising that some candidates were successful that, unfortunately

---

1. Journals of Continental Congress, January 23, March 15, 1777.
2 Ibid., July 25, 1777.

for the navy, had tasted little salt water.[1]

In military services questions of promotion and rank are perennial sources of heartburning and jealousy. The advancing of an officer on any other principle than that of seniority in service rarely fails to arouse feelings of injustice and suspicions of partiality, which are only too often warranted. The discontent and insubordination that such a promotion incites must always be weighed against its beneficial results. When, on October 10, 1776, Congress, in determining the rank of twenty-four captains and two lieutenants, disregarded the dates of their commissions and appointments, it was unable to defend its act on the usual, and under some circumstances, tenable ground of the conspicuous services, marked talents, and signal professional skill of those favored. Once more Southern influences prevailed, and James Nicholson, of Maryland, commander of the frigate "Virginia," was made the senior captain of the navy. This distinguishing of Nicholson, who was appointed captain on June 6, 1776, worked

---

1. Journals of Continental Congress, June 25, October 10, 1776; Scribner's Magazine, XXIV, 29, Mahan, John Paul Jones in the Revolution, quotes a member of Congress writing to Jones probably in the fall of 1776: "You would be surprised to hear what a vast number of applications are continually making for officers of the new frigates, especially for the command."

a hardship to the officers, and especially to the four captains, appointed on December 22, 1775. John Paul Jones, who stood fifth in rank in the list of December 22, and now found himself eighteenth, smarted under the injustice which was done him.[1] It is noteworthy that from March, 1777, when Esek Hopkins was suspended from his position of commander-in-chief of the fleet, until the end of the Revolution, the head of the Continental army and the ranking officer of the navy came from adjoining Southern states.[2]

On November 15, 1776, Congress fixed

---

1. Jones made a copy of the list of captains of the navy arranged in accordance with their respective ranks, upon which copy he commented: "Whereby No. 18 is superseded by..........13 [men].....altho their superior Merits and Abilities are at best Presumptive, and not one of them was in the service the 7th day of December, 1775, when No. 18 was appointed Senior Lieut of the Navy."—Jones Manuscripts, Library of Congress.

2. Nicholson, while at times displaying conspicuous bravery, was less fortunate in his naval service than Hopkins. Two frigates under his command were at different times captured by the enemy. On May 1, 1777, Congress suspended him from his command, "until he shall have made such satisfaction as shall be accepted by the executive powers of the state of Maryland, for the disrespectful and contemptuous letter written by him to the governor of that state."—Journals of Continennental Congress, May 1, 1777.

the relative rank of army and naval officers as follows:[1]

Admiral, with General.
Vice-Admiral, with Lieutenant-General.
Rear-Admiral, with Major-General.
Commodore, with Brigadier-General.
Captain of a ship of 40 guns and upwards, with Colonel.
Captain of a ship of 20 to 40 guns, with Lieutenant-Colonel.
Captain of a ship of 10 to 20 guns, with Major.
Lieutenant of the navy, with Captain.

In this legislation on rank once more the influence of British models is apparent. The Committee was evidently building for the future, for the four higher ranks were not established at this time, nor during the Revolution. The present relative rank of army and naval officers is based on the above table.

On March 23, 1776, Congress passed most important resolutions supplementary to those of November 25, 1775, concerning captures and the shares of prizes. The resolutions of November 25 legalized the capture of the enemy's vessels of war and transports. The new resolutions permitted for the first time the capture of all ships and cargoes, "belonging to any inhabitant, or inhabitants of Great Britain, taken on the

---

[1]. Journals of Continental Congress, November 15, 1776.

high seas, or between high and low water mark," by American privateers, vessels of the Continental navy, or ships fitted out by any of the colonies. In brief, the new resolutions legalized reprisals on British commerce. In the case of Continental vessels, one-third of the prize went to the officers and crew; in the case of privateers, the whole of the prize fell to the owners and captors. Each colony was permitted to fix the shares of the proceeds of merchantmen captured by its own ships of war.[1] On October 30, 1776, the share of prizes taken by vessels of the Continental navy was increased to one-half of merchantmen, transports, and store ships; and to the whole of ships of war and privateers.[2]

On April 2, 1776, Congress agreed to a form of commission for privateers. On the next day it resolved to send blank commissions, signed by the President of Congress, to the legislatures, provincial congresses, and committees of safety of the United Colonies. These were to be filled out and delivered to privateersmen. Blank bonds, which were to be executed by the owners or masters of privateers, were also sent. These bonds, which prescribed a penalty of five or ten thousand dollars, according to the size of the ship, were intended to

---

1. Journals of Continental Congress, March 23, 1776.
2. Ibid., October 30, 1776.

discourage or prevent misconduct and unwarrantable acts on the part of officers and crews. Congress also drafted a form of instructions to the commanders of privateers.[1]

Congress on November 15, 1776, established a new pay-table. Officers were now divided into three classes, those serving on board of vessels of 20 guns and upwards, vessels of 10 to 20 guns, and vessels below 10 guns. The vessels of the first two classes were commanded by captains, and of the third class by lieutenants. The pay of the higher officers, which the new table generally raised, varied for each of the three classes, the commanding officers of which received, respectively, $60, $48, and $30 a month. Seamen were now paid a monthly wage of $8. The pay of officers below the captain ranged from $30 to $8.34 a month. A bounty of $20 for every cannon and $8 for every seaman captured on board a British ship of war was now voted.[2] On July 25, 1777, the "subsistence" of officers while in foreign or domestic ports was fixed.[3] On January 19, 1778, Congress resolved that officers not in actual service should be allowed pay, but not rations. While prisoners of war, their allowance

---

1. Journals of Continental Congress, April 2, April 3, 1776.
2. Ibid., November 15, 1776.
3. Ibid., July 25, 1777.

for rations was to be diminished by the value of the supplies which they received from the enemy.[1] Pursers for vessels of 16 guns and upwards were authorized on November 14, 1778.[2]

Additional interest attaches to the initial legislation on pensions of the American government because of the unprecedented liberality which now marks its treatment of its veterans. The first legislation on naval pensions dates from the adoption by Congress on November 28, 1775, of a form of naval contract according to which certain bounties were granted officers, seamen, and marines disabled from earning a livelihood.[3] These bounties were derived from the proceeds of prizes captured by the aid of the beneficiaries. A more typical pension law was passed on August 26, 1776.[4] It had, however, a vital defect in that it was left to the enforcement of the individual states. According to its provisions every naval officer, seaman, or marine, "belonging to the United States of America, who shall lose a limb in any engagement in which no prize shall be taken, or be therein otherwise so disabled as to be rendered incapable of

---

1. Journals of Continental Congress, January 19, March 20, 1778.
2. Ibid., November 14, 1778.
3. See Chapter I, page 46.
4. Journals of Continental Congress, August 26, 1776. This law applied to both the army and the navy.

getting a livelihood, shall receive during his life, or the continuance of such disability, one half of his monthly pay." When a prize was captured at the time the disability was contracted, the disabled person's share of prize money was considered as a part of his half-pay. If the disabled person was rendered incapable of serving in the navy, although not totally disabled from earning a livelihood, he received a monthly sum, judged to be adequate by the legislature of the state in which he resided. Each state was to determine which of its citizens were entitled to a pension under this law, to pay such persons their half-pay or allowance, and to make a quarterly report of its work to the secretary of Congress. The distinguishing characteristic of the law lay in its dependence on the states for its enforcement. As might be expected, it was very imperfectly carried out.

On September 25, 1778, Congress extended the advantages of the law to all persons whose disabilities were acquired previous to August 26, 1776.[1] It is to be carefully noted that this was a pension for disabilities and not for service—a fundamental classification in pension law. An agitation for a service pension for life for the officers of the army was made in and out of Congress for a long time, until in 1780 it

---

1. Journals of Continental Congress, September 25, 1778.

was at last successful.¹ Such emoluments were not at this time granted to naval officers; it was probably argued that their sharing in captured prizes offset the pensions of the army officers. Then, too, the army had ways of gaining the attention of Congress that the weak and insignificant navy did not possess.

Few more important duties fall to naval offices than the enforcing of discipline in the navy by means of naval courts. Adams's rules of November 28, 1775, made provision for holding courts-martial, but not courts of enquiry, which are a sort of grand jury or inquest. They also provided that courts-martial should consist of at least six naval officers, with six officers of marines, if so many of the latter were convenient to the court.² The Committee and Navy Boards at times found it impossible to assemble so many officers. No definite procedure in investigating the loss of vessels was prescribed by Adams's rules. Additional legislation was therefore demanded. On May 6, 1778, Congress adopted new regulations on naval courts, which were to be operative for one year.³ They provided that, when a vessel of war was lost by cap-

1. Harvard Historical Studies, X, L. C. Hatch, Administration of American Revolutionary Army, Chapter V, Pay and Half-pay.
2. See Chapter I, page 45.
3. Journals of Continental Congress, May 6, 1778.

ture or otherwise, a court of enquiry should be held, "consisting of that navy board which shall, by the marine committee of Congress, be directed to proceed therein, or any three persons that such navy board may appoint." If the court of enquiry found that the loss of the vessel was caused by the negligence or malconduct of any commissioned officer, the Navy Board might suspend such officer pending his trial by a court-martial, which, in the event that six naval officers could not be assembled, was to consist of five men appointed by the Navy Board. The permitting of civilians to sit upon naval courts is the salient feature of these new resolutions, and is an anomaly in naval judicature. They also provided that in cases where one or more vessels out of a fleet were lost by capture or otherwise, the commanders of the escaping vessels were to be tried by a similar procedure. If a court-martial found that the loss of a vessel was caused by the cowardice or treachery of the commanding officer, it was directed to inflict the death penalty. On August 19, 1778, the procedure established on May 6 was extended to "all offences and misdemeanors in the marine department."[1] The proceedings of courts-martial were forwarded to the Marine Committee, which laid them, together with its recommenda-

---

1. Journals of Continental Congress, August 19, 1778.

tions thereupon, before Congress for final action.

During the incumbency of the Marine Committee a number of interesting and important naval trials were held. Captain Thomas Thompson in 1778 and Captain Dudley Saltonstall in 1779 were broken by courts-martial. Other captains who lost their vessels were tried, but escaped so severe a punishment. The cases growing out of Commodore Hopkins's expedition to New Providence, his engagement with the "Glasgow," and the immediately succeeding events of his fleet in the spring of 1776 deserve more extended notice. During the summer of 1776 the Marine Committee ordered Commodore Hopkins and Captains Dudley Saltonstall and Abraham Whipple to leave the fleet, which was then stationed in Rhode Island, and to come to Philadelphia for trial. After calling before it the inferior officers of the "Alfred" and "Columbus," and hearing their complaints against the two captains, the Committee reported to Congress on July 11 that the charge against Captain Saltonstall was not well founded, and that the charge against Captain Whipple "amounts to nothing more than a rough, indelicate mode of behaviour to his marine officers." Congress ordered the two captains to repair to their commands, and recommended Captain Whipple "to cultivate harmony with his officers."[1]

Commodore Hopkins was not to get off so easily. His whole conduct since he left Philadelphia early in January, 1776, was investigated. The principal charge against him was the disobeying of the instructions of the Naval Committee of January 5, 1776, to attack the forces of the enemy in the region of Virginia and the Carolinas. Hopkins based his defence on the statement that the enemy in that region had become too strong to attack by the time his fleet had sailed on February 17, and also on a certain clause in his instructions granting him discretionary powers.[2] After the Marine Committee had investigated the case, and reported upon it, Congress, on August 12, took into consideration the "instructions given to Commodore Hopkins, his examination and answers to the Marine Committee, and the report of the Marine Committee thereupon; also, the farther defence by him made, and the testimony of the witnesses." On the 15th, Congress came to the resolution: "That the said commodore Hopkins, during his cruise to the southward, did not

---

1. Journals of Continental Congress, July 11, 1776.
2. Edward Field's Esek Hopkins, 154-56, quotes words of Hopkins in his own defence. Washington feared the plan of the Naval Committee would fail as the enemy must know it, so long had the fleet been fitting for sea.—Ford, Writings of Washington, III, 319.

pay due regard to the tenor of his instructions . . . . . and, that his reasons for not going from Providence immediately to the Carolinas, are by no means satisfactory." The next day Congress resolved, "that the said conduct of commodore Hopkins deserves the censure of this house, and this house does accordingly censure him."[1]

This action seems more severe than the facts justify. John Adams, who defended Hopkins, had with difficulty prevented Congress from cashiering the Commodore. According to Adams's view, Hopkins was "pursued and persecuted by that anti-New-England spirit which haunted Congress in many other of their proceedings, as well as in this case."[2] The action of Congress may be interpreted differently. Hopkins had not met the expectations of Congress or the Marine Committee. As the head of the fleet, blame naturally fell upon him, whether he deserved it or not. He had his shortcomings as a naval officer, and failure magnified them. By placing the blame upon him, the skirts of Congress, of the Marine Committee, and of the other naval officers were cleared, and the hopes of a few self-interested men were brightened.

Commodore Hopkins's failure to carry out the plans of the Marine Committee dur-

---

1. Journals of Continental Congress, August 12, 15, and 16, 1776.
2. Quoted in Field's Esek Hopkins, 158.

ing the fall of 1776, together with the partial inaction of the fleet under his command, increased his disfavor with Congress and the Marine Committee. His praiseworthy endeavors to man and prepare his fleet for sea won for him the enmity of the owners of privateers at Providence, for his success would mean the taking of men and materials sorely needed by the privateersmen. Hopkins's intemperate language, lack of tact, and naval misfortunes bred a spirit of discontent, and gave an excuse for insubordination among his inferior officers. Encouraged by the discontented privateersmen of Providence, ten of the inferior officers of the "Warren," the Commodore's flagship, signed a petition and certain letters containing complaints and charges against Hopkins, and sent their documents to the Marine Committee. They were taken to Philadelphia by the chief "conspirator," Captain John Grannis of the marines. These documents asserted that Hopkins had called the members of the Marine Committee and of Congress "ignorant fellows—lawyers, clerks—persons who don't know how to govern men;" that he was "remarkably addicted to profane swearing;" that he had "treated prisoners in a most inhuman and barbarous manner;" that he was a "hindrance to the proper manning of the fleet;" and that "his conversation is at times so wild and orders so unsteady that I have sometimes thought he was not in his right mind." Besides these accusations, there were a few others of even less substantial character.[1]

On March 25, 1777, the Marine Committee laid before Congress the complaints and charges against Commodore Hopkins, and on the next day Congress took them into consideration; whereupon it resolved that "Esek Hopkins be immediately, and he is hereby, suspended from his command in the American navy."[2] Hopkins remained suspended until January 2, 1778. The Journals of Congress for this date contain the following entry: "Congress having no farther occasion for the service of Esek Hopkins, esq. who, on the 22nd of December, 1775, was appointed commander in chief of the fleet fitted out by the naval committee, Resolved, That the said Esek Hopkins, esq. be dismissed from the service of the United States."[3]

Hopkins's suspension and removal did not in any way improve the navy. Indeed, it was far less fortunate in 1777, than it had been in 1776. That its chief officer should have been suspended without a hearing, on flimsy charges, offered by a small number of inferior officers whose leader

---

1. Edward Field's Esek Hopkins, Chapter VI, Conspiracy and Dismissal, contains many original documents.
2. Journals of Continental Congress, March 25, March 26, 1777.
3. Ibid., January 2, 1778.

was guilty of insubordination, convicts Congress of acting with undue haste and of doing a possible injustice, and arouses the suspicion that it was not actuated wholly by a calm and unbiased judgment. The wording of Hopkins's dismissal seems needlessly curt, and harsh. Since Hopkins had lost the confidence of Congress, the Marine Committee, and many of his countrymen, his removal from the office of commander-in-chief to that of a captain might have been justified.

On January 13, 1778, Hopkins brought a suit for libel against the ten officers concerned in the "conspiracy," fixing his damages at £10,000. On July 30 Congress passed a resolution for defraying the reasonable expenses of the ten officers in defending their suit.[1] The case was tried before a jury in the Inferior Court of Common Pleas of Rhode Island. The decision was unfavorable to Hopkins, as the jury brought in a verdict for "the defendants and their costs." The victory of the opposition to the Commodore was complete. He had not, however, lost the confidence of his fellow townsmen. He served in the General Assembly of his state, representing North Providence from 1777 until 1786, and he was from 1777 until the end of the Revolution a member of the Rhode Island Council

---

1. Journals of Continental Congress, July 30, 1778.

of War.[1] No one who knew Hopkins intimately ever doubted his courage, his patriotism, or his honesty of purpose.

The arrival off the Delaware Capes, on July 8, 1778, of twelve sail of the line and four frigates under the command of Count D'Estaing, Vice-Admiral of France, threw additional work upon the Naval Department. No sooner did the Marine Committee learn of the presence of the French, than it exerted itself to supply the table of its naval guests with eatables and drinkables. Casks of fresh water, several hundred barrels of bread and flour, and a small supply of fresh provisions, were at once sent to the Count, and the Committee ordered a commissary to collect for the use of the French fleet fifty bullocks, seven hundred sheep, a number of poultry, and a quantity of vegetables. After the ill-starred expedition against Rhode Island in August, 1778, when the French fleet put into Boston for repairs, its provisioning again became a care to the Naval Department. The Marine Committee ordered three thousand barrels of flour to be sent on from Albany for the use of the French.[2]

The distinction of having performed the first work of a consular bureau in the United

---

1. Edward Field's Esek Hopkins, 237-38.
2. Marine Committee Letter Book, Committee to Count D'Estaing, July 12, July 17 1778.

States belongs to the Marine Committee, since it had charge of the publication and record of the first consular appointments to this country. In accordance with the first commercial treaty between the United States and France, Gerard, the French minister, soon after his arrival in America in July, 1778, appointed John Holker, consul for the port of Philadelphia, and in September named a vice-consul for the same place. The latter appointment Congress referred to the Marine Committee "in order that the same may be made public." A similar disposition was made of the appointments of consuls for Maryland, South Carolina, and Boston, and of the vice-consuls for Alexandria (Virginia), and Virginia. In the case of the vice-consul for Virginia, Congress ordered the Marine Committee to "cause the commission of Mr. d' Annemours to be recorded in the book by them kept for that purpose, and his appointment made known to all concerned." The Committee was instrumental in obtaining the settling of the powers and duties of consuls as regards the United States and France. On August 2, 1779, the control of consular affairs was removed from the Marine Committee and vested in the Secretary of Congress.[1]

---

1. Journals of Continental Congress, July 23, September 24, October 27, November 4, 1778; January 21, June 7, 22, 23, July 30, August 2, 1779.

CHAPTER V

THE CONDITIONS OF THE CONTINENTAL NAVAL SERVICE

The nineteenth century worked its marvels on sea as well as on land. The progress of invention, the discovery of new sources of wealth and power in nature and in man, and the development of powerful states, have revolutionized transportation and communication by sea, maritime pursuits, and naval science. Commerce has found fleeter wings; and it no longer waits on the caprice of Aeolus. Countless steamships with enormous tonnage and high rates of speed have in large measure supplanted the small, snail-like sailing craft of our fathers. The hazards of sea-going trade have been greatly reduced. Invention has pacified Neptune's fierce temper. The breed of pirates and corsairs has been exterminated by the long muscular arm of the modern state. The privations of ocean-travel which were distressing accompaniments of the colonial period in America, were succeeded about the middle of the last century by the comforts of the first steamships, and these within the memory of young men have yielded to the luxuries of the floating palaces of the sea.

Complementary to these transformations in commerce, navigation, and travel by sea, have come improved methods of their defence. Modern naval science in all of its aspects has been developed. Glancing for a moment in retrospect at the long line of naval progress, one sees it pass from the ancient row-galleys, to the sailing ship of the early Modern Age, and from thence to the steamships of to-day. The motive power has changed from human muscle to wind, and from wind to steam. Placed beside the iron-clad battleships, the light, wooden frigates of the Revolution look almost as antiquated as the Greek galley with its figured prow. Smart, trim, beautiful vessels were the Revolutionary craft, but how small, simple, and crude they now appear. Indeed, a new type of poet, one who loves raw force first, and the picturesque afterwards, has risen to sing the glories of new navies and new seas.

Other naval changes have been made, as significant as those in style of vessel and motive power. Ships of war now wear heavy coats-of-mail. The "great guns" and the "long guns" of the Revolution are neither great nor long beside modern cannon. A new type of sea officer has been trained to meet the new conditions of naval service. It would puzzle a modern officer to take a schooner from Boston to Plymouth, for his seamanship is now fitted to steamships. By over-study of modern armament, torpedo boats, and the latest naval manœuvres, his "weather eye" has lost something of its skill for reading in the skies the coming of storms or sunshine. Trim and immaculate in their uniforms, the American naval officers of to-day, who have entered the naval profession by the way of their technical studies at Annapolis, little resemble their hardy prototypes in the Continental navy, to whom clung the barnacles of their apprenticeship aboard merchantmen.

Notwithstanding this revolution in naval science, a consideration of the conditions of the Continental naval service and of the naval policy of the Marine Committee has to-day a practical value for naval experts. Certain fundamental principles in naval science do not change. Captain Mahan, in his "Influence of Sea Power upon History," has pointed out that, while naval tactics vary with the improvements in the motive power and armament of fleets, the basic principles of naval strategy do not. They are as enduring as the order of nature. For example, one cannot conceive that there will come a time when an inversion will be made of the strategic principle, that an enemy should be struck at his weak point. Captain Mahan even finds it worth while, for the benefit of his fellow-experts, to set forth with some detail the naval strategy of the Carthaginian wars.

When America, in these first years of the twentieth century, makes an invoice of her resources, she counts first her great prairies of the Mississippi basin, her rich mines of the Alleghanies and Rockies, and her wealth of manufactories and their products. In 1775 her assets were of a different sort. America then was a mere strip of seacoast, cut into a series of peninsulas by the lower courses of a number of navigable rivers. Her interests and her wealth then were much more largely maritime than now. Attention has already been directed to the wide pursuit of commerce, shipbuilding, fishing, and whaling in New England. It remains to be said that in the Middle and Southern colonies commerce and shipbuilding were important industries. During the Revolution Virginia put more naval ships afloat than any other colony. In the colonial period communication between the towns of the colonies was best by water. The inhabitants of America, during this period, were amphibious. They have lost this quality, for their character is now fixed by the "West," and not by the Atlantic seaboard. In 1775 America had, relatively, many more seamen than in 1898.

In the light of these facts it seems somewhat singular that the Revolutionary navy was forced to spend most of its days in port,

cleverly recited the many advantages of the Continental service, were displayed in sundry taverns.[1]

All these efforts were defeated by the seductive allurements of privateering. The Revolutionary Congress was poor and paid poor wages. After its seamen had enlisted, they were toled away by mercenary privateersmen. These same privateersmen were accused of taking the naval stores and the artisans of Congress in order to fit out their own ships. The owners and commanders of privateers, as they received the whole of their captures, could afford to treat their crews liberally. It was generally asserted that they paid higher wages than did Congress or the states. Privateering was more popular, more elastic, and more irregular than the other naval services. When no one was looking, parts of cargoes could more readily be appropriated for private use without waiting the tedious process of the admiralty courts. Privateersmen could devote all their time and energy to commerce-destroying, unfettered by the miscel-

---

[1]. A facsimile of a most interesting and rare broadside will be found in C. K. Bolton's Private Soldier under Washington, page 46. This broadside was designed to attract recruits to the ship "Ranger," Captain John Paul Jones, fitting out in the summer of 1777 at Portsmouth, New Hampshire, to sail for France.

laneous duties which often fell to naval ships.

The backbone of the privateering interest was in New England. Silas Deane said in 1785 that four out of every five of the privateers of the Revolution came from the states north and east of the Delaware river. This probably overstates the proportion in favor of the northern states.[1] Pennsylvania and Maryland did considerable business, but farther to the southward the industry was less flourishing. The Virginia privateers did little. Massachusetts sent out one-third of all the privateers. From 1777 until 1783, inclusive, the Massachusetts Council issued 998 commissions. In 1779, 184 prizes captured by privateers were libelled in the three admiralty courts of this state. The average burden of these captured vessels was one hundred tons. Rhode Island's best year was probably in 1776, when thirty-eight vessels were libelled at Providence. A list of 202 privateers has been made out for Connecticut. In 1779 twenty-nine vessels taken from the British by privateers were libelled in the Pennsylvania court of admiralty. During the last six years of the war Maryland issued about 250 commissions. Boston was the chief center for fitting out privateers and for selling their prizes, al-

---

1. Collections of New York Historical Society, Deane Papers, V, 466.

bargoes upon privateers;[1] bounties were paid to seamen enlisting for a year;[2] inducements were offered to those captured from the enemy to get them to enter the American service;[3] some seamen were impressed; glowing advertisements were inserted in the public prints;[4] and broadsides, which

[1] Rhode Island Colonial Records, VIII, 53.
[2] Journals of Continental Congress, July 11, 1780.
[3] Ibid., August 5, 1776.
[4] In July, 1778, when a joint American and French attack on Newport was planned, the Navy Board at Boston inserted a notice in the Providence Gazette, requiring sailors who were enlisted to repair to their vessels, and calling for recruits. This call was in the following language: "All seamen now in America, who regard the Liberty of Mankind, or the Honor of the United States of America, as well as their own advantage, are now earnestly entreated to enter immediately on board some of the Continental Vessels, in order to afford all possible Aid and Assistance to His Most Christian Majesty's Fleet, under the Command of the Count de Estaing, the Vice-Admiral of France, now in the American Seas, for the Purpose of assisting these American States in vanquishing a haughty and cruel Enemy, too long triumphant on these Seas. Now is the Time to secure to yourselves Safety in your future Voyages, and to avoid the cruelties which all those experience who have the Misfortune to be captured by the Britons; and now is the time to make your Fortunes."—Providence Gazette, July 25, 1778. See also advertisement in Connecticut Gazette, March 7, 1777.

vainly trying to enlist seamen for its depleted crews. To be sure the lack of sufficient armament, naval stores, and provisions was felt, but it was the lack of sailors that constituted the chief obstacle to the success of the Continental navy. Those vessels that finally weighed anchor were wanting as a rule in this prime naval requisite. The same causes that prevented seamen from enlisting lowered the quality of those that did enlist, and kept them from entering for longer than a single cruise. A ship's complement of sailors was often ill-assorted. Seamen were improvised from landsmen; captured British seamen were coaxed into service; and for one cause or another many nationalities at times shipped side by side. These conditions made for insubordination, and even mutiny. On one occasion seventy or eighty British sailors, who were enlisted on board the Continental frigate "Alliance," bound for France, planned to mutiny and carry the frigate into an English port. In order to obtain seamen many measures were resorted to by Congress, the states, the Marine Committee, Navy Boards, and commanders of vessels. Premiums for importing seamen were given to foreigners;[1] wages were advanced to recruits;[2] attempts were made to place em-

---

1. Journals of Continental Congress, April 17, 1776.
2. Ibid., March 29, 1777.

though towns like Salem and Marblehead did a thriving business.[1]

Not a few of the failures and misfortunes of the Continental navy are to be laid at the doors of the Yankee privateersmen, whose love for Mammon exceeded that for their country.[2] A more patriotic course was to have been expected of certain substantial merchants who embarked in the business of commerce-destroying. But on the other hand, one might easily be too severe on many bold, simple, seafaring folk. The war, which deprived them of their gainful pursuits at sea, now pointed the way, as a recompense, to a new and attractive calling. Wives and babies were still to be fed, and plans for sweethearts to be realized. The new trade was as alluring as a lottery. Had not a neighbor drawn a competence sufficient for almost a lifetime

---

1. For additional information and appropriate references concerning privateers, see Part II, State Navies.

2. There is much evidence on this point. See especially Publications of Rhode Island Historical Society, VIII, 256, William Vernon, Commissioner of Navy Board at Boston, to John Adams, December 17, 1778; Force, American Archives, 5th, II, 1105, John Paul Jones to Robert Morris, October 17, 1776; Ibid., 599, Mrs. John Adams to John Adams, September 29, 1776; Ibid., 337 and 622; Ibid., 5th, III, 1513, Benjamin Rush to R. H. Lee, December 21, 1776; and C. K. Bolton, Private Soldier under Washington, 45, 46.

by a successful haul of the enemy's rich West Indiamen? It was true that another neighbor, who but recently sailed proudly for sea with women-folk waving a last good-bye, now languished in a prison-ship off New York, or was starving in the old Mill prison at Plymouth, England. "But then a man must take his chances," each privateersman argued, "and it may be I, who by a fortunate cruise shall bring home enough Jamaica rum to fairly float my schooner, and every pint of it is as good as gold coin."

Due credit must always be given to the hardy and venturesome privateersmen for supplying the army and navy with the sinews of war, which they captured. To be sure, if Congress or the states wished their captured property, it was to be had by paying a good round price for it in the open market. Even here the government's agents sometimes suspected collusions between the buyers and the agents of the captors to run up prices to the disadvantage of the government.[1] The privateersmen were engaged

---

[1] In the case of Continental prizes the Navy Board at Boston discovered collusions which were detrimental to the government. Ordered to buy the Continental prize "Thorn," it writes to the Marine Committee that the agents and captains interested in the prize refuse to let it have the "Thorn" at a price to be fixed by three disinterested appraisers; and that "taking our chance, in the purchase by auction, amongst such circles of men in com-

not in patriotic, but business ventures. Could one-half of this irregular service have been enlisted in the Continental and state navies, the other half could not have been better employed than in its work of distressing the enemy's commerce, transports, and small letters of marque. Zealous eulogists of the privateers have overrun the cup of their merit. They have not always pointed out that the number of American privateers, merchantmen, fishermen, and whalemen captured by British privateers and small naval craft was comparable to the number of similar British vessels taken by the American privateers. The prison ships and naval prisons of the enemy at New York, in Canada, the British West Indies, and England were at times crowded with Americans captured at sea.[1] A few of these men England enlisted in her navy; and with others she manned a whaling-fleet for the coast of Brazil composed of seventeen vessels. It is, however, worthy of note that

binations is a miserable one." In the same letter the Board writes also concerning the "Thorn" that "bets run high that she will sell for two hundred thousand pounds."—Records and Papers of Continental Congress, 37, pp. 145, 147.

1. See Chapter IX, page 267; also Gomer Williams, Liverpool Privateers, Chapter IV, Privateers of the American War of Independence. From August, 1778, to April, 1779, Liverpool fitted out one hundred and twenty privateers.

the supplies captured from the British were often almost indispensable to the colonists; while similar captures made by the British had to the captors little value.

Another factor in the naval situation of the Americans was the existence of state navies in Massachusetts, Rhode Island, Connecticut, New York, Pennsylvania, Maryland, Virginia, North Carolina, and South Carolina. The fleet of Massachusetts, comprising sixteen armed vessels, was the most active and effective of the state fleets. The Virginia navy numbering about fifty vessels was poorly equipped and rendered little service. These fleets were made up of all sorts of naval craft; sailing vessels variously rigged, fire-ships, floating batteries, barges, row-galleys with and without sails, half-galleys, and boats of all sizes. Most of this craft was designed for the defence of coasts, rivers, and towns. This was especially true of the galleys, which were shallow vessels, some seventy or eighty feet in length, carrying two or three cannon, sometimes as large as 36's or 42's. Only some sixty of these vessels of the state navies were well adapted for deep-sea navigation.[1]

To a limited extent both privateers and state vessels were placed at the service of the Marine Committee. There were cruises, expeditions, and defences of towns, in which

1. See Part II, State Navies.

two, or the three, services participated. In such cases the senior Continental captain was regularly the ranking officer, or the commodore of the fleet, as it was then expressed. To the extent that state vessels and privateers might be concerted with the Continental vessels, it would seem at first blush that they undoubtedly were elements of naval strength to the Marine Committee. This was by no means true. These concerted expeditions proved disappointing, and when too late the Committee became wary of them. Proper subordination, upon which naval success so much depends, could not be obtained in these mixed fleets. The commander of a state vessel or the master of a privateer, for aught either could see, subtended as large an angle in maritime affairs, as an officer of Congress, which body was to them nebulous, uncertain, and irresolute.

If the location and physical form of colonial America with reference to the sea tended to develop a maritime people, they also made most difficult the problems of naval defence. As has been pointed out, the territory of the revolting colonies comprised a narrow band of seacoast divided into a number of peninsulas. All the large towns were seaports. Had the peninsulas been islands, their defence against the great sea-power of England would have been an impossibility. The connections by land on the west side of the thirteen colonies gave Washington a most valuable line of communications from Canada to Florida. Had the revolting territory lain compactly, approaching a square in shape, with a narrow frontage on the sea, its naval defence would have been a simple problem.

Having decided late in 1775 to make a naval defence, Congress early in 1776 took into consideration the establishing of one or more bases for naval operations.[1] There were needed one or more strongly fortified ports where the Continental fleet and its prizes would be comparatively secure from attack, and where the armed vessels could equip, man, and refit. The ports best adapted for naval stations were Boston, New York, Philadelphia, some point on or near the James river in Virginia, and Charleston, South Carolina. Lesser towns had their advocates and their hopes. In February, 1776, Gurdon Saltonstall of Connecticut wrote to Silas Deane that New London would be "the Asylum of Cont. Navey," for "one they must have of necessity."[2] The Southern ports were not available for several reasons, but chiefly on account of their distance from the center of maritime interests in New England. New York was

1. Journals of Continental Congress, March 23, 1776.
2. Papers of Silas Deane in the Library of the Connecticut Historical Society.

occupied by the British. Philadelphia had many points in its favor, not the least of which was the location there of Congress and the Marine Committee. Its occupation for a time by the enemy in 1777 and 1778, and the close watch which his armed vessels maintained at the mouth of Delaware Bay, greatly impaired its usefulness as a harbor of refuge for the Continental vessels. Boston was by far the most available port. After its abandonment by the British in March, 1776, and the shifting of the theater of the war first to the Middle and later to the Southern states, it was left comparatively free from British interference. It was the naval emporium of the Revolution, where naval stores, armament and equipment for vessels of war, seamen, and ships could be procured, if they were to be had at all.

The British had naval bases in America that left little to be desired. When they seized New York in September, 1776, they obtained not only a military point of the highest strategic value, but also a secure naval station for fitting out and refitting their privateers and naval ships. From New York, centrally situated with reference to the revolting colonies, their vessels proceeded along the Atlantic coast both northward and southward on the outlook for American merchantmen, privateers, and naval craft. Their favorite patrolling grounds were off the entrances of Delaware, Chesapeake, and Narragansett bays. British vessels were also to be found off Boston Bay, Ocracoke Inlet, Cape Fear, Charleston, and Savannah. The British occupation of Newport from 1776 to 1779, and of Savannah from 1778, and Charleston from 1780, to the end of the war, afforded other convenient stations for British operations against the shipping of the colonies. St. Augustine was a port of much importance in the movements of the enemy's smaller ships. The naval stations at Halifax, Jamaica, and the Bermudas, while not so convenient as those enumerated, were sources of naval strength to the British. Halifax was a base for the naval operations against New England. It scarcely needs to be said that the ports mentioned were in a way secondary bases of operations, and that England's center for ships, seamen, and supplies of all sorts was the British Isles.

From this account of the respective naval stations in America of the two combatants, one proceeds naturally to a comparison of their fleets. The rude naval craft of the Americans, two-thirds of which were made-over merchantmen, was outclassed by the vessels of the Royal Navy at every point. Disregarding the fleets of Washington and Arnold, there were during the Revolution fifty-six armed vessels in the American navy, mounting on the average about twenty guns. The vessels in the British navy when the Revolution opened in 1775 numbered 270, and when it closed, 468.[1] Of this latter number, 174 were ships of the line, each mounting between sixty and one hundred guns. The naval force of the Americans when it was at its maximum in the fall of 1776 consisted of 27 ships, mounting on the average twenty guns.[2] At the same time the British had on the American station, besides a number of small craft, 71 ships, which mounted on the average twenty-eight guns.[3] Of these, two were 64's; one, a 60; seven, 50's; and three, 44's. The British vessels, being so much larger than the American, were naturally armed with much heavier guns. Very few 18-pounders were to be found in the Continental navy. The frigates were usually mounted with 12's, 9's, and 6's; and many of the smaller craft with 6's and 4's. The guns on the larger British ships mounted 18's, 24's, 32's, and 42's.

An exhibition of figures showing the difference in size between one of the largest of

---

1. Clowes, Royal Navy, III, 328.
2. Few of these vessels were ready for sea for lack of crews. The British also suffered greatly during the Revolution owing to the scarcity of seamen. This the First Lord of the Admiralty attributed to the loss of 18,000 American sailors, who had contributed to the manning of the British fleets in former wars. —Annual Register, 1778, 201.
3. Boston Gazette, November 4, 1776.

the frigates built by the Marine Committee in 1776 and a typical 100-gun ship of the line of the Royal Navy is interesting not only by way of comparison, but also as giving a notion of the size of Revolutionary naval craft. The figures in feet for the American 32-gun frigate, "Hancock," and for the British 100-gun ship, "Victory," respectively, were as follows: Length of gun deck, 137 and 186; length of keel, 116 and 151; width of beam, 34 and 52; depth, 12 and 22. The tonnage of the "Hancock's" companion frigate, the "Boston," was 515 tons; of the "Alfred," the first ship fitted out by Congress, 200 tons.[1] Continental naval craft, such as the "Cabot," "Wasp," and "Fly," were smaller still than the "Alfred."

The number of seamen and marines in the Continental navy is believed not to have exceeded at any time three thousand men. The exact number of commissioned officers in the Continental navy and marine corps may not as yet have been ascertained. Owing to the diffusion of the power of appointment, the Naval Department of the Revolution seems to have prepared no perfect list of its officers. The best list of commissioned officers, and one that in all probability needs few corrections was com-

---

1. A battleship building in 1903 at the New York navy yard has a displacement of 16,000 tons.

piled in 1794 in the Auditor's Office, Department of the Treasury.[1] This gives the names of 1 commander-in-chief, 45 captains, and 132 lieutenants, or 178 commissioned officers in all, in the navy proper; and 1 major, 31 captains, and 91 lieutenants, or 123 commissioned officers, in the marine corps. With the exception of the years 1776 and 1777, when the total number of officers in actual service was about one-half of the above figures, the number of officers at sea or attached to vessels in ports was much less than one-half. In 1902 the American navy consisted of 899 commissioned officers of the line, arranged in eight grades.

In 1775 the British navy contained 18,000 seamen and marines, and when the war closed in 1783 this number had risen to 110,000. The total "extra" and "ordinary" expenses of the Royal Navy from 1775 to 1783, as voted by Parliament, amounted to £8,386,000.[2]

Both Continental and state naval services suffered from the lack of *esprit de corps*, naval traditions, and a proper subordination and concert of action between officers and crews. Bravery is often a poor substitute for organization and naval experience and skill. Navies can be grown, but not created. The quality of the Continen-

---

1. Manuscript list, in Division of Manuscripts, Library of Congress.
2. Clowes, Royal Navy, III, 327.

tal naval officers, diluted it is true by the presence of a few "political skippers," was upon the whole as high as the circumstances of their choice and the naval experience of the country admitted. Many of them were drawn from the merchant service, and a few had had some months' experience in state navies. Six captains appointed by Washington entered the service of the Marine Committee.

The vessels of the Continental navy were procured and managed under several Continental auspices. The Marine Committee, with its predecessor and its successors in naval administration was the chief naval administrative organ of the Revolutionary government. We have already seen, however, that Washington fitted out one fleet in New England and another in New York; and that Arnold fought with still another fleet, one of the most important naval engagements of the Revolution. In a succeeding chapter we shall find that the American representatives in France, who were responsible to the Foreign Office of Congress, and the Continental agent at New Orleans, who worked chiefly under the Committee of Commerce, fitted out fleets, and were vested with important naval duties. At one and the same time three committees of Congress, the Marine Committee, the Committee of Foreign Affairs, and the Committee of Commerce, were fitting out armed vessels.

CHAPTER VI

MOVEMENTS OF THE CONTINENTAL FLEET UNDER THE MARINE COMMITTEE

Many duties fell to the Marine Committee and its fleet which were not of a purely military character. The Committee was obliged to employ some of its vessels in keeping open the commercial and diplomatic communications of the United States with Europe and the West Indies; upon this intercourse with foreign countries largely depended the successful issue of the war. The Committee detailed vessels to carry abroad ambassadors, and foreign agents; letters and dispatches; tobacco, fish, flour, indigo, and such other colonial products as exchanged well for naval stores, clothing, and the munitions of war. Among the distinguished men who took passage on board the Continental vessels were John Adams, Lafayette, and Gerard, the first French minister to the United States. In this work it coöperated with other committees of Congress, and most especially with the Committee of Secret Correspondence, or its successor, the Committee of Foreign Affairs; and with the Secret Committee, or, as it was later called, the Committee of Commerce. Owing to the close connection of the work of the Marine Committee and the Committee of Commerce in exporting colonial products and in importing supplies, their accounts became inextricably confused. While running errands for the various administrative organs of Congress, the Marine Committee often at the same time ran errands of its own. A commander who had been selected to carry abroad a minister or foreign agent, might be ordered to pick up any prizes which fell in his way, or to cruise for a brief period in European waters while waiting for letters and packets from Paris addressed to Congress; or if on the other hand, it was a voyage in which dispatch was of the highest importance, he would be specifically forbidden to do these very things.

Turning now to the strictly military work of the Committee, one finds that clearness in presentation will be obtained by making a classification of naval operations. These will be divided into primary and secondary operations. A primary operation will be defined as one directed against the enemy's naval vessels at sea. Any other naval operation whatsoever will be called a secondary one. Primary operations will be divided into major and minor operations. In major primary operations fleets of considerable size and force are matched against each other, as was the case at the battles of Santiago, Trafalgar, and Martinique. Minor primary operations are engagements between some two or three of the smaller vessels of the combatants. A good example of these is the fight between the "Bon Homme Richard" and the "Serapis." Secondary operations are of several forms, chief of which is "commerce-destroying." Continental vessels during a single cruise sometimes engaged in both primary and secondary operations.

In the light of the comparison which has been made showing the relative strength of the Continental and British navies, the reader does not need to be told that the Marine Committee did not engage its fleet in major primary operations. The very existence of the Continental vessels depended upon their success in keeping outside the range of the larger guns of the Royal Navy. The Marine Committee sometimes gave specific orders to its captains to avoid the British "two-deckers." In the minor primary operations of the Revolution some thirty or thirty-five engagements may be counted. The honors here are upon the whole evenly divided. The Americans captured ten or twelve naval vessels of the enemy. With the exceptions of the frigate "Fox," 26, captured by Captain John Manly between New England and Newfoundland; and the sloop "Drake," 20, and the ships "Countess of Scarborough," 20, and "Serapis," 44, captured by Captain John Paul Jones in European waters, the prizes of the Americans were minor naval craft, averaging ten or twelve 4's and 6's. The British captured or destroyed about the same number of vessels as they lost, but their prizes on the average were larger and better armed vessels than were those of the Americans. Seven of them were frigates. On the other hand the British had no victory as brilliant as that of Jones off Flamborough Head.

The secondary operations of the Continental navy were more important than its primary operations. They mainly involved the protection of American commerce, the defence of certain Atlantic ports, the striking of the lines of communication of the British military forces, the attacking of the enemy's commerce at sea, and the threatening and assailing of her unprotected coasts and ports both at home and in her outlying dependencies. Each of these forms of secondary operations will now be briefly considered.

The Committee defended American commerce by ordering its cruisers to "attack, take, burn, or destroy" the enemy's privateers. One illustration of such orders will suffice. In November, 1778, the Committee wrote to the Navy Board at Boston that "at present we consider it an Object of importance to destroy the infamous Goodrich who has much infested our Coast, cruising with a squadron of 4, 5, or 6 armed Vessels, from 16 guns downwards, from Egg Harbour to Cape Fear in North Carolina."[1] In its orders the Committee as a rule included the small naval ships of the enemy with the privateers. Of the three naval captains who lost their lives in the Continental service, two of them were killed in engagements with privateers. On March 4, 1778, the brigantine "Resistance," Captain Samuel Chew, while cruising in the West India seas had a desperate and indecisive encounter with a letter of marque of 20 guns. Chew and his lieutenant, George Champlin, both of New London, were killed; Chew was a native of Virginia.[2] Late in the summer of 1778 the "General Gates," 18, Captain John Skimmer, captured the brigantine "Montague" in an engagement in which Captain Skimmer lost his life.[3]

In addition to defending the American commerce by cruising against the privateers and small naval ships of the enemy, the

---

1. Marine Committee Letter Book, Committee to Navy Board at Boston, November 16, 1778.
2. F. M. Caulkins, History of New London, 539-40; Records and Papers of New London Historical Society, Part IV, I, 9.
3. Journals of Continental Congress, September 14, 1778.

Continental vessels often threw their protecting arm directly around the trade of the states. Vessels were often detailed to convoy to sea American merchantmen and packets. At times when the trade was bound for France, the Continental vessels accompanied it even as far as the Grand Banks of Newfoundland, but as a rule their services did not extend beyond a few leagues from the American coast. Sometimes the Continental vessels were ordered to cruise off the Delaware Bay, or similar channel, to guide and protect incoming shipping.

The Marine Committee coöperated with the army in the defence and in the attack of certain ports. In the campaigns around Philadelphia in 1777 and 1778 the Continental navy lost some ten vessels, including three of the thirteen original frigates; and at the siege of Charleston in 1780 it lost four vessels. The British occupation of New York caused the destruction of the two frigates built at Poughkeepsie. In 1779 a Continental vessel aided a Spanish expedition in capturing Mobile. Several times the Committee placed part of its fleet under the control of Washington and the Admiral of the French naval forces, when they were planning an attack upon some seaport held by the enemy.

In 1779 Gerard, the French minister, devised a plan which contemplated a joint expedition of the French and American fleets against the British colonies to the northward. Gerard's purpose was "to give the King of France Halifax and Newfoundland." In May, 1779, he consulted with Washington in his camp about the proposed expedition. By September Gerard's plan, or a similar one, had so far matured that the Marine Committee ordered the Navy Board at Boston to prepare the Continental vessels for a three months' cruise and to hold them ready to sail at a moment's warning to join the French fleet, or to proceed to such other place as Washington or Count D'Estaing might direct. The Board was to provide a sufficient number of pilots for Newfoundland, Halifax, Rhode Island, and the Penobscot river. This expedition was not abandoned until November, 1779.[1]

The Committee struck at the enemy's lines of communication between his army and navy in America, and the British Isles, Canada, the Bermudas, Florida, and the West Indies. After the transfer of the war to the Southern states in 1778 and 1779, transports running between New York and Savannah and Charleston were vulnerable craft. The capture of British transports laden with munitions of war, provisions, and troops had the advantage of obtaining for

---

[1]. Bancroft, History of United States, V, 319; Marine Committee Letter Book, Committee to Navy Board at Boston, September 28, November 10, 1779.

the Americans the very sinews of war, of which the enemy were deprived. When troops were captured, they could be exchanged for an equal number of American prisoners. The reader may recall that it was for the purpose of intercepting British transports that Congress fitted out the first Continental vessels in October, 1775.

The most successful capture of the enemy's transports was made in the spring of 1779. In order to protect the trade of the Southern states, depredations upon which were most frequent and destructive, the Marine Committee in February of that year, ordered the Navy Board at Boston to send certain of the Continental vessels to sweep the coast from Cape May to the bar of South Carolina. This detail of the armed vessels was made partly to satisfy the merchants of Baltimore, who had complained to Congress that their interests were being neglected. On March 13 a fleet consisting of the "Warren," 32, Captain J. B. Hopkins, as commodore, the "Queen of France," 28, Captain Joseph Olney, and the "Ranger," 18, Captain Thomas Simpson, sailed from Boston, for the coast of the Southern states. On April 7 they captured the privateer schooner, "Hibernia." This vessel told them of the sailing of a fleet of transports from New York, bound for Brigadier-General Campbell's army in Georgia, and laden with stores and supplies. The next day fifteen leagues off Cape Henry, Hopkins fell in with the fleet; and meeting with a trifling resistance, he made prizes of seven out of its nine vessels. These prizes were all sent to New England. On April 22, the "Queen of France" arrived in Boston with the ship "Maria," 16, carrying eighty-four men, the schooner "Hibernia," 8, also carrying eighty-four men, and the brigs "John," 200 tons, "Batchelor," 120 tons, and "Prince Frederick," 160 tons. Another prize, His Majesty's ship "Jason," 16, with one hundred men, also reached Boston. The "Ranger" put into Portsmouth with the schooner "Chance" and a brig. The Marine Committee wrote to Captain Hopkins congratulating him and his fellow captains on the fortunate outcome of their cruise.[1]

The most important objective of the Marine Committee in its naval operations was the capture of England's commerce in transit at sea. The Committee planned to intercept her sugar ships of the West Indies, her Newfoundland fishing craft, her Hudson bay fleet laden with skins and peltries, her Guineamen with cargoes of ivory and

---

1. Marine Committee Letter Book, Committee to Captain Olney, to Captain Harding, and to Navy Board at Boston, February 10, 1779; Committee to Merchants of Baltimore, February 23, 1779; Boston Gazette, April 26, 1779; Publications of Rhode Island Historical Society, VIII, 259.

slaves, and her Mississippi trade with its lumber and furs. The Committee's agents and the naval officers abroad hoped to ensnare the enemy's Baltic trade, the Irish linen ships, the Brazil whaling fleet, and homeward bound East Indiamen. The sending of frigates to the Coromandel Coast to intercept the enemy's China ships and the trade of India was seriously considered. On one occasion the Committee designed to attack English vessels bound for Canada with cargoes of "Indian goods." But generally the blows were aimed at the fleets of rich merchantmen returning to England, for their many vessels were like honey-laden bees flying homeward to their hives.

The British fishing fleet on the Grand Banks of Newfoundland and the homeward bound West Indiamen were found most vulnerable. It is not practicable for a combatant to prey upon commerce far from his base of operations. The frequent manning of prizes depletes his crews and compels him to make an early return home. The chance of prizes being retaken is increased with the distance they must travel to reach safe ports. The operations of the Continental vessels in European waters were made possible by their use of French ports as naval stations. In attacking England's commerce the Marine Committee found most promise of substantial reward by directing its vessels to cruise during the summer or the early fall some leagues to the eastward of the Bermudas in the track of the homeward bound West Indiamen, laden with rum, sugar, cotton, coffee, and other Colonial products. These fleets sometimes consisted of as many as 200 merchantmen under the convoy of a few ships of war. Skilful seamanship found it comparatively easy to cut out a few sail. In three instances Continental vessels made captures which netted them more than one million dollars each.

Two of these fortunate cruises were made while the fleet was under the direction of the Marine Committee. On May 4, 1779, the Committee wrote to the Navy Board at Boston that it desired that the "Confederacy," "Warren," "Queen of France," "Ranger," "Jason," "Hibernia," and two of the lately built packets as tenders, and the "Deane," which it should send from Philadelphia, should be joined together and sail in company to the southward and attack the sea force of the enemy on the coast of Georgia. After routing the enemy there, the fleet was to throw itself in the way of the West India ships, bound to England. A fortnight later the Committee wrote that it had reason to lay aside the expedition to Georgia, and that it was their intention to place the collected naval force in such manner as to accomplish the double purpose of intercepting the enemy's transports, coming to and going from New York, and of attacking her homeward bound West India ships.

In accordance with the latter plan of the Committee, sometime during the summer a fleet was sent to sea from Boston, consisting of the "Providence", 28, Captain Abraham Whipple, commodore of the fleet, the "Queen of France," 28, Captain John P. Rathburn, and the "Ranger," 18, Captain Thomas Simpson. In August the American vessels fell in with the Jamaica fleet, bound for London, and convoyed by a 32-gun frigate and three other armed vessels. The Americans succeeded in cutting out from the fleet ten large merchantmen, heavily laden with rum and sugar. Of the ten vessels, seven arrived at Boston and one at Cape Ann. The names of these eight ships, whose average burden was 285 tons, were as follows: "Holderness," "Dawes," "George," "Friendship," "Blenheim," "Thetis," "Fort William," and " Neptune." This was one of the richest captures which the Continental fleet made during the Revolution. The ships with their cargoes sold for more than one million dollars.[1] Early in

---

1. Marine Committee Letter Book, Committee to Navy Board at Boston, May 4, May 20, 1779; Continental Journal and Weekly Advertiser, August 26, 1779; Boston Gazette, September 20, 1779. "Last Saturday noon this town was alarmed by the Appearance of Seven Topsail Vessels in the Offing, which,

the year the ship "General Gates" and the sloop "Providence" sent prizes into Boston which sold for £240,000.[1]

The Marine Committee threatened and attacked the enemy's coasts and towns in the British Isles, Canada, and the West Indies. Two Continental vessels visited the mouth of the Senegal river on the west coast of Africa. An attack on the shipping of the Bermudas was ordered to be made, if it was found practicable. Nassau, New Providence, was twice captured by Continental vessels, and a third time by a Spanish fleet and a ship of war of the South Carolina navy. Robert Morris, when vice-president of the Marine Committee, planned to send a fleet of five vessels against the British possessions in the West Indies and the Floridas. The movements of Captains Wickes, Conyngham, and Jones in attacking and alarming the British Isles are well known.[2]

however, soon subsided, for between the Hours of Three and Five in the Afternoon were safe anchored in this Harbour the Continental Ships of War, 'Providence,' 'Queen of France,' and 'Ranger,' with Four Prize Ships laden with Rum and Sugar, being part of a Jamaica Fleet bound to London captured by the above Vessels."—Continental Journal and Weekly Advertiser, August 26, 1779, published at Boston.

1. Publications of Rhode Island Historical Society, VIII, 259.

2. See Chapter IX and X, Naval Duties of American Representatives in Foreign Countries.

These expeditions against British coasts, towns, and dependencies had several objects in view. One, of course, was the capture of booty. To the extent that the expeditions were directed against the shipping and commerce of the attacked ports, their object was similar to that of fleets which cruised against shipping and commerce at sea. Another object is discovered in the thought of Morris when he planned to attack England in the West Indies. Such a move Morris believed would force the enemy to withdraw part of his fleet from the coasts of the United States for the defence of his attacked colonies; and to the extent that he did so, the states would be relieved. The cruises made in the waters around the British Isles had in view the lessening of the prestige of Great Britain, the shaking of her credit, the alarming of her inhabitants, and the raising of her marine insurance; and also the impressing of Europe with the power and courage of the new American nation, and perchance, creating a diversion in its favor. Both a psychological and a political element entered into the purpose of the cruises in British waters. They realized to both Britain and the Continent the existence of a new flag and a new state in the family of nations.

The naval plan devised by Morris, as vice-president of the Marine Committee, deserves additional notice. It was to be put into operation by John Paul Jones, with a fleet composed of the "Alfred," "Columbus," "Cabot," "Hampden," and sloop "Providence." Jones was first to proceed to St. Christopher in the West Indies, which island was almost defenceless, capture the cannon, stores, and merchandise there deposited, and then sail for Pensacola, Florida. Morris thought Jones might find it best to pass along the south side of Hispaniola, and alarm Jamaica by putting in to some of its ports. Arriving at Pensacola, he would find it defended by two or three sloops of war, which could be easily silenced, and the town would fall into his hands with its munitions of war, including one hundred pieces of artillery. Having reduced Pensacola, Jones was to send a brigantine and sloop to cruise at the mouth of the Mississippi, in order to waylay the British merchantmen leaving there in March and April with cargoes of indigo, rice, tobacco, skins, and furs, to the value of £100,000 sterling. Returning from the Gulf, he might alarm St. Augustine, and finally he might refit in Georgia, or South or North Carolina. He was directed to carry as many marines as possible for his operations on shore.

Morris's object in this expedition involved a nice bit of naval policy. He purposed not so much the taking of booty, as the alarming of the whole British nation, and the forcing of the enemy to withdraw some of her naval forces from the coast of the United States. "It has long been clear to me," he said, "that our infant fleet cannot protect our coasts; and the only effectual relief it can afford us, is to attack the enemy's defenceless places, and thereby oblige them to station more of their own ships in their own countries, or to keep them employed in following ours, and either way we are relieved so far as they do it." Morris proposed his plan as a substitute for one of Jones, which contemplated a descent on the west coast of Africa; and to the carrying out of which the Marine Committee had given its consent. Morris thought that the same results as Jones sought could be obtained with less risk by "cruizing Windward of Barbadoes as all their Guinea Men fall in there."[1]

The Marine Committee naturally planned and carried out naval enterprises which had in view two or more forms of secondary operations. Sometimes it ordered its vessels to take stations at sea where they would be in position to intercept both the West India trade, and the enemy's transports plying between New York and England. Often it left the specific object of a cruise to the Navy Board at Boston, or to

---

1. Marine Committee Letter Book, Morris to Jones, February, 1, 1777; Morris to Commodore Hopkins, February 5, 1777.

the commander of a ship, and issued merely the general order to proceed to sea and cruise against the enemy. Any plan of the Committee which was directed towards meeting an immediate emergency was rarely carried out. The movements of the vessels were rendered uncertain by reason of depleted crews, deficient equipments, and the position of the British fleets. The Committee was often in the dark as to the exact state of a vessel in New England with reference to its preparation for sea. Consequently it made many plans and gave many orders which could not be put into operation. The telegraph, cable, and rapid postal services have revolutionized the direction of naval movements.

In prize-getting the Marine Committee's most successful years were 1776 and 1779. Beginning with 1776 the number of prizes taken by the Continental vessels for each year of the Committee's incumbency was, respectively, sixty, twenty, twenty, and fifty. The fifty prizes captured in 1779 were probably more valuable than the one hundred taken in the other three years. As regards the number of Continental vessels lost, the years 1776 and 1779, when the fleet was decreased by but three ships, again prove to be the most fortunate years. In 1777 and 1778 twenty-six vessels, ten of which were frigates, were lost.[1] With the

---
1. Files of newspapers for the period of the Revolution.

memory of the misfortunes of the past two years in mind, well might the Marine Committee write, towards the end of 1778, of "the bad success that hath hitherto attended our Navy." In May, 1778, it wrote to the Navy Board at Boston, that the "Committee are entirely of Opinion with you that it will be proper to send out a Collected force to Cruise against our enemies that we recover the injured reputation of our Navy and the losses we have sustained."[1]

In 1779 the navy retrieved the bad effects of some of its disasters. Its changed fortunes can in part be easily accounted for. The transference of the scene of war to the Southern states late in 1778, removed a part of the British land and sea forces from the North, and thereby gave the Naval Department a freer hand in its operations, and rendered the movements of the fleet less perilous. The Department this year had larger success in manning and equipping its fleet. It was, therefore, able not only to send the armed vessels to sea more frequently, but also to send several of them cruising in company. Such little fleets had a decided advantage over single cruisers, both in defensive and offensive operations. No doubt, too, the experiences and past failures of the navy were now telling in a better

---

1. Marine Committee Letter Book, Committee to Navy Board at Boston, May 8, November 9, 1778.

understanding of naval tactics, and were bringing about a proper subordination and concert of action between officers and men. Possibly, something should be attributed to the Department's increased experience in marine affairs.

The reader has probably already drawn parallels, far from fanciful, between the solutions of the naval problems of the Revolution made by the Marine Committee and those of the Spanish-American war made by the Naval Board of Strategy at Washington. The naval problems presented to the two bodies were in certain respects widely different. Equally striking similarities appear. In both wars the United States was fighting a European power with possessions in the West Indies and in the Asiatic seas. The attacks on Nassau and Morris's proposed expedition against the British West Indies correspond to the movements of the American fleet in the West Indies during the late war. The operations of Wickes, Conyngham, and Jones off the coasts of the British Isles are matched by the proposed descent on the Spanish coast in 1898. The plan made in 1777 to send a fleet of frigates to Mauritius and from thence to operate against the English trade in the Indian seas looks singularly like Admiral Dewey's movement from Hong Kong against Manila.

The hope is to be cherished that America will never again cross swords with her kin beyond seas, but if moved by some untoward fate she should, it is not too much to say that a Naval Board of Strategy at Washington will devise plans of naval attack and defence quite similar to those of the Marine Committee. The weak spots in a nation's armor often prove to be its outlying dependencies, especially when they are situated near the enemy's coast. The principles of naval strategy which led the Marine Committee either to attack, or to plan to attack, Canada, the Newfoundland fisheries, the Bermudas, and the British West Indies, are still operative, notwithstanding the vast changes which the past century and a quarter have witnessed in the methods of naval warfare, and in the distribution of the territory of the Western Hemisphere among nations, new as well as old. In a world of change the fundamental principles of naval strategy remain immutable.

CHAPTER VII

THE BOARD OF ADMIRALTY

It is speaking tritely, although accurately, to say that our present executive departments at Washington did not spring into perfect being in 1789 like panoplied Minerva from the head of Jove. Not a little of the interest and value of a study of the administration of the Revolution comes from the fact that the administrative practices and experiences of this period gave rootage to the later and more perfect executive organs. The development of the Continental Naval Department, both in the variety and in the character of its forms, is typical of that of the other administrative departments of the Revolution. We have already seen how the naval business of the Continental Congress was first vested in the small Naval Committee; and how this Committee, early in 1776, was overshadowed and absorbed by the more numerous and more active Marine Committee. We now come to the third step in this evolution, the superseding of the Marine Committee by the Board of Admiralty.

The Marine Committee had proved slow,

cumbrous, inexpert, and irresponsible. The wiser members of Congress had long seen that it was a prime defect in governmental practice to add to the duties of a legislative committee, those of an executive office; for it threw upon the same men too much work of too diverse kinds, and it removed from the administrative organ its most essential attributes of permanency, technical skill, and responsibility. In December, 1776, Robert Morris had urged the employment of a corps of executives chosen outside the membership of Congress, as a requisite to a proper and orderly management of the business of the Revolutionary government.[1]

As early as February 26, 1777, William Ellery, a member of the Marine Committee from Rhode Island, wrote to William Vernon at Providence, who was soon to become a member of the Navy Board at Boston, that a proper Board of Admiralty was very much wanted. "The members of Congress," he said, "are unacquainted with this Department. As one of the Marine Committee I

---

[1]. Force's Archives, 5th, III, 1336, Robert Morris to American Commissioners at Paris, December 21, 1776. Morris wrote as follows: "So long as that respectable body persist in the attempt to execute, as well as to deliberate on their business, it never will be done as it ought, and this has been urged many and many a time by myself and others, but some of them do not like to part with power, or to pay others for doing what they cannot do themselves."

sensibly feel my ignorance in this respect. Under a mortifying Sense of this I wrote to you for Information in this Matter. Books cannot be had here; and I should have been glad to have been pointed to proper Authors on this Subject when I should be in a Place where Books may be had."[1] Early in 1779 when Congress was groping in search of a more efficient naval executive, Ellery again expressed regret at the lack of technical skill in the management of the navy. He said that the marine affairs would never be "well conducted so long as the supreme direction of them is in the hands of Judges, Lawyers, Planters, &c."[2] Even before Morris and Ellery had declared for better executives, John Paul Jones, while distressed by a loss in naval rank caused by the appointing and the placing above him of certain "political skippers," wrote that efficient naval officers could never be obtained, until Congress "in their wisdom see proper to appoint a Board of Admiralty competent to determine impartially the respective merits and abilities of their officers, and to superintend, regulate, and point out all the motions and operations of the navy."[3]

---

1. Publications of Rhode Island Historical Society, VIII, 205, Papers of William Vernon and Navy Board.
2. Ibid., 257, Ellery to Vernon, March 23, 1779.
3. Force's Archives, 5th, II, 1106, Jones to Morris, October 16, 1776.

During 1778 and 1779 Congress hit upon a system of executive departments that did little violence to its lust for power, and at the same time secured a permanent body of administrators and advisors. This was the system of executive boards, composed jointly of commissioners selected outside the membership of Congress, and of members of Congress. Congress and the Marine Committee probably derived a part of their knowledge of executive boards from the practice of the English government and of the states. "Board of Admiralty" was the name during the Revolution, as now, of the British Naval Office. Pennsylvania, Virginia, and South Carolina had early in the Revolution established "Navy Boards." In October, 1777, Congress had formed a Board of War composed of five commissioners. In October, 1778, Congress attempted to clip the wings of this Board and bring it under Congressional control by substituting two members of Congress for two of its five commissioners.[1] On July 30, 1779, a Board of Treasury was constituted on exactly this plan, being composed of three commissioners and two members of Congress.[2]

In the spring of 1779 the feeling was general that some change must be made in the

---

1. Journals of Continental Congress, October 29, 1778.
2. Ibid., July 30, 1779.

management of the navy. Both 1777 and 1778 had been lean, empty, and disastrous years for the Continental fleet. The blame for this failure was placed upon the Marine Committee and the naval commanders. It was in April, 1779, that Washington wrote to John Jay asking questions and making suggestions about the management of the navy, which may be briefly summarized as follows: What are the reasons for keeping the Continental vessels in port? Had not Congress better lend them to "commanders of known bravery and capacity" for a limited term? If additional encouragement is necessary in order to induce seamen to enlist, why not give them the whole of their captures? Great advantage might result from placing the whole fleet under "a man of ability and authority commissioned to act as commodore or admiral." Under the present system the Continental ships are not only very expensive and totally useless, but sometimes they require a land force to protect them.[1]

This arraignment of the navy is somewhat severe. The last clause in the above paragraph refers to an incident which took place at New London in the spring of 1776. The reader may recall that Commodore Hopkins put into this port on his return from

---

1. Johnston, Correspondence and Public Papers of John Jay, I, 207-08, Washington to Jay, April, 1779.

New Providence and just after his unfortunate engagement with the "Glasgow." He then received a temporary loan from Washington of one hundred and seventy troops, with whom, for the time being, he replenished his depleted crews. He kept the troops less than six weeks.

In his reply to Washington's letter, Jay ascribed the naval inefficiency to a defective Naval Department. He said: "While the maritime affairs of the continent continue under the direction of a committee, they will be exposed to all of the consequences of want of system, attention, and knowledge. The marine committee consists of a delegate from each state; it fluctuates, new members constantly coming and old ones going out; three or four, indeed, have remained in it from the beginning; and few members understand even the state of our naval affairs, or have time or inclination to attend to them. But why is not this system changed? It is in my opinion, inconvenient to the family compact."[1] The "family compact" is supposed to refer to the Lees. During the Revolution the Lees and the Adamses formed the nucleus of a faction, which was generally opposed to constructive legislation in the field of administration.

---

1. Johnston, Correspondence and Public Papers of John Jay, I, 209, Jay to Washington, April 26, 1779.

When this letter of Jay's was written a new naval system was forming.[1] On June 9 Congress resolved to vest in "commissioners all business relating to the marine of these United States."[2] Apparently this resolution of Congress meant that the naval affairs were to be given over to a board chosen outside the membership of Congress; if so, Congress soon retracted it. On October 1, 1779, Congress discharged the committee that had had the new project in hand, and directed the Marine Committee "to prepare and report a plan of regulations for conducting the naval affairs of the United States."[3] The Marine Committee reported on October 28, 1779; thereupon, Congress passed resolutions making provision for a Board of Admiralty, "to be subject in all cases to Congress." These resolutions were in important respects based upon those of October 17 and November 24, 1777, establishing a Board of War.[4] This was natural, as the work of a war and a naval office are quite similar. In the composition of the two boards there was a vital difference. The Board of War, as has been said, consisted of five commissioners; the Board of Admir-

---

1. Marine Committee Letter Book, Committee to Navy Board at Boston, April 27, 1779.
2. Journals of Continental Congress, June 9, 1779.
3. Ibid., October 1, 1779.
4. Ibid., October 17, November 24, 1777.

alty consisted of three commissioners and two members of Congress, being modeled after the Board of Treasury. Any three members of the Board of Admiralty were empowered to form a quorum. No two members were permitted to come from the same state. The Board must have its office in the same town in which Congress was sitting. It selected its clerks, but Congress chose its secretary.

The powers and duties of the Board of Admiralty were practically the same as those of the Marine Committee. The Board was to order and direct the movements of all ships and vessels of war. It was to superintend and direct the navy boards and see that they kept fair entries and proper accounts of all the business transacted by them. It was to keep a complete and accurate register of the officers of the navy, giving their rank and the date of their commissions; these were to be signed by the President of Congress and countersigned by the secretary of the Board. The Board was to have the care and direction of the marine prisoners. It was to obtain regular and exact returns of all warlike stores, clothing, provisions, and miscellaneous articles belonging to the marine department. Lastly the Board of Admiralty was to "execute all such matters as shall be directed, and give their opinion on all such subjects as shall be referred to them by Congress, or as they may think necessary for the better regulation and improvement of the navy of the United States; and in general to superintend and direct all the branches of the marine department."[1]

The officers of the navy were enjoined to obey the directions of the Board of Admiralty. The proceedings, records, and papers of the Board were to be open at all times to the inspection of the members of Congress. The Board of Admiralty was ordered to examine at once the unsettled accounts of the navy boards and naval agents, and report thereon to Congress. It was further directed to form proper plans for increasing the naval force of the United States and for the better regulating of the same.

The salary of each commissioner was fixed at $14,000, and that of the secretary of the Board at $8,000 a year. On September 13, 1780, these salaries were decreased to $1,850 and to $1,100 a year, respectively, to be now paid quarterly in specie or its equivalent.[2] When Congress increased the salary of its Commissioners of the Treasury from $1,850 to $2,000, the Commissioners of Admiralty, exhibiting that delicate sense of the fitness of more pay which characterizes the employees of

---
1. Journals of Continental Congress, October 28, 1779.
2. Ibid., September 13, 1780.

governments, petitioned for a similar increase in their salaries;[1] and Congress, in accord with its subsequent character under the Constitution, refused a favor to the navy which it granted to a more popular branch of its public service.[2] The Congressional members received no pay for their services on the Board.

When Congress came to select Commissioners of Admiralty, it found no easy task. Men who were eager for distinction and honor felt that they were cultivating a surer field in their home governments or in the army. The prestige of the Continental government was now declining. The dilution of salaries caused by the depreciation of the currency lessened the attractiveness of the Continental offices. Employees of Congress found it hard to support their families on their pay. Then too, the navy business had become a thankless and disheartening task. The class of men who will accept a disagreeable office with little pay and no glory is a small one at any time.

The first three commissioners elected by Congress were William Whipple of New Hampshire, chairman of the Marine Committee, Thomas Waring of South Carolina, and George Bryan of Pennsylvania. Each

---

1. Force Transcripts, Library of Congress, 37, p. 207, Report of Board of Admiralty, April 12, 1781.
2. Journals of Continental Congress, July 7, 1781.

declined. On December 7 Francis Lewis of New York was chosen commissioner, and on the next day he accepted the office. Congress on the 3rd had named the two Congressional members of the Board, William Floyd of New York, and James Forbes of Maryland. The appointment of Lewis vacated the position of Floyd, as two members from the same state could not serve on the Board. William Ellery of Rhode Island was now elected as the second Congressional member. Congress had already chosen John Brown, the secretary of the Marine Committee, to be secretary of the Board of Admiralty. Lewis, Forbes, and Ellery were sufficient to organize the Board. Accordingly on December 8, 1779, Congress resolved "that all matters heretofore referred to the marine committee be transmitted to the board of admiralty."[1] On December 10 the Board of Admiralty wrote to the Navy Board at Boston, informing it of the dissolution of the Marine Committee, and directing it to address in the future all letters and applications relating to the navy to the "Commissioners of the Admiralty of the United States."[2]

Upon the organization of the Board of Admiralty, its difficulties in obtaining quo-

1. Journals of Continental Congress, November 26, December 3, 7, 8, 1779.
2. Marine Committee Letter Book, Board of Admiralty to Navy Board at Boston, December 10, 1779.

rums began; and the troubles of Congress in its search for additional commissioners continued. On January 22, 1780, Congress gave Brigadier-General Thomas Mifflin of Pennsylvania an opportunity to decline a commissionership.[1] On March 21 Lewis was complaining to Congress that Forbes was sick, and that consequently there had been no Board since the 4th instant. He hoped Congress would fill up the vacancy and prevent the navy business from being longer suspended.[2] On the death of Forbes on March 25, Congress elected James Madison to fill his place. Madison had but recently arrived at Philadelphia as a delegate from Virginia.

In June, 1780, Lewis was again in trouble and was writing to Congress. He conceived that the addition of members of Congress to the Board of Admiralty was principally intended to lay such information before Congress from time to time as the Board desired to give, to explain its reports, and in the absence, or during the sickness, of a commissioner to make a quorum. He said that, notwithstanding the attention which Madison and Ellery had been disposed to give, their necessary attendance

---
1. Journals of Continental Congress, January 22, 1780.
2. Records and Papers of Continental Congress, 78, XIV, 309, Lewis to President of Congress, March 21, 1780.

on Congress did not admit of their being daily and constantly present at the sessions of the Board; that Ellery had been superseded in Congress; and that at present there was no Board for lack of a quorum.[1] Congress once more came to the rescue of Lewis and his Board by appointing Ellery and Thomas Woodford as commissioners.[2] Ellery at once accepted, but Woodford for some reason declined the appointment. Congress never obtained a third commissioner. In the fall of 1780 Daniel Huntington of Connecticut and Whitmill Hill of North Carolina were the Congressional members of the Board. On their being supplanted in November, 1780, by new delegates to Congress from their respective states, it took the urgent solicitation of Lewis to get Congress to fill the vacancies.[3] When the Board was discontinued in July, 1781, it had but one Congressional member, Daniel of St. Thomas Jenifer of Maryland.

To all intents and purposes Lewis and Ellery were the Board of Admiralty; and in many respects they were well qualified for their positions. Both were able men, though

1. Records and Papers of Continental Congress, 78, XIV, 337-43, 349, Lewis to President of Congress, June 6, June 12, 1780.
2. Journals of Continental Congress, June 23, 1780.
3. Force Transcripts, Library of Congress, 37, pp. 291, 294, Lewis to President of Congress, November 4, 6, 1780.

not brilliant. Both had passed the meridian of life; Lewis was in his sixty-seventh year, and Ellery in his fifty-second. Both had taken prominent parts in the Revolutionary counsels in their respective states; both had been members of the Continental Congress and of the Marine Committee. Both were among the immortal Signers of the Declaration of Independence. Lewis had amassed a fortune as an importing merchant in New York, and had served in the French and Indian war. Ellery had been a merchant, and later a lawyer in Newport, Rhode Island. Both men were interested in naval affairs, and had rendered good service on the Marine Committee. Lewis's work on the Board of Admiralty exceeded that of Ellery.

From the first the Board of Admiralty was more dependent on Congress than the Marine Committe had been. Congress, always jealous of its prerogatives, naturally permitted a freer exercise of power to a committee of its own members, than to a mixed board, whose work was almost entirely that of commissioners selected outside the membership of Congress. To the Board's dependence on Congress for its organization was added that for means to carry out its naval program. The frequency with which it went to Congress asking for quorums and money indicates its helplessness and weakness.

The work of the Board of Admiralty was, generally speaking, that of the Marine Committee under a change of name. It managed the dwindling business of the navy from December, 1779, until July, 1781. It was served by the Navy Boards and naval agents of its predecessor, the Marine Committee. Immediately after its organization, the Board of Admiralty, in compliance with the resolutions of Congress, urged the Navy Boards and naval agents to transmit to it accurate accounts of their transactions up to December 31, 1779. Owing to the loose methods of business which obtained during the Revolution, the agents of the Board found it in most cases impossible to make such statements.

The failure of the agents properly to report their accounts, together with a diminution in the naval business of Congress, now led to some decrease in naval machinery. In August, 1780, the Board recommended that the two Philadelphia prize agents be discharged, since it had not been able to induce them by means of its repeated written and verbal requests to exhibit their accounts. Congress now discontinued their office and gave their work to the Board of Admiralty.[1] In the winter of 1780-81 the

---

1. Force Transcripts, Library of Congress, 37, p. 125, Board of Admiralty to President of Congress, August 14, 1780; Journals of Continental Congress, August 18, 1780.

resignations of Winder and Wharton, as commissioners of the Navy Board at Philadelphia, were accepted by Congress, and the duties of this Board were vested in its remaining member, James Read.[1] On May 7, 1781, Congress accepted the resignation of Deshon of the Navy Board at Boston.[2] The work of the Navy Boards and naval agents had now greatly diminished. Already the settling of naval accounts was becoming one of their principal tasks. After 1779 there were few Continental prizes to libel. Upon the resignation of the naval agents at Philadelphia, those at Boston, Portsmouth, and New London were the only ones of consequence.

The Board of Admiralty was called to act upon divers letters, petitions, and memorials, differing little from the similar communications which Congress referred to the Marine Committee. It also fell to its lot to prepare and report not a little important legislation. The reports of the Board, which were in writing, were chiefly the work of Lewis and Ellery, and were presented to Congress by the Congressional members of the Board. Congress usually referred these reports to a committee, before it discussed them or took final action upon them. Not a few of the reports of the Board were,

---

1. Journals of Continental Congress, December 5, 1780; January 11, 1781.
2. Ibid., May 7, 1781.

however, pigeon-holed by Congress, and no action was taken upon them. The naval legislation of Congress during the incumbency of the Board of Admiralty was in part rendered necessary by the decline of the navy. Certain other legislation was caused by the putting into effect of the Articles of Confederation on March 1, 1781; and a few Congressional resolutions on naval affairs may be attributed to the special legislative activity and enterprise of the Board of Admiralty.

In January, 1780, Congress on the recommendation of the Board of Admiralty passed a resolution which was no doubt in harmony with administrative economy and thrift, but which pressed hard upon many naval officers. The pay of all officers in the navy not in actual service was at once to cease. Their commissions were to be deposited with the most convenient Navy Board, until the officers should be again called into service; each officer was to retain his rank.[1] This was merely a courteous way of disestablishing the larger part of the navy. Owing to the capture and destruction of many Continental vessels, most of the naval officers were not in actual service. The number of commissioned officers in actual service in

1. Records and Papers of Continental Congress, 37, pp. 175-77, Report of Board of Admiralty, January 24, 1780; Journals of Continental Congress, January 22, January 25, 1780.

both navy and marine corps at this time was about twenty. It is clear that the Continental Congress was unfriendly to the theory that an employee of a government has a vested right in his office.

On July 11, 1780, naval salaries, subsistence money, and bounties were ordered to be paid in specie; forty Continental dollars were considered equal to one of specie. On the same day, in order that the depleted crews might perchance be recruited, Congress voted a bounty of twenty dollars to able, and ten dollars to ordinary seamen who should enlist in the navy for twelve months.[1] On August 7 it provided that officers who had served aboard vessels of twenty guns or upwards, and who should afterwards be detailed to vessels of less armament, should suffer no diminution in pay.[2] These provisions all indicate a declining government and navy.

On February 8, 1780, the Board of Admiralty secured the re-enaction of the resolutions of May 6, 1778, concerning the holding of courts of enquiry and courts-martial.[3] The most important provision of these resolutions, it is recalled, lessened the require-

---

1. Journals of Continental Congress, July 11, 1780; Records and Papers of Continental Congress, 37, pp. 261-63, Report of Board of Admiralty, July 10, 1780.
2. Journals of Continental Congress, August 7, 1780.
3. Ibid., February 8, 1780.

ments for the membership of courts-martial as fixed by Adams's rules. On the partial disestablishment of the navy in January it became increasingly difficult to assemble courts-martial composed entirely of naval officers. The only naval captain cashiered by a court-martial held under the direction of the Board of Admiralty was the eccentric Peter Landais.[1]

On May 4, 1780, the Board of Admiralty reported and Congress adopted the following device for a seal: "The arms, thirteen bars mutually supporting each other, alternate red and white, in a blue field, and surmounted by an anchor proper. The crest a ship under sail. The motto, sustentans et sustentatus. Legend, U. S. A. Sigil. Naval."[2] The anchor and ship under sail are still a part of the seal of the Department of the Navy. Instead of the arms, motto, and former legend, there now appear an eagle with outstretched wings, and the words "Navy Department, United States of America."

On April 20, 1780, Congress adopted a new form of commission for naval officers, which the Board of Admiralty had drafted.[3] This varied little from the one which had been used since the beginning of the Revo-

---

1   See Chapter X, pages 298-300.
2.   Journals of Continental Congress, May 4, 1780.
3.   Ibid., April 20, 1780.

lution. With slight changes in phraseology made to adapt it to the government under the Constitution, it is still used in the Department of the Navy at Washington. It is this form properly filled out which constitutes our present Admiral's title to his rank and office. The Board also prepared a form of commission, of bond, and of instructions for commanders of private vessels of war.[1] In the instructions the rights of neutrals were especially guarded. Following the lead of "Her Imperial Majesty of all the Russias," Congress declared that the goods of belligerents on board neutral vessels, with the exception of contraband, were not subject to capture. It confined the term contraband to those articles expressly declared to be such in the treaty of amity and commerce of February 6, 1778, between the United States and France.[2]

Congress on March 27, 1781, passed an ordinance relative to the capture and condemnation of prizes. This law was enacted by virtue of the ninth article of the Articles of Confederation, which vested the war powers in Congress. It codified the resolutions of November 25, 1775, and March 23, 1776. It was more severe than these reso-

---

1. Journals of Continental Congress, May 2, November 27, 1780, April 7, 1781; Records and Papers of Continental Congress, 37, pp. 225-41.
2. Journals of Continental Congress, October 5, 1780; Wharton's Diplomatic Correspondence, III, 860, 867.

lutions, and omitted certain indulgences and exemptions, which they contained. It prescribed the penalty of forfeiture of vessel without trial for those captors who destroyed or falsified their ship papers. One of its provisions related to salvage.[1] This law and also the one of April 7, 1781, fixing the instructions of commanders of private armed vessels, brought former legislation into conformity with the Articles of Confederation.

The Board of Admiralty and Congress were inclined to disagree as to the proper construction to be placed upon the ninth article of the Articles of Confederation, which gave Congress "the sole and exclusive right and power of determining on peace and war." In a report which it made to Congress under date of May 29, 1781, after referring to the commissions which Massachusetts had issued to the "Protector" and "Mars," two ships of the navy of that state, it said that "the Board humbly conceives that Commissions issuing from different Fountains of Power, is a matter which may merit the attention of the United States in Congress assembled who are the supreme power in Peace and War." The Board was inclined to take the view that Massachusetts had no right to issue these commissions. The committee of Congress to whom the report was re-

---
1. Journals of Continental Congress, March 27, 1781.

ferred interpreted more narrowly the war powers of Congress than did the Board of Admiralty. It conceived that each state had the right to issue commissions to ships of war under the regulations established by Congress, and that the only step necessary to be taken for the present was for the Board to transmit to each state a copy of the present regulations governing the issuing of commissions.[1] This incident is noteworthy in its indicating the existence of "strict" and "loose" constructionists within three months after the Articles of Confederation were adopted.

If another illustration is needed to show the dependence of the makers of the American navy upon British models, some words of the Board of Admiralty are in point. For a long time it had under consideration a revision of the rules and regulations of the Continental navy. Concerning its intention to inspect the British rules and incorporate into its new code such of them as were adapted to the American navy, it observed that it did not "think it unlawful to be taught by an enemy whose naval skill and power, until the reign of the present illustrious King of France, were superior to

---

1. Force Transcripts, Library of Congress, 37, pp. 241-44. The Board of Admiralty probably had in mind the sixth as well as the ninth article of the Articles of Confederation.

that of any kingdom or state on earth."[1] It is believed that the work of the Board in this particular was not brought before Congress.

On January 15, 1780, Congress created a permanent Court of Appeals for the trial of prize cases appealed from state admiralty courts. Since January 30, 1777, such cases had been heard and determined by a standing committee composed of five members of Congress. Such a committee naturally lacked permanency, expertness, and technical and legal knowledge. The Court established in January, 1780, was to consist of three judges, who were to try, in accordance with the law of nations, questions of fact as well as law. On January 22, 1780, Congress chose as the three judges of the Court, George Wythe of Virginia, William Paca of Maryland, and Titus Hosmer of Connecticut.[2]

When the Board of Admiralty took charge of the navy in December, 1779, there were ten Continental cruisers in American waters. The "Deane," 32, was fitting for sea at

---

1. Records and Papers of Continental Congress, 37, pp. 277, 281, Reports of Board of Admiralty, July 24, July 26, 1780.
2. Journals of Continental Congress, January 30, 1777; January 15, January 22, 1780; Jameson, Essays in the Constitutional History of the United States, Chapter I, Predecessor of the Supreme Court; Carson, Supreme Court of the United States, Part I, 50-57.

Boston; the "Trumbull," 28, was still in the Connecticut river; the "Providence," 28, "Boston," 24, "Queen of France," 28, and "Ranger," 18, were on their way to Charleston, South Carolina, in whose defence they were to assist; the "Confederacy," 32, was at Martinique repairing and refitting; and three vessels were still on the stocks, the "America," 74, at Portsmouth, "Bourbon," 36, at Chatham on the Connecticut river, and "Saratoga," 18, at Philadelphia. The "Alliance" was at the Texel in Holland where she had arrived after playing an ignominious part in the celebrated fight of Jones off Flamborough Head. This is not a formidable fleet, and its future movements have little bearing upon the great naval conflict now being waged between the mistress of the seas on the one side and France and Spain on the other. The Continental navy, however, still had some important errands to run, both Washington and the French were to ask its assistance, and on a few occasions the enemy was to find its officers and sailors no mean combatants.

In completing the vessels which were building and in refitting those which were in commission, the Board of Admiralty was from the first sorely embarrassed by a lack of money. The difficulties which the Marine Committee had encountered were now intensified by the prostration of the country's finances and credit. The Board resorted to all means within reason in its attempts to obtain the requisites for prosecuting its work. In January, 1780, it wrote to the Board of Treasury that unless money was at once forthcoming the Naval Department would be at a standstill; and that not less than one hundred thousand dollars would be sufficient for its needs.[1] It eagerly sought the proceeds to be derived from the sale of rum, wine, fruit, and sugar, taken from Continental prizes. In the summer of 1780 in order that its vessels might be in condition to render assistance to the expected French fleet, the Board solicited aid from the governors of New Hampshire, Massachusetts, and Connecticut; pressed the Commissary-General of Issues of the Continental Army to furnish it with "62,820 weight of Bread and 13,260 weight of Flour" with all despatch;[2] and finally, applied to John Holker, the Consul-General of France at Philadelphia, for a loan of 60,000 pounds of bread, promising to take special pains to repay it.[3]

Thus hampered, the Board was unable to accomplish much with its little fleet. Dur-

---

1. Marine Committee Letter Book, Board of Admiralty to Board of Treasury, January 7, 1780.
2. Ibid., Board of Admiralty, to Commisary-General of Issues, August 21, 1780.
3. Ibid., Board of Admiralty to Holker, August 29, 1780.

ing its incumbency some half-dozen cruises were made by the Continental vessels. Twenty prizes were captured; half of them only reached safe ports. Two of the prizes were His Majesty's brigs "Atalanta," 16, and "Trepassey," 14, which were taken by the "Alliance," 36, Captain John Barry, in May, 1781, when returning from France. During the fight, which lasted four hours, the gallant Barry was wounded in the shoulder. This voyage of Barry, during which he captured seven prizes, was the most successful one made under the direction of the Board of Admiralty.

In June, 1780, one of the most hotly contested engagements fought at sea during the Revolution occurred to the northward of the Bermudas between the "Trumbull," 28, Captain James Nicholson, the ranking officer of the Continental navy, and the Liverpool privateer "Watt," 32, Captain Coulthard. After a fight of two hours and a half both vessels withdrew seriously disabled, and with difficulty made their ways to their respective ports—the "Trumbull" to Boston and the "Watt" to New York. A British account of the engagement places the loss of the "Watt" at eighty-eight men, and that of the "Trumbull" at "considerable more." The Americans gave their own loss as thirty-eight men, and the British as ninety-two. The "Trumbull" had two lieutenants killed. Gilbert Saltonstall, the captain of marines on board the "Trumbull," wrote a vivid account of the fight. He was in the thick of it, and received eleven wounds. He said that "upon the whole there has not been a more close, obstinate, and bloody engagement since the war. I hope it won't be treason if I don't except even Paul Jones'. All things considered we may dispute titles with him."[1] This was the first cruise of the "Trumbull." The other twelve frigates of the original thirteen were at this time either destroyed or captured.

In July, 1780, a futile plan for an attack on New York was made. The Continental navy and army were to coöperate with the French fleet under the Admiral the Chevalier de Ternay. Under the direction of the Board of Admiralty, the Continental vessels continued to make voyages to France and the West Indies. The losses suffered by the navy during 1780 and the first half of 1781 were considerable. The "Boston," "Providence," "Queen of France," and "Ranger" were surrendered to the British on the fall of Charleston in May, 1780. The "Confederacy," 32, Captain Seth Harding, returning from Cape Francois with a load of military stores and colonial produce, was, on April 14, 1781, captured by the British

---

1. Records and Papers of New London Country Historical Society, part IV, I, 47-56; Boston Gazette, July 24, 1780 ; Gomer Williams, Liverpool Privateers, 272-75.

naval ships, "Roebuck," 44, and "Orpheus," 32. The "Confederacy" was taken into the British navy under the name of "Confederate." In March, 1781, the "Saratoga," 18, Captain John Young, foundered at sea and all on board were lost.[1]

Early in 1781 Congress resolved to supersede the Board of Admiralty with a Secretary of Marine, but failed to find a man who was willing to accept the new office. In June, 1781, the plan of appointing an Agent of Marine, and vesting in him the duties of the Board of Admiralty, pending the selection of a Secretary of Marine, was brought forward in Congress. The commissioners of admiralty were able to forecast the results of this agitation for a new naval system.[2] On July 9, 1781, Ellery informed Congress "that his family affairs pressed his return home, and therefore requested leave of absence."[3] As there was at this time but one Congressional member serving on the Board, on the absence of Ellery no quorum could be obtained. Lewis now prayed Congress to permit him to resign, or to give him such further directions "as they in their

---

1. List of Officers in Revolutionary Navy, miscellaneous manuscripts in the Library of Congress.

2. See Chapter VIII, Secretary of Marine and Agent of Marine.

3. Journals of Continental Congress, July 9, 1781.

wisdom shall deem meet."[1] On July 17 Congress accepted his resignation.[2] On July 18 Congress put the marine prisoners in charge of the Commissary of Prisoners of the army, and ordered the seal of the admiralty to be deposited with the Secretary of Congress until a Secretary of Marine should be appointed.[3] The Revolutionary Naval Department was without a head.

The Board of Admiralty was not a satisfactory executive. It was at all times dependent on its Congressional members for quorums. It proved to be slower, more cumbersome, and less responsible than the Marine Committee. The management of the navy still lacked unity and concentration. On the other hand, had the Board not been superseded, its commissioners would no doubt in time have developed greater expertness and technical skill than did the members of the Marine Committee. It should also be said that under more favorable auspices the Board of Admiralty would have shown a higher administrative efficiency than it did; for its lines had indeed fallen in unpleasant places, and a bankrupt federal treasury and a decadent Congress denied it the means requisite to the successful prosecution of its work.

---

1. Records and Papers of Continental Congress, 78, XIV, 445-47.
2. Journals of Continental Congress, July 17, 1781.
3. Ibid., July 18, 1781.

CHAPTER VIII

THE SECRETARY OF MARINE AND THE AGENT OF MARINE

On the question of the proper organization of the executive departments, the leaders of the Revolution were divided into two factions. Moved by their love of liberty, their distrust of governments, and their jealousy of delegated and concentrated powers, the members of one faction favored the vesting of the executive business in Congressional committees. The members of the other faction, who stood for governmental authority and control, for constructive legislation in the field of administration, and for the application of the principles of business to the affairs of state, declared for a system of permanent and single-headed executives chosen outside of the membership of Congress. The issue that was here joined in the special field of administration was of course a part of that perennial and perpetual conflict between the freedom of the individual and social control. In this case, as everywhere and always, the political doctrinaires, the iconoclasts and radicals, and the men of heart rather than of head, lined up on the side of liberty; while the practical and conservative men, the representatives of vested interests, and the cold, logical thinkers, stood together on the side of governmental control.

The faction which distrusted power and wished to keep it scattered, may be called the "dispersive school;" and the faction which wished to gather up the power and lodge it with a few men, may be called the "concentrative school." To the "dispersive school" belonged Samuel Adams, the Lees, Patrick Henry, and William Whipple; to the "concentrative school", Hamilton, Washington, the Morrises, and Jay. Early in the Revolution the advantage lay with the "dispersive school." Its executive plan of Congressional committees needed little work to put it into operation; it was more flexible than the scheme of permanent single-headed executives; and it was more in harmony with the ultra anti-monarchical spirit of the times. The Revolutionary government, originating as a congress of delegates, organized itself, after the manner of congresses, by means of committees of its own members. When the Congress became a Government, and had entrusted to it a multiplicity of executive duties, it naturally continued and adapted the old organization for the transaction of its new business. The executive system of Congressional committees, in this way becoming fixed, could not be easily changed.

By 1780 the "concentrative school" was winning its way. Indeed, the adoption in 1779 of mixed boards composed of men both in and out of Congress was a compromise between the two schools, in which the "concentrative school" gave up its contention for simplicity in the executive organs, in order to secure, in part at least, another of its objectives, permanency in the tenure of the administrators. By 1780 both committees and boards had been tried and found wanting. Then too, there was a greater need for a change in the executive system, than in the first years of the war. As Congress became imbecile, the quality of its committees and of their work deteriorated; and as the country wearied of the war, and its finances tightened, the necessity for greater economy and efficiency in administration increased. In 1780 the feeling among the leaders was general that a crisis in the army, in the finances, and in the business of the government, which could be met only by some thorough and far-reaching reform, was approaching. The leaders of the "concentrative school" proposed a complete change in the administrative system of Congress as a solution of the serious problems that confronted the country. By the end of 1780 a movement for a reform of this sort was in progress. It was diligently furthered by one school and zealously opposed by the other.

"If Congress," Washington wrote in December, 1780, "suppose that Boards composed of their own body, and always fluctuating, are competent to the great business of war (which requires not only close application, but a constant and uniform train of thinking and acting), they will most assuredly deceive themselves. Many, many instances might be adduced in proof of this." Washington was convinced that extravagant and improper expenditures of the public money, inexpertness in the transacting of business, and needless delays resulted from vesting all or a part of the duties of an executive office in Congress.[1] Hamilton declared specifically for the substitution of single executives for plural ones, and he named three men whom he considered especially qualified for departmental posts, General Schuyler for Minister of War, General McDougall for Minister of Marine, and Robert Morris for Minister of Finance. He conceived that there were always more knowledge, energy, responsibility, decision, despatch, zeal, and attraction for first-rate

---

1. Ford's Washington, IX, 75-76, Washington to James Duane, December 26, 1780; 33-5, Washington to John Sullivan, November 20, 1780; 125, Washington to R. R. Livingston, January 31, 1781; 131-34, Washington to John Sullivan, February 4, 1781; 246, Washington to John Sullivan, May 11, 1781.

ability "where single men, than where bodies are concerned."[1] Gouverneur Morris contributed to the agitation in behalf of better executives an enumeration of the qualifications requisite in the men who were to become heads of the leading departments. He held, as still do some of the writers on naval administration, that a Minister of Marine should possess a practical and technical knowledge of naval affairs; and he presented a unique list of his qualities in the following words:

"A minister of the marine should be a man of plain good sense, and a good economist, firm but not harsh; well acquainted with sea affairs, such as the construction, fitting, and victualling of ships, the conduct and manœuvre on a cruise, and in action, the nautical face of the earth, and maritime phenomenon. He should know the temper, manners, and disposition of sailors; for all which purposes it is proper, that he should have been bred to that business, and have followed it, in peace and war, in a military, and commercial capacity. His principles and manners should be absolutely republican, and his circumstances not indigent."[2]

It has been said that the debate in Congress over the change in the executive sys-

---

1. Hamilton's Hamilton, I, 127, note, Hamilton to Robert Morris, 1780; 154-55, 159 Hamilton to James Duane, September 3,1780'.
2. Sparks's Gouverneur Morris, I, 229-30.

tem was long, and was marked by the workings of party spirit, the self-interest of some members, and the doubts and fears and divided opinions of others.[1] Samuel Adams placed himself at the head of the advocates of the old system. On January 10, 1781, the friends of the new system gained their first decisive victory; for on this day Congress resolved to establish a Department of Foreign Affairs, and to appoint for its chief officer a Secretary for Foreign Affairs.[2] Five days later Adams wrote to Richard Henry Lee a letter which is almost pathetic in its earnestness and seriousness. "My friend," he said, "we must not suffer anything to discourage us in this great conflict. Let us recur to first principles without delay. It is our duty to make every proper exertion in our respective States to revive the old patriotic feelings among the people at large, and to get the public departments, especially the most important of them, filled with men of understanding and inflexible virtue. Our cause is surely too interesting to mankind to be put under the direction of men, vain, avaricious, or concealed under the hypocritical guise of patriotism, without a spark of public virtue." Adams recognized that the public service needed reforming. This he

1. Sparks's Gouverneur Morris, I, 227-28; Reed's Reed, II, 296.
2. Journals of Continental Congress, January 10, 1781.

would accomplish, not by a change of the administrative system, but by the introduction of more competent and more virtuous men into Congress and into its committees. This latter was to be brought about by a revival of civic interest in the several states.[1]

On February 7, 1781, Congress "resumed the consideration of the plan for the arrangement of the civil executive departments." It this day resolved that there should be a Superintendant of Finance, a Secretary of War, and a Secretary of Marine. It summed up the duties of the Secretary of Marine in the following brief paragraph:

"It shall be the duty of the secretary of marine to examine into and to report to Congress the present state of the navy, a register of the officers in and out of command, and the dates of their respective commissions; and an account of all the naval and other stores belonging to that department; to form estimates of all pay, equipments, and supplies necessary for the navy; and from time to time to report such estimates to the superintendant of finance, that he may take measures for providing for the expences, in such manner as may best suit the condition of the public treasury; to superintend and direct the execution of all resolutions of Congress respecting naval

---

1. Wells, Samuel Adams, III, 127, Adams to Lee, January 15, 1781; 128, extract from a letter of Luzerne, French minister to the United States.

preparations; to make out, seal, and countersign all marine commissions, keep registers thereof, and publish annually a list of all appointments; to report to Congress the officers and agents necessary to assist him in the business of his department; and in general to execute all the duties and powers specified in the act of Congress constituting the board of admiralty."

Speaking generally, the Secretary of Marine was to succeed to the duties and powers of the Board of Admiralty. It is, however, significant that the Secretary was not specifically charged with the ordering and directing of the movements of the vessels of war, as was the Board. The specified duties of the new office are largely secretarial. Congress was disposed to be less liberal in granting powers to a Secretary chosen outside its membership than to a Board partly composed of Congressmen. On February 9th the salary of the Secretary of Marine was fixed at $5000 per annum.[1]

On February 27, 1781, Congress, with a promptness which was exceptional, elected Major-General Alexander McDougall of New York to be Secretary of Marine, for which position he had been recommended by Alex-

---

1. Journals of Continental Congress, February 7, February 9, 1781. On October 1, 1781, the salary of the Secretary of Marine was fixed at $4,000 per annum, payable in specie.

ander Hamilton. McDougall's qualifications for the office were above the average. In the French and Indian War he had been a commander of privateers. Later he became a merchant in New York City. He was a leader of the Revolution in that state, and had risen to the rank of a major-general in the Revolutionary army. McDougall declined to accept the position proferred him unless permitted to hold his rank in the army, and to retain the privilege of returning to the field when his services were required. He based this partial refusal on patriotic grounds. Congress did not wish a Secretary of Marine on these conditions; and it therefore voted that it did not expect the acceptance of Major-General McDougall, and that it had a due sense of his zeal "for the safety and honour of America, and applaud his magnanimity in declining 'to retire from the toils and perils of the field in the present critical condition of the United States in general, and that of New York in particular.' "[1] Congress made no other choice of a Secretary of Marine.

During the summer of 1781 the control of naval affairs gravitated towards Robert Morris. Soon after assuming the office of

---

1. Journals of Continental Congress, February 27, March 30, 1781. Three states were willing to accept McDougall on the conditions he proposed. Samuel Adams and his friends voted against acceptance.

Superintendant of Finance in May, 1781, he was brought into close relation with the navy. He was invited to take upon himself more or less of the naval business by the urgent need of sending the cruisers on important errands, the helplessness of the Board of Admiralty, the inertia of Congress, and the interregnum in the headship of the Naval Department, which lasted from the discontinuance of the Board of Admiralty early in July, 1781, until the appointment of an Agent of Marine on September 7. The figure that Morris presents at this time is that of the strong and confident man of affairs, sagacious, expeditious, and painstaking, who is surrounded by weaker men, hesitating, vacillating, and procrastinating in their administrative attempts.

In June, 1781, Morris wrote to the President of Congress recommending the appointment of a captain for the 74-gun ship "America," and explaining how money for completing her might be obtained. He says that he is aware that John Jay has liberty to sell this ship at the Court of Madrid; that he thinks and hopes that Jay will not succeed, for the sale of the "America" would be injurious to the United States; and that it would be "more consistent with Oeconomy and with the dignity of Congress to have her finished than to let her Perish." On the receipt of this letter, Congress authorized Morris to take measures for launching the

"America" and fitting her for sea.[1] Morris now hinted to the Board of Admiralty that the frigate "Trumbull" could perform an essential public service if put under his direction, and pursuing his plan, he obtained a resolution of Congress giving him control of this vessel.[2] During the summer of 1781, while the reorganization of the Naval Department was in suspense, Morris, on his own initiative, directed the fitting out of the "Alliance" and "Deane," and ordered them to proceed to sea, "being convinced that while they lay in port, an useless Expence must necessarily be incurred."[3]

Meanwhile, a movement to place the Naval Department under the control of Morris had been set on foot in Congress. On June 26 Meriwether Smith of Virginia reported a series of resolutions providing for the reorganization of the Naval Department, a work which he considered necessary because the present naval system was "inefficient

---

1. Records and Papers of Continental Congress, 137, I, 47, 55, Morris to President of Congress, June 22, 1781; Ibid., 28, p. 145, Report of Committee respecting "America"; Journals of Continental Congress, June 23, 1781.

2. Records and Papers of Continental Congress, 137, I, 77; Journals of Continental Congress, July 11, 1781.

3. Records and Papers of Continental Congress, 137, I, 137, Morris to President of Congress, September 10, 1781.

and expensive."[1] The most important of these resolutions was one which dissolved the offices of the Board of Admiralty, the navy boards, and the naval agents; and another, which empowered the Superintendant of Finance to appoint some discreet agent to manage the navy under the order and inspection of the said superintendant, until a Secretary of Marine should be appointed, or until the further pleasure of Congress. On the day of their introduction these resolutions were referred to a committee, consisting of Meriwether Smith of Virginia, Roger Sherman of Connecticut, and Daniel of St. Thomas Jenifer, of Maryland. On July 2, having made a slight change in the phraseology of the resolutions, this committee reported them to Congress;[2] and on July 6 it again reported them, having now added a few additional resolutions. One of the latter was to the effect that the election of a Secretary of Marine should be postponed until the first Monday in November. On the putting of this resolution, it passed in the negative. The states divided sectionally; the four New England states and Delaware voted in the negative; Pennsylvania and the five Southern states, except South Carolina which was divided,

1. Records and Papers of Continental Congress, 28, p. 135, Resolutions of M. Smith.
2. Ibid., p. 133, Report of Committee on Smith's resolutions.

voted in the affirmative; delegates from New York and New Jersey were not present in Congress. The vote seems to indicate the defeat of those who were in favor of placing the navy under the control of Morris. On the same day, July 6, the remaining resolutions were referred to a committee consisting of Thomas McKean of Delaware, Oliver Ellsworth of Connecticut, and Theodoric Bland of Virginia.[1]

On July 18 the new committee reported a series of resolutions, differing little from those which had been referred to it, with the exception of one important change; the Agent of Marine was now to be appointed, not by Morris, but by Congress. On this day Congress passed two of the committee's resolutions. One of these transferred the care of the marine prisoners from the Board of Admiralty to the Commissary of Prisoners of the army; and the other ordered the seal of the admiralty to be deposited with the Secretary of Congress, and empowered him to use it in countersigning naval commissions. The remaining resolutions again went over. Congress was able to agree on the discontinuance of the Board of Admiralty, but not on the arrangements for its successor.[2]

---

1. Records and Papers of Continental Congress, 28, p. 149, Resolutions of Committee; Journals of Continental Congress, July 6, 1781.

2. Records and Papers of Continental Con-

Finally, the whole business of the reorganization of the Naval Department was referred to a third committee, composed of Theodoric Bland of Virginia, James M. Varnum of Rhode Island, and James Duane of New York. On the report of this committee on August 29, Congress agreed "that for the present an agent of marine be appointed, with authority to direct, fit out, equip, and employ the ships and vessels of war belonging to the United States, according to such instructions as he shall, from time to time, receive from Congress." The Agent of Marine was to direct the selling of all prizes. He was to settle and pay the naval accounts, and keep a record of his work. As soon as he entered into the execution of his office, the functions and appointments of the board of admiralty, the several navy boards, and all civil officers, appointed under them, should cease and be determined. The salary of the new head of the Naval Department was fixed at $1,500 a year, and that of his clerk at $500. Both the Agent of Marine and his clerk were required to take an oath "well and faithfully to execute the trust reposed in them, according to the best of their skill and judgment"; and to give good and sufficient bond.[1]

---

gress, 28, p. 147, Report of Committee on July 18; Journals of Continental Congress, July 18, 1781.

1. Records and Papers of Continental Con-

These resolutions of August 29 were to be only temporary; and they did not displace those of February 7, 1781, which provided for a Secretary of Marine. A second temporary expedient was resorted to on September 7, when Congress resolved: "That until an agent of marine shall be appointed by Congress, all the duties, powers, and authority assigned to the said agent, be devolved upon and executed by the said superintendant of finance."[1]

The reason why Congress appointed an Agent of Marine instead of a Secretary of Marine is not at all points clear. Having failed to secure the acceptance of McDougall as Secretary of Marine, Congress may have decided that the small and disheartening business of the navy would not attract first-rate talent; or that for the transaction of this business a full-fledged executive department was not necessary. It is more probable that the appointment of an Agent of Marine, under the circumstances of a disagreeing Congress, the failure of the Board of Admiralty, and the improbability of securing an efficient Secretary, was merely a temporary and feasible expedient for conducting the affairs of the navy. There are obvious reasons why the proposal to give the Superin-

---

gress, 28, p. 157; Journals of Continental Congress, August 29, 1781.

1. Journals of Continental Congress, September 7, 1781.

tendant of Finance the power to appoint the Agent of Marine, or the selection of Morris as Agent, should have aroused vigorous opposition. Men of Samuel Adams's way of thinking would oppose it, among other reasons, because it placed too much power in the hands of one man. The friends of the navy would dislike to see the Naval Department swallowed up by the Department of Finance. But on the other hand, many considerations recommended the step which was finally taken. It was the most economical disposition of the naval business which could be made. Morris had superior qualifications for the office, and he was at once available. Indeed, he was the only man in sight that promised to be equal to the task of straightening out the tangle of marine accounts, of financing a bankrupt navy, and of wielding effectively that arm of the military service. He was admirably qualified for the headship of the Naval Department by his experience as a man of business, familiar with accounts and the selection of employees, as the owner of a fleet of merchantmen, and as one of two or three of the most influential members of the Marine Committee during the years 1776 and 1777, when the navy was founded. Whatever may have been the shortcomings of the navy while Morris was directing it, they did not spring from the lack of an efficient executive.) For the first time during the Revolution its management was marked by despatch, decision, and an expert and adequate understanding of its problems.

On September 8, 1781, Morris wrote to the President of Congress accepting, in words of modesty and reluctance, his appointment as Agent of Marine. "There are many Reasons," he said, "why I would have wished that this Burthen had been laid on other Shoulders, or that at least I might have been permitted to appoint a temporary Agent untill the further Pleasure of Congress. As it is I shall undertake the Task however contrary to my Inclinations and inconsistent with the many Duties which press heavily upon me, because it will at least save Money to the Public." He then added, in a characteristic way, some observations on his new task. "True Oeconomy in the public business," he declared, "consists in employing a sufficient Number of Proper persons to perform the Public Business." He wished the accounts of the marine department to be speedily settled.[1]

Morris filled the office of Agent of Marine from September 7, 1781, until November 1, 1784. It is believed that he received no salary as Agent of Marine. In addition to Mor-

---

1. Records and Papers of Continental Congress, 137, I, 133, Morris to President of Congress, September 8, 1781.

ris the personnel of the Marine Office consisted of James Read, Secretary to the Agent of Marine, at a salary of $1,000 a year; Joseph Pennell, paymaster, at a salary of $1,000; and George Turner, Commissary of Naval Prisoners, at a salary of $1,200; the latter officer was authorized on July 24, 1782.[1] Read, who had been one of the commissioners of the Navy Board of the Middle Department, was of great service to Morris in conducting the business of the Marine Office. The clerical work of the Office was performed by the clerks of the office of the Superintendant of Finance, an instance of Morris's economies.

According to the resolutions of September 7, 1781, the positions of the commissioners of the navy boards were abolished and the positions of the prize agents were vacated. The Navy Board at Boston continued however to fit out vessels until March, 1782. It was not until some time later that it delivered over the books and papers of the Board to John Brown, the former secretary of the Board of Admiralty, whom Morris had appointed naval agent for settling the business of the navy in New England. In the four New England states, North and South Carolina, and Georgia, Morris either re-appointed the prize agents of the Board of Admiralty, or appointed new

---

1. Records and Papers of Continental Congress, 137, II, 183.

ones; in the other states, he served in this capacity himself.[1]

The Agent of Marine, like the Board of Admiralty, communicated with Congress by means of written reports, which that body referred to special committees of its own members. Accordingly, when naval business was discussed in Congress, it usually came up in the form of a "report of a committee on the report of the Agent of Marine." The subjects upon which the Agent of Marine reported were similar to those dealt with by his predecessors in naval administration. Not a few of his reports were concerned with the settling of marine accounts, and the satisfying of claimants against the government, which business was now insistent. During his tenure of the office of Agent of Marine, Morris prepared the larger part of the naval legislation of Congress. The changes or additions to his work which were made by committees of Congress were unimportant.

The law that provides for a change in a governmental system is often incomplete, and experience under the new order of business soon suggests the need of supplementary legislation. This was the case with the laws which transferred the naval business from the Board of Admiralty to the Agent of Marine. Morris, in one of his first

[1]. M. I. J. Griffin, Commodore John Barry, 169.

reports, explained to Congress that he had no power to hold courts of enquiry; thereupon, Congress, on November 20, 1781, revived the law of February 8, 1780, on the holding of courts of enquiry and courts-martial, which had lapsed with the passing of the Board of Admiralty. Morris's business-like care for the saving of time and effort is well shown, when in this report he tactfully suggests that Congress adapt their act not only to the Agent of Marine, but also to the Secretary of Marine, so that when the latter is appointed, "it may not be necessary for him to bring this matter again under Consideration."[1]

By the law of November 20 Morris was empowered to constitute a court of enquiry with three persons; and to constitute a court-martial with three captains and three first lieutenants of marines, "if there shall be so many of the marines then present". But in the event that so many officers for a court-martial could not be conveniently assembled, he might appoint any five persons to hold it. Morris, convinced of the impropriety of constituting naval courts with civilians, did not wish to avail himself of this latter alternative. Accordingly, on June 8, 1782, he made a report on naval

---

1. Records and Papers of Continental Congress, 137, I, 233, Morris to President of Congress, November 17, 1781; Journals of Continental Congress, November 20, 1781.

courts, which became the basis of the resolutions of Congress of June 12 on this subject. These provided that in the future a marine court of enquiry or court-martial for enquiring into and trying capital cases should consist of five navy and marine officers, two of whom should be captains; and in all cases not capital, should consist of three navy and marine officers, one of whom should be a captain in the navy. No sentence in capital cases was to be executed until approved by the Agent of Marine. All naval courts for commissioned officers must be appointed by the Agent of Marine. A captain in the navy might appoint a court-martial for the trial of offences committed by any other than a commissioned officer, provided that the sentencing of a warrant officer to be cashiered should have the confirmation of the Agent of Marine.[1]

During the incumbency of Morris, no captain in the navy was cashiered. The findings of a court-martial, which was held in Boston in the early summer of 1781, possess a peculiar interest, because of the light which they throw upon the penal code of the Continental navy, and because this case is one of the first in which a seaman in the American navy was sentenced to be hanged.

---

1. Records and Papers of Continental Congress, 137, I, 543, Report of Morris, June 3, 1782; Journals of Continental Congress, June 12, 1782.

Three seamen, who were enlisted on board the "Alliance," were tried for a breach of the 29th article of the rules and regulations of the navy.[1] Of Patrick Sheridan, the court adjudged that he should be whipped three hundred and fifty-four lashes upon the naked back, one hundred and seventy-seven thereof alongside the ship "Alliance," and the remainder alongside the ship "Deane." John Crawford was sentenced to wear a halter around his neck, and receive fifty lashes. Sheridan and Crawford were to lose certain wages and their share of prize money. The court found the third seaman, William McClehany, "peculiarly Guilty of a breach of all the Clauses in the Article aforesaid," and it adjudged that he should "suffer the punishment of death, and that he be hanged by the neck on the starboard fore Yard Arm of the said ship 'Alliance' until he is dead."

The Board of Admiralty laid the proceedings of this court-martial before Congress in July, 1781, but owing to the confusion of the naval business at this time, and to the carelessness of Congress, no action was taken on them. When John Brown, the naval agent of the Agent of Marine, reached

1. The 29th article of Adams's rules as adopted by Congress in 1775 fixed penalties for desertion and cowardice. It is not likely that the numbering was changed. I know of no earlier instance of the sentencing of a seaman in the American navy to be hanged.

Boston, towards the end of 1781, he found the three men in prison, waiting the execution of their sentences, and "perishing with cold for want of Cloathing." The fate of the three men is best told in Brown's words: "Under these circumstances it was the opinion of the Board (and I agreed with them) that as the proceedings had lain so long before Congress without anything being done, and it being uncertain when they would act upon them, to save expence it was best to dispose of the Men in the best manner we could. Accordingly the two who were sentenced to be whipped were put on board the Deane, the other was sold by the Sheriff to pay his bill of fees, keeping, &c., and with the surplus of the money he procured us three good seamen for the Deane. My motive for concurring in this proceeding was to save expence and preserve the public Money in my hands for more Material purposes."[1]

In December, 1781, and January, 1782, Congress passed an ordinance, "in pursuance of the powers delegated by the Confederation," which codified in great part the previous legislation on captures and condemnation of prizes, recaptures and salvage, contraband, and the sharing of prizes

---

1. Records and Papers of Continental Congress, 137, I, 367, Finding of Court Martial, dated June 28, 1781; 365, Morris to President of Congress, March 25, 1782, containing extract from Brown's letter.

between the captors and the government and between the captors themselves. Several changes were made in previous resolutions, and a few new ones were added. On their receiving a reasonable salvage, the recaptors of negroes, mulattoes, Indians, and indented servants, were to return all such property to its owners. The new ordinance specified in some detail the various forms of property which were subject to capture. It contained a revised list of articles of contraband. It declared that the rules of decision in the several admiralty courts should be "the resolutions and ordinances of the United States in Congress assembled, public treaties when declared to be so by an act of Congress, and the law of nations, according to the general usages of Europe;" public treaties were given precedence over the two other classes of rules.[1] This ordinance went into operation on February 1, 1782. Its importance is diminished by reason of its being in force during only the last year of the war, when the naval activities of the American fleets had decreased.

It is believed that this ordinance was entirely the work of Congress. Indeed, it soon appeared that there was at least one provision, the giving of the whole of certain prizes to captors on board of Continental vessels, which the Agent of Marine disap-

---

[1]. Journals of Continental Congress, December 4, 1781, January 8, 1782.

proved. In June, 1782, Morris made a report to Congress in which he showed that, owing to the government's liberality to its officers and seamen, it had lost ten thousand dollars on the late successful cruise of the frigate "Deane," during which she had captured five prizes of considerable value. He thought that wages, bounties, and one-half of prizes were quite sufficient inducements for manning the fleet. In all cases, however, in which the capture of a vessel of the enemy was especially meritorious, Morris would have Congress encourage and stimulate effort and merit in the navy by giving the captors, by a special act of Congress, the whole of their prizes. On July 10, 1782, Congress passed an ordinance embodying Morris's recommendations.[1]

When Morris, on September 7, 1781, became Agent of Marine, the direction of the movements of the Continental vessels was vested in him, but with a serious limitation; he was authorized to employ the armed cruisers "according to such instructions as he shall, from time to time, receive from Congress." Morris could never abide indefinite grants of power which confused authority; and he therefore, by means of a cleverly written letter, elicited a resolution from Congress giving him full power "to fit

---

1. Records and Papers of Continental Congress, 137, I, 559, Morris to President of Congress, June 20, 1782; Journals of Continental Congress, July 10, 1782.

out and employ the ships of war belonging to these United States, in such manner as shall appear to him best calculated to promote the interest of these United States."[1]

When Morris fell heir to the duties of the Naval Department, in the summer of 1781, the Continental navy was reduced to small numbers. There were in active service only five captains and seven lieutenants in the navy, and three captains and three lieutenants in the marine corps. Including with these, those officers who were unemployed, were in private service, were prisoners, or were on parole, there were twenty-two captains and thirty-nine lieutenants in the navy, and twelve captains and twelve lieutenants in the marine corps.[2] Only three vessels were now in commission; the frigate "Trumbull," 28, at Philadelphia, and the "Alliance," 36, and "Deane," 32, at Boston. The "America" and "Bourbon" were still on the stocks. About the first of September, 1782, Morris purchased the ship "Washington," 20, and in October he took over into the Continental service in payment for a debt the ship "Duc de Lauzun," 20.

The movements of the fleet under Morris's direction were marked, as formerly, by bits

1. Records and Papers of Continental Congress, 137, I, 137, Morris to President of Congress, September 10, 1781; Journals of Congress, September 12, 1781.
2. Records and Papers of Continental Congress, 37, p. 473.

of good and bad fortune, encounters with naval ships, privateers, and merchantmen, and voyages to France and the West Indies. From the summer of 1781 until the end of the war the little fleet captured twenty prizes, some fifteen of which reached safe ports. The last of his Majesty's vessels to surrender to a Continental ship was the schooner "Jackall," 20, Commander Logie, which was taken in the spring of 1782 by Captain Samuel Nicholson, when in command of the "Deane," or the "Hague," as she was now called. By a singular coincidence the first, and the last, valuable prize captured by a Continental ship during the Revolution, were taken by Captain John Manly. On one of the last days of November, 1775, he received the surrender of the brig "Nancy," a transport; and in January, 1783, while in command of the "Hague" he captured the ship "Baille" of 340 tons burden, with a cargo consisting of sixteen hundred barrels of provisions.[1]

One of the most interesting, varied, and fortunate cruises of the war was made by Captain John Barry in the "Alliance," 36, one of the largest and best-built vessels of the Continental navy. Barry left New London on August 4, 1782, and having visited the region of the Bermudas, and the Grand Banks of Newfoundland, he sailed eastward and overhauled a fleet of Jamai-

1. Boston Gazette, January 27, 1783.

camen, and arrived at L'Orient on October 17. He had captured nine prizes, four of which he carried into L'Orient. These four ships were Jamaicamen, and with their rich cargoes of rum and sugar, they sold for £620,610, one of the largest sums realized on any cruise during the Revolution. On December 8, Captain Barry left France for the West Indies. Having made a call at Madeira, Barry early in January, 1783, anchored at St. Pierre, Martinique, where he found a letter from the Agent of Marine ordering him to proceed to Havana and convoy the "Duc de Lauzun" to Philadelphia. About the first of February the "Alliance" arrived at Havana, after she had put into St. Eustatius and Cape Francois, and had been chased by one fleet off Porto Rico and another off Hispaniola. On account of the closing of the port of Havana, Barry was detained here a month. After considerable correspondence with the Governor of Havana, Barry on March 6 was permitted to sail with his convoy, which had on board seventy-two thousand dollars in specie. On March 10, 1783, Barry fell in with a British vessel, which is said to have been the frigate "Sibylle," 32, and he now fought the last naval engagement of the Revolution. It lasted forty-five minutes, ended indecisively, and resulted in the loss of ten men on board the "Alliance;" the loss of the British is unknown. The two American vessels now parted company, and each soon reached a safe port; the "Alliance" arrived at Newport, Rhode Island, on March 20, and the "Duc de Lauzun" anchored at Philadelphia on March 21. It was now two months since the Preliminary Articles of Peace had been signed at Versailles.[1] The naval movements of the Continental vessels during the Revolution ended with the arrivals of these two vessels.

While Morris had the direction of the fleet, only one vessel was captured by the enemy, and this before he became Agent of Marine. In July, 1781, he ordered the "Trumbull," 28, Captain James Nicholson, to proceed to Havana with despatches, letters, and a cargo of flour. The "Trumbull" had scarcely cleared the Capes of the Delaware, on August 8, when she was chased by the frigate "Iris," 32, Captain George Dawson. Encountering a storm, the "Trumbull" was dismasted, and thus crippled she was overtaken by the "Iris." The "Trumbull's" crew were a sorry lot; some of them were British deserters, and others were cowardly and disaffected. It was late in the evening when the fight began. Many of the crew now put out their battle lanterns and flew from their quarters. Captain

---

1. Records and Papers of Continental Congress, 137, II, 103; M. I. J. Griffin, Commodore John Barry, 162-248, prints many contemporaneous papers relating to Barry's cruise.

Nicholson and his officers, with a handful of seamen, bravely defended their ship against impossible odds for an hour before they surrendered. Nicholson lost sixteen men; two of his lieutenants were wounded. It is recalled that the "Iris" was originally the "Hancock," of the Continental navy, and that she was the first of the thirteen original frigates to surrender to the enemy. The "Iris" was a fast ship, and is said to have made the fortunes of all the British captains that commanded her. It was the irony of fate that the first of the thirteen frigates to be captured should receive the surrender of the last remaining one. A letter from New York, dated August 11, 1781, informs us that "this day arrived the celebrated rebel frigate named the Trumbull."[1]

The attempts of Morris, in 1782, to obtain an increase in the naval force of Congress, form one of the most interesting and characteristic parts of his naval work. The surrender of Cornwallis on October 19, 1781, was not considered by many contemporaneous Americans as an event that must necessarily end the Revolution. Indeed, the final outcome of the war was in doubt for more than a year. The Agent of Marine was too cautious and conservative to count on peace before its actual accomplishment had been sealed by a formal treaty. After

---

1. Clowes, Royal Navy, IV, 72, 73; Pennsylvania Packet, August 16, 1781.

the surrender of Cornwallis he not only continued to send the Continental cruisers against the enemy, but whenever an occasion presented, he vigorously urged on Congress the necessity of a naval increase. To the mind of Morris the need of a navy in 1782 was greater than it had been at any previous time during the Revolution. He conceived that up to this time Britain had attempted to conquer the Colonies on land by means of her army; since she had been defeated in this, it was now her purpose to starve the Colonies into submission by means of her navy and superior sea-power. The United States must meet the enemy's change of tactics by building a navy.

In April, 1782, Morris took steps to have the frigate "Bourbon" completed. Congress was not convinced of the expediency of this, and was inclined to sell the frigate in its unfinished state. Morris wrote reprovingly to Congress that the most economical thing to do was to complete the vessel; and that "there is also a degree of Dignity in carrying through such measures as Congress have once adopted, unless some change of circumstances renders the execution improper." He then added: "The present circumstances of the United States I apprehend to be such as should induce our attention to the re-establishment of a Naval Force, and altho' former attempts have proved unfortunate, we must not take it for granted that future Essays will be unsuccessful. Altho' the Naval Force of our enemy is powerful, and their Ships Numerous, yet that Force is opposed by equal Numbers, so as to give them much more employment than at the time our infant Fleet was Crushed."[1]

On May 10, 1782, in response to a request of Congress, Morris submitted an exhaustive report on the state of American commerce. Referring to the intentions of the British, he declared that having been compelled to abandon the idea of conquest, their avowed design was to annihilate the American commerce. The plans of the enemy could be frustrated and the American trade protected by so small a fleet as two ships of the line and ten frigates. The ships of the line, together with two frigates, should be stationed in the Chesapeake, to cruise as occasion might require. The frigates should be divided into two equal squadrons, each of which should serve as a convoy of the American trade between the United States and France. By each squadron making two round trips a year, a quarterly communication both ways between these two countries would be established. The United States of course could not provide this service, but the ships which the plan required might

---

1. Records and Papers of Continental Congress, 137, I, 415, Morris to President of Congress, April 24, 1782.

be detailed from the French or Spanish fleet. "It is to be hoped," Morris said, "that if the war continues much longer, the United States will be able to provide the necessary force for themselves, which at present they are not, tho' if the above arrangements take place, they might now provide for the trade from America to the West Indies." Congress authorized Morris to apply to both Spain and France for the needed vessels.[1]

But a more extensive naval plan than this was in Morris's mind, and one which could be undertaken independent of foreign ships. On July 30, 1782, he submitted to Congress an estimate for the public services of the United States for the year 1783, amounting in all to eleven millions of dollars. More than one-fifth of this sum was to be spent on the navy. "Congress will observe," he said, "that the estimates for the Marine Department amount to two Millions and a half, whereas there was no Estimate made for that Service in the last year any more than for the civil list." Morris based this most remarkable recommendation for a naval increase on the belief that the enemy had changed his mode of warfare, and that it was now his purpose to annihilate the commerce of America, and thus starve her into submission. With this sort of a campaign, conducted by the enemy, an American army

---

1. Records and Papers of Continental Congress, 137, I, 447, Report of Morris, May 10, 1782.

without a navy would be burdensome without being able to accomplish anything. With a navy, we could prevent the enemy from making predatory excursions, ruining our commerce, and capturing our supplies; he would either be compelled to keep a superior naval force in this country, which would give our allies a naval superiority elsewhere; or else he must permit the balance of naval strength in America to be on our side; in which latter case we could protect our trade, annoy his commerce and cut off the supplies which he would be sending to his posts in America. Then, concluded Morris in words which remind one of the annual report of some recent Secretary of the Navy asking for the yearly quota of battleships: "By oeconomizing our Funds and constructing six ships annually we should advance so rapidly to Maritime importance that our enemy would be convinced not only of the Impossibility of subduing us, but also of the Certainty that his forces in this Country must eventually be lost without being able to produce him any possible Advantage;" and we should in this way regain the "full Possession of our Country without the Expence of Blood, or treasure, which must attend any other Mode of Operations, and while we are pursuing those Steps which lead to the Possession of our natural Strength and Defence."[1]

---

1. Records and Papers of Continental Con-

The signing on November 30, 1782, of the Provisional Articles of Peace between the United States and Great Britain, news of which reached America early in the spring of 1783, removed the necessity of a naval increase, and in the minds of many the need of a navy at all. Morris did not at once give up the notion that the government on a peace footing should maintain a respectable marine. In May, 1783, he asked Congress to relieve him of his naval duties. "The affairs of the Marine Department," he writes, "occupy more time and attention than I can easily spare. This Department will now become important, and I hope extensive. I must therefore request that Congress will be pleased to appoint an Agent of Marine as soon as their convenience will admit."[1] He became convinced however that not much could be done for the navy until the finances of Congress were placed on a better and more permanent basis. In July, 1783, Morris made a report on a proposition of Virginia offering to sell her naval ship "Cormorant" to the United States. Congress agreed to his report, which was as follows: "That although it is an object highly desirable, to establish a respectable marine, yet the situation of the

gress, 137, I, 713, Estimate for public services for 1783, July 30, 1782.

1. Records and Papers of Continental Congress, 137, II, 425, Morris to President of Congress, May 3, 1783.

public treasury renders it not advisable to purchase ships for the present, nor until the several states shall grant such funds for the construction of ships, docks, naval arsenals, and for the support of the naval service, as shall enable the United States to establish their marine upon a permanent and respectable footing."[1]

Meanwhile, Congress had been rapidly going out of the naval business, by formally ending the war at sea, by providing for the settlement of marine accounts, and by disposing of its naval stock. On March 24, 1783, it ordered the Agent of Marine to recall all armed vessels cruising under the American colors. On April 11 it issued a "Proclamation, Declaring the Cessation of arms, as well by Sea as by Land, agreed upon between the United States of America and His Britannic Majesty; and enjoining the observance thereof." On April 15 it ordered the Agent of Marine to set free all the naval prisoners of the enemy.[2]

During the last year of the Revolution and for several years after its close, one of the principal administrative tasks of the government was the settling of the outstanding accounts of the several executive de-

   1. Records and Papers of Continental Congress, 137, II, 725, Report of Morris, July 31, 1783; Journals of Continental Congress, August 5, 1783.
   2. Journals of Continental Congress, March 24, April 11, April 15, 1783.

partments. This was a work fraught with extraordinary difficulties. The administration of a government founded and conducted amid the distractions of war was necessarily marked by irregularities in official procedure, the lack of system in accounting, and in general by haphazard ways of business. On February 27, 1782, Congress acting on the recommendation of Morris authorized him to appoint five commissioners with full power and authority to liquidate and finally settle the Revolutionary accounts. Each commissioner was paid $1,500 a year; he was permitted to employ a clerk. The states were recommended to empower the commissioners to examine witnesses under oath. Each commissioner was given charge of a certain class of accounts; to one of the five men fell the settling of the accounts of the Naval Department. Owing to Morris's caution in making appointments, and to the obstacles that stood in the way of a wise choice, the "commissioner for settling the accounts of the marine department" was not selected until June 19, 1783, when Joseph Pennell, the paymaster of the Marine Office, was named for the place.[1] By the fall of 1783 Pennell was settled in his work, and was complaining of its arduousness. He soon found himself involved in a dispute with the members of the old Naval Com-

---

1. Journals of Continental Congress, February 27, 1782, June 19, 1783.

mittee. He said that they had received money from Congress for which they had not accounted; and that, according to the vouchers, they had paid one debt twice. He found that the members of the Marine Committee were individually charged with the moneys they had received; and that when they left the Committee, they made no settlement. In many instances vouchers were lacking. Statements from members of the Navy Boards and from the naval agents could be obtained only with great difficulty, as these men were now discharged, and they were often scattered. He discovered that the prize agents made no uniform charge for their services; some exacted five, and others two and a half per cent on the receipts from the sale of prizes. Offices for settling the naval accounts were opened in Philadelphia, New York, and Boston. On the retirement of Morris, Pennell became responsible to the new Board of Treasury.[1]

In the last year of the war Congress began to dispose of its naval craft. On September 3, 1782, the 74-gun ship "America" now at last almost ready for launching was on the recommendation of the Agent of Marine given to France to replace the ship of the line "Magnifique," 74, which the 'rench

---

1. Records and Papers of Continental Congress, 137, III, 651, 655, Morris to President of Congress, May 26, 1784, enclosing extract of letter of Pennell.

fleet had recently lost in Boston harbor. Congress, "desirous of testifying on this occasion to his Majesty, the sense they entertain of his generous exertions in behalf of the United States," directed the Agent of Marine to present the "America" to Luzerne, the French minister at Philadelphia, for the service of His Most Christian Majesty.[1] It was a gracious act of international friendship. In April, 1783, the "Duc de Lauzun" was lent to the French minister to carry home some French troops, after which service she was to be sold.[2] In July Morris ordered the "Hague" to be sold, and recommended to Congress a like disposition of the "Bourbon," which latter ship in all probability had been recently launched.[3] In March, 1784, Morris recommended the sale of the "Alliance," as she was "now a mere bill of costs;" and also the "Washington," because much money would be required to repair her, and there was no need to employ her as a packet, since the French and English had established a mail service.[4] Lieutenant Joshua

---

1. Journals of Continental Congress, September 3, 1782.
2. Ibid., April 21, 1783.
3. Records and Papers of Continental Congress, 137, III, 677, Report of Morris, July 22, 1783.
4. Force Transcripts, Library of Congress, 137, 3, p. 243, Report of Morris, March 19, 1784.

Barney, acting as the agent for the Naval Department, sold the "Washington" in Baltimore in the summer of 1784.

The members of Congress were not unanimous on the question of the proper disposition of the "Alliance." On January 15, 1784, a committee of three reported: "That the honour of the Flag of the United States and the protection of its trade and coasts from the insults of pirates require that the Frigate of Alliance should be repaired."[1] A committee in March, 1784, and another in May, 1785, recommended her sale.[2] Finally, on June 3, 1785, Congress directed the Board of Treasury "to sell for specie or public securities, at public or private sale, the frigate Alliance, with her tackle and appurtenances."[3] In August, 1785, the Board of Treasury sold this vessel for £2,887, to be paid in United States certificates of public debt. The purchasers afterwards sold the "Alliance" at a great profit to Robert Morris. In June, 1787, this vessel sailed for Canton, China, as a merchantman.[4]

1. Records and Papers of Continental Congress, 28, p. 221, Report of Committee, January 15, 1784.
2. Ibid., 28, pp. 213, 225-27, Reports of Committees.
3. Journals of Continental Congress, June 3, 1785.
4. Records and Papers of Continental Congress, 140, II, 45, Board of Treasury to President of Congress, August 5, 1785; M. I. J. Griffin, Commodore John Barry, 258-59.

From the sale of the "Alliance" until the establishment of a new navy under the Constitution in 1794 it was left to the stars and stripes floating from American merchantmen to familiarize foreign ports and seas with the symbol of the new Nation.

Congress did not formally end the naval establishment by act or resolution, unless one considers that such was the effect of the resolution of January 25, 1780, which provided that the pay of all naval officers except those in actual service should cease. After this date it would seem that as the vessels were captured, sold, or thrown out of commission, the names of the officers were taken from the pay-roll. In September, 1783, an unsuccessful attempt was made in Congress to discontinue the Agent of Marine.[1] Morris continued in office until November 1, 1784, when he retired from public service. Congress made no move to fill his place as Agent of Marine, for there was little need for such an official. Certain unimportant naval business, chiefly concerned with the settlement of naval accounts, remained, however, to be transacted. This for the most part naturally fell to the Board of Treasury, organized in the spring of 1785. This Board, aided by the commissioner for settling the marine accounts, and by James Read, the efficient secretary to the Agent

---

1. Journals of Continental Congress, September 16, 1783.

of Marine, with whom Morris on retiring left the books and papers of the Naval Department, wound up the small, unimportant, and dwindling business of the navy.

CHAPTER IX

NAVAL DUTIES OF AMERICAN REPRESENTATIVES IN FOREIGN COUNTRIES

On the outbreak of the war between the Colonies and the mother-country, Congress turned with true political insight to France for aid. The self-interest of no other country in Europe gave so good a basis for friendship and alliance with America. To France, the success of the revolting British Colonies meant the humbling of a victorious rival, the turning of a part of Britain's valuable colonial trade into French channels, and probably a reopening of the trial at arms of the Seven Years' War and a reversal of some of its humiliating decisions. Common interests led the two countries to coöperate in achieving and furthering their objects and ambitions; and this led to the establishing of intimate diplomatic, commercial, and naval relations between them. Many of the duties that grew out of these three classes of relations had to be transacted in France, and they therefore necessitated the appointment of American representatives to be resident in that country. The naval duties of these representatives were numerous and important. They involved the renting, purchase, and building of naval vessels; the officering, manning, and fitting out of vessels; the directing of cruises; the purchase of naval supplies; the disciplining of officers; the paying of officers and crews; the disposing of prizes; the devising of naval plans; the commissioning of privateers; the caring for naval prisoners and the negotiating for their exchange; and the disseminating of naval intelligence. The vesting of these duties in the American representatives in France virtually constituted the establishment of a Branch Naval Office at Paris.[1]

Besides the above duties, which may be considered strictly naval in character, the American representatives had other business closely related to their admiralty work, but which was also intimately connected with their diplomatic and commercial work. For instance, dealings with breaches of neutrality committed by American ships had to do equally with diplomatic and naval affairs. The selling of colonial products which the Commercial Committee of the Continental Congress exported to France,

---

1. For convenience the term "Naval Office" will be used in this chapter. It will be understood of course that there existed no "Naval Office" apart from the Office of the American representatives at Paris, in whom were vested diplomatic, naval, and commercial duties.

and the buying of French manufactures which the American representatives shipped to America, were of course commercial duties. These transactions, however, came into contact with naval affairs when the goods purchased in France happened to be naval stores, or when naval ships carried the goods or convoyed the merchantmen which carried them. For the sake of obtaining a complete view of the admiralty work of the American representatives in France, this chapter will touch upon naval duties of all sorts even though their diplomatic and commercial aspects stand out the most prominently.

The first naval business of the Colonies in France fell to Silas Deane, a political and commercial agent of the Continental Congress, who arrived at Paris in July, 1776. In December, 1776, Deane was succeeded by three American commissioners to the Court of France, Benjamin Franklin, Silas Deane, and Arthur Lee. These three men shared the naval duties of their office until the spring of 1778, when Deane was superseded by John Adams. In February, 1779, Franklin, who had been chosen Minister Plenipotentiary at the Court of France, fell heir along with the other duties of the commissioners to those of a naval character; and he continued·in this office until the end of the Revolution. Of the first three commissioners Silas Deane had the most to do with the naval business. He says that the management of the Continental ships of war and of their prizes which was a "most complicated and embarrassing part of our affairs" fell entirely upon himself.[1] When Deane was superseded, it would seem that his naval duties fell to Franklin rather than to Adams. Franklin had at all times the chief part of the work of exchanging naval prisoners with Great Britain; and Adams excelled the other commissioners in transmitting to the home government naval intelligence.

The headquarters of the Naval Office were of course situated at Paris, several hundred miles from the ports frequented by the Continental vessels. This was a great disadvantage, as it caused delays in communicating with the naval officers and naval agents, besides other inconveniences. The Office gave its orders as a rule by letter, but now and then when its officers and agents visited Paris, it communicated with them by word of mouth. Its official correspondence with the home government was carried on almost exclusively with the "Foreign Office" at Philadelphia—that is, at first with the Committee of Secret Correspondence, then with the Committee of Foreign Affairs, and finally with the Secretary for Foreign Affairs. A few letters passed between the Naval

---

1. Ingraham, Papers relative to Silas Deane, 67.

Office at Paris and the Naval Department in America. The secretary and the clerks, first of the Commissioners, and later of the Minister at the Court of France, assisted in transacting the naval business.

The American representatives at Paris employed agents in a number of the chief Atlantic ports of France to transact their naval and commercial business. The principal agencies were at Nantes, L'Orient, Bordeaux, Brest, and Dunkirk. There were also agencies at Bilbao, and Coruña, Spain; and in Holland. It is difficult to separate the naval and commercial duties of these agencies, as they were vested in the same men. The whole subject is exceedingly complicated. For transacting naval business, Nantes was the most important agency, although L'Orient was not far behind it. At Nantes in 1777 within a comparatively short period of time one finds Thomas Morris, a half-brother of Robert Morris, William Lee, a brother of Richard Henry Lee, Jonathan Williams, a nephew of Franklin, John Ross, a Philadelphia merchant, and a certain German merchant by the name of Schweighauser exercising similar duties. William Lee was for a time commercial agent for all of France, and his authority of course came in contact with that of the Commissioners at Paris.[1] Such divisions and duplications

---
1. Wharton's Diplomatic Correspondence and Ford's Letters of William Lee are the best sources for the work of these agents.

of powers resulted in much contention, misunderstanding, and jealousy. John Adams tells us that when he arrived in France in the spring of 1778 he found in some places two or three persons claiming the character of American agents; and that at one port, three agents had been appointed, one by the Commissioners at Paris, another by the commercial agent of France, and a third by the Commercial Committee of Congress. "We have such abuses and irregularities every day occurring as are very alarming. Agents of various sorts are drawing bills upon us, and the commanders of vessels of war are drawing upon us for expenses and supplies which we never ordered." Moved by the reformatory zeal that so often characterizes the new appointee to public office, Adams attempted to reduce the business of Congress in France to some system.[1]

The Naval Office at Paris appointed several naval officers by filling out blank commissions and warrants, which had been signed and sent by the President of Congress for that purpose. Late in the war the question arose as to the proper rank in the navy of some of these appointments. In certain specific cases which were referred to Robert Morris as Agent of Marine, he recommended that new commissions be granted

---

1. Wharton, Diplomatic Correspondence II, 595, Adams to Commercial Committee, May 24, 1778.

dated as the old, and that the officers receiving them take rank according to the dates of their old commissions. The Naval Office granted commissions of captain to Gustavus Conyngham, Samuel Nicholson, Peter Landais, and John Green. On the recommendation of John Paul Jones it appointed Richard Dale to be a lieutenant on board the "Bon Homme Richard." Dale became an officer of distinction in the new navy under the Constitution, where he rose to the rank of commodore. Landais was the only Frenchman who received a permanent commission as captain in the Continental navy.

Silas Deane had a penchant for recommending French officers; and he was very credulous as to the compliments expressed by themselves and their friends in their behalf. On November 28, 1776, Deane wrote to the Committee of Secret Correspondence as follows, having just referred to certain army officers whom he was sending to America: "As to sea officers, they are not so easily obtained, yet some good ones may be had, and in particular two, one of whom I have already mentioned; the other is quite his equal, with some other advantages; he was first lieutenant of a man-of-war, round the World with Captain Cook, and has since had a ship, but wants to leave this for other service where he may make a settlement and establish a family. These two officers would engage a number of younger ones, should they embark. I send herewith the plans of one of them for burning ships." The French officer who designed these plans, also made "drafts of ships and rates for constructing and regulating a navy," of which Deane had the "highest opinion." This officer, Deane said, "has seen much service, is a person of study and letters, as well as fortune, and is ambitious of planning a navy for America, which shall at once be much cheaper and more effectual than anything of the kind which can be produced on the European system."[1]

That Deane gave too ready an ear to the soft words of the French, is clear from his extravagant recommendations of the erratic and troublesome French captain, Peter Landais. Deane said that Landais would be a "valuable acquisition to our Navy;" and that he was a "skilful seaman of long Experience in every Part of the World, of good judgment and the most unsuspicious honor and Probity." In May, 1778, Congress continued Landais in the naval service; but directed "the commissioners of the United States at foreign courts" not to "recommend any foreign sea-officers, nor give any of them the least expectation of

---

1. Wharton, Diplomatic Correspondence II, 191, 200, Deane to Committee of Secret Correspondence, November 6, November 28, 1776.

being employed as captains in the navy."[1]

The Naval Office at Paris issued a few commissions to privateers. As early as October, 1776, Deane was writing to the Committee of Secret Correspondence for blank commissions. Private as well as public interests were involved in the cruises of Captain Gustavus Conyngham in European waters. Carmichael, a Marylander and an employee in France of Congress and the Commissioners at Paris, asserted that Deane in 1777 intended to equip a vessel in the Mediterranean sea partly on public and partly on private account, that an agent was employed who succeeded in buying a vessel, but that the state of Genoa interposed and stopped the enterprise.[2] Two famous, or better infamous, letters of marque were fitted out at Dunkirk and commissioned by the Naval Office in 1779. They were named the "Black Prince" and the "Black Princess." Their crews were a malodorous medley, containing "a few Americans, mixed with Irish and English smugglers." These smugglers had recently broken prison in Dublin, recaptured their smuggling vessel, and escaped to Dunkirk. Should they be recaptured by the English

---

1. Collections of New York Historical Society, Deane Papers, II, 122; Journals of Continental Congress, May 9, 1778.
2. Ingraham, Papers relative to Silas Deane, 141-49.

and their identity be discovered, they would be forced to suffer the penalty for smuggling. As they spoke English, it was thought that their past character might be best concealed by giving them an American commission, instead of a French one. These two privateers captured or destroyed upwards of one hundred and twenty sail of the British, and insulted "the coasts of these lords of the ocean." In the summer of 1780, the "Black Prince" was wrecked on the coast of France, and the commission of the "Black Princess," upon the request of Vergennes, the French Minister of Foreign Affairs, was recalled by Franklin.[1] In 1780 certain American prisoners, who had escaped, fitted out a privateer at Cadiz in Spain and asked Jay, the American minister at Madrid, for a commission. He referred them to Franklin.[2]

When the American Commissioners assembled in Paris in December, 1776, to begin their mission, they had with them the orders of Congress to purchase, arm, and equip a frigate and two cutters. They were to send the frigate cruising against the enemy in the English channel, and were to employ the cutters in transporting supplies to

1. Wharton, Diplomatic Correspondence, III, 802-03; IV, 26, 33; Hàle's Franklin in France, I, chapter XVI, Privateers from Dunkirk.
2. Wharton, Diplomatic Correspondence III, 731.

America. The Commissioners were further directed to hire or buy at the French Court eight line of battle ships.[1] They began to carry out these orders in January, 1777, when Captain Samuel Nicholson was sent to Boulogne to purchase one of the cutters; in the spring a lugger was obtained at Dover, England; and in the early summer another cutter was bought at Dunkirk. In the two latter transactions William Hodge, a merchant from Philadelphia, acted as the agent of the Commissioners. Early in the year Captain Lambert Wickes, who had in December, 1776, arrived in France in the Continental sloop "Reprisal" with Dr. Franklin on board, was inspecting vessels for the Commissioners. Nicholson's cutter was named the "Dolphin;" and Hodge's two vessels were called, respectively, the "Surprise" and the "Revenge." It is believed that the "Revenge" was purchased jointly on public and private account. After this vessel's first cruise it is known that Hodge and possibly others were pecuniarily interested in its ventures.

By the fall of 1777 the Commissioners had completed the construction of a 32-gun frigate at Nantes, which they called the "Deane." They also purchased a ship which they fitted out as a 28-gun frigate

---

1. Journals of Continental Congress, October 3, 1776; Wharton, Diplomatic Correspondence, II, 177.

and named the "Queen of France." Early in 1778 they sent the "Deane" under the command of Captain Samuel Nicholson, and the "Queen of France" under the command of Captain John Green, both vessels laden with supplies, to Boston. The "Deane" remained in the navy until the end of the Revolution. The "Queen of France" was surrendered to the British in May, 1780, on the fall of Charleston, South Carolina. On the application of the Commissioners to the French Court for the loan or sale of some ships of the line, they were told that the French government considered it absolutely necessary to keep the whole of its fleet at home ready for the defence of France in case of a rupture with Great Britain; but, that, since England was apprehensive of a war with France, such a disposition of the French naval forces was serviceable to America in so far as it forced England to retain an equal force in the British seas.[1]

In the spring of 1777 the Commissioners received orders from Congress to build six vessels of war; but before this, they had on their own responsibility contracted with "one of the ablest sea officers of France, skilled in all the arts relating to the marine," who had offered "his services to our States, with the permission of the minister," to "superintend the building of two ships of

1. Wharton, Diplomatic Correspondence, II, 284.

war, of a particular construction, which, though not of half the cost, shall be superior in force and utility to ships of sixty-four guns." This officer had already built a vessel of this type for the King of France which the Commissioners were told "exceeds everything in swift sailing."[1] Only one of these frigates, which was named the "Indian," was placed upon the stocks, and this one at Amsterdam. To conceal its ownership and destination it was built in the name of a private individual. The Commissioners wrote in the fall of 1777, when the ship was almost finished, that it was a large frigate and was supposed to equal a ship of the line, as it would carry thirty 24-pounders on one deck. The ship did not get to sea under Continental colors. Owing to the many difficulties of equipping and manning so large a ship in a neutral port, and to the lack of money necessary for such work, the Commissioners sold it to the King of France for a sum equal to that which they had expended upon it; the King at the same time agreed to pension well the officer who had built it.[2] With the sale of this frigate the work of the Naval Office at Paris in naval construction came to a close. The "Indian" was finally rented to the state

---

1. Wharton, Diplomatic Correspondence, II, 284-85.
2. Ibid., 433, Commissioners to Committee of Foreign Affairs, November 30, 1777.

of South Carolina. In 1779 and 1780 the French government loaned several vessels to the Naval Office.

During the years 1777, 1778, and 1779, the fitting out of Continental armed vessels, as well those which were sent to France from America, as those which were originally obtained by the Commissioners, was a severe tax on the slender resources of the Continental treasury at Paris. After a long voyage or cruise a wooden sailing vessel needed much repairing. Perchance it must be careened and cleaned or repaired below the water line; new masts and spars were often needed; and old sails had to be mended and new ones provided. Always, the vessel before beginning a new cruise must be freshly provisioned; and its crew, depleted by battle, desertion, and the dispensations of Providence, had to be replenished. The enlisting of a few recruits was not a difficult thing at this time, for there was human driftwood in every port of Christendom, of divers nationalities, willing to ship under any flag. Many Frenchmen enlisted in French ports on board American vessels. In 1782 Franklin said he was continually pestered by such Frenchmen, who, being put on board prizes, had been captured by the English, and were now demanding arrears of pay.[1] In May, 1779, Franklin was complaining to Congress

---

1. Wharton, Diplomatic Correspondence, V, 512, 13.

that the expense of fitting out each Continental cruiser which it sent to France amounted to 60,000 or 70,000 livres. He said that Mr. Bingham, the Continental agent at Martinique, had recently drawn upon him for the expense of fitting out two Continental cruisers which had recently put in to that island, but for lack of money he would be obliged to protest Bingham's bill.[1] The American representatives in France fitted out and loaded with supplies for America both Continental vessels and French and American merchantmen. This work properly forms a part of their commercial duties. Deane tells us that while he was in France he expended more than ten million livres for stores, goods, and ships; and that he loaded sixteen ships for America.[2] The commercial agents had much to do with this work; Nantes was the principal shipping port.

Before the treaties of February, 1778, between the United States and France, the disposing of prizes captured by American vessels in French ports was exceedingly informal. Since France was obliged to at least make a pretence of observing her treaties with England and the laws of neutrality, she could not permit a trial of American

1. Wharton, Diplomatic Correspondence, III, 189, 193, Franklin to Committee of Foreign Affairs, May 26, 1779.
2. Collections of New York Historical Society, Deane Papers, IV, 159.

prize cases in her admiralty courts. Consequently, prizes captured by American vessels were disposed of without trial and legal condemnation; they were taken into the offing of French ports and secretly sold to French merchants at a great sacrifice to the captors. After February, 1778, the prizes were legally tried, but not according to a uniform practice. Some cases were tried by the French admiralty courts; but in other cases the French courts prepared the *procès verbaux,* which they sent to Franklin; he then condemned the prizes and ordered the court to sell them. After July, 1780, Franklin ceased to exercise such judicial functions.[1]

One of the objects of the cruises of Continental vessels in European waters was to capture Englishmen and exchange them for American naval prisoners languishing in prisons in England. These imprisoned Americans were confined chiefly at Forton prison at Portsmouth, and Mill prison at Plymouth. A list of prisoners confined at Mill prison during the Revolution, which contains 947 names, has been made out.[2] In April, 1782, there were eleven hundred

---

1. Wharton, Diplomatic Correspondence, III, 801-03, 880-81; Bigelow's Franklin, VII, 54-55, 58-59.
2. Pennsylvania Packet, May-June, 1782. Another list will be found in New England Historical and Genealogical Register for 1865, 74, 136, 209.

Americans in the jails of England and Ireland, all committed to prison as charged with high treason.[1] A few Americans were confined at Gibraltar. These prisoners often suffered greatly from a lack of sufficient food, clothing, bedding, and fuel. This was in part caused by the cruelty and fraud of those whom the British government entrusted with the supply and control of its prisons. The rigors of their captivity were softened, and their deprivations in a measure relieved by money which Franklin sent from Paris, and by private subscriptions in their behalf made by generous Englishmen.

To escape their penury and distress some prisoners enlisted in the enemy's navy, or joined the British whaling fleets. Others escaped from prison; some of these burrowed their way out, committing treason through His Majesty's earth, to use a phrase of Captain Conyngham, who, with sixty companions, in this way escaped from Mill prison in November, 1779. These escaped prisoners gradually found their way into Holland, the seaports of France, or even Paris; and they often became a tax upon Franklin's pity, and the Continental treasury in his keeping. Franklin was deeply moved by the sufferings of these men, whether confined in England or at liberty in France. His

---

1. Wharton, Diplomatic Correspondence, V, 326-27.

efforts in their behalf are an important part of his work and achievements in France.

A long correspondence directed towards securing an exchange of Englishmen captured by American vessels and confined in France for Americans confined in England was conducted by Franklin with his friend Hartley in England. Hartley was a noble-minded and humane Englishman, who was, at the time, a member of the House of Commons. The first letters on the exchanging of prisoners were written, however, by the American Commissioners, to Lord Stormont, the British Ambassador at Paris. The Commissioners stated that Captain Wickes, of the Continental cruiser "Reprisal," had in his possession one hundred captured British seamen, and they wished to exchange them for an equal number of American seamen, prisoners in England. The first letter of the Commissioners Lord Stormont ignored. To the second letter, or possibly to the third, he replied in those well-known words: "The King's Ambassador receives no applications from rebels, unless they come to implore His Majesty's mercy." The reply of the Commissioners was equally spirited: "In answer to a letter which concerns some of the most material interests of humanity, and of the two nations, Great Britain and the United States of America, now at war, we received the enclosed indecent paper, as coming from your

Lordship, which we return for your Lordship's more mature consideration."[1]

Until after the treaties of February, 1778, between the United States and France, Great Britain resisted the exchange of naval prisoners, confined in England, on three grounds: that it involved the recognition of belligerent rights in the insurgents; that France being neutral, the Colonists would be compelled either to free captured British seamen taken in European waters, or else to take them to America; and that since British seamen were far more numerous than American, an exchange would tell more favorably for the Americans than for the British.[2] Not until France had entered into the war, did Britain take a broader and more generous position, and begin to listen to Franklin's overtures for an exchange of prisoners. During 1778 the negotiations proceeded slowly and vexatiously, and it was not until March, 1779, that the first exchange was made. One hundred American prisoners from the Mill prison at Plymouth were then sent to France by the British government in the Milford cartel-ship; and in August one hundred more were exchanged.

In October, 1779, when Captain Jones ter-

---

1. Hale's Franklin in France, I, Chapter XI, American Prisoners, prints many original letters.

2. Wharton, Diplomatic Correspondence, II, 724.

minated his famous cruise, he carried into the Texel, Holland, 472 prisoners; and Franklin had high hopes that at last considerable numbers of the unfortunate American prisoners would be released. Since the Texel was a neutral port, complications growing out of the laws of neutrality now arose. If Jones's prisoners were to be exchanged for Americans, it was decided that they must first be brought to France. Rather than risk their recapture, Franklin agreed to permit them to be considered as the prisoners of France and to be exchanged for an equal number of Frenchmen imprisoned in England. In return, the French were to give Franklin 472 English prisoners confined in French prisons, which were to be exchanged for American prisoners. Franklin had difficulty in securing the Englishmen from France; after England had sent over one hundred prisoners, misunderstandings arose, and in May, 1780, she refused to exchange Americans except for Englishmen taken by American cruisers. One of the main objects of Jones's famous cruise, the releasing of American prisoners in England, seems to have partly failed.[1] In March, 1782, Franklin considered a proposed plan for rescuing the American prisoners in Forton prison, and bringing them to France on

---

1. Wharton, Diplomatic Correspondence, III, 535, 608, 681-82, 745-46.

smuggling vessels, but he concluded that the project was impracticable.[1]

After France and Spain entered into the war, the American Commissioners confined British prisoners in French and Spanish prisons. Before the French treaties, the Commissioners had no place, except in their own ships, to stow away their prisoners. The American captains were therefore forced to free many captives. They often exacted of a prisoner a pledge or parole that he would, on returning to England, be responsible for the release of an American prisoner; but of course the British government refused to take cognizance of such pledges, or to listen to the claims of the Commissioners that these released captives should be considered as returned prisoners. Beginning with 1778, the burden upon the Commissioners for the maintenance of English prisoners was considerable. In May, 1779, Franklin thought it would take more than 100,000 livres to pay all the accounts arising from expenditures in their behalf.[2] Could satisfactory and expeditious exchanges have been effected with England, this item of expense would have been greatly reduced. When the Revolution came to an end, there was still a considerable number of Americans in English prisons.

---

1. Wharton, Diplomatic Correspondence, V, 276.
2. Ibid., III, 189.

A number of alleged breaches of neutrality, said to have been made by American armed vessels, was brought to the attention of the American representatives at the Court of France. For example, in 1777 the French, Spanish, and Dutch governments complained that either their ships or their merchandise had been unlawfully captured. In 1778 the Spanish and Swedish Courts asserted that Captain Conyngham had violated the laws of neutrals. The Dutch found fault with Captain Jones for sending the brigantine "Berkenbosch" to America. In 1780 the Portuguese Ambassador at Paris presented Franklin with papers which alleged that the Massachusetts state cruiser "Mars" had illegally taken a Portuguese ship and had sent it to New England. The American representatives at Paris regularly disposed of such cases as the above by referring them to Congress, and to the American courts of admiralty. In the case of the Portuguese ship, Franklin wrote to Congress that he hoped that it would forward a speedy decision; and that it would give orders to the American cruisers not to meddle with neutral vessels, for this was a practice "apt to produce ill blood." Complaints having been made of violences done by American armed vessels to neutral nations, the Commissioners, in November, 1777, issued a proclamation enjoining the American commanders to obey the laws of neutrality. In

1780, in view of the First Armed Neutrality which had been proposed by Catherine of Russia, and which was then being concerted by certain European nations, Franklin wrote to Congress, asking whether it would not be proper to confine American captures to the principle that "free ships shall make free goods," since it was likely that this would become the law of nations.[1]

Many miscellaneous duties, more or less naval in character, fell to the Commissioners at Paris and to their successor, the American Minister. In August, 1778, the Commissioners offered a few observations on some regulations for prizes and prisoners, which Sartine, the French Minister of Marine, had prepared with a view of making uniform certain rules of France and the United States on these subjects.[2] In June, 1778, Franklin issued a curious passport in the form of a proclamation to all commanders of American armed vessels, not to attack a certain British vessel, which was bound to the Moravian mission on the coast of Labrador. "I do therefore hereby [inform you] that the sloop 'Good Intent,' burthen about 75 tons, Capt. Francis Mugford, carrying

1. Wharton, Diplomatic Correspondence, II, 425, 435, 784, 827; IV, 24, 180; Stevens's Facsimiles, 1967, 1969; Bigelow's Franklin, VII, 308; C. H. Lincoln, Calendar of John Paul Jones Manuscripts, 163.
2. Wharton, Diplomatic Correspondence, II, 682-83, 684-87.

in the present voyage about 5000 bricks for building chimneys, with provisions and necessaries for the missionaries and their assistants, and some ironmongery and tin ware for the Indians—the crew consisting of the Captain, Mate, three men, and a boy, and the passengers one man and three women—is the vessel employed in the above service this year."[1] Coming amid the cruelties, resentments, and misunderstandings of war, this document, which breathes a humane spirit and declares that the philanthropic interests of nations are inviolable, is indeed a most welcome one. In October, 1778, the Commissioners provided the Ambassador of Naples at the Court of France, whose country had lately opened its ports to American vessels, with a description of American flags. After describing the flag of the United States, they added: "Some of the States have vessels of war distinct from those of the United States. For example, the vessels of war of the state of Massachusetts Bay have sometimes a pine tree; and those of the state of South Carolina a rattlesnake in the middle of thirteen stripes. Merchant ships have only thirteen stripes, but the flag of the United States ordained by Con-

---

1. Hale's Franklin in France, I, 245. Franklin issued a similar proclamation in behalf of the celebrated navigator, Captain Cook.—Wharton, Diplomatic Correspondence, III, 75.

gress is the thirteen stripes and the thirteen stars above described."[1]

The Naval Office at Paris served as a channel for the communication of foreign naval intelligence; it also proposed to Congress several important naval plans. John Adams, while Commissioner, and later while on a diplomatic mission in Holland, wrote long letters to Congress on the armament of the foreign navies, the movements of the British, French, and Spanish fleets, and the captures made by these fleets. In November, 1776, Silas Deane, always fertile in schemes, proposed to the Committee of Secret Correspondence the sending of frigates against the Newfoundland fisheries; after destroying these, the frigates were to sail for the Baltic and cruise after the enemy's ships bound for Russia. In the same letter he proposed a second project. A number of frigates with merchantmen under their convoy should be loaded with tobacco, rice, wheat, and other colonial products, and should sail for Bordeaux. After unloading their cargoes and refreshing their crews the frigates should strike a blow on the British coast which would "alarm and weaken Great Britain most effectually. The city of Glasgow might at any hour be destroyed by a single frigate capable of landing two hundred men." After their descent on England

---

1. Wharton, Diplomatic Correspondence, II, 759-60.

the frigates should sail northward and intercept the Baltic ships, or else return to France and wait for a good opportunity to strike a second blow. Ships engaging in such expeditions could obtain any number of recruits in France. By issuing commissions, individuals would "join you in the adventure under your flag, with stout frigates, several of which are now building absolutely with the design, viz., the hopes of getting into the service of the United States of North America."[1] Deane's letters at this time are somewhat extravagant, nor are they always based on an accurate knowledge of the facts. "Would it not be well," he asks, "to purchase at Leghorn five or six stout Frigates, which might at once transport some companies of Swiss and a quantity of stores and the whole be defended by the Swiss soldiers on their passage?"[2]

In May, 1777, the recommendations made by Deane in November, 1776, were in substance repeated by the Commissioners at Paris to the Committee of Foreign Affairs. These new recommendations were in all

---

1. Collections of New York Historical Society, Deane Papers, I, 339-40. The letter of Deane here published, it is believed, was written to the Committee of Secret Correspondence, and not to the Secret Committee as given.

2. Wharton, Diplomatic Correspondence, II, 199. Deane to Committee of Secret Correspondence, November 28, 1776.

probability drafted by Deane. The Commissioners thought that a blow might be struck on the coast of England which would "alarm and shake Great Britain, and its credit, to the center." The burning and plundering of Liverpool or Glasgow would do more essential service to the Colonies than a million of treasure and blood spent in America. It would raise our reputation to the highest pitch, and lessen in the same degree that of our enemy. The Commissioners were confident that the plan was practicable, and could be carried out with very little danger. They also recommended the sending of two or three Continental frigates with some small cruisers into the German ocean, where, about the middle of August, they might seize the greater part of the enemy's Baltic and northern trade. One frigate, they said, would be sufficient to destroy the "Greenland whale fishery, or take the Hudson Bay ships returning."[1]

In the fall of 1778 the Commissioners called the attention of both the Committee of Foreign Affairs and the French Minister of Marine to the ease with which a single frigate or privateer of twenty or twenty-four guns could capture the valuable whale fishery which the English maintained off the coast of Brazil. The seventeen vessels employed in this industry were manned and officered

---

1. Wharton, Diplomatic Correspondence, II, 324-27.

almost entirely by Americans belonging to Nantucket and Cape Cod. These men had been captured by Great Britain, and having been given their choice of entering the British naval service or the whale fishing industry, had chosen the latter. By their recapture four hundred and fifty of the best kind of American seamen would be added to the Continental service, and moreover the cargoes of oil which would be taken were very valuable.[1]

In December, 1777, the Committee of Foreign Affairs proposed to the Commissioners at Paris the most extensive naval expedition planned for the Continental fleet during the Revolution. The plan was to be carried out by two or three of the frigates which the Marine Committee were sending to France. These, being well manned, were early in February, 1778, to be despatched to the French island of Mauritius in the Indian ocean, where they should refit and replenish their stores. The frigates should next proceed to the Coromandel Coast, a twenty days' sail from Mauritius. Here they should intercept the enemy's China ships, and also distress the internal trade of India. The prizes could be sold in Mauritius and the proceeds sent to Paris by bills of exchange. Gorée was recommended as a better port of call than the Cape of Good Hope,

---

1. Wharton, Diplomatic Correspondence, II, 818-19, 832-33.

where there was danger to be apprehended from British vessels. In the same letter the Committee wrote that "another beneficial attempt may be conducted along the coasts of Africa. The French and Dutch settlements, and perhaps the Portuguese, will purchase the prizes, and give bills on Europe."[1] No reply was made by the Commissioners relative to the proposed East Indian expedition until in July, 1778, when Arthur Lee wrote to the Committee of Foreign Affairs that the Commissioners considered the plan "impracticable at the present." "Better order," he said, "must be established in our marine, and the ships' companies better sorted, before it will be safe to attempt enterprises at such a distance, and which require a certain extent of ideas in the captain and entire obedience in the crew."[2] One must agree with Lee's conclusion, although more weighty objections to the complicated plan of the Committee might be adduced.

1. Wharton, Diplomatic Correspondence, II, 440-41.
2. Ibid., 673-74.

CHAPTER X

NAVAL DUTIES OF AMERICAN REPRESENTATIVES IN FOREIGN COUNTRIES

(Continued)

In 1777 the work of the Naval Office at Paris was greater and more varied than during any other year. Naval vessels were both built and purchased. Continental ships, and merchantmen chartered from the French, were laden for America with muskets, cannon, powder, cordage, duck, tents, blankets, and clothing. The naval prisoners in England and the violations of neutral rights committed by Continental ships and by privateers demanded much attention. In the spring the Continental brig "Lexington," and in the fall the "Raleigh," "Alfred," and "Independence," arrived in France. The "Reprisal," 16, "Lexington," 14, "Dolphin," 10, "Surprise," 10, and "Revenge," 14, were fitted and refitted in French ports and sent cruising off the British coasts; and the prizes of these vessels were sold in France. The "Dolphin," "Surprise," and "Revenge" were officered and manned in

France. The task of conducting all these naval activities in a neutral country the Commissioners found to be a most delicate one.

Among the earlier undertakings of the American representatives at Paris were their attempts to obtain the freedom of French ports for American vessels. Nor was their work of this sort confined wholly to the French Court, for in the spring of 1777 Arthur Lee sought at Madrid permission for American vessels to sell their prizes and to refit in Spanish ports; and later in the year he went on a similar errand to Berlin. Both the Spanish and Prussian Courts refused his requests.[1] Prizes were, however, without difficulty secretly disposed of in Spain.

As early as August, 1776, Deane wrote from Paris that he was "not without hopes of obtaining liberty for the armed vessels of the United Colonies, to dispose of their prizes in the ports of this Kingdom, and also for arming and fitting out vessels of war directly from hence."[2] When Franklin arrived in France, early in December, 1776, he carried instructions for the Commissioners to apply immediately to the Court of France for the protection of its ports to

---

1. Wharton, Diplomatic Correspondence, II, 296-97, 355-58, 370.
2. Ibid., 119-20, Deane to Committee of Secret Correspondence, August 18, 1776.

American ships of war, privateers, and prizes. If this favor were granted, he was to ask for permission to sell American prizes and their cargoes in French ports. In case both requests met with favorable responses, the Committee of Secret Correspondence would obtain the consent of Congress to empower the Commissioners to appoint a judge of admiralty in France; this judge would try all American prize cases, arising in the ports of France, in accordance with the rules and regulations of Congress. Pending the obtaining of the consent of Congress, the Commissioners were authorized to consult with the French Ministry whether it would permit the erection of American admiralty courts in France and the French West Indies.[1] Of course France could not grant such requests as these if she wished to remain at peace with England. During 1776 the Americans generally overestimated the friendliness of France. They either failed to see that the laws of neutrality must set quite definite limits to her overt favors, or else they thought her eager for an excuse to go to war with Great Britain. The attitude of France towards permitting American vessels of war and their prizes the freedom of French ports was disclosed sooner than the Commissioners had reason to expect.

It is remembered that the "Reprisal" ar-

---

1. Wharton, Diplomatic Correspondence, II, 178-79.

rived in France with Franklin on board early in December, 1776. She was the first Continental vessel to reach European waters. Not far from the French coast she captured two small British brigantines, and carried them into Nantes. These were the first American prizes to enter French ports. It may be guessed that the captains of the two prizes were not long in communicating with Lord Stormont, the British Ambassador at Paris, and that Lord Stormont was not long in communicating with the French government. On December 17 he held a conference with Vergennes, the French Minister of Foreign Affairs, to whom he declared that the prizes were unlawfully captured, since the "Reprisal" had no commission from a sovereign power as a letter of marque; that he expected that the prizes would be immediately restored to their owners; and that the permitting of their sale would be a violation of the treaty of Utrecht between Great Britain and France. Though conciliatory, Vergennes's reply was not altogether satisfactory to the British Ambassador, who records that the French Minister ended "with expressions which seemed to shew an Intention of taking some Middle Way, and leaving the Point undetermined."[1]

During 1777 Lord Stormont held many

---

[1] Stevens's Facsimiles, 1392, 1-2, Lord Stormont to Lord Weymouth, December 18, 1776.

similar conferences with Vergennes in which the naval liberties permitted the Americans in French ports were the subject of discussion. Vergennes set forth the position of his government in a way that was reasonably acceptable to England. He declared that its purpose was to prevent every violation of its treaties and of the law of nations. He gave orders that the prizes captured by the Americans should not be sold in French ports. At different times he commanded the American vessels of war to sail within twenty-four hours from French harbors. When the British wrath flamed out at some overt act of the Americans, Vergennes appeased it by vigorous and decisive acts of repression, aimed at the American captains and agents. A past master in soft and plausible answers, he excused flagrant violations of British rights by explaining that every government had some tempestuous spirits which were hard to control, and that the "avidity of gain" in merchants could not always be restrained.

The British government could not object to the public acts of the French government, or to the reception which it gave to the American Commissioners, whom it received "privately with all civility," but avoided an open reception, as it was "cautious of giving umbrage to England." As regards its observance of the treaty of Utrecht, and its inability to grant the freedom of its ports to

American vessels and their prizes, its declarations to the Commissioners were in line with those which it made to Lord Stormont. On the other hand, the Commissioners were given to understand, through secret and informal channels, that the Colonies had the sympathy of the French government; that so far as was consistent with French treaties, they might expect favors and indulgences; that the ports of France were open to American ships "as friends;" that ways of disposing of American prizes which would not be offensive to England might be found; and that other irregularities would be permitted unnoticed.[1] The Commissioners pressed their favors as far as they could safely go; indeed, so far, that at one time they endangered the continuance of their friendly relations with the French Court.

The two prizes which the "Reprisal" carried into Nantes in December, 1776, were taken into the offing of that port and privately sold. The "Reprisal" was quietly refitted, and in February, 1777, she made a cruise off the coast of Spain and returned to L'Orient with the Falmouth packet and four other English vessels. Lord Stormont made vigorous remonstrances. The French government at once ordered the "Reprisal" and her prizes to put to sea within twenty-four hours. Nothing of this sort was done. The

---

1. Wharton, Diplomatic Correspondence, II, 283-84, 364, 379.

"Reprisal" remained in port, on the ground that she had sprung a leak; and her prizes were secretly sold for one-seventh of their value to French merchants, who, for the sake of large profits, eagerly overlooked the irregularity of the transaction.[1] Confident of the accuracy of the cues they were receiving, the Commissioners now fitted out, manned, and officered at Dunkirk the "Surprise," Captain Gustavus Conyngham, and early in May, 1777, sent her cruising. Within a few days after his leaving Dunkirk, Conyngham returned with the Harwich packet, and one other prize. The storm raised by the British at so open and undoubted a violation of their rights could be pacified only by more rigorous measures. The French government therefore imprisoned Captain Conyngham and his crew, and returned his prizes to their owners.[2]

Not at all disconcerted, the Commissioners fitted out a fleet, consisting of the "Reprisal," "Lexington," and "Dolphin," to intercept the Irish linen ships. Captain Wickes was placed at its head as commodore, and was instructed not to return to France unless he found it absolutely necessary. Wickes got to sea during the first

---

1. Wharton, Diplomatic Correspondence, II, 379-80; Stevens's Facsimiles, 1445, 1536, 1568.
2. Stevens's Facsimiles, 1529, Lord Stormont to Lord Weymouth, May 8, 1777.

of June. Missing the linen ships, he sailed quite around Ireland, and captured or destroyed seventeen or eighteen sail of vessels; he "most effectually alarmed England, prevented the great fair at Chester, occasioned insurance to rise, and even deterred the English merchants from shipping goods in English bottoms at any rate, so that in a few weeks forty sail of French ships were loading in the Thames, on freight, an instance never before known."[1] The three vessels returned to French ports about July 1.

Obviously there was a limit to the forbearance of the English government, and it made it plain that this limit had been reached. Lord Stormont was instructed to tell the French government that, however desirous the British king might be to maintain peace, he would not submit "to such strong and public instances of support and protection shewn to the Rebels by a Nation that at the same time professes in the strongest terms its Desire to maintain the present Harmony subsisting between the two Crowns. The shelter given to the armed Vessels of the Rebels, the facility they have of disp sing of their Prizes by the connivance of overnment, and the conveniences allowed them to refit, are such irrefragable proofs of support, that scarcely more could

---

1. Stevens's Facsimiles, 703, 1539; Wharton, Diplomatic Correspondence, II, 379-80, Deane to Robert Morris, August 23, 1777.

be done if there was an avowed Alliance between France and them, and We were in a state of War with that Kingdom."[1]

This last cruise of Wickes also threatened to endanger the friendliness of the French Court and the Commissioners. Vergennes wrote to them with some spirit, and insinuated that they had broken their promises. "After such repeated advertisements," he said, "the motives of which you have been informed of, we had no reason to expect, gentlemen, that the said Sieur Wickes would prosecute his cruising in the European seas, and we could not be otherwise than greatly surprised that, after having associated the privateers the Lexington and the Dolphin to infest the English coast, they should all three of them come for refuge into our ports. You are too well informed, gentlemen, and too penetrating, not to see how this conduct affects the dignity of the king, my master, at the same time it offends the neutrality which his majesty professes."

In their reply the Commissioners exhibited some knowledge of the pleasing phrases of diplomacy. They said that they were "very sensible of the protection afforded to us and to our commerce since our residence in this kingdom, agreeable to the goodness of the king's gracious intentions and to the law of na-

[1] Stevens's Facsimiles, 1562, Lord Weymouth to Lord Stormont, July 4, 1777.

tions, and it gives us real and great concern when any vessels of war appertaining to America, either through ignorance or inattention, do anything that may offend his majesty in the smallest degree." They tried to shift the blame of their captains' return to French ports to the British men of war that had chased the American vessels into safe retreats. "We had," they continued, "some days before we were honored by your excellency's letter, dispatched by an express the most positive orders to them to depart directly to America, which they are accordingly preparing to do." There can be no doubt about the honesty of these orders, for it was plain to the Commissioners that the French government was not disposed to forgive further infringements of neutral rights. By express orders of the French king the fleet of Wickes was sequestered until it gave security that it should return directly to America.[1]

Meantime the Commissioners had obtained the release of Conyngham and his crew. He was now placed in command of the "Revenge;" and in July, eluding the British, he sailed from Dunkirk, ostensibly for America. He first cruised along the eastern coast of England, into the North

---

1. Stevens's Facsimilies, 1677; Wharton, Diplomatic Correspondence, II, 364-66, Vergennes to Commissioners at Paris, July 16, 1777, and Franklin and Deane to Vergennes, July 17, 1777.

Sea and the region of the Baltic, then back through the straits of Dover and into the Irish Channel, and finally into the Bay of Biscay, anchoring at Ferrol, Spain, about the first of October. The terror of his name, which his recklessness and daring greatly increased, spread great alarm among the inhabitants of the British Isles. He did not return again to France with the "Revenge." This fact made his cruise less annoying to the Commissioners, than the last cruise of Wickes. Hodge, the agent of the Commissioners, who had given bond to the French admiralty that the "Revenge" would not engage in operations against the British, was arrested and thrown into the Bastile; and Vergennes wrote a most severe letter, to be shown to the Commissioners. Presently, when the wrath of the British had abated, Hodge was released on the representation of the Commissioners that he was a person of character, and that they could not "conceive him capable of any willful offence against the laws of this nation."[1]

About the middle of September the "Reprisal" and the "Lexington" sailed for America; the "Reprisal" foundered on the Grand

---

1. C. H. Jones, Captain Gustavus Conyngham, 15-17; Outlook for January 3, 1903, 71-83, James Barnes, Tragedy of the Lost Commission; Hale's Franklin in France, I, 139; Wharton, Diplomatic Correspondence, II, 375, 377, 406.

Banks of Newfoundland, losing all on board except the cook; and the "Lexington" was taken by the British off Ushant. With the departure of these vessels the movements of the Continental fleet for 1777 in European waters came to an end; as did also the nice task of the Commissioners of conducting a naval war from a neutral country as a base, without losing the friendship of that country, or involving it in war. Had not hostilities broken out in 1778 between France and England by reason of other causes, a repetition of the naval operations of 1777, if permitted by the French, would very likely have brought them on.

During 1778 two cruises were made in European waters, one by Captain Tucker, and the other by Captain Jones. On April 1, 1778, the frigate "Boston," Captain Samuel Tucker, arrived at Bordeaux with John Adams, the new Commissioner who was to succeed Silas Deane, as a passenger. After refitting, Tucker made a short cruise in which he captured four prizes. In August the "Boston," in company with the frigate "Providence," and the ship "Ranger," sailed for America. Some months previous the "Ranger," when under the command of Captain Jones, had made an important cruise. Jones arrived in this vessel in France on December 2, 1777. He expected to receive command of a frigate or a ship of the line; but in this he was disappointed.

On January 18, 1778, the Commissioners wrote to him that they could not procure such a ship as he expected; and that they advised him, "after equipping the 'Ranger,' in the best manner for the cruise you propose," to proceed "with her in the manner you shall judge best for distressing the enemies of the United States, by sea or otherwise, consistent with the laws of war and the terms of your commission."[1]

From these orders it may be seen that Jones had in mind a descent on the British coast. On April 10, 1778, he sailed for the Irish sea. After capturing or destroying four vessels, he made an unsuccessful attempt to burn the shipping at Whitehaven in Cumberland. He next tried to take prisoner the Earl of Selkirk from his summer home at St. Mary's Isle, off the southwest coast of Scotland, but failed to find him. These movements ashore naturally struck terror to the inhabitants of the British Isles. Jones now crossed to Ireland, and in the neighborhood of Belfast attacked the British naval ship "Drake," 20, Commander George Burdon. After an engagement of seventy-four minutes, during which the "Ranger" was "skillfully handled and well-fought," the "Drake" struck her colors. Jones arrived in Brest with his prize on May

---
1. Wharton, Diplomatic Correspondence, II, 471-72.

10.[1] Many plans and suggestions were now made by both the Commissioners and the French government to supply Jones with some large ship from the French navy, or to give him the command of a small fleet, but they all miscarried. The ambitious and energetic American captain, chafing under his enforced idleness, was not to make another cruise until fifteen months had elapsed.

During 1779 and 1780 the Naval office at Paris was chiefly concerned with the movements, conduct, and achievements of two captains in the Continental navy, John Paul Jones and Peter Landais. Never have the fortunes of war thrown into close association two men of more striking contrasts. Jones was ardent, hopeful, and magnetic; Landais sullen, quarrelsome, and repellent. Jones was a master of men; from unpromising materials, swept together by the winds and waves of diverse fortunes, he made most effective crews. Landais was seldom on good terms with his officers or seamen, some of whom were always dissatisfied and mutinous. Called to play their parts on the same theater of war, the Scotchman achieved signal success and distinction, and won the plaudits of the French king, of Congress, and of his countrymen; while to the Frenchman fell the ill-will of his own government,

---

1. Sherburne's John Paul Jones, 43-53, Jones to Commissioners, May 27, 1778; Clowes, Royal Navy, IV, 11-13.

the hatred of Americans, and, in his dismissal from the navy of the United States, dishonor and professional disgrace.

In the spring of 1779 Franklin—now American minister at the Court of France—the French government, and Lafayette planned an expedition against the coast of England, which had in view especially the striking of some of the larger English towns. Lafayette was to command the French troops which were to be lent for the expedition, and Jones, to whom the French government had, in February, given the command of the "Bon Homme Richard," formerly the "Duras," an old East Indiaman, was to command the sea forces. The "Alliance," Captain Landais, which vessel had recently arrived in France from America, was to be a part of Jones's fleet. This plan miscarried.

It was not until August 13 that Jones finally got to sea with a fleet consisting of five naval vessels and two privateers. The two chief vessels of the little fleet were the "Bon Homme Richard," 42, Captain Jones, and the "Alliance," 36, Captain Landais. These two officers had of course permanent commissions in the Continental navy; the three French officers in command of naval vessels were given temporary commissions in the Continental navy. The expense of the cruise was borne by the French government; and the fitting out of the fleet was superintended by Chaumont, the joint agent of the French government and the American minister.[1] The destination of the fleet was determined by the French government; and the orders of Jones, the commodore of the fleet, were prepared by the French Minister of Marine, translated and signed by Franklin, and sent to Jones by Chaumont. The fleet sailed under the American flag. Its principal object was the intercepting of the Baltic fleet of the enemy.

The details of this memorable cruise are familiar to the reader, and need not be repeated here. The fleet was scarcely at sea before Landais became insubordinate, asserted his independence of Jones, and left and rejoined his commodore when and where he chose. Sailing first along the west coast of Ireland and then around Scotland, Jones reached the east coast of Yorkshire, on September 23. He had by this time taken seventeen ships, and had made an unsuccessful attempt to reach Leith and Edinburgh, and lay them under contribution. Off Flamborough Head Jones's fleet, which was now reduced to the "Bon Homme Richard," "Alliance," and "Pallas," fell in with the Baltic trade of forty-one sail and convoyed by His Majesty's ships, "Serapis," 44, Captain Richard Pearson, and "Countess

---

1. Wharton, Diplomatic Correspondence, III, 242.

of Scarborough," 20, Commander Thomas Piercy. There now ensued an engagement between the "Bon Homme Richard" and the "Serapis," which lasted more than three hours. It was one of the fiercest fights recorded in the annals of naval warfare. For the greater part of the engagement the two vessels were lashed together, stem to stern, starboard to starboard, and with the muzzles of their guns touching. Both ships were set on fire in various places, and the "scene was dreadful beyond the reach of language," to use Jones's phrasing. The "Bon Homme Richard" won the fight only through the brilliant daring, the remarkable naval skill, and the intelligence in action of her commander. She was so badly injured that she sank the second day after the fight; her own crew were transferred to the "Serapis." The loss to the "Bon Homme Richard" was 116 men; to the "Serapis," 129. During the fight of the "Bon Homme Richard" and the "Serapis," the "Pallas," Captain Cottineau, and the "Countess of Scarborough," Commander Piercy, engaged each other, with the result that the British ship was compelled to surrender. The "Alliance" took little or no part in the contest, as her commander was sulking throughout the engagement. The two prizes, the "Alliance," and the "Pallas" arrived at the Texel in Holland on October 3, 1779.[1]

---

1. Sherburne's John Paul Jones, 111-125,

A naval discord now arose, which tried the patience and temper of Franklin. No sooner did Jones and Landais reach the Texel, than each wrote to Franklin making charges against the other. Jones accused Landais of gross insubordination and misbehavior and specifically charged him with intentionally firing into the "Bon Homme Richard" and killing a "number of our men and mortally wounding a good officer." The French government, which was inclined to attribute the loss of the "Bon Homme Richard" and so many of her crew to the conduct of Landais, took a hand in the dispute, and asked Franklin to call Landais to account at Paris. In cases of this sort the Naval Office had little authority or means to effect discipline in the navy. A sufficient number of commissioned officers could not be assembled in France to hold a court-martial; and if they could, it was doubtful whether the Naval Office had the power to order such a court. Their inability to hold courts-martial had been regretted more than once by the American Commissioners. Landais came to Paris, and Franklin investigated the case before friends of the two disputants; but satisfactory evidence and witnesses could not be obtained to prove or disprove the charges, so Franklin did the only thing

---

Jones to Franklin, October 3, 1779, giving an account of cruise; Clowes, Royal Navy, IV, 33-39.

possible, by referring the dispute to Congress, and a properly constituted court-martial in America. Franklin thought his inquiry had one good effect, the preventing of a duel in Holland between the two officers.[1]

On the coming of Landais to Paris, Franklin placed Jones in command of the "Alliance." After cruising through the English Channel to Spain, Jones, in February, 1780, brought his vessel into L'Orient. Acting under Franklin's orders, Jones now refitted his vessel with the purpose of returning to America with a cargo of supplies. In the spring of 1780 Landais began to beseech Franklin to restore him to the command of the "Alliance," and he soon raised the question whether the American minister at Paris had the power to remove him from the command of a vessel to which Congress had appointed him. His request was refused by Franklin in bald and vigorous terms. "I think you," Franklin wrote, "so imprudent, so litigious, and quarrelsome a man, even with your best friends, that peace and good order, and consequently the quiet and regular subordination so necessary to success, are, where you preside, impossible."[2]

---

1. Wharton, Diplomatic Correspondence, III, 375-77, 378-79, 535, 547-49, 562-63; IV, 293; Bigelow's Franklin, VII, 108-09.

2. Hale, Franklin in France, I, 327-28; Chapter XVII, Captain Landais, prints many original letters connected with the dispute.

Later he charged Landais "not to meddle with the 'Alliance' or create any disturbance on board her, as you will answer the contrary at your peril."[1] About the first of June Jones left his vessel, and came up to Paris to hasten the sale of his prizes. Landais now appeared at L'Orient, raised a mutiny on board the "Alliance," and, acting on Arthur Lee's advice, took charge of her. Early in July, without taking the stores which had been assigned to his ship, Landais sailed for America. It was on this passage that he developed a strangeness, a madness, some say, that incapacitated him for his command. He was removed, and the "Alliance" was sailed into Boston in charge of her lieutenant. Landais was now tried by a court-martial and dismissed from the naval service.

Meantime Jones and Franklin had succeeded in obtaining from the French government the loan of the "Ariel." Having loaded her with supplies, Jones sailed for America on October 7, 1780; but, encountering a storm which dismasted his vessel, he was compelled to return to port. On December 18 he again put to sea; and in February, 1781, he reached Philadelphia.

With the departure of Jones, the European waters, for the first time in four years, were clear of the armed vessels of the Continental fleet. The venerable Franklin, vexed

1. Hale, Franklin in France, I, 330-31.

with the discords and details of naval affairs, must have drawn a sigh of relief when the last Continental vessel and captain had withdrawn from France. The most disagreeable of his duties as "Admiral," to use John Adams's word in this connection, now came to an end. Concerning his vexations, Franklin wrote to one of his agents in the summer of 1780: "I have been too long in hot water, plagued almost to death with the passions, vagaries, and ill humours, and madnesses of other people. I must have a little repose."[1] He had now for some time been writing to Congress, asking to be relieved of his naval duties. An example of his requests may be extracted from a letter of March 4, 1780, to the President of Congress: "As vessels of war under my care create me a vast deal of business (of a kind, too, that I am unexperienced in), I must repeat my earnest request that some person of skill in such affairs may be appointed, in the character of consul, to take charge of them. I imagine that much would by that means be saved in the expense of their various refittings and supplies, which to me appears enormous."[2]

From the beginning of 1781 until the close of the Revolution the duties of the Naval

---

1. Bigelow's Franklin, VII, 97-98, Franklin to Jonathan Williams, June 27, 1780.
2. Wharton, Diplomatic Correspondence, III, 535.

Office at Paris were comparatively light. Few armed vessels were sent from America to France; and those that were, remained only long enough to refit, load with supplies, and receive letters and despatches for America. Over such ships Franklin exercised little or no control. The Agent of Marine, not wishing his vessels to slip from his grasp when within the reach of orders from Paris, sometimes directed his captains who were about to sail for France to return home on a specified date. In May, 1782, he wrote disapprovingly to Congress concerning the "delays and exorbitant expenses which have accrued from the detention of public vessels in Europe."[1] Acting under the direct orders of Morris, Captain Barry, in the "Alliance," in February, 1782, left L'Orient and cruised without success for seventeen days. This was the last cruise in European waters which was made by a Continental vessel during the Revolution.

On July 10, 1781, Congress gave Thomas Barclay a commission as vice-consul to France in the place of William Palfrey, who had, in November, 1780, been appointed consul to France, and had gone down with the vessel on which he took passage.[2] In addition to his strictly consular duties, Bar-

---

1. Force Transcripts, Library of Congress, 137, 3, p. 313.
2. Journals of Continental Congress, November 4, 1780; July 10, 1781.

clay was authorized to "assist in directing our Naval affairs."[1] When Barclay entered upon his duties in France, our naval business was narrowing to the settling of accounts. He was in time, however, to represent his country in the trial and sale of a few prizes, to assist in the shipping of some supplies, and to sell the Continental ship, "Duc de Lauzun." In November, 1782, Congress appointed Barclay a commissioner for settling the Revolutionary accounts of the United States in Europe; and in December Morris gave him his instructions.[2] Barclay was directed to inquire into the accounts of the agents for fitting out armed vessels in Europe, and to make a settlement with the various prize agents into whose hands prizes or moneys derived from their sale had come. Barclay's duties, both as consul and as commissioner, came to an end in the fall of 1785, when he was appointed to negotiate a treaty with Morocco.

Some of the duties of Barclay as commissioner for settling accounts were in December, 1783, vested in John Paul Jones. In accordance with a resolution of Congress, Franklin appointed Jones agent of the United States to solicit the payment of prize

---

1. Force Transcripts, Library of Congress, 137, 1, p. 463, Instructions to Barclay.

2 Journals of Continental Congress, November 18, 1782; Force Transcripts, 137, p. 55, Instructions to Barclay.

money, "in whose hands soever the money may be detained," arising from prizes captured by vessels under Jones's command in European waters.[1] Jones was engaged in this work during 1784 and 1785. Under the sanction of Thomas Jefferson, the American Minister at Paris, Jones in 1786 set out for Copenhagen, to settle a dispute with the Danish Court over three of his prizes. These ships had been captured, in 1779, by the fleet under his command, and had been sent into Bergen, Norway. The Danish government had restored them to the British. Jones's journey was interrupted and he did not reach Copenhagen until 1788. The Danish government now transferred the settlement of the disputed claims to Paris, pleading that Jones had not sufficient authority to treat. By June, Jones had left Copenhagen, had accepted the commission of Vice-Admiral in the Russian navy, and was writing from his flagship "Wolodimer" to his friend Jefferson at Paris. The Revolutionary accounts in Europe possessed the usual vitality, not to say immortality, of government claims. Certain Revolutionary claims of South Carolina, growing out of expenses which that state incurred in Europe in connection with the ship "Indian," are

---

1. Journals of Congress, November 1, 1783; C. H. Lincoln, Calendar of John Paul Jones Manuscripts, 188, Franklin to Jones, December 17, 1783.

now pending before the government at Washington.

In the West Indies the chief naval station for the Continental vessels was St. Pierre, Martinique. Bound on commercial errands, our vessels occasionally visited St. Eustatius, until its capture by the British in February, 1781; Cape Francois, Hispaniola; and in the late years of the war, Havana. The United States had commercial agents at these three ports. But at Martinique our vessels were refitted, repaired, and provisioned whenever convenience suggested, or stress of weather compelled, the seeking of a friendly harbor in this part of the Atlantic. In June, 1776, William Bingham, who had been the secretary of the Committee of Secret Correspondence, went to Martinique as the commercial agent of Congress; and in March, 1780, he was succeeded by Parsons, Alston and Company.

The commercial agent at Martinique did a varied and lively business. He was employed in shipping supplies, obtaining convoys for his merchantmen, refitting privateers, and now and then Continental vessels, disposing of prizes, and forwarding to Congress naval intelligence concerning the West Indies and Europe. Congress at times sent despatches and supplies to France by the way of Martinique; and the American representatives and commercial agents in France, now and then, communicated with the United States through the same island. In October, 1777, Bingham wrote to Congress that, if France should declare war against Great Britain, many prizes would naturally be sent into Martinique, and that he wished to be directed about proper forms and methods for trying and selling them.[1] In December American prizes and privateers were being publicly received into the ports of Martinique, and Bingham was shipping arms to America on board American vessels under the convoy of a frigate which he had hired for that purpose. In January, 1778, the permitting of these favors was causing spirited letters between the "General" of Martinique and the Governor of the British island of Antigua.[2]

During 1779 three Continental vessels, the "Deane," "General Gates," and "Confederacy," put into Martinique to refit, repair, and obtain provisions. The expense to which Bingham's empty treasury was subjected caused him to complain to Congress. The only Continental armed vessel purchased at Martinique was the little schooner "Fame," 7 guns. The commercial agent made this purchase on his own responsibility in February, 1781, in order to carry to Philadelphia the news of the capture of St. Eustatius by the British. But unfortun-

1. Records and Papers of Continental Congress, 90, p. 9.
2. Ibid., 90, pp. 21, 27.

ately, the "Fame" was forced to bequeath her errand to a better-fated conveyance, as the British carried her into Antigua.[1]

Our naval affairs on the Mississippi during the Revolution, although conducted on a small scale, are not devoid of interest; nor do they entirely escape the glamour of romance which seems to touch everything connected with the early history of this region. Oliver Pollock, originally a Pennsylvanian, and a man of ability, integrity, and patriotism, who freely spent his private fortune for his country, was the commercial agent at New Orleans during the Revolution, and to him fell sundry naval duties. Pollock was responsible to the Commercial Committee, the third committee of Congress that was simultaneously purchasing and arming vessels. He was intelligently and heartily assisted in his work at New Orleans by the Governor of Louisiana, Galvez, "that worthy Nobleman," as Pollock called him, who "gave me the delightful assurance that he would go every possible length for the interest of Congress."[2] It is refreshing to find for once American and Spanish officials acting in concert and inspiring mutual confidence and affection. Early in 1777, immediately after

1. Force Transcripts, Library of Congress, 137, 1, p. 357.
2. Records and Papers of Continental Congress, 50, pp. 1-13, Pollock to President of Congress, a *résumé* of Pollock's services as commercial agent at New Orleans.

Galvez became governor, he, with slight limitations, opened the port of New Orleans to American vessels of war and their prizes. Galvez's favors to Americans called down upon him the threats of the British at Pensacola to have his conduct brought to the attention of the Court at Madrid.

Pollock received from Congress blank commissions both for officers in the Continental navy and for privateers. One of the privateers which he commissioned, the "Reprisal," Captain Calvert, sent into a safe port, in April, 1778, a prize whose cargo consisted of flour, sugar, coffee, and forty-eight slaves.[1] In March, 1778, Captain Willing and a small party of men arrived in New Orleans from Pennsylvania, having come by the way of the Ohio and Mississippi rivers. They captured several prizes on the Misssissippi, which were sold in New Orleans to the value of $37,500. One of these, the "Rebecca," Pollock bought for Congress on his own responsibility. He obtained permission from Galvez to fit out his ship in a warlike manner; and he decided upon an armament, consisting of "16 six pounders upon one Deck, 2 Bow and 2 Stern Chacers, 8 four pounders upon her quarter Deck, with Swivels, Cohorns, &c."[2] He intended to enlist one hundred and fifty men and send his ship

---
1. Records and Papers of Continental Congress, 50, p. 66.
2. Ibid., 50, pp. 77-81.

against His Majesty's sloop of war "Sylph," which was defending Manchac on Lake Pontchartrain. Pollock planned to obtain most of his armament from Havana, but the Spanish authorities refused to permit its shipment even after Galvez had written to the Cuban government.[1]

By July, 1779, Pollock had succeeded in obtaining and mounting twenty-four guns on the decks of his ship, which he had now christened the "Morris" in honor of his well-known friend at Philadelphia. He had appointed a full quota of officers; and he had engaged seventy-six men, with "English deserters arriving daily" to swell the complement. The captain of the "Morris" was William Pickles, a man found to be "capable and steady to our Cause." Pollock had now for some time been waiting for orders for his vessel from Philadelphia; and tired of delay he was on the point of sending the "Morris" cruising, when a severe hurricane swept over New Orleans doing great damage to the town and its shipping. The "Morris" was lost, and eleven of her crew were drowned; the rest were rescued nine miles below the city clinging to the wreckage of their vessel.

Governor Galvez's heart was touched by the loss of the Americans. He now "spared" Pollock an armed schooner, which was soon

---

1. Records and Papers of Continental Congress, 50, p. 97.

fitted out, and by September Pickles was cruising on Lake Pontchartrain. On September 10 Pickles had a short, but hot, dispute with the British armed sloop "West Florida," which was forced to surrender, although it lost but four men to Pickles's eight. Pollock now fitted out the "West Florida," and sent her cruising on the Lake. On September 21 Pickles captured a small British settlement on the north side of Lake Pontchartrain. He made prisoners of all the inhabitants who refused to swear allegiance to the United States. This capitulation, Pollock wrote to Congress, gave them an undoubted right to that part of the colony of West Florida which lay along Lake Pontchartrain; and he conceived, in language that sounds familiarly like that of later expansionists, that the capitulation was "a proper Ground on which to claim (at any convenient period) the Sovereignty of the Soil and the Allegiance of the Inhabitants."[1]

In October, 1779, the "West Florida" cruised on the Lake at the request of Galvez for the protection of trade. Letters from Philadelphia now made it evident to Pollock that Congress wished the naval force on the Mississippi to proceed to that town. He therefore on January 20, 1780, gave

1. Records and Papers of Continental Congress, 50, p. 120, Copy of Capitulation of Inhabitants of the Settlements on Lake Pontchartrain, dated October 16, 1779, with signatures of nineteen men.

Pickles orders to sail for Philadelphia after taking on a cargo of tafia and sugar at Havana; but he directed Pickles, before entering on this detail, to join the fleet of Galvez and to assist in the reduction of Mobile and Pensacola.[1] This was an undertaking which Pollock had long assigned to an American fleet and army; and since 1777 he had urged it most audaciously upon Congress. After aiding in the capture of Mobile and taking a small prize which she sent into that town, the "West Florida" proceeded to Philadelphia, where she arrived about the first of June, 1780. Since it appeared to a committee of Congress that the "West Florida" was not fit for a cruiser, she was sold, and her crew was assigned to other Continental vessels.[2] Captain Pickles was placed in command of the "Mercury" packet and detailed to take Henry Laurens to Amsterdam. Here ends the story of the Revolutionary navy on the Mississippi.

1. Records and Papers of Continental Congress, 50, pp. 123-25, Pollock to Pickles, January 20, 1780.
2. Force Transcripts, Library of Congress, 137, 2, p. 281; 37, p. 95.

PART II

THE STATE NAVIES

CHAPTER XI

THE NAVY OF MASSACHUSETTS

With the exception of New Jersey and Delaware, each of the thirteen original states during the Revolution owned one or more armed vessels. Massachusetts, Connecticut, Pennsylvania, Maryland, Virginia, and South Carolina had the largest fleets. New Hampshire with its one ship and Georgia with its four galleys just escaped from being in the same class with New Jersey and Delaware. The navies of Rhode Island, New York, and North Carolina were small. The navy of no one state was so large as that of Congress. The total number of state craft, however, greatly exceeded the number of vessels in the Continental navy. The state vessels on the average were smaller and not so well armed as the Continental vessels. The states generally had less means for naval purposes at their disposal than had Congress, and were therefore not so well able to build large vessels. Then, too, the chief need of each state for a navy was to defend its seaports, coasts, and trade. For such service small craft, adapted for running in and out of shallow harbors, rivers, and bays, was demanded. The states therefore provided themselves with armed boats of various sizes, galleys with and without sails, half-galleys, floating batteries, barges, and fire-ships. Besides such vessels as these, most of the states had a few larger and stouter sailing craft, mounting generally from ten to twenty guns, and fairly well fitted for deep-sea navigation. The one state whose deep-sea exceeded its inshore craft was Massachusetts.

The history of naval administration in the several states possesses some common features. It will be recalled that in most of the states the provincial government about the year 1775 was superseded by a revolutionary government, and this in turn about a year later was succeeded by a permanent state government. The revolutionary government consisted of a legislative body, or provincial congress, and an executive body, or committee of safety. The permanent state government consisted of a legislature of one or two houses and an executive, which was either a council, or a governor and council. The initial naval administration in the states usually fell to the committee of safety, or revolutionary executive, which, upon the change to a permanent state government, bequeathed its naval duties to the council or to the governor and council. In most of the states the details of naval administration were at some time during the Revolution lodged with an executive board. Some states had separate boards for naval and military affairs; in other states, one board performed both functions.

The history of naval administration in the states falls into two periods, one embracing the years from 1775 to 1778, the other the years from 1779 to 1783. In the first period each state procured a naval armament, as a rule, for the general purpose of providing a naval defence, and not to meet some specific call for armed vessels. By 1779 the first naval craft had been largely captured, destroyed, or sold; and often the first machinery of naval administration had been in large part removed. In response to special needs for armed vessels, calls for which came most often from those who were suffering from the ravages of the British fleets, the states now procured additional vessels, and often devised new administrative machinery to manage them.

In defensive warfare, the problem in each state was to provide for the defence of its ports, trade, coasts, and shipping. The offensive warfare of the state navies, which was quite secondary in importance, consisted chiefly of commerce-destroying, conducted along the great ocean-paths of British trade. The principal problem here was for the American vessels in leaving home ports and in returning with their prizes to elude the British vessels, which hovered along the American coast, especially at the mouths of the Chesapeake, Delaware, and Narragansett bays. It is always to be remembered that in all the states the privateers exceeded the state craft, which were often insignificant in comparison.

The reader recalls that in June, 1775, the battle of Bunker Hill was fought, a British army occupied Boston, and British vessels sailed the New England seas with little or no opposition. These vessels had already committed depredations and "piracies" upon the coasts and trade of Massachusetts, and were obstructing the importation of ammunition and provisions for the Continental army. It was under these circumstances that Massachusetts took her first step towards procuring a naval armament. On June 7 her third Provincial Congress appointed a committee of nine "to consider the expediency of establishing a number of small armed vessels, to cruise on our sea coasts, for the protection of our trade, and the annoyance of our enemies." The Provincial Congress, which moved very cautiously, enjoined secrecy on the committee. On June 10 three additional members were added to the committee; but later in the day a new committee consisting of seven members was apparently substituted for the old one. On June 12 the committee "appointed to consider the expediency of establishing a number of armed vessels" made a report which provided for the fitting out of not less than six vessels, to mount eight to fourteen carriage guns, and to cruise under the orders of the Committee of Safety—the chief executive organ of the Provincial Congress consisting of nine members, three of whom were from Boston. This report came up several times between June 12 and June 20. Finally on the latter date "the matter was ordered to subside."[1] The Battle of Bunker Hill which was fought on June 17 may have had something to do with this action of the Provincial Congress.

On July 19, 1775, the Revolutionary government in Massachusetts was superseded by a permanent government consisting of a House of Representatives and a Council of eighteen members elected by the House; the two houses were called the General Court. The continued depredations of the British now caused several endangered ports to ask the General Court to provide them with a naval defence. The part of Massachusetts which during the Revolution was most exposed to the attacks of the British,

1. Journals of Third Provincial Congress of Massachusetts, June 7, June 10, June 11, June 12, June 13, June 16, June 19, and June 20, 1775. All references to the state records of Massachusetts refer to the manuscripts or early printed copies to be found in the State Library or State Archives at Boston.

and which was most troublesome to defend, was the coast of Maine, then often referred to as the Eastern Coast. In August, 1775, a petition came to the General Court from Machias, a town situated on the Maine coast a few miles west of the present Eastport, asking that commissions be granted to officers and men on board two armed vessels which citizens of Machias had fitted out for the defense of their town. In response the General Court took into the service of the state the sloop "Machias Liberty" and the schooner "Diligent."[1] Jeremiah O'Brian, one of the men who had signed the petition, was commissioned by the Council commander-in-chief of the two vessels; and he was directed to enlist a number of men, not to exceed thirty, for each vessel. The "Machias Liberty" and the "Diligent" were in the service of the state until October, 1776, when they were discharged. About the first of October, 1775, Salem and Newburyport each asked the General Court for naval aid similar to that granted to Machias, but did not receive it.[2]

The General Court of Massachusetts next turned its attention to privateering. The

---

1. Journals of Massachusetts House of Representatives, August 21, 1775. O'Brian's name is found spelled in various ways.

2. Ibid., September 29, October 2, October 4, 1775; Records of General Court of Massachusetts, October 4, 1775.

acts of the states on this head fall into two general classes; those which in terms established state privateering, and those which adopted Continental privateering or accommodated state laws to the same. After the first half of 1776 all the states used Continental commissions and bonds. Massachusetts, moving in this matter before Congress, necessarily established state privateering. On September 28, 1775, her House of Representatives, having such establishment in view, appointed a committee of seven to consider the "Expediency of fitting out a Number of Armed Vessels." On October 9, this committee reported in favor of instituting privateering and a prize court to try cases of capture. On October 14 a bill embodying the committee's recommendations was introduced. It now passed slowly through the legislative mill, and on November 1 it became a law.[1] John Adams once referred to this statute of Massachusetts as one of the most important documents in the history of the Revolution. Its preamble was the work of Elbridge Gerry, and the body of the law was drafted by James Sullivan, many years later Governor of Massachusetts.[2] Gerry stated the sanctions for

---

1. Journals of Massachusetts House of Representatives, September 28, October 6, 9, 14, 17, 18, 19, 27, November 1, 1775.

2. Austin's Gerry, I, 94-95; Works of John Adams, X, 37.

the law. These he found in the arbitrary and sanguinary acts of Great Britain, in the charter of Massachusetts granted by King William and Queen Mary, and lastly in the resolution of the Continental Congress of July 18, 1775, recommending each colony to provide by armed vessels or otherwise for the protection of its harbors and navigation.

The Massachusetts law provided that all vessels convicted of making unlawful invasions or attacks on the seacoasts or navigation of any part of America should be forfeited. The Council was authorized to grant letters of marque and reprisal to masters and owners of vessels upon their entering into bond faithfully to discharge the duties of their office and to observe the naval laws of the colony. Three admiralty districts embracing the counties on the Massachusetts seacoast were established. The Southern district with the seat of its court at Plymouth embraced Plymouth county and the counties to the southward; the Middle district with the seat of its court at Ipswich embraced the counties of Suffolk, Middlesex, and Essex and extended from Plymouth county to New Hampshire; and the Eastern district with the seat of its court at North Yarmouth embraced the seacoast counties of Maine. The form of procedure in these courts was fixed for both captured and recaptured vessels. In the latter case salvage was from one-third to one-fourth of the selling price of the vessel. The facts in prize cases were to be tried by twelve good and lawful men. At this time the people of Massachusetts were so enraged at the judges of the former Provincial admiralty court that they would have universally condemned the trying of facts in prize cases by judges.[1]

The Council soon appointed three judges of admiralty, Nathan Cushing for the Southern district, Timothy Pickering for the Middle district, and James Sullivan for the Eastern district. Elbridge Gerry declined the judgeship for the Middle district. After trying about one hundred and fifty prize cases, Pickering in June, 1777, resigned, and was succeeded by Nathan Cushing, who now served as judge in both the Southern and Middle districts.[2] Comparatively few cases were tried in the Southern and Eastern districts. Timothy Langdon was for a long time judge of the Eastern district.

During the fall of 1775 the General Court took no steps towards establishing a state navy. It was at this time assisting Washington in obtaining and arming vessels for

1. Amory's Sullivan, II, 378-79, James Sullivan to Gerry, December 25, 1779.
2. Records of Massachusetts Council, November 14, December 9, December 12, 1775; Pickering's Pickering, I, 79-80; Amory's Sullivan, I, 63.

the Continental military service around Boston. Early in December the House of Representatives, acting on a recommendation contained in a letter from John Adams at Philadelphia, resolved to obtain statistics on the number of officers, seamen, and vessels, suitable for naval purposes, in the seaports of Massachusetts. On December 29 the Council declared for a navy by passing the following resolution: "Whereas several of the United Colonies have of late thought it expedient and necessary to fit out armed Vessels for the Defence of American Liberty, and it appears to this Court necessary that Measures be taken by this Colony for our further Protection by Sea: Therefore, Resolved that John Adams and Joseph Palmer, Esqurs. with such as the Hon. House shall join be a committee for fitting out one or more Vessels for the Defence of American Liberty."[1]

The House at once appointed its members of the committee, which on January 12, 1776, made a report favorable to the establishment of a navy.[2] Accordingly, on Feb-

---

1. Records of General Court of Massachusetts, December 29, 1775.
2. Journals of Massachusetts House of Representatives, January 12, 1776. On January 11 the Council resolved that two ships, one of 36, and the other of 32 guns, should be built. On the same day both House and Council voted to recommit the resolution in order that the committee which prepared it might report on the expense to be incurred

ruary 7 a resolution passed the General Court to build ten sloops of war, of 110 or 115 tons burden, each, suitable for carrying fourteen to sixteen carriage guns, 6-pounders and 4-pounders. A joint committee of the two houses was appointed to build the vessels, and £10,000 was voted for that purpose.[1] On the 16th the committee was authorized to contract for the building of only five vessels, until there was a prospect of procuring materials for ten; it was authorized to buy five vessels, if it thought best.[2] By July, 1776, the sloop "Tyrannicide" built at Salisbury, the brigantine "Rising Empire" built at Dartmouth, and the brigantine "Independence" built at Kingston were ready for sea; and by September the sloops "Republic" and "Freedom" built at Swanzey, and the "Massachusetts" built at Salisbury were completed.

Meanwhile the General Court had prepared and adopted the legislation necessary to establish a navy. It had drafted proper naval forms; and it had appointed a number of naval officers. A partial pay-table was

---

in building and fitting the two ships. It does not appear that further action was taken.— Records of Massachusetts Council, January 11, 1776.

1. Journals of Massachusetts House of Representatives, February 6, 1776; Records of Massachusetts Council, February 7, 1776.

2. Journals of Massachusetts House of Representatives, February 16, 1776.

established on February 8.¹ This on April 12 was succeeded by a new one, which generally raised wages, and which provided for a number of new offices. A captain was now to receive a monthly wage of £8; a first lieutenant, £5, 8s.; a second lieutenant, £5; a master, £4; a mate, £3; a surgeon, £7; and an ordinary seaman, £2. Each vessel was to be provided with 115 officers and seamen. No better proof of the rawness of the naval service is needed than that afforded by the regulation that recruits, whether officers, seamen, or marines, should furnish themselves with "a good effective Fire Arm, Cartouch Box, Cutlass, and Blanket." The captains were ordered to recommend to the Council a list of inferior officers and to enlist the proposed number of seamen and marines. Captors were given one-third of the proceeds of prizes.²

On April 27, 1776, the General Court fixed the respective shares of the proceeds of prizes for officers and seamen: a captain was to receive six shares, and "all the Cabbin Furniture;" a first lieutenant, five shares; a drummer, one and one-fourth shares; a seaman, one share; and a boy, one-half a share.³ On April 29, in order to en-

---

1. Journals of Massachusetts House of Representatives, February 7, 1776; Records of Massachusetts Council, February 8, 1776.
2. Journals of Massachusetts House of Representatives, April 12, 1776.
3. Ibid., April 27, 1776.

courage enlistment, an advance of one month's wages was voted to recruits. On the same day it was decided that "the Uniform of Officers be Green and White, and that the Colours be a white Flagg, with a green Pine Tree, and an Inscription, 'Appeal to Heaven.'"[1] On July 26 the Council appointed a prize agent in each of the three admiralty districts, whose duty was to represent the state in receiving, trying, and selling prizes.[2] At times the prize agents assisted in fitting out vessels.

During the first half of 1776 the law of November 1, 1775, establishing privateering, was three times amended and remodelled.[3] The law was thereby accommodated to the resolutions of the Continental Congress fixing the kinds of property subject to capture, and the respective shares of captors and recaptors. Doubts which had arisen as to the proper construction of the original act were now removed. The procedure before admiralty courts was made more specific. In cases of captures made by Continental vessels, appeals were permitted from state admiralty courts to the Continental Congress; in all other cases, appeals were allowed to the superior state courts. In each

---

1. Journals of Massachusetts House of Representatives, April 29, 1776; Records of Massachusetts Council, April 29, 1776.
2. Ibid. (Records), July 26, 1776.
3. Goodell, Laws of Massachusetts, February 14, April 13, May 8, 1776.

of the three admiralty districts in Massachusetts additional towns were named where court might be held. The towns named for the Middle district were Boston, Salem, Ipswich, and Newburyport.

During the summer and fall of 1776 the instructions and orders to the captains of the armed vessels were issued to them by the Council, having been previously prepared by a committee. The following instructions, which were drafted by Thomas Cushing and Daniel Hopkins, were given to Captain John Fisk, and will suffice as a sample of such documents:

"The Brigantine Tyrannicide under your Command being properly Armed and Man'd and in other respects fitted for a Cruise you are hereby Ordered and directed immediately to proceed to sea and use your utmost Endeavors to protect the Sea Coast and Trade of the United States and you are also directed to exert yourself in making Captures of all Ships and other Vessels Goods Wares and Mechandise belonging to the King of Great Britain or any of his subjects wherever residing excepting only the Ships and Goods of the Inhabitants of Bermuda and the Bahama Islands—You are directed not to Cruize further Southward than Latitude Twelve North nor farther East than Longitude Nine Degrees West from London nor farther West than the Shoals of Nantucket. At all times using necessary precautions to prevent your Vessel from falling into the hands of the Enemy.

"And Whereas you have received a Commission authorizing you to make Captures aforesaid and a set of Instructions have been delivered you for regulating your Conduct in that matter; these Instructions you are Hereby directed diligently to attend to, and if you are so fortunate as to make any Captures you are to Order them to make the first safe Harbor within the United States.—and you are further Ordered not to expend your Ammunition unnecessarily and only in time of Action or firing Alarm or Signal guns."[1]

Until October, 1776, the Massachusetts navy was administered by the General Court, committees of its members, the Council, and naval agents. The General Court for the period of its recess in May, 1776, placed the armed vessels in the charge of "the committee for fortifying the harbor of Boston." By the fall of that year it realized that "secrecy, dispatch, and economy in conducting the war" demanded a special executive department. Accordingly, on October 26 it established a Board of War consisting of nine members, any five of whom constituted a quorum. The Board

---

1. Records of Massachusetts Council, October 29, 1776. The naval documents introduced in the narrative on the Massachusetts navy are typical of similar ones in other states.

of War was "empowered to Order and Direct the Operations of the Forces in the Pay of this State, both by sea and land, by giving the Commanders of the Troops, Garrisons, and Vessels of War, such Orders for their Conduct and Cruizes from time to time as they shall think proper."[1] It organized by electing a president and secretary; and it rented permanent quarters near the State House in Boston. In December, 1776, James Warren, later Commissioner for the Continental Navy Board at Boston, was president of the Board of War. Philip Henry Savage was for a long time its president. Savage presided at the meeting in 1773 at Old South Church which decided that the tea should not be landed.[2] The Board of War entered upon its work with vigor in November, 1776. It was yearly renewed, until it was dissolved in February, 1781.

The principal business of the Board of War was the administration of the naval, commercial, and military affairs of the state. Its naval and commercial duties were quite engrossing. The Board kept fairly distinct the activities of its "armed" and "trading" vessels. It is true that the armed vessels were now and then sent on commercial errands, or combined in a single voyage naval

---

1. Resolves of Massachusetts, October 26, 1776.
2. Winsor's Memorial History of Boston, II, 543.

and trading duties. The sloop "Republic," used for a short time as a naval vessel, was taken into the commercial service. The Massachusetts Archives contain a list of thirty-two trading vessels owned or chartered by the Board of War.[1] These vessels visited Nantes, Bilbao, Martinique, Guadaloupe, St. Eustatius, Cape Francois, Baltimore, and the ports of North and South Carolina. They carried as staple exports, fish, lumber, and New England rum.

1. Massachusetts Revolutionary Archives, XL, 110-11. The influence on the naming of vessels of the friendly relations existing between the United States and France during the Revolution early manifested itself. On December 27, 1776, the Massachusetts Board of War changed the names of its trading vessels as follows: ships, "Julius Cæsar" to "Bourbon," "Venus" to " Versailles," and "Friend" to "Paris;" brigantines, "Charming Sally" to "Penet," and "Isabella" to "Count D'Estaing." The brigantine "Penet," which was named for a French merchant at Nantes, a member of the firm of Pliarne, Penet and Company, agents for the United States, has been sometimes confused with the brigantine "Perch," which was obtained by Massachusetts in the fall of 1777 for the sole purpose of conveying the news of Burgoyne's surrender to the American Commissioners at Paris. The letters and dispatches were intrusted with Jonathan Loring Austin, secretary of the Board of War, who after a passage of thirty days reached the Commissioners at Passy on December 4, 1777.—Board of War Minutes, December 27, 1776; Hale's Franklin in France, I, 155.

As a rule the work of the Board of War in looking after its trading vessels exceeded its naval work. At times, as in the case of the Penobscot expedition, the naval duties were the important ones. A week's work of the Board in behalf of its armed vessels shows a curious mixture of orders on the commissary-general for clothing and provisions, and on the state storekeeper for naval stores; and of directions to the prize agents, the agents for building armed vessels, and the naval captains. The General Court permitted the Board a rather free hand in its management of the navy. The Board carried on a considerable correspondence with the commanders of the armed vessels. The following letter written to the Board by Captain John Clouston of the armed sloop "Freedom" on May 23, 1777, from Paimboeuf, France, will illustrate this correspondence from the Captain's side. Clouston's disregard of orthography and punctuation is exceptional even for a Revolutionary officer.

"Gentlemen:

I have the pleasure of Informing your Honours by Capt. Fisk of the 'Massachusetts' That on the first Instant I arrived safe in this Port after taking twelve Sail of Englis Vessels Seven of which I despatched for Boston Burnt three gave one smal Brigg to our Prisners and one Retaken by the

'Futereange' which Chast us fore Glasses and finding she Could not Cume up with us she gave Chase to our Prize and toock her in our sight—I have Cleaned & Refited my Vessel and Taken in forty Tons of War like Stores and have bin waiting for a wind to go this fore days—Capt. Fisk being short of Provisions I have supplied him with foreteen Barels of Pork and Eleven of Beef and have Suffisantse for my Vessel left."[1]

In January, 1777, a new sea establishment was effected. Wages were generally raised, no doubt chiefly to meet their decrease caused by the depreciation of the currency. A captain was now to receive a monthly wage of £14, 8s.; a lieutenant or a master, £7, 4s.; a seaman, £2, 8s.; and a boy, £1, 4s. The offices established in the Massachusetts navy, while not quite so many, were in general the same as those in the Continental navy. The Massachusetts navy, however, had the offices of prizemaster, pilot, and boy, which did not occur in the Continental list. Following the regulations of Congress, the General Court now gave captors one-half of their captures. The rations for seamen were modelled on the Continental bill of fare.[2] On March 21, 1777,

---

[1]. Board of War Letters, Massachusetts Revolutionary Archives, May 23, 1777.

[2]. Massachusetts Resolves, January 8, January 24, 1777. On December 6, 1776, six naval offices were established, which included a captain's clerk, prizemaster, and sergeant of marines.

the General Court adopted rules and regulations for its ships of war; and it ordered that they should be read by the commanding officer of a vessel at least once a week. These rules, while briefer than the Continental rules, naturally followed the same general lines. They show either the influence of the Continental rules or of the English rules upon which the Continental rules were based. The following curious rule in part parallels quotations made from the Continental rules in Chapter I:

"And if any Person belonging to either of such Vessels shall be convicted of Theft, Drunkenness, profane Cursing, or Swearing, disregarding the Sabbath, or using the Name of God lightly, or profanely, or shall be guilty of quarreling or fighting, or of any reproachful or provoking Language tending to make Quarrels, or of any turbulent or mutinous Behavior, or if any Person shall sleep upon his Watch, or forsake his Station, or shall in any wise neglect to perform the Duty enjoined him, he shall he punished for any of the said Offences at the Discretion of the commissioned Officers of such Vessel, or the Major Part of them, according to the Nature and Aggravation of the Offence, by sitting in the Stocks, or wearing a wooden Collar about his Neck, not exceeding 4 Hours, nor less than one, or by whipping, not exceeding 12 Lashes, or by being put in Irons for so long Time as the said Officers shall judge the Safety and well being of the Ship and Crew requires, or otherwise shall forfeit to the State not more than six, nor less than two Days Pay for each offence."[1]

During every year of the Revolution attempts were made to increase the Massachusetts navy. In the fall of 1777 the brigantine "Hazard" was added. On August 6, 1777, the General Court resolved that, since the armed vessels at the lowest computation had netted the state £55,000, the Board of War should purchase or build two vessels mounting 28 and 32 guns, respectively. In January, 1778, it reduced the sizes of these vessels almost one-half; and finally it gave up building them.[2] In the spring of 1779 a prize of the "Hazard," the brigantine "Active," taken in April off the island of St. Thomas in the West Indies, was purchased.[3] In April, 1778, the Gen-

1. Massachusetts Resolves, March 21, 1777.
2. Ibid., August 6, 1777; January 17, 1778.
3. The following is an extract from the enlisting contract of the armed brig "Active," which was signed by officers, seamen, and marines: "And we hereby bind ourselves to Submit to all orders and regulations of the Navy of the United States of North America and this State and faithfully to observe and obey all such orders, and Commands as we shall receive from time to time from our Superior Officers on board or belonging to the said Brig Active and on board any Such Boats or Vessel or Vessels as foresaid.

eral Court resolved to build a frigate of 28 guns, which would carry two hundred officers and men.¹ This vessel was built at Newburyport and was named the "Protector." In the fall of 1779 it was nearing completion. The launching of the "Protector," which was the largest ship in the Massachusetts navy, was a matter of more than usual local interest. Stephen Cross who was in charge of the construction of the frigate wrote a letter to the Board of War in July, 1779, which throws light upon the minor naval duties of the Board. Cross's language is somewhat involved, but his meaning is clear; it is hardly necessary to say that the "souring" refers to lemons.

"Gentlemen.

it being customary for the owners of Vessels when they are Launched to give the Workmen something Better than New England Rum to drink & Likewise some thing to Eat and also all those Persons who

---

"And it is on the part of the State that such persons as by Land or sea shall loose a Limb in any Engagement with the Enemies of these United States of America or be otherwise so disabled as to be rendered incapable of getting a Lively Hood Shall be entitled to the same Provisions as the disabled Persons in the Continental Service."—Massachusetts Revolutionary Archives, XL, 20.

1. Massachusetts Resolves, April 21, 1778.

Attend the Launching Expect to be asked to Drink and Eat something and Especially Publick Vessells it will be Expected that something be Provided and it is my opinion about sixty Galls of West India Rum & sugars for the same & souring if to be had and one Quarter Cask of Wine and A Hamper of ale or Beer together with a Tierce hams Neet Tongs or Corn Beef will be necessary to comply with the Customs in these Cases."[1]

After August, 1779, when the disaster on the Penobscot occurred, the naval duties of the Board of War were slight. For a time the "Protector" was the only vessel in the navy. With the coming in of a new government under a Constitution on October 25, 1780, there was no longer much need for a Board of War. According to the provisions of the new Constitution, the Governor was commander-in-chief of the navy; and he was authorized to "train, instruct, exercise, and govern it," and to call it into service in time of war. On February 8, 1781, the Board of War was discontinued, and Caleb Davis, who was appointed Agent of the Commonwealth, succeeded to its ministerial duties.[2] The Governor and the Agent

---

1. Massachusetts Revolutionary Archives, XLIV, 279.
2. Massachusetts Resolves, February 8, 1781. Three members of the Board of War and two clerks were continued for a few months to settle the accounts of the Board.

now shared the naval duties. The Governor commissioned officers, issued orders to the naval commanders, and was responsible to the General Court; the Agent had direct oversight of the fitting out of vessels, the selling of prizes, and was responsible to the Governor. As the Revolution spent itself the simplification of the administrative machinery of the state continued. On January 1, 1783, the Agent was discontinued. His naval duties fell to the Commissary-General.[1]

During each year from 1780 to 1783 the General Court made one or more attempts to increase the naval force of the state. It was spurred to action by the ravages of the British cruisers on the Eastern Coast. On March 21, 1780, two armed vessels mounting not less than ten or more than fourteen 4's or 6's were ordered. The expense incurred was to be met by the sale of the "Rising Empire" and of the confiscated estates of Loyalists, and from the rents of the property of absentees. On March 6, 1781, the Agent was directed to obtain a small vessel of eight to twelve guns to serve as a tender for the "Mars;" and on April 23, he was ordered to procure by hire or purchase two small craft to be employed as "guarda coasta." On November 12, 1782, a committee was appointed to purchase a vessel of twelve or sixteen guns to be used in pro-

[1]. Massachusetts Resolves, October 4, 1782.

tecting the coast. On March 26, 1783, the Commissary-General was ordered to obtain a small vessel and a whale boat to cruise against the enemy in Casco Bay and along the Eastern Shore.[1] As the result of these resolutions, four armed vessels were added to the navy: in the spring of 1780 the "Mars;" in the summer of 1781, the "Defence;" in the winter of 1781-1782, the "Tartar," which was built by the state; and in the spring of 1782, the "Winthrop."

Private naval enterprise throughout the Revolution was exceedingly active in Massachusetts. In 1775, some months before the General Court granted letters of marque, Massachusetts citizens, unauthorized, were capturing the vessels of the enemy. Scarcely a fortnight after the battles of Lexington and Concord men from New Bedford and Dartmouth fitted out a vessel and attacked and cut out from a harbor in Martha's Vineyard a prize of the British sloop of war "Falcon," 16. This act was called forth by the captures which the "Falcon" had made from the people of Buzzard's Bay. On June 12, 1775, the inhabitants of Machias, Maine, had captured the King's sloop "Margaretta," Lieutenant Moore, after mortally wounding the commander and inflicting a loss of fourteen men. Still other British

---

1. Massachusetts Resolves, March 21, 1780; February 19, March 6, April 23, 1781; November 12, 1782; March 26, 1783.

340 *Navy of the American Revolution*

vessels were captured off the coast of Maine during the summer of 1775.[1]

With the act of November 1, 1775, granting to the Council the power to issue letters of marque and reprisal, all such private enterprises as the above, when done under the authority of a commission, were legal. It does not appear however that Massachusetts granted many commissions until the second half of 1776. In 1777 she granted 96 commissions. The best year was 1779 when she issued 222 commissions; the year 1781 with 216 commissions was not far behind. The total number of commissions issued by Massachusetts for the years 1777 to 1783 was 998.[2] In 1779 one hundred and eighty-four prizes captured by privateers were libelled in the Massachusetts prize courts.[3] The privateering industry for this year was very active. The following is an extract from a letter dated May 16, 1779, written from a Massachusetts seaport:

"Privateering was never more in vogue than at present; two or three privateers sail every week from this port, and men seem

---

1. Winsor, Narrative and Critical History, VI, 564; Maclay, History of American Privateering, 52-60.
2. Massachusetts Revolutionary Archives. The total numbers of privateering commissions always exceed the total numbers of vessels, as the same vessels were often commissioned two or more times.
3. Boston Gazette for 1779.

as plenty as grasshoppers in the field; no vessel being detained an hour for want of them. We have near 1,000 prisoners on board the guard-ships in Boston, and a great balance due us from the enemy. Cruisers from New York, &c are daily brought in, and often by vessels of inferior force; our privateers-men being as confident of victory, when upon an equal footing with the English, as these were of gaining it of the French in the last war."[1]

The rivalry between the state service and the privateers for seamen was exceedingly active. The latter service was always the more popular. In 1779 the Council recommended that some effectual measures be taken to prevent the owners of private ships of war and merchantmen from seducing seamen away that were engaged in the public service. It declared that proper encouragement must be given to state officers and seamen, and that commanders must have the aid of the government in manning their vessels, "or they will lie by the Walls and so be of little or no service."[2] In 1778 the General Court found some difficulty in securing commanders.

The movements of the armed vessels of the Massachusetts navy are quite similar to the movements of the naval vessels of Con-

---

1. Virginia Gazette, June 19, 1779.
2. Journals of House of Representatives, January 6, 1779.

342 *Navy of the American Revolution*

gress.[1] The smaller fleet like the larger cruised in European waters, in the region of the West Indies, and to the eastward of the Bermudas in the path of the richly-laden West Indiamen. The Massachusetts vessels, however, cruised more frequently nearer home. About the first of June, 1779, the "Hazard" and "Tyrannicide" were in the region of Nantucket. After 1779 the vessels were frequently ordered to protect the

---

1. The vessels in the Massachusetts navy with the approximate periods of their service were as follows: Sloop "Machias Liberty," 1775-1776; schooner "Diligent," 1775-1776; brigantine (at first a sloop) "Tyrannicide," 1776-1779; brigantine "Rising Empire," 1776-1777; brigantine "Independence," 1776-1777; sloop "Republic," 1776-1777; sloop "Freedom," 1776-1777; brigantine "Massachusetts," 1776-1778; brigantine "Hazard," 1777-1779; brigantine "Active," 1779; frigate "Protector," 1779-1781; ship "Mars," 1780-1781; sloop "Defence," 1781; ship "Tartar," 1782-1783; sloop "Winthrop," 1782-1783; and galley "Lincoln," 1779-1781. Most of these vessels mounted from ten to twenty guns, 4's and 6's. The only larger vessel was the "Protector," 26. Vessels such as the "Tyrannicide," "Hazard," and "Winthrop" carried about 125 officers and men. The following captains or commanders were the chief officers in the Massachusetts navy: Jeremiah O'Brian, John Lambert, John Fisk, John Foster Williams, John Clouston, Jonathan Haraden, Daniel Souther, Simeon Samson, Richard Welden, Allen Hallet, James Nevens, John Cathcart and George Little. Massachusetts did not establish the rank of commodore.

Eastern Coast. In the spring of 1777 the "Tyrannicide," Captain Jonathan Haraden, "Massachusetts," Captain John Fisk, and "Freedom," Captain John Clouston, cruised eastward as far as the coasts of France and Spain, capturing some twenty-five prizes, many of which however, were recaptured by the British.[1] This was a most fortunate venture, for all told one can not now count more than seventy prizes captured by the Massachusetts navy. In the summer of 1780 the Board of War turned over the "Mars," Captain Simeon Samson, to the Massachusetts Committee for Foreign Affairs which sent her to France and Holland for supplies.

---

1. These three vessels captured the four prizes mentioned in the following advertisement, which appeared in the Continental Journal and Weekly Advertiser for July 3, 1777, a paper published at Boston. The advertisement is introduced here to illustrate the final disposition of prize vessels:

"To be sold by Public Auction at eleven o'clock on Wednesday the 23rd of July instant at Mr. Tileston's wharf in Boston the following prizes with their appurtenances.

"The Ship Lonsdale, about 250 tons
Brig Britannia, about 140 "
Brig Penelope, about 130 "
Snow Sally, about 180 "

"The above prizes lay at Tileston's wharf. They are all good vessels and well found. Inventories to be seen at the sheriff's office Cornhill, and at the place of sale.

"W. Greenleaf, Sheriff."

The state vessels were at times joined in cruises with privateers or with Continental vessels; and enterprises were concerted with all three classes of armed craft. In April, 1777, the state took into its service for a month nine privateers, mounting 130 guns and carrying 1,030 men, to cruise with the Continental frigate "Hancock" and "Boston" after the British frigate "Milford" which had been especially annoying and destructive to the trade of the state.[1] In February, 1781, the "Protector" was cruising with the Continental frigate "Deane" thirty leagues windward of Antigua. In March, 1781, the Admiral of the French fleet at Newport was requested to send two French ships to cruise with the "Mars" on the Eastern shore; and a bounty was offered to privateersmen who would cruise against the "worthless banditti" in that region.[2]

The capture of a prize often amounted to little more than the chasing of a merchantman and the firing of a few shots as a signal for surrender. At times however when the merchantman was armed, or when the enemy's vessel happened to be a privateer, the action was more serious. One of the most severe single engagements in which a

---

1. Massachusetts Resolves, April 26, 1777; Massachusetts Revolutionary Archives, XL, 29, 55.
2. Massachusetts Resolves, March 2, 1781.

Massachusetts vessel was concerned was that between the "Protector," 26, Captain John Foster Williams, and the privateer frigate "Admiral Duff," 32, Captain Stranger. It occurred on June 9, 1780, in latitude 42° N. and longitude 47° W. The engagement was heavy for an hour and a half when the "Admiral Duff," having caught fire, blew up; all on board were lost except fifty-five men who were picked up by the "Protector." The American vessel lost six men.[1] The following brief account of one of these minor engagements, told in the simple and direct language of the Massachusetts captain who took part in it, is taken from a letter of Captain Allen Hallet to the Board of War. It is dated at sea on board the "Tyrannicide," latitude 28° N., longitude 68° W., March 31, 1779. This simple and vivid description shows with clearness the character of the minor engagements of the Revolution.

"I have the pleasure of sending this to you by Mr. John Blanch who goes prize-master of my Prize, the Privateer Brig Revenge, lately commanded by Capt. Robert Fendall belonging to Grenada, but last from Jamaica, mounting 14 Carriage Guns, 6 & 4 pounders, 4 swivels & 2 Cohorns, & sixty ablebodied Men, which I took after a very smart & Bloody Engagement, in which they had 8 men killed & fourteen wounded, the

1. Boston Gazette, July 24, 1780.

Vessell cut very much to pieces by my Shott, so that they had no command of her at all—amongst the killed was the 1st Lieut. & one Quarter Mr.—amongst the wounded is the Capt. 2nd. Lieut. & Gunner—I captured her as follows: on the 29 Inst. at 4 P M. I made her about 4 leagues to windward coming down upon us, upon which I cleared the Ship and got all hands to Quarter, ready for an Engagement, I stood close upon the Wind waiting for her, about half past six PM. she came up with me, and hailed me, ask'd me where I was from, I told them I was from Boston & asked where they were from, they said from Jamaica & that they were a British Cruizer, I immediately told them I was an American Cruizer, upon which they ordered me to Strike, & seeing I did not intend to gratify their desires, they rang'd up under my Lee & gave me a Broadside, I immediately return'd the Compliment & dropping a Stern, I got under their Lee and then pour'd Broadsides into her from below and out of the Tops, so fast & so well directed that in one hour & a Quarter we dismantled two of her Guns & drove them from their Quarters & compell'd them to Strike their Colors, during the whole Engagement we were not at any one time more than half Pistol Shott distant & some part of the Time our Yards were lock'd with theirs—I had Eight men wounded only two of which are Bad—

amongst the wounded are my first Lieut. & Master, I intended to man her and keep her as a Consort during the Cruize, but having twenty wounded Men on board, of my own men & prisoners I thought it Best to send her home, with all the wounded men on board under the Care of the Surgeons Mate."[1]

By far the largest naval undertaking of the Revolution made by the Americans was the Penobscot Expedition. Until 1779 the general policy of those who managed the fleet of Massachusetts was to send its vessels cruising against the British transports, merchantmen, and small privateers, and to leave the coast to be defended by the seacoast establishment and by local forces. In August, 1777, the Council agreed with this policy for it then spoke of the Continental vessels, the state vessels, and the privateers as "improper" to be employed in clearing the coasts of these "vermin."[2] In April, 1779, however, it disapproved this policy. It now in a message to the House submitted whether, instead of sending the armed vessels on long cruises after prizes, it would not have been vastly more to the advantage and profit of the state to have employed them cruising on the coast of Massachusetts for the protection of trade

---

1. Massachusetts Revolutionary Archives, XLIV, 408.
2. Ibid., 268.

and the defence of harbors and seacoast, "which have been left in such an unguarded and defenceless Situation that where we have taken one Vessel of the Enemy their small privateers out of New York have taken ten from us."[1] It would seem that the Board of War was right in employing its fleet in prize-getting rather than in defensive warfare. The capturing of small privateers and of merchantmen were the only enterprises for which the Revolutionary fleets were adapted. Those vessels that cruised continually near the American coast, sooner or later, fell foul of the stouter and better armed ships of the enemy. Moreover, the Board of War, had it not responded to the commercial spirit of the times, would have been compelled to adopt the methods of the privateers, did it wish to succeed in its competition with them for seamen.

During the first half of 1779 the British vessels were very destructive to the trade and shipping of Massachusetts and New Hampshire. On June 9, eight hundred of the enemy, encouraged by certain Tories in Maine, effected a lodgment on the Maine coast at a place called Bagaduce, now Castine, near the mouth of the Penobscot river.[2] This made a fine vantage-point as

---

1. Journals of Massachusetts House of Representatives, April 7, 1779.
2. Amory's Sullivan, II, 376-78, James Sulli-

a base for naval operations. The appeal for naval protection which the inhabitants of Massachusetts now made upon her was a strong one. Towards the close of June the Massachusetts government began concerting with the Continental Navy Board at Boston and with the government of New Hampshire an expedition to capture and destroy this British station. Samuel Adams, who had recently retired from the chairmanship of the Marine Committee of Congress and had returned to Boston, furthered the enterprise. To the fleet which was now formed, New Hampshire contributed the "Hampden," 22; the Navy Board at Boston, the Continental vessels, "Warren," 32, "Providence," 12, and "Diligent," 12; and Massachusetts, the three state brigantines, "Tyrannicide," 16, "Hazard," 14, and "Active," 14, together with thirteen privateers, which were temporarily taken into the state service. These twenty armed vessels mounted in all 324 guns, and were

---

van to John Sullivan, August 30, 1779. James Sullivan says that, on the occupation of Bagaduce by the British, Boston and neighboring seaports were greatly alarmed at the prospect of a scarcity of wood; and that men who had made their fortunes by war, for once and for a moment, felt a public spirit, and freely offered their ships to the government. They were careful to have them appraised and insured by the state, which of course suffered the loss on the failure of the expedition.

manned by more than 2,000 men. Besides the armed fleet there were twenty transports which carried upwards of 1,000 state militia. The naval forces were under the command of Captain Dudley Saltonstall of the Continental navy; and the troops were commanded by Brigadier-General Solomon Lovell of the state military forces of Massachusetts. Paul Revere was Chief of Artillery with the rank of Lieutenant-Colonel.

The assembling, manning, provisioning, and fitting of so many vessels greatly taxed the resources of Massachusetts. The fleet left Boston on July 19, and during the last days of the month appeared off the Penobscot, and attacked Bagaduce with only partial success, since it failed to take the main fort. Before a second attempt was made, a British fleet from New York under the command of Sir George Collier, who had received news of the expedition, appeared in the Penobscot. The British fleet consisted of the "Raisonnable," 64; "Blonde," and "Virginia," 32's; "Greyhound," "Camilla," and "Gallatea," 20's; and "Otter," 14; together with three small vessels at the garrison, the "Nautilus," 16, "Albany," 14, and "North," 14. The British fleet mounted 248 guns and carried more than 1,600 men. In number of guns and men the advantage lay with the Americans, but in weight of metal and tonnage it was probably with the British. On the morning of August 14 the British fleet came in sight of the American. The two fleets were barely in range of each other's guns when the Americans were seized with a panic, and fled with their vessels helter skelter up the river, pursued by the British. The Americans offered almost no resistance whatever, but ran their ships ashore, set fire to them, and escaped afoot, when not too closely pursued. With the exception of two or three vessels which were captured, the American fleet was annihilated. The British lost 13 men; the American loss has been placed at 474 men. The larger part of the American sailors and soldiers returned by woods to New Hampshire and Massachusetts.

The total cost of this expedition to Massachusetts as calculated by the Board of War was £1,739,175. The larger part of this sum, £1,390,200, was charged to the account of the navy. It suffered the loss of three state armed vessels and a victualer, nine privateers, and twenty transports. Among the twenty transports, with possibly one exception, was the whole trading fleet of the state. Soon after the disaster a joint committee of the Massachusetts House of Representatives and Council with Artemas Ward as president, held an inquiry and made a report on the causes of the failure of the expedition. In answer to the question, "What appears the principal reason of the failure," the committee decided unanimously, "want of proper Spirit and Energy on the part of the Commodore." A court-martial, which was held on the frigate "Deane" in Boston harbor about the first of October, decided against Captain Saltonstall; and he was dismissed from the navy. Rarely has a more ignominious military operation been made by Americans than the Penobscot expedition. A New Englander with some justice has likened it to Hull's surrender at Detroit. Had it been successful, it would not have been worth the effort it cost. Its object had no national significance; it was an eccentric operation. "Bad in conception, bad in preparation, pad in execution, it naturally ended in disaster and disgrace."[1]

Besides the "Tyrannicide," "Hazard," and "Active" the Massachusetts navy lost to the enemy at least three other vessels. Towards the close of 1777 the British captured the "Freedom" and "Independence." On May 5, 1781, His Majesty's ships "Roebuck," 44, and "Medea," 28, captured the

---

1. Massachusetts Revolutionary Archives, CXLV, 199-203, 350; Weymouth Historical Society Publications, I, chapters VII-X, gives the best account of the Penobscot expedition, also contains the Original Journal of General Solomon Lovell kept on the expedition; Massachusetts Historical Society Collections, 7th, II, 430; Proceedings of Massachusetts Historical Society, 2nd, XII, 201-202; Clowes, Royal Navy, IV, 28-29.

"Protector," 26, with more than one hundred and thirty men on board.[1] She was added to the Royal Navy as the "Hussar." In the latter half of 1782 Captain George Little in the "Winthrop" cruised on the Eastern Coast, and captured and sent into Boston "nearly the whole of the arm'd force they possessed at Penobscot;" he thus in part retrieved the naval honor of his state.[2] Acting under orders of Governor Hancock, Little in the "Winthrop" made the last cruise of the Massachusetts navy, when in the winter of 1782-1783 he visited Martinique. On his return, he was fitting for a cruise on the Eastern Coast, when about April 1 news of permanent peace arrived. On June 4, 1783, the Commissary-General was directed to sell the "Winthrop," the last vessel in the navy. The "Tartar" had been sold during the past winter.[3] Captain Little's accounts were being settled in March, 1785.

---

1. Massachusetts Revolutionary Archives, XXXIX, 45.
2. Ibid., CLVIII, 274, Message of Governor Hancock to House of Representatives, February 6, 1783.
3. Massachusetts Resolves, June 4, 1783. Those naval vessels which were not captured, destroyed, or sold, were either returned to their owners, or were thrown out of commission and employed in other services.

CHAPTER XII

THE NAVY OF CONNECTICUT

An introductory word about the government of Connecticut during the Revolution may not be amiss. Speaking generally, the power of legislation was vested in the Governor, Council, and House of Representatives; and of administration in the Governor and Council of Safety.[1] The Legislature or General Assembly met two or three times a year. Jonathan Trumbull, the only Provincial governor in the thirteen colonies who was not displaced by the dominance of the Patriot party, was governor of Connecticut throughout the Revolution. On October 10, 1776, Connecticut, by a resolution of the General Assembly, which made no change in the frame-work of the government, ceased to be a colony and became a state. The Council of Safety, appointed to assist the Governor in administration, was elected each year. Its membership varied in numbers; in 1775 there were five members; in 1779, twenty. About half of its members attend-

---

1. One must distinguish between the Council and Council of Safety. A few members were common to both bodies.

ed its meetings, which were principally held at Hartford, and at Lebanon, the home of Governor Trumbull. Roger Sherman, Oliver Ellsworth, and other leaders of the Revolution in Connecticut served in the Council of Safety.

Connecticut's first step towards obtaining a naval armament was made early in July, 1775, when her General Assembly resolved to fit out and arm two vessels of suitable burden for the defence of the seacoasts of the colony, and authorized the Governor and Council to procure, furnish, and employ the two vessels.[1] On July 24, 1775, the Governor and Council of Safety thoroughly considered the "affair of the two armed vessels;" and letters relating thereto from men in New Haven, Middletown, Wethersfield, and other towns were read. Captain John Deshon and Nathaniel Shaw, jr., both of New London, and Captain Giles Hall of Norwich attended the meeting and offered information and advice. A committee of four, consisting of two members of the Council of Safety together with Deshon and Hall, was appointed to visit the principal ports of the colony and ascertain the terms

---

1. Colonial Records of Connecticut, XV, 99-100. The published Colonial and State Records of Connecticut to which I refer, consist of two parts, the Records of the General Assembly, and the Jounrals of the Council of Safety. The reader can easily tell from the context to which part each reference refers.

upon which vessels, officers, and men might be had.[1]

On August 2 this committee reported that sundry vessels could be obtained at reasonable prices, but that none of them were perfectly adapted for vessels of war. The committee said that the people of the colony disagreed as to the propriety of arming vessels; many thought that it would be impossible for America to compare by sea with the British, and that to attempt it would provoke insult and would expose the seacoast and trade of Connecticut to increased danger; but others thought that a naval armament would be an advantage, and would afford protection to the colony. The Governor and Council of Safety expressed a doubt whether they had a right to suspend the measure of the General Assembly, even if they should think it advisable. They now resolved to fit out an armed vessel, the brig "Minerva," of about 108 tons burden, belonging to Captain William Griswold of Wethersfield; and to obtain a smaller and faster vessel of some twenty-five tons burden to be employed as a "spy vessel, to run and course from place to place, to discover the enemy, and carry intelligence." Captain Samuel Niles of Norwich was appointed captain of the spy-vessel; and Benjamin Huntington of the Council of Safety and

---

[1]. Colonial Records of Connecticut, XV, 108, 109.

John Deshon were appointed a committee to obtain, fit out, and furnish it.[1]

On August 3 the Governor and Council of Safety appointed Captain Giles Hall of Norwich captain and commander of the "Minerva." A pay-table and a small list of officers were now established. Captain Hall was to receive a monthly salary of £7; the first lieutenant, £5; the second lieutenant, and master, £4 each; seamen, £2, 5s.; and marines, £2. Hall was instructed to raise forty seamen and forty marines.[2]

When the committee for obtaining the spy-vessel reported on August 14, the Governor and Council of Safety resolved to buy the schooner "Britannia," belonging at Stonington, at a price not to exceed £200. Robert Niles was made captain of the "Spy," the name now given to the schooner, in place of Samuel Niles.[3] The "Spy" was cruising early in October, 1775, when she recaptured and brought into New London a large ship containing eight thousand bushels of wheat,[4] the first capture of the Connecticut navy.

By October the "Minerva" was ready for sea, and on the ninth of this month, in response to a request of the Continental Congress, the Governor and Council of Safety

1. Colonial Records of Connecticut, XV, 109, 110.
2. Ibid., 111-13.
3. Ibid., 117.
4. Connecticut Gazette, October 13, **1775**.

ordered this vessel to intercept two transports bound from England for Quebec.[1] This detail was not carried out by the "Minerva" for the very sufficient reason "that all the hands or soldiers and marines on board, except about 10 or 12, being duly noticed of said orders, utterly declined and refused to obey the same and perform said cruise," which through their disobedience wholly failed.[2] The Governor and Council of Safety ordered the mutinous men discharged, and others enlisted in their places; but before the "Minerva" was again ready for service, the General Assembly in December directed Captain Hall to return his vessel to its owner and dismiss his crew.

In December, 1775, the General Assembly deciding to increase the naval forces of the colony, appointed Colonel David Waterbury of Stamford and Captain Isaac Sears of New Haven to examine a certain brigantine at Greenwich with a view to ascertaining its fitness for the naval service; and it resolved to build or otherwise procure an additional armed ship and four row-galleys "for the defence of this and the neighboring colonies." Waterbury and Sears reported that the Greenwich brigantine was a new vessel which had made one voyage to the West Indies,

1. See Chapter I, Naval Committee, page 35; Colonial Records of Connecticut, XV, 176.
2. Colonial Records of Connecticut, XV. 176.

Navy of the American Revolution 359

and that she would mount sixteen six-pounders and twenty-four swivels.¹ The Governor and Council of Safety at once purchased the brigantine, which they named the "Defence," and appointed Captain Seth Harding of Norwich to command her. By April, 1776, the "Defence" was manned and ready for sea.

On January 9, 1776, the Governor and Council of Safety appointed Benjamin Huntington of the Council of Safety and Captain Seth Harding a committee to visit Middletown and other towns on the Connecticut river to ascertain the terms upon which the second vessel could be purchased or built.² In the end the Governor and Council of Safety decided to build a ship of 200 tons burden at Saybrook, and they employed Captain Uriah Hayden at six shillings a day to undertake the task.³ The ship was built during the spring and summer of 1776. An important event in the history of the "Oliver Cromwell," as the new ship was called, is thus chronicled in the Connecticut Gazette of August 23, 1776, published at New London: "Last Lord's Day, the new Ship of War belonging to the State of Connecticut, built at Say-Brook, and commanded by William Coit, Esq., came out of the River

---

1. Colonial Records of Connecticut, XV, 200-02.
2. Ibid., 223-24.
3. Ibid., 229, 232.

and arrived here Tuesday: she is the largest Vessel that has ever come over Say Brook Bar, and was piloted by Capt. James Harris."[1]

Before building the row-galleys the Governor and Council of Safety sent one builder to Philadelphia and another to Providence in order to take advantage of the experiences of Pennsylvania and Rhode Island in constructing this sort of craft. Of the four galleys ordered in December, 1775, but three were built, the "Whiting" at New Haven, the "Shark" at Norwich, and the "Crane" at East Haddam. They were rigged as schooners; and by July, 1776, their construction was completed and they were officered and manned.

The General Assembly permitted the Governor and Council of Safety a free hand in their control of naval affairs. They were given full power and authority to order, direct, furnish, and supply the navy, during the recess of the General Assembly. It does not appear, however, that the sessions of the General Assembly caused much change in the management of the naval affairs. It was not in session longer than a few weeks or a few days at a time. In October, 1776, the General Assembly directed the Governor and Council of Safety to execute and continue all naval business which they had begun, the sessions of the Assembly notwith-

1. Connecticut Gazette, August 23, 1776

standing.[1] Matters, which in some states were determined by legislation, such as the establishing of naval rules and regulations, the shares of prizes, and the naval pay, were in Connecticut for the most part left to administrative orders. In such work the Governor and Council of Safety often followed Continental models. In July, 1776, they ordered Richard Law, a member of the Council of Safety, to "compile a Code of Laws for the Naval Service of this Colony, as much in conformity to the laws of the naval service of the United Colonies as may consist with the service of this colony."[2]

The Governor and Council of Safety transacted the naval business, as has already been seen, by means of committees of the Council of Safety, naval agents, and mixed committees composed of members of the Council of Safety and men from the outside. The sending of prizes captured by Connecticut ships of war into the ports of Massachusetts, and the refitting of the state's vessels in Boston, necessitated the employment of a naval agent in Massachusetts. In April, 1777, Samuel Elliot of Boston was acting for the Governor and Council of Safety in this capacity. In October, 1777, the General Assembly authorized the appointment

---

1. Records of the State of Connecticut, I, 11.
2. Colonial Records of Connecticut, XV, 492

of a naval agent for Massachusetts, and on the 22nd of this month the Governor and Council of Safety appointed Elliot agent in all marine affairs to be transacted by Connecticut in Massachusetts.[1]

During the Revolution the chief seaport of Connecticut was New London, then one of the largest and most important towns in New England. The most complete naval news of the time is to be found in the Connecticut Gazette published at New London, and not in the Hartford Courant, or in the New Haven paper, the Connecticut Journal. New London was the naval station of the Connecticut fleet, the port where it was refitted and repaired. One of the most wealthy, influential, and public-spirited merchants of New London was Nathaniel Shaw, jr. He was an ardent patriot and was on intimate terms with Washington and other Revolutionary leaders.[2] The Govern-

---

1. Records of State of Connecticut, I, 212, 214, 418, 452. This is either Samuel Elliot, a Boston merchant, or Samuel Eliot, a most distinguished Boston merchant, a benefactor of Harvard college, and grandfather of the present President Eliot.—See New England Historical and Genealogical Register, XXIII (1869), 338-39. I find the agent's name spelled Elliot, Eliott, and Eliot.

2. Better evidence of the social standing of the Shaw family in New London may not be needed than that afforded by the statistics contained in the following newspaper clipping: "A great wedding dance took place

or and Council of Safety naturally turned to Shaw when naval duties were to be performed in New London. We have already seen that Shaw was present at a meeting of the Council of Safety in July, 1775, and was consulted on the initial naval project of the colony. From 1775 to 1779 the Governor and Council of Safety availed themselves of his services in fitting out their naval vessels. In July, 1776, they appointed him "Agent for the Colony, for the purpose of naval supplies and for taking care of such sick seamen as may be sent on shore to his care."[1] In October, 1778, the General Assembly appointed Shaw Marine Agent for Connecticut and authorized him to equip the state vessels, to direct their cruises, and to receive and sell their prizes, in all, taking the advice of the Governor and Council of Safety from time to time.[2]

The Governor and Council of Safety showed an enterprising willingness to experiment in naval warfare, when in February, 1776, they permitted David Bushnell to

---

at New London at the house of Nathaniel Shaw, Esq., June 12, 1769, the day after the marriage of his son Daniel Shaw and Grace Coit; 92 gentlemen and ladies attended, and danced 92 jigs, 52 contra-dances, 45 minuets, and 17 horn-pipes, and retired 45 minutes past midnight."—F. M. Caulkins, History of Norwich, Connecticut, 332.

1. Colonial Records of Connecticut, XV, 474.
2. Records of State of Connecticut, II, 136.

explain to them his machine for blowing up ships, and voted him £60 to complete his invention.[1] Bushnell's "American Turtle," as his contrivance was called, anticipated modern inventions in submarine warfare. It consisted of a tortoise-shaped diving boat which could be propelled under water. It contained a supply of air sufficient to last the operator a half-hour, and was guided by means of a compass made visible by phosphorus. Upon reaching the doomed vessel a screw was driven into it by the operator. A magazine of powder was attached by a string to the screw. The casting of the magazine from the diving-boat set going a certain clock-work which gave the operator time to get beyond the reach of danger before it ignited the powder. In 1777 a trial of the "Turtle" against the British ship "Eagle," 84, in New York Harbor was unsuccessful. The operator succeeded in getting under the "Eagle," but was unable to drive the screw into her bottom.

Connecticut did not establish state privateering. In May, 1776, the General Assembly authorized the Governor to fill out the blank privateering commissions which the President of Congress should send from time

---

[1]. Colonial Records of Connecticut, XV, 233-36. I have followed the familiar accounts of this invention. Washington gave Jefferson an account of Bushnell's invention in September, 1785.—Ford, Writings of Washington, X, 504-06.

to time, and to deliver them to such persons as should execute the bond prescribed by Congress.[1] A list of Connecticut privateers in which some vessels are counted two or more times has been made out. The totals of this list give 202 vessels, 1,609 guns, and 7,754 men.[2] In order to enlist her quota of troops for the Continental army, Connecticut in May, 1780, placed an embargo upon privateers.[3] In May, 1776, the General Assembly, in pursuance of the recommendations of the Continental Congress relative to the establishment of admiralty courts by each state, vested the county courts of Connecticut with the power to ''try, judge, and determine, by jury or otherwise, as in other cases, concerning all captures that have or shall be taken and brought into said respective counties.'' The courts were to follow the rules of the civil law, the law of nations, and the resolutions of Congress. Appeals were allowed to the Continental Congress agreeable to its directions and resolves. Connecticut was more liberal in granting appeals to Congress than Massachusetts, which state,

---

1. Colonial Records of Connecticut, XV, 318-19.
2. Records and Papers of New London County Historical Society, I, pt. 4, p. 32.
3. State Archives, Acts of Connecticut, May, 1780. The laying of embargoes on privateers for short periods in order to obtain men for different purposes was common during the Revolution.

it will be recalled, permitted such appeals only in cases of captures made by the vessels of the Continental navy.[1]

The reader may recollect that on August 26, 1776, the Continental Congress recommended that each state should grant certain pensions to its citizens who should receive serious disabilities in the Continental naval service. In May, 1777, the Connecticut General Assembly granted such pensions; and in imitation of the resolutions of Congress it granted half-pay to all officers, seamen, and marines in the Connecticut navy, who were wounded in action so as to be disabled from earning a livelihood; and a fraction of half-pay for lesser disabilities.[2]

In October, 1777, the House of Representatives passed a bill providing an elaborate list of rules and regulations relating to naval discipline, naval courts-martial, pay of officers and seamen, and the sharing of prizes. The bill, however, was rejected by the Council.[3] In April, 1779, when too late to be of much service, the General Assembly passed a statute creating a naval establishment, which was modelled on that of Congress. Two scales of wages were established, one for vessels under twenty guns, and the other

1. Colonial Records of Connecticut, XV, 280-81.
2. See Chapter IV, page 129; Records of State of Connecticut, I, 246-49.
3. Connecticut Revolutionary Archives, VIII, 1777-1778.

for vessels of twenty guns or upwards. Captains of the two classes received a monthly wage, respectively, of $48 and $60; lieutenants and masters, $24 and $30; and boatswains, $13 and $15. The wages for seamen and marines did not vary, being $8 for seamen, and $6.67 for marines. The sharing of prizes among officers and seamen varied for the two classes. In general, the same offices were established as in the Continental navy; there were, however, not so many of them. Following the regulations of Congress, the General Assembly gave the officers, seamen, and marines the whole of captured ships of war and privateers, and one-half of all other vessels.[1]

Besides the vessels already mentioned, there were, in the Connecticut navy, for a short time in 1777, the schooner "Mifflin" and the sloop "Schuyler;" and for an equally brief period in 1779, the sloop "Guilford."[2]

---

1. Records of State of Connecticut, II, 230-33.
2. The vessels of the Connecticut navy with the approximate periods of their service were as follows: Brigantine "Minerva," 1775; schooner "Spy," 1775-1778; ship "Defence," 1776-1779; ship "Oliver Cromwell," 1776-1779; galleys "Crane" and "Whiting," 1776; galley "Shark," 1776-1777; schooner "Mifflin," 1777; sloop "Schuyler," 1777; and sloop "Guilford," 1779. The galley "New Defence," belonging to Branford, received arms, ammunition, and stores from the state. The sloop "Dolphin," a prize of the "Spy," was pur-

By far the most important vessels in the navy were the "Oliver Cromwell", 18, "Defence", 14, and "Spy", 6. The principal cruising ground of the Connecticut vessels was in and near Long Island Sound. This region was fairly alive with British craft of all sorts. Long Island was a nest of Tories, and New York was of course headquarters for the British in America. Connecticut, being convenient to both places, found much service for her navy in protecting her coasts and in preventing illicit trade with the enemy.

The cruises of the "Oliver Cromwell," "Defence," and "Spy" were by no means confined to the waters near home. Several times they visited the ports of Massachusetts. In the summer of 1777 the "Oliver Cromwell" cruised to the northward of the Azores, in the path of the homeward bound West Indiamen, where she captured and sent into Massachusetts the brigantine "Honor" and the "Weymouth" packet. In the spring of 1777 the "Defence" and a privateer met with success to the windward of the Lesser Antilles in capturing British

---

chased in the fall of 1777, and sent to Philadelphia for flour. The following captains were the chief officers of the navy: Giles Hall, Robert Niles, William Coit, Seth Harding, Timothy Parker, and Samuel Smedley. Coit had commanded the "Harrison" in Washington's fleet, and Harding was given a commission in the Continental navy.

vessels bound for the West Indies. In the following spring the "Oliver Cromwell" and the "Defence" were cruising in the same region, where they captured the letter of marque "Admiral Keppel," eighteen six-pounders, the most valuable prize taken by the Connecticut navy. The "Admiral Keppel" and her cargo sold in Boston for £22,321. In June and July, 1778, the "Oliver Cromwell" and the "Defence" refitted in Charleston, South Carolina. Towards the end of July the "Oliver Cromwell" sailed for Nantes with a load of indigo, which she expected to exchange for clothing. Encountering a storm, this vessel was dismasted, and forced to return to Connecticut. Some thirty prizes, most of which reached safe ports, were captured during the Revolution by the Connecticut navy.[1]

Upon the urgent and repeated solicitations of Washington, the three Connecticut galleys were sent by the Governor and Council of Safety in the summer of 1776 to New York to assist in the campaign on the Hudson. The "Crane" and "Whiting," after giving a good account of themselves in an attack on two British vessels near Tarrytown, were lost to the enemy in the fall of 1776. The "Shark" probably met a similar

---

1. Revolutionary Files of Connecticut Gazette, Hartford Courant, and Connecticut Journal.

fate.[1] The "Spy," Captain Robert Niles, was one of several vessels which were selected to carry to France the news of the ratification by Congress of the French treaties of February, 1778. Captain Niles had the honor of reaching France first with his important message and packet. On his return voyage Niles and his vessel were captured. In March, 1779, the "Defence" struck on a reef near Waterford, Connecticut, and sank.[2] On June 5, after a severe fight to the southward of Sandy Hook, the "Oliver Cromwell" surrendered to a superior force.[3] About July 1 the "Guilford," 8, which had been recently added to the navy, was taken by the enemy.[4] With the capture of this vessel, the navy of Connecticut came to an end.

The warfare of "armed boats" participated in by Connecticut deserves notice. During the Revolution much smuggling was carried on between men in Connecticut and the British and Tories on Long Island and at New York. The feeding of the British army at New York, the supplying

---

1. Colonial Records of Connecticut, XV, 481, 488; Records of State of Connecticut, I, 85, 201; Hartford Courant, August 12, 1776; Connecticut in Revolution, 593-94.
2. Records of State of Connecticut, II, 372; Wharton, Diplomatic Correspondence, II, 642, 650. Hartford Courant, March 16, 1779.
3. Hartford Courant, June 15, 1779.
4. Records of State of Connecticut, II, 360.

of the Tories on Long Island, and the demand for manufactured articles in Connecticut, naturally made good markets. Political law was in rivalry with economic law, and proved, in large part, powerless. In 1778, 1779, and 1780, the Connecticut General Assembly passed a number of stringent acts forbidding illicit commerce with the enemy. Many patriot refugees had fled to Connecticut from Long Island. Some of these men would obtain a license to return to their former homes for their property, and under its cover would engage in smuggling. To prevent this abuse, the General Assembly in April, 1779, recalled the power to issue licenses, which it had previously vested in the selectmen of towns.[1]

Since the trade had assumed alarming proportions, the General Assembly, in May, 1780, authorized the Governor and Council of Safety to commission not more than twelve armed boats to suppress the trade.[2] In October, Colonel William Ledyard, who was in command of the forts at New London and Groton, was ordered to provide three more whaleboats, besides the two which he already had obtained, to be used in the Sound against the smugglers; and the Commandant of the French navy at Newport was asked to send two vessels to aid in the work.[3] These

---
1. Records of State of Connecticut, II, 222.
2. State Archives, Acts of Connecticut, May, 1780.
3. Ibid., October, 1780.

efforts of the state were in large part unavailing. Some of the boats commissioned to stop the trade became participants in it. "On consideration of the Many Evils committed by the armed Boats in this State commissioned to cruise on their own acct. for the pretended purpose of making captures on the enemy and preventing illicit Trade and Traders," the General Assembly on January 23, 1781, revoked all the commissions which it had given to the armed boats.

A more successful attempt to stamp out the abuse was that made by Norwich, in January, 1782. Certain associators agreed to hold no social or commercial intercourse with those persons detected in evading the laws. They provided boats which kept watch at suspected places; smuggled goods, wherever found, were seized and sold, and the proceeds were devoted to charitable purposes.[1]

---
1. History of Norwich, F. M, Caulkins, 398.

CHAPTER XIII

THE NAVY OF PENNSYLVANIA

The two objects of Pennsylvania's naval enterprises were the defence of Philadelphia and the protection in Delaware river and bay of the outward and inward bound trade of the state. These two needs determined the form and size of her armed vessels and the character of their operations. Pennsylvania therefore adapted her fleet to shallow waters. Only in a few instances did her armed vessels pass beyond the Capes of the Delaware into the Atlantic.

On July 5, 1775, the Pennsylvania Committee of Safety, the first Revolutionary executive of this state, visited "Red Bank," situated a few miles below Philadelphia, near the mouth of the Schuylkill, for the purpose of deciding on the character of the defences which were to be made at this point on the river. On the 6th, having returned to Philadelphia, the Committee reported the results of its inspection; whereupon it came to its first naval resolution, that Robert White and Owen Biddle be a committee for the construction of boats and machines for the defence of the River.[1] On July 8 it ordered John Wharton to immediately build a "Boat or Calevat," 47 or 50 feet keel, 13 feet broad, and 4 1-2 feet deep. By October, thirteen such galleys or armed boats had been built, at a cost of about £550 each. They were armed chiefly with 18-pounders.[2] During the late summer and the fall of 1775 the Committee of Safety attended to the numerous details of officering, manning, arming, and provisioning these galleys. It chose a captain and lieutenant for each of them; and on October 23 it appointed Thomas Read commodore of the fleet. It organized a naval staff consisting of a muster master, a pay master, a surgeon, an assistant surgeon, a ship's husband, and a victualer. The distinguished scholar, Dr. Benjamin Rush, was made surgeon. The Committee of Safety prepared a form of commission for officers, a list of rules and regulations, general instructions for the captains, and general instructions for the commodore.[3]

The rules and regulations of the Pennsyl-

1. Colonial Records of Pennsylvania, X, Minutes of Committee of Safety, July 4, 6, 8, 1775.
2. Pennsylvania Archives 2nd, I, 246; Wallace's William Bradford, 203.
3. Colonial Records of Pennsylvania, X, Minutes of Committee of Safety, August 26, September 1, October 2, 12, 16, 23, November 6, 1775. See also the Minutes of the Committee of Safety for each day of this period.

vania navy were concerned with little else than the establishing of a penal code. All penal offenses were to be tried by a court-martial, which, in capital cases, was to consist of fifteen naval officers; and in all other cases, of five officers, unless so many could not be assembled, when it might consist of three. A majority of the court was sufficient to convict, except in capital cases, where two-thirds were necessary. In returning a verdict, the officers of lowest rank voted first. Except in cases of mutiny, or of cowardice in time of action, all sentences of death needed the approval of the General Assembly, or, in its recess, of the Committee of Safety. Besides the death penalty, a court-martial could inflict no punishment other than "degrading, cashiering, drumming out of the fleet, whipping, not exceeding thirty-nine lashes, fine, not exceeding two months' pay, and imprisonment, not exceeding one month." All fines were to go to the relief of those maimed and disabled in the service, or to the widows and families of such as should be killed. These rules, apparently, were not influenced by those of the Continental navy prepared by John Adams.[1]

On November 7, 1775, the Committee of Safety decided to build a ship for the service on the Delaware, which would mount

---

1. Colonial Records of Pennsylvania, X, Minutes of Committee of Safety, August 29, 1775.

twenty 18-pounders; and it appointed six of its members, among whom were Robert Morris and John Nixon, a committee to build and arm the vessel. This committee estimated that £9,000 would be necessary to construct the ship. Later, owing to the unfitness of the season for shipbuilding, it was authorized to purchase a vessel.[1] By April, 1776, it had obtained and equipped the ship "Montgomery," and Thomas Read had been given command of it. A number of small and unimportant craft were gradually added to the navy. On December 28, 1775, Captain John Hazelwood was appointed commander of ten fire-rafts. These rafts were thirty-five feet long and thirteen feet wide, were loaded with oil barrels, rosin casks, turpentine, brimstone, and various other inflammables, and were designed to float down stream and set fire to the enemy's ships through direct contact.[2] An inventory of the navy, dated August 1, 1776, shows the following vessels and men: the ship "Montgomery," 138 men; the floating battery "Arnold," 82 men; thirteen galleys, 35 men each; six guard boats, 12 men each; six small vessels, including fire-ships, a total of 27 men. The total number of officers,

[1]. Colonial Records of Pennsylvania, X, Minutes of Committee of Safety, November 7, November 10, 1775.
[2]. Ibid., December 28, 1775; Pennsylvania Archives, 2nd, I, 248, note.

seamen, and marines was 768; the Pennsylvania land forces at this time amounted to 1,365 men.[1] In August, 1776, the schooner "Delaware" and the brig "Convention" were added; and in the fall the "Putnam" floating battery.

I have found no mention of the uniform of the officers of the Pennsylvania navy. The uniform of the Pennsylvania marines was "a brown coat faced with green, letters 1. P. B. on the buttons, and a cocked hat." In October, 1776, the flag for the naval vessels had not been provided. The following memorandum, taken from the minutes of the Pennsylvania Navy Board of May 29, 1777, shows that flags had then been procured: "An Order on William Webb to Elizabeth Ross, for fourteen pounds twelve shillings and two pence, for Making Ships' Colours etc."[2]

The Committee of Safety was assisted and directed in its naval work by committees of its own members, of which the principal ones are as follows: "ship committee,"

---

1. Pennsylvania Archives, 1st, V, 3-5. The names of the thirteen galleys were as follows: "Bull Dog," "Burke," "Camden," "Chatham," "Congress," "Dickinson," "Experiment," "Effingham," "Franklin," "Hancock," "Ranger," "Warren," and "Washington." The "Delaware" and "Convention" were at times referred to as galleys.

2. Pennsylvania Archives, 1st, V, 46; 2nd, I, Minutes of Pennsylvania Navy Board, May 29, 1777; 2nd, I, 251.

"armed boat committee," "committee for fitting out two of the armed boats," "committee for building two galleys for the Bay Service," and "committee for fitting out four guard boats to cruise at Cape May." The Committee of Safety was composed of twenty-five members, any seven of whom formed a quorum. Benjamin Franklin was its first president. Robert Morris was for a time its vice-president. In the absence of Franklin, Morris or John Nixon often presided. On July 23, 1776, the Pennsylvania Convention appointed a Council of Safety to succeed the Committee of Safety, a succession which involved merely a change of personnel and of name. From July 24, 1776, until March 4, 1777, when the Supreme Executive Council, the executive under the first state constitution, assumed control, the administration of the Pennsylvania navy was vested in the Council of Safety.

Much difficulty was experienced by the several Pennsylvania executives in finding suitable commodores for the fleet. The office on October 23, 1775, first fell to Thomas Read. On January 13, 1776, Thomas Caldwell was made commodore; and on March 6, 1776, Read was formally placed second in command. Failing in health, Caldwell, on May 25, resigned, and on June 15 the Committee of Safety appointed Samuel Davidson. This succession met with serious and continued opposition on the part of the officers of the navy. They declared that the appointment of Davidson violated the rule of promotion according to seniority in service; and they made vigorous remonstrances, which received countenance and support from men of influence in Philadelphia. So serious was the clamor and insubordination, that the Committee of Safety was compelled to yield to the demands of a resolution of the Provincial Conference of Committees, and remove Davidson from the command of all the vessels except the ship "Montgomery" and the "Arnold" floating battery. The Committee, however, in an "Address to the Inhabitants of Pennsylvania," upheld the propriety and justice of their appointment; and it declared that by the support which the dissatisfied officers had received "mutiny was justified and abetted and disobedience triumphed over Authority."[1]

When the Council of Safety assumed control of the navy on July 24, 1776, it found the spirit of dissatisfaction and insubordination so strong among the naval officers that it removed Davidson from the navy; at the same time, however, it declared that the charges made against him

---

1. Colonial Records of Pennsylvania, X, Minutes of Committee of Safety, July 2, 1776; Proceedings of Provincial Conference of Committees of Pennsylvania, June 23, June 24, 1776.

were frivolous.[1] On September 2, 1776, the Council of Safety gave Samuel Mifflin an opportunity to decline the office of commodore. Thomas Seymour was named for the place on September 26, 1776. Early in 1777 Captain John Hazelwood, "Commander-in-Chief of the Fire Vessels, Boats and Rafts belonging to the State," objected to being subject to the orders of Commodore Seymour, who was an old man, infirm, and incapacitated for his position. On September 6, 1777, when Philadelphia was threatened by the British, Seymour was discharged, and Hazelwood was appointed in his place.[2] Hazelwood was the sixth commodore within less than two years.

The Committee of Safety and the Council of Safety passed a number of resolutions fixing the naval pay. For a time the officers on board the ship "Montgomery" and the two floating batteries were generally paid larger wages than those on board the galleys. On February 22, 1777, the Council of Safety adopted a new pay-table, which gave the same salary to officers of the same rank, on whatever vessel employed. The monthly wages of the leading officers were as follows: commodore, $75; captains, $48; first lieu-

---

1. Colonial Records of Pennsylvania, X, Minutes of Council of Safety, August 22, August 27, 1776.
2. Ibid., XI, Minutes of Supreme Executive Council, September 6, 1777.

tenants, $30; second lieutenants, $20; and surgeons, $48. Seamen were paid $12 a month. A bounty of $12 was now given to recruits.[1] On June 25, 1777, the salary of the commodore was raised to $125 a month.[2] On February 4, 1776, the Committee of Safety gave captors two-thirds of the proceeds of the prizes taken on the Delaware river, and reserved the remaining one-third for the maintenance of disabled sailors and the widows and families of those who should be killed.[3]

Recognizing the navy's need of a permanent body of administrators, the Council of Safety on February 13, 1777, appointed a Navy Board of six members who were authorized to take under their care all the vessels of the navy. On February 19 four additional members were added.[4] On March 13, 1777, the Supreme Executive Council, which on March 4 had become the executive of the state, reconstituted the naval board. It was now to consist of eleven members, any three of whom formed a quorum. It was given "full power and authority to do and perform all Matters and

---
1. Colonial Records of Pennsylvania, XI, Minutes of Council of Safety, February 22, 1777.
2. Ibid., Minutes of Supreme Executive Council, June 25, 1777.
3. Ibid., X, Minutes of Committee of Safety, February 4, 1776.
4. Ibid., XI, Minutes of Council of Safety, February 13, February 19, 1777.

things Relating to the Navy of this State, subject nevertheless to the directions and examinations of the Council, from time to time, as we may judge expedient, and saving to ourselves always the power of appointing officers." William Bradford and Joseph Blewer, who each served for a time as chairman of the Board, were its most useful members. On the same day, March 13, the Supreme Executive Council constituted a Board of War.[1]

The work of the Navy Board consisted of a great variety of details relating to provisioning, arming, equipping, officering, and manning the numerous craft of the navy. Soon after entering into office it reported to the Council that it found the armed boats needing repairs and alterations, and that owing to the better wages paid to the seamen on board privateers there was a shameful deficiency in the armed boats' complement of men. The Board recommended the laying of an embargo to prevent the sailing of private ships until the navy should be re-

---

1. Colonial Records of Pennsylvania, XI, Minutes of Supreme Executive Council, March 13, 1777. The members of the Navy Board as constituted by the Supreme Executive Council were as follows: Andrew Caldwell, Joseph Blewer, Joseph Marsh, Emanuel Eyre, Robert Ritchie, Paul Cox, Samuel Massey, William Bradford, Thomas Fitzsimmons, Samuel Morris, jr., and Thomas Barclay.

cruited. It found that additional officers were needed.[1] The Council immediately ordered the Board to appoint the requisite number of warrant officers and to recommend proper commissioned officers.

During 1777 the naval business of Pennsylvania was large and complicated. A list of stores issued to the navy for one month during the year contains the names of fifty-one vessels. Many of these are minor and unimportant craft, such as half-galleys, fire-ships, and accommodation sloops. A return of the Naval Department on February 1, 1777, shows 71 commissioned officers, 2 staff officers, 123 non-commissioned officers, and 513 privates; total officers and men in the navy, 709. Many men who enlisted in the navy had little or no experience at sea. The amount of the pay rolls for May, 1777, was £6,325.[2]

The salient event in the history of the Pennsylvania navy was the campaign on the Delaware river which followed the occupation of Philadelphia by the British in September, 1777. Before this time the navy had rendered miscellaneous services on the Delaware river and bay, which had been useful though not at all brilliant. Now

---

1. Captains Nicholas Biddle, Thomas Read and Charles Alexander, and Lieutenant James Josiah resigned from the Pennsylvania navy to enter the Continental navy.
2. Pennsylvania Archives, 2nd, I, 416-24.

and then some of the vessels were ordered down the river to protect incoming and outgoing merchantmen, or to drive back the venturesome craft of the enemy. On May 8, 1776, the galleys had a spirited engagement with the "Roebuck," 44, and the "Liverpool," 28, in the Delaware river near the mouth of Christiana Creek. Little injury was done on either side. The British vessels returned to the Delaware Capes, and the Americans returned to their station at Mud Island, which was generally the headquarters for the state fleet.

The reader is familiar with the military movements of Howe during the summer and fall of 1777; his irretrievable blunder in sailing from New York for Philadelphia, instead of coöperating with Burgoyne in the campaign on the Hudson; his landing with an army at the head of Elk in Maryland late in August; his march to Philadelphia; and after fighting the battle of Brandywine, his entry into that city late in September. Upon occupying Philadelphia the British were forced to open a communication with the sea. This was for the time being prevented by the American defences at Mud Island and Red Bank just below the mouth of the Schuylkill. Here were situated Forts Mercer and Mifflin; and here were stationed the vessels of the Pennsylvania and Continental navy under the command of Commodore Hazelwood. During October and November, 1777, the Pennsylvania navy did its best fighting and rendered its most valuable services. At this time the Pennsylvania Navy Board made its headquarters near the fleet on board the sloop "Speedwell."

On October 22 and 23, when the British fleet below the American defences on the Delaware attempted to pass them, Commodore Hazelwood with two floating batteries and twelve galleys forced them to retire, and succeeded in burning two of their vessels, the "Augusta," 64, and "Merlin," 18, which ran aground. Congress voted Hazelwood an elegant sword in recognition of his merit. On the fall of Forts Mifflin and Mercer the American fleet was left without support. At a council of war held on board the sloop "Speedwell" on November 19, it was decided to pass Philadelphia with the fleet in the night and gain a point of safety to the northward of the city. Thirteen galleys, twelve armed boats, the brig "Convention," and a number of minor craft passed the city without receiving a shot. Before the ship "Montgomery," schooner "Delaware," floating batteries "Arnold" and "Putnam," and several Continental vessels could get under sail, the wind died away; and thus becalmed it was found necessary to set fire to them in order to prevent their capture.[1]

---

1. Wallace's William Bradford, 252-53, 366-67; Pennsylvania Archives, 1st, VI, 21, 47-50.

On October 11, 1777, Commodore Hazelwood reported a capture of fifty-eight prisoners. About seventy men were killed or wounded in the different actions of the navy in the fall of 1777. Hazelwood wrote in October, 1777, that he had lost two hundred and fifty men through desertion owing to their cowardice and disaffection; and in February, 1778, that a great many men had run away since he had been in winter quarters.[1]

Several cases of the desertion of commissioned officers which took place during the campaign on the Delaware, were tried by courts-martial during the summer of 1778. First Lieutenant Samuel Lyon of the "Dickinson" galley was charged with deserting his vessel and going over to the enemy with seven men. Lyon pleaded guilty to the charge, and a court of fifteen fellow officers sentenced him "to suffer Death by being Shott." On September 1 Lyon, together with Samuel Ford, a lieutenant lately attached to the "Effingham" galley who also had been convicted of desertion, were executed on one of the guard boats in the Delaware. The first conviction for a capital crime in the Pennsylvania navy is said to have been made in the case of the boatswain of the "Montgomery," who was sentenced to death for desertion on June 25, 1778. On the trial

---

1. Pennsylvania Archives, 1st, V, 663, 721; VI, 235; VII, 165.

of John Lawrence for desertion, a gunner on board the "Dickinson" galley, the accused acknowledged that he "took the Oath of Allegiance to the King of Great Britain, and received three and a half Guineas for his share of the Boat and Arms," which he assisted in carrying to the enemy. The court sentenced him to "suffer Death by being hung with a Rope around his Neck till he is Dead, Dead, Dead." Lawrence together with the lieutenant of the galley "Ranger" were reprieved on September 1, 1778.[1] These desertions from the Pennsylvania navy are but one instance of many which prove that it was without *esprit de corps*, and that its officers and men were often raw, undisciplined, and insubordinate. Used to a free and easy life, they did not take kindly to the routine and discipline of the naval service.

During the winter of 1777–1778 when the British were in Philadelphia, the navy and Navy Board were some miles up the Delaware. A few members of the Board continued to hold its sessions at Bordentown, Trenton, or other convenient points. The navy was disorganized at this time, and the work of the Board was naturally dull and disheartening. In January, 1778, William Bradford, its chairman, wrote from Trenton to President Wharton of the Supreme Executive Council: "I am left here alone, none

---

1. Pennsylvania Archives, 2nd, I, 425-31.

of the Board being with me. I am also tired of being here, had much rather be in action with the Militia."[1]

In April, 1778, the Navy Board, acting reluctantly on Washington's advice who feared that the British would make a raid and capture the fleet, dismantled and sank all or nearly all of the state craft in the Delaware river.[2] On May 8 the British made their expected foray on the shipping to the northward of Philadelphia, and destroyed some forty-five vessels, among which were the two Continental frigates, "Effingham" and "Washington," and probably a few of the minor craft belonging to the Pennsylvania navy.[3]

As soon as the British received intelligence of the sailing of a French fleet under D'Estaing for America, they prepared to evacuate Philadelphia. In anticipation of this event Hazelwood was in June raising and refitting his fleet, and wishing that he had it in his "power to give the enemy a scouring before they got out of the river." On July 19 he reported his vessels afloat and ready for use. Already the Supreme Executive Council had ordered the navy to be put into commission, and the brig "Convention" to make a cruise down the Bay.

The Pennsylvania navy had cost the state

---
1. Pennsylvania Archives, 1st, VI, 204.
2. Ibid., 332-33.
3. Almon's Remembrancer, 1778, 148-50.

at the rate of £100,000 a year.[1] It had been serviceable in defending the Delaware, but it had in the end failed to hold it. Always hampered by a lack of seamen, of naval supplies, and of an armed force comparable to that of the enemy, the Navy Board found the greatest difficulty in enforcing the orders of the Council. It was naturally blamed for a part of the inactivity and the misfortunes of the fleet. Since the British had abandoned Philadelphia, and a strong French fleet was in American waters, the need for a naval defence of the Delaware seemed more remote than it did in the first years of the Revolution. These considerations moved the Supreme Executive Council on August 14, 1778, to recommend to the General Assembly the dismissal of the Navy Board, and all the officers and men of the navy, except those that were necessary to man two or three galleys, two or three guard boats, and the brig "Convention." The General Assembly at once agreed to the recommendation. Finally, on Friday, December 11, the following vessels were sold at the "Coffee House" in Philadelphia: "Ten galleys, Nine armed Boats, the Brig 'Convention,' the sloops 'Speedwell,' 'Sally,' 'Industry,' and 'Black Duck;' and the schooner 'Lydia.'"[2]

1. Scharf and Westcott, History of Philadelphia, I, 300.
2. Colonial Records of Pennsylvania, XI,

In March, 1779, there remained in the navy six small craft, namely, the galleys "Franklin," "Hancock," and "Chatham," and the armed boats, "Lion," "Fame" and "Viper;" and there were still in commission five captains, six lieutenants, and one hundred and eighteen men.[1] This little fleet was quite insufficient to protect the commerce of the state. In March, 1779, the Supreme Executive Council, in response to a petition from the merchants of Philadelphia praying for the protection of their trade, purchased the ship "General Greene," at a cost of £53,000; and placed it in charge of two agents, who were to fit it for sea, and receive and dispose of its prizes. Part of the money which was used in fitting the "General Greene," 14, was raised by private subscription. During the summer and fall of 1779 the new ship, under the command of Captain James Montgomery, cruised along the Atlantic coast between Sandy Hook and the Virginia Capes either alone, in company with the Continental frigates, "Boston," "Deane," and Confederacy," or in company with the well-known Philadelphia privateer,

---

Minutes of Supreme Executive Council, August 14, August 16, December 9, 1778. The capture of the sloop "Active" by the "Convention" in the fall of 1778, gave rise to the most celebrated prize case of the Revolution. —Jameson, Essays in Constitutional History of United States, 17-21.

1. Pennsylvania Archives, 2nd, I, 255.

"Holker." The "General Greene" was quite fortunate, as she sent into Philadelphia six prizes. In the spring before a full complement of men could be enlisted, President Reed of the Supreme Executive Council was compelled to lay an embargo on privateers. Her crew were a mutinous rabble. In June Captain Montgomery wrote that he had arrived at New Castle with a "Great number of Prisoners on board and a Great Part of my own Crew Such Villons that they would be glad of an opportunity to take the Ship from me. Som of the Ringleaders I have sent up in Irons." On October 27 the Council ordered the "General Greene" to be sold, as this was more economical than laying her up for the winter. Her sale, much below her real value, aroused suspicions of collusion and corruption.[1]

Naval legislation in Pennsylvania was not extensive. In 1775, 1776, and 1777 almost all naval rules and provisions were established by executive decrees. Before the middle of January, 1776, the Committee of Safety had established courts for the trying of prize cases.[2] It permitted appeals from the state prize courts to Congress. On September 9, 1778, however, the General As-

1. Pennsylvania Archives, 1st, VII, 320, 476; Colonial Records of Pennsylvania, XI, 724, 750; XII, 150; Scharf and Westcott, History of Philadelphia, I, 403.
2. J. F. Jameson, Essays in Constitutional History of United States, 9.

sembly established a Court of Admiralty. A law passed in 1780 provided that a judge of admiralty should be appointed and commissioned for seven years by the Supreme Executive Council.[1] On September 17, 1777, an act was passed for the relief of officers, seamen and marines, who, being in the service of the United States and residents of Pennsylvania, should be disabled from earning a livelihood. In all probability this was passed in accordance with the recommendations of the Continental Congress of August 26, 1776. On March 1, 1780, the General Assembly granted officers, seamen, and marines in the Pennsylvania navy, who were in actual service on March 13, 1779, and who should continue therein until the end of the war, half-pay for life.[2]

It is believed that Pennsylvania did not establish state privateering. Her executives in commissioning privateers in all probability followed the regulations of Congress. The Pennsylvania Archives contain a list of 448 privateering commissions issued for the years from 1776 to 1782. Most of the privateers were small vessels, mounting six to twelve cannon, and carrying twenty-five to fifty men. Out of the 448 commissions, only 14 commissions were for vessels mounting twenty or more guns. In 1779 Penn-

---
1. Laws of Pennsylvania, September 9, 1778, March 8, 1780.
2. Ibid., September 17, 1777; March 1, 1780.

sylvania issued commissions for one hundred different vessels.[1]

The spring of 1782 was marked by a renewal in naval enterprise similar to that in the spring of 1779. Armed ships, refugee boats, and picaroon privateers fitted out at New York, had been greatly distressing the shipping and trade of Philadelphia. Within eight months the British frigate "Medea" had taken nine Philadelphia privateers; the whale-boat "Trimmer" from New York had been very destructive to the shipping on the Delaware; and the British naval ship "General Monk," formerly the American privateer "Washington," was inflicting serious losses on Pennsylvania's commerce.[2] The merchants and traders of Philadelphia now appealed by petition to the General Assembly for protection. Accordingly, on April 9, that body appointed three commissioners to procure and equip a naval armament for the defence of Delaware river and bay. The commissioners were authorized to borrow £50,000, which was to be repaid from certain old tonnage and impost duties, and from a new impost on certain specified articles. The act also provided for a distribution of the proceeds of prizes. This act is significant in its being the first instance where the General Assembly authorized a naval increase and appointed a committee to take

---
1. Pennsylvania Archives, 2nd, I, 388-402.
2. Scharf and Westcott, History of Philadelphia, I, 421-22.

charge of naval vessels. It met with considerable disfavor. The Supreme Executive Council informed the General Assembly that it considered the appointment of commissioners and the conferring upon them of full administrative powers unconstitutional and an encroachment of the legislative on the administrative body.[1]

Anticipating the act of the legislature, the merchants of Philadelphia had fitted out the ship "Hyder Ally," 18, and had appointed Lieutenant Joshua Barney of the Continental navy to command her. Proceeding down the Bay, Barney on April 8 made his memorable capture of the "General Monk," 18, Captain Josias Rogers. Both the "Hyder Ally" and the "General Monk" were now taken into the service of the state. The "General Monk," which was renamed the "Washington," was in May, 1782, loaned to Robert Morris, the Continental Agent of Marine, who sent her on a commercial errand to the West Indies. On the return of the "Washington." Morris purchased her for the service of Congress. The "Hyder Ally" under different commanders cruised for the rest of the year with little success. In December the commissioners ob-

---

1. Laws of Pennsylvania, April 9, April 15, 1782; Mary Barney, Memoirs of Commodore Barney, 303-04. Pennsylvania Archives, 1st, IX, 531-32. The three Commissioners were John Patton, Francis Gurney, and William Allibone,.

tained permission from the Supreme Executive Council to sell her, and build a vessel of more suitable construction for the defence of the Delaware, for which purpose they were already equipping an armed schooner. When the "Hyder Ally" was offered for sale, the commissioners bid her in for the state, as the bidders refused to give her full value.[1]

The establishment of officers and seamen on board the "Hyder Ally" and the "Washington" was a new one. On February 13, 1781, the officers and seamen of the first establishment were all discharged, except Captain Boys and certain disabled seamen; and on December 20 Boys was dismissed, since the service in which he was engaged was at an end.[2] When peace was declared in the spring of 1783, a few men were probably in naval employ under the new establishment. That the state still owned a few small vessels is certain. On April 10, 1783, the Supreme Executive Council endorsed a letter from the commissioners saying "that as no doubt appears to remain that Hostilities are ceased, we conceive it our Duty to request your permission to dispose of the Armed vessels under our direction belonging to the State, in order to enable us to close our accounts with the Public."[3]

---

1. Colonial Records of Pennsylvania, XIII, Minutes of Supreme Executive Council, December 6, 1782.
2. Pennsylvania Archives, 2nd, I, 256.
3. Ibid., 1st, X, 26.

CHAPTER XIV

THE NAVY OF VIRGINIA

In July, 1775, Virginia began to raise and officer an army of more than one thousand men. By fall Lord Dunmore, the Provincial Governor of Virginia, who in June had retreated to His Majesty's ship "Fowey" at Yorktown, had collected a small flotilla, and had begun a series of desultory attacks upon the river banks of Virginia. On October 25 he was repulsed at Hampton; on December 9 he was beaten by the Virginia patriots at Great Ridge; and on January 1 he burned Norfolk. His movements excited so much alarm that the leading patriot families on the James, York, Rappahannock, and Potomac rivers retreated inland for safety. In order to prevent the depredations of Lord Dunmore, and to provide effectually for the general defence of the state, the Virginia Provincial Convention in December authorized the Committee of Safety of the state "to provide from time to time such and so many armed vessels as they may judge necessary for the protection of the several rivers in this colony, in the best manner the circumstances of the country will admit." The Committee of Safety was further directed to raise a sufficient number of officers, sailors, and marines; and settle their pay, which was not to exceed certain specified rates. The maximum wage of "the chief commander of the whole as commodore" was fixed at fifteen shillings a day.[1]

Between December, 1775, and July, 1776, the Committee of Safety procured and established a small navy. On April 1 it fixed the naval pay, generally at the maximum rates permitted. Captains in the navy were to receive a daily wage of 8s.; captains of marines, 6s.; midshipmen, 3s.; marines, 1s., 6d. The Committee resolved that two years ought to be a maximum period of service. It appointed a number of the most prominent officers in the Virginia navy, among whom were Captains James Barron, Richard Barron, Richard Taylor, Thomas Lilly, and Edward Travis. It fixed the relative rank between army and navy officers. It purchased the boats "Liberty" and "Patriot," the brigs "Liberty" and "Adventure," and the schooner "Adventure." It contracted for the construction of a number of galleys on the different rivers of the state.[2]

---

1. Hening, Statutes of Virginia, IX, 83.
2. Calendar of Virginia State Papers, VIII, 75-240, Journal of Committee of Safety of

George Mason and John Dalton were appointed a committee to build two row-galleys, and buy three cutters for the defence of the Potomac. In April, 1776, Mason wrote that the galleys were well under way, and that three small vessels had been purchased, of which the largest was a fine stout craft of about 110 tons burden, mounting fourteen 8's and 4's, carrying ninety-six men, and named the "American Congress." A company of marines for this vessel, he said, were being exercised in the use of the great guns.[1] The Committee of Safety chose a "Lieutenant of Marines in the Potomac river Department."

The Provincial Convention of Virginia, which met at Williamsburg on May 6, 1776, being convinced that the naval preparations would be conducted more expeditiously and successfully if proper persons were appointed to superintend and direct the same, chose a Board of Naval Commissioners, consisting of five persons.[2] The

---

Virginia, February 7 to July 5, 1776. Virginia had a class of vessels which she referred to as "armed boats." They were smart craft, and appear to have been schooner-rigged.

1. Miss Rowland's George Mason, I, 214, 218.
2. Hening, Statutes of Virginia, IX, 149-51. The Provincial Convention which met May 6, 1776, adopted a Constitution which provided for a Legislature of two houses, and an Executive consisting of a Governor and a Privy Council of eight members.

Board was authorized to appoint a clerk and assistants, and to elect from their membership a First Commissioner of the Navy— the title of a well-known officer in the English naval service. No member of the Board could sit in the legislature or hold a military office. Each Commissioner was to receive twenty shillings a day, when employed. On the depreciation of the currency this was doubled.[1] A majority of the Board constituted a quorum. Thomas Whiting served as First Commissioner of the Board throughout its existence.

In general, the business of the Navy Board was "to superintend and direct all matters and things to the navy relating." It had charge of the building, purchase, fitting, arming, provisioning, and repairing of all armed vessels and transports. It had charge of the shipyards and the public ropewalk. In case of vacancies in the navy or marines it recommended officers to the Governor and Council. It could suspend an officer for neglect of duty or for misbehavior. It was to keep itself informed on the state of the navy through reports from the naval officers. It was authorized to draw warrants on the treasury for money expended in the naval department, and to audit the naval accounts.

The Navy Board had charge of naval af-

1. Hening, Statutes of Virginia, IX, 521-22' October session of General Assembly in 1778.

fairs in Virginia for three years, from the summer of 1776 until the summer of 1779. During 1776 and 1777 vessels were built on the Eastern Shore of Virginia, on the Potomac, Rappahannock, Mattapony, Chickahominy, and James rivers, and at Portsmouth, Gosport, and South Quay. After 1777 vessels were chiefly built at the Chickahominy and Gosport shipyards. No other state owned so much land, property, and manufactories, devoted to naval purposes, as Virginia. In April, 1777, the Navy Board purchased 115 acres of land, for £595, on the Chickahominy, twelve miles from its confluence with the James.[1] On this site was located the Chickahominy shipyard. Virginia's ships found here a safer retreat than at Gosport, which lay convenient for the enemy's ships. It is said that before the Revolution the British had established a marine yard at Gosport, and named it for Gosport, England, where many supplies for the Royal Navy were manufactured. In some way Virginia came into possession of the shipyard at this place.[2] Two ships were built for the defence of Ocracoke Inlet, the chief entrance to Albemarle Sound, at South Quay, on the Blackwater, a few miles north of the North Carolina line.

    1. Southern Literary Messenger, 1857, 14. The references to this magazine refer to a series of valuable articles entitled "The Virginia Navy of the Revolution."
    2. E. P. Lull, History of U. S. Navy Yard,

At Warwick, on the James, a few miles below Richmond, the state built and operated a rope-walk. The state owned a manufactory of sail-duck and a foundry. In July, 1776, four naval magazines were established, one each for the James, York, Rappahannock, and Potomac rivers. For each magazine one or two agents were appointed to collect and issue provisions, ships' supplies, and naval stores.[1] For the location of the magazine on the Potomac the General Assembly authorized the Navy Board to purchase an acre of land at the head of "Potomack Creek."[2] In January, 1777, the Navy Board appointed James Maxwell, Naval Agent, to superintend the shipyards, and the building, rigging, equipping, and repairing of the naval vessels. He was to follow the instructions of the Board, and keep it informed on the state of the navy.[3] Maxwell's annual salary was £300, payable quarterly. He lived at the Chickahominy shipyard.

Virginia had a naval staff consisting of pay masters, muster masters, surgeons, and chaplains. The captains and recruiting of-

---

at Gosport, Virginia, 8-11; Hening, Statutes of Virginia, XI, 407.
 1. Journals of Virginia Navy Board, Virginia State Archives, June 25, June 26, 1776.
 2. Hening, Statutes of Virginia, IX, 235-36.
 3. Journals of Virginia Navy Board, January 7, 1777.

ficers enlisted seamen. Their task was rendered difficult, not so much because of the superior attractions of privateering, as in New England, as because of the small number of seamen resident in the state. The first commodore of the Virginia navy was John Henry Boucher. He was serving as lieutenant in the Maryland navy, when, in March, 1776, Virginia called him to the command of her Potomac fleet, and soon promoted him to the head of her navy.[1] He served as commodore for only a few months, resigning in November, 1776. Walter Brooke was commodore from April, 1777, until September, 1778. Brooke's successor, James Barron, was not appointed until July, 1780; he served until the end of the war. The commodore of the navy made his headquarters regularly at or about Hampton, and superintended the armed vessels in that part of the state.[2]

In Virginia, as in the other states and in the Continental Congress, naval enthusiasm and interest was at its height in 1776. In the fall the Navy Board contracted for the building of twenty-four small transports.[3] The General Assembly in its October session authorized the Navy Board to con-

1. Maryland Archives, XI, 293-94.
2. Journals of Virginia Navy Board; State Navy Papers, I; Southern Literary Messenger, 1857, 3.
3. Journal of Virginia Navy Board, September, October, 1776.

struct two frigates of thirty-two guns each, and four large galleys, adapted "for river or sea service." For manning these galleys and those already building, the Navy Board was empowered to raise thirteen hundred men, exclusive of officers, to serve three years from March 3, 1777. It was to recommend proper officers to the Governor and Council. Having been commissioned by the Governor, the officers were to enlist the crews for their respective galleys. Since to secure a sufficient number of experienced seamen would be impossible, it was provided that each crew should consist of three classes of men: able seamen, at a daily wage of 3s.; ordinary seamen, at 2s.; and common landsmen, at 1s., 6d. As the men in the second and third classes became proficient, they were to be promoted. Every recruit was given a bounty of $20.[1]

The Provincial Convention, in its December session in 1775, erected a Court of Admiralty, consisting of three judges, to enforce the Continental Association against trading with England. In its May session in 1776, it gave this court jurisdiction over all captures of the enemy's vessels. The General Assembly, at its October session in 1776, superseded all previous admiralty legis-

---

1. Hening, Statutes of Virginia, IX, 196-97. In August, 1776, the Navy Board drew up a list of naval rules which were endorsed by the Governor and Council.—Journals of Virginia Navy Board, August 2, 1776.

lation by an "Act for Establishing a Court of Admiralty." Such court was to consist of three judges, elected by joint ballot of the two houses of the General Assembly. The judges were to hold their offices "for so long time as they shall demean themselves well therein." The court, which was to be held at some place to be fixed by the General Assembly, was to have cognizance of "all causes heretofore of admiralty jurisdiction in this country." Its proceedings and decisions were to be governed by the regulations of the Continental Congress, the acts of the General Assembly of Virginia, the English statutes prior to the fourth year of the reign of James, and by the laws of Oleron and the Rhodian and Imperial laws, so far as they have been heretofore observed in the English courts of admiralty. In cases which related to captures from a public enemy with whom the United States should be at war, and in which a conflict should arise between the regulations of Congress and the acts of the General Assembly, the regulations of Congress should take precedence; in all other cases of conflict, the acts of Virginia were to prevail. This provision is of particular interest. It is one of the first instances in which a state recognized the superiority of federal law when in conflict with state law. Virginia was liberal in granting appeals to Congress, as she permitted them in all cases of the capture of the enemy's vessels.[1]

The Admiralty Court of Virginia tried few prize cases. Governor Thomas Jefferson in writing to the President of Congress in June, 1779, no doubt understates the truth when he says that "a British prize would be a more rare phenomenon here than a comet, because one has been seen, but the other never was." His state, he said, had long suffered from a lack of blank letters of marque, and he wished fifty to be sent to him.[2] Virginia did not establish state privateering, but followed the regulations of Congress on the subject. Because of the lack of seamen and the continual presence of the enemy's vessels at the mouths of the Virginia rivers, the privateering interest was not important in this state.

The Navy Board superintended both the trading and armed vessels of the state until April, 1777, when the trading vessels were placed in charge of William Aylett.[3] Writers on the Virginia navy have not, as a rule, distinguished one class of vessels from the other, nor is it always easy to do so. During 1776 seven vessels were employed

---

1. Hening, Statutes of Virginia, IX, 103, 131-32, 202-06.
2. Ford, Writings of Thomas Jefferson, II, 241-43.
3. Journals of Virginia Navy Board, April 8, 1777.

chiefly in commerce.[1] In the fall, most of them were ordered to the West Indies with cargoes of flour and tobacco; one, the brig "Adventure," was directed to proceed to Dunkirk, France. The armed fleet for 1776 consisted of sixteen small craft adapted chiefly for service in the rivers of Virginia and in Chesapeake Bay.[2] In 1777 the galleys "Accomac" and "Diligence" were built and stationed on the Eastern Shore; and the ships "Caswell" and "Washington" were built at South Quay on the Blackwater, for the defence of Ocracoke Inlet, which Virginia was undertaking jointly with North Carolina. Besides these four vessels, two brigs, one armed boat, and the ships "Gloucester," "Protector," "Dragon," and "Tartar," were this year added to the navy. In 1778 an armed boat and the ships "Tem-

---

1. These vessels were the brig "Adventure;" the schooners "Hornet," "Peace and Plenty," "Revenge," and "Speedwell;" the sloop "Agatha;" and the armed boat "Molly." The lists of vessels here given were compiled from the Virginia naval archives.

2. These vessels were the galleys "Henry," "Hero," "Lewis," "Manly," "Norfolk Revenge," "Page," and "Safeguard;" the brigs "Liberty," "Mosquito," "Northampton," and "Raleigh;" the schooners "Liberty" and "Adventure;" the sloop "Scorpion;" and the armed boats "Liberty" and "Patriot." The schooner "Liberty" was taken into the trading fleet as the "Hornet." It is believed that this list does not contain the vessels in Mason's Potomac fleet.

pest" and "Thetis" were built; and in 1779 two armed boats, the brig "Jefferson" and the ship "Virginia," were added.[1]

This fleet is formidable only in its enumeration. It was poorly armed, incompletely manned, and in almost every respect ill fitted for service. But few of its vessels went beyond the Chesapeake Bay. It showed most activity during 1776 and the spring of 1777. From 1775 until 1779 fifteen small prizes were captured. In May, 1776, Captain Taylor seized four small merchantmen; in June, one of the Barrons brought up to Jamestown the transport "Oxford," with 220 Highlanders on board; in the spring of 1777 the "Mosquito," Captain Harris, carried into St. Pierre the ship "Noble," valued at 75,000 livres; and a few months earlier the brig "Liberty" captured the ship "Jane," whose cargo of West India goods was valued at £6,000. These were the most fortunate captures made by the Virginia navy.[2]

---

1 The names of the vessels not mentioned in the text, which were added during 1777, 1778, and 1779 were the brigs "Greyhound" and "Hampton" and the armed boats "Nicholson," "Experiment," "Fly," and "Dolphin." The names of several other vessels which were probably used in trade, occur during this period. Some of the ships are at times referred to as galleys.

2. Files of Virginia Gazette; Journals of Virginia Convention, May 8, 1776; Virginia

Virginia's naval craft met with the usual misfortunes. During the first half of 1777 His Majesty's ship "Ariadne" captured the "Mosquito." About the same time the frigate "Phœnix" took the "Raleigh." The British made two raids into Virginia which were destructive both to the shipping of the state and to private individuals. The first was ordered by Clinton in the spring of 1779; the troops were under the command of Matthews and Collier. At the Gosport shipyard they destroyed five uncompleted vessels, three of which were frigates, besides a large quantity of masts, yards, timber, plank, iron, and other ships' stores. The shipyards on the Nansemond were looted; and twenty-two vessels with a considerable quantity of powder were taken or destroyed on the "South Branch of the navy." Suffolk was burned, and upwards of two thousand barrels of Continental pork and fifteen hundred barrels of flour were destroyed. In all one hundred and thirty vessels were burned.[1] The raid of Arnold and Phillips will be considered later.

The General Assembly at its May session in 1779 discontinued the Navy Board, and

---

Historical Register I, 77; Calendar of Virginia State Papers, III, 365.

1. Almon's Remembrancer, 1779, 289-95, account given by British officers; Records of State of North Carolina, XIV, 85-86, 94-95. Some of the vessels destroyed at Gosport probably belonged to Congress.

vested its strictly naval duties with the newly created Board of War, consisting of five members. The Board of War was empowered to appoint a Naval Commissioner. A Board of Trade was now given charge of the trading vessels of the state, and of the state manufactories of military supplies.[1]

The General Assembly in its May session, 1780, "for the purpose of introducing oeconomy into all the various departments of government, and for conducting the publick business with the greatest expedition," abolished the Boards of War and Trade, and authorized the Governor to appoint a Commissioner of War, a Commercial Agent, and coördinate with these two, a Commissioner of the Navy. This act is the outgrowth of the same movement for economy and efficiency in administration, which resulted in the establishment in January and February, 1781, of the single-headed executive departments of the Continental Congress. The salary of the Commissioner of the Navy was fixed at thirty thousand pounds of tobacco a year, and that of his clerk at ten thousand pounds.[2] The Commissioner was to be under the "controul and direction of the governour and council." Governor Jefferson appointed James Maxwell, the naval agent under the Navy Board, Commissioner of the Navy.

1. Hening, Statutes of Virginia, X, 15-18, 123.
2. Ibid., 278, 291-92.

The General Assembly in the May session of 1779, as an inducement to enlistment, granted seamen and marines additional bounties and pensions. Recruits entering for the rest of the war were now to receive $750 and one hundred acres of land. They were to be furnished upon enlistment, and once a year thereafterwards, with a complete suit of clothes. Naval officers were entitled to a "grant of the like quantity of lands as is allowed to officers of the same rank in the Virginia regiments on continental establishment." Disabled sailors and the widows of the slain were entitled to immediate relief, and an annual pension. At the October session of this year, moved by the need for money and the impossibility of fitting out the whole fleet, the General Assembly ordered the governor to sell nine of the armed vessels, and to equip and man the remaining six with all diligence. For some reason the governor did not carry out the order. There was probably little market for the vessels.[1]

The years 1780 and 1781 were marked by a renewed naval activity in Virginia. It is recalled that the theater of war had now shifted to the Southern states. Savannah was in the hands of the enemy. Charleston surrendered in May, 1780. By the fall of that year the lowlands of the states to the south of Virginia were generally in the possession

---

1. Hening, IX, 537; X, 23-24, 217.

of the British. Apparently Virginia would be the next to feel the rough hand of the conquering enemy. British privateers and naval craft lay off the mouths of the Virginia rivers, and captured all her vessels that ventured towards the Bay or the sea. Early in 1780 it was apprehended that the enemy meditated an invasion of the coasts of the state.

When the General Assembly came together in May, 1780, it at once took measures for the protection of the coasts. It passed "an act for putting the eastern frontier of this commonwealth into a posture of defence." This act, after providing for calling out the militia in the seaport counties, ordered the Governor and Council to direct the Commissioner of the Navy to immediately make ready for service in the Bay and on the seacoast the ships "Thetis," "Tempest," and "Dragon," the brig "Jefferson," and the galleys "Henry," "Accomac," and "Diligence." Three hundred marines, to be commanded by five captains and fifteen lieutenants, were to be recruited. Marines and sailors who enlisted for three years were to receive a bounty of $1,000. Naval officers were put upon the same footing in regard to pay, rations, and privileges as officers of the same rank in the land service.[1]

When the Legislature came together in October, since the situation was still more

---

1. Hening, X, 296-99.

critical, it was moved to pass an additional act for the defence of the seacoast. This act shows that the navy was in sore need for seamen and money. It provided drastic measures to obtain both. Naval officers were now authorized, under certain restrictions and limitations, to impress seamen. The eastern counties of the state were directed to bind to the sea, "under the most prudent captains that can be procured to take them," one-half of all orphans of certain descriptions living below the falls of the Virginia rivers. A hospital for seamen was established at Hampton, to be maintained by a tax of nine pence a month on the salaries of all mariners and seamen in either the navy or the merchant service of the state. Officers and seamen were given the whole of their captures; and still other inducements to enlistment by way of pay and clothing were held out.

Two new galleys, of the same construction as those built by Congress in 1776, carrying two 32's at the bow and at the stern, and 6's at the sides, were ordered for the defence of the Chesapeake. Five vessels of the state fleet were to be immediately made ready for service; and all the other naval vessels were to be sold and the proceeds devoted to naval purposes. For the use of the navy import duties were laid upon rum, gin, brandy, and other spirits; on wine, molasses and sugar; and on all imported dry goods, except salt, munitions of war, and iron from Maryland. Tonnage was laid upon merchant vessels. Despite these efforts few seamen and little money were raised, and the fleet during 1780 accomplished almost nothing.[1]

The salient event in the history of the Virginia navy in 1781 was the invasion of Arnold and Phillips during the first half of the year. Arnold was first reported on the coast of Virginia on December 29, 1780, when his fleet consisting of twenty-seven sail was seen at Willoughby Point.[2] Governor Jefferson began at once to make strenuous efforts to get the Virginia fleet in condition to oppose Arnold. The rôle of admiral was an odd one for Jefferson. In February he sent Benjamin Harrison, speaker of the Virginia House of Delegates, to Philadelphia to request of the French minister the aid of the French fleet.[3] A half-dozen or more privateers were taken into the service of the state. Twelve vessels of the state fleet of 1776-1779 still remained. Most if not all of these vessels were either at the Chickahominy shipyard and near by on the James, or else at the mouth of the James. Few of them were sufficiently manned to render much service. On April 26 Maxwell reported 78 men on board seven vessels, whose complement was

---

1. Hening, X, 379-86.
2. Ford, Writings of Jefferson, II, 392.
3. Ibid., 443-44.

520 men. Other ships had neither arms nor men.[1]

In April, 1781, Arnold and Phillips made their raid up the James, penetrating as far as Richmond. On April 21 and 22, a detachment under Lieutenant-Colonel Abercrombie destroyed the shipyard on the Chickahominy, including a number of naval craft and the warehouses. On April 27, at Osbornes on the James a few miles below Richmond, the Virginia fleet, supported by two or three hundred militia upon the shore opposite the British army, drew up to oppose the enemy. It consisted of six ships, eight brigs, five sloops, two schooners, and several smaller craft. Its chief vessels were the "Tempest," 16, "Renown," 16, and "Jefferson," 14. The British sent a flag of truce to the Commodore of the Virginia fleet, proposing to treat with him for its surrender. He sent back the spirited reply that "he was determined to defend it to the last extremity." A few cannon planted on the shore soon gave the enemy a command of the situation. After a short engagement, the Virginians scuttled or set fire to several of their vessels and fled to the opposite shore. None of the fleet escaped. The British captured twelve vessels, which the Virginians were unable to destroy. On this expedition the British burnt the state rope-walk at Warwick. After

1. Virginia Calendar of State Papers, I 588; II, 74.

the raid of Arnold and Phillips, but one vessel remained in the Virginia navy, the armed boat "Liberty."[1]

The officers and seamen of the Virginia navy, thrown out of employment by the destruction of the fleet, aided the allied forces at the siege of Yorktown in collecting supplies and transporting troops. The boat "Liberty" was used as a transport; and also the ships "Cormorant," "Loyalist," and "Oliver Cromwell," which three vessels, it is believed, Virginia purchased for this purpose. Soon after the surrender of Cornwallis the Virginia General Assembly, recognizing that "during the continuance of the present expensive war it is necessary to husband the resources of the state with the utmost oeconomy," dismissed almost all the officers and seamen, the Commissioner of the Navy, the chaplains, surgeons, pay masters, and all others on the naval staff.[2]

A number of times during the Revolution, and now for the last time in 1782, Virginia and Maryland undertook to concert a naval defence of their trade on the Chesapeake. The General Assembly of Virginia which met in May, 1782, appointed three commissioners to superintend the work of

---

1. Almon's Remembrancer, 1781, II, 62-63, Arnold to Clinton, Petersburg, May 12 1781.
2. Hening, Statutes of Virginia, X, 450; Virginia Navy Papers, I, and II.

protecting the Bay. The "Cormorant" and "Liberty" were to be immediately prepared for this service. Two galleys and two barges or whale boats were to be built. For this work the state appropriated £1,000, the proceeds arising from the sale of the "Loyalist," and certain tonnage and import duties. The commissioners were to fix the pay and subsistence of the seamen; the fleet was not to be sent outside of the Capes.[1]

The commissioners managed a small naval force during 1782 and 1783 until the war came to an end. Commodore Barron, stationed at Hampton, was chiefly occupied at this time with the exchanging of prisoners. Beyond the building of a few naval craft, it does not appear that this final naval enterprise of Virginia was attended with fruitful results. When peace was declared in the spring of 1783, the commissioners had in different stages of construction the schooners "Harrison," "Fly," and "Patriot," and the barges "York" and "Richmond." Virginia now disposed of all her fleet except the "Liberty" and "Patriot," which she retained as revenue cutters.[2] In order to keep these two armed vessels in time of peace, Virginia, in accordance with a pro-

1. Hening, Statutes of Virginia, XI, 42-44. In March, 1783, the three commissioners were Paul Loyall, Thomas Brown, and Thomas Newton, jr.—Virginia Calendar of State Papers, III, 456.
2. Virginia Navy Papers, II.

vision in the Articles of Confederation, obtained the permission of Congress.[1] These two boats were still in the employ of the state in 1787. The "Liberty" saw more service than any other state or Continental vessel of the Revolution. She was in the employ of Virginia from 1775 until 1787.

---

1. Journals of Continental Congress, October 3, 1783.

CHAPTER XV

THE NAVY OF SOUTH CAROLINA[1]

South Carolina employed her first armed vessels in obtaining a supply of gunpowder, the need of which article was so keenly felt throughout the colonies during the first years of the Revolution. In July, 1775, the South Carolina Council of Safety sent Captains John Barnwell and John Joyner of Beaufort with forty men in two large and well-armed barges to assist the Georgians in taking an English supply-ship, which was daily expected at Savannah. The enterprise was wholly successful. The ship with its cargo of sixteen thousand pounds of gunpowder was captured by the combined forces of the two colonies. South Carolina sent four thousand pounds of her share of the powder to the Continental Congress at Philadelphia.[2]

---

1. In writing this chapter I have been much assisted by Mr. A. S. Salley, Jr., Secretary of the Historical Commission of South Carolina.
2. Drayton, Memoirs of American Revolution, I, 269-71. Collections of South Carolina Historical Society, II, 50.

In the same month of July the Council of Safety planned to seize certain gunpowder stored at Nassau, New Providence, and for this purpose the "Commerce," a sloop belonging to citizens of New York, was temporarily taken into the service of the state. It will be recalled that Commodore Esek Hopkins in the initial essay of the Continental fleet in February and March, 1776, attempted to capture this gunpowder. Before the "Commerce" was ready to set sail, word came that the brigantine "Betsey" from London with a cargo of ammunition was soon to arrive at St. Augustine. Captain Clement Lemprière, the commander of the "Commerce," was therefore ordered to cruise off St. Augustine in watch for the expected vessel. On August 8 he captured the "Betsey" with her load of gunpowder amounting to almost twelve thousand pounds.[1]

Neither of these two episodes led to a permanent naval armament. This, as was to be expected, was brought about by the necessity of protecting Charles Town, the capital and chief port of the Province. The critical month in South Carolina in 1775 was September. During this month two of His Majesty's vessels, the "Tamar," 16, and "Cherokee," 6, lay in Charles Town harbor. It was in September that Lord William

---

1. Collections of South Carolina Historical Society, II, 43, 44, 57, 59, 62, 63. Drayton, Memoirs of American Revolution, I, 304-06.

Campbell, the Royal Governor of the Province, fled from Charles Town on board the "Tamar." In September the South Carolina Council of Safety began to seize the forts commanding the channel leading to Charles Town from the sea. The executive of the Revolutionary government at this time consisted of the Council of Safety of thirteen members. About the first of October the Council of Safety obtained the schooner "Defence" and placed it under the command of Captain Simon Tufts, a native of Massachussetts, but now a resident of Charles Town. The Council of Safety fixed the pay of officers and men on board the schooner.

During November, naval affairs were chiefly in the hands of the Second Provincial Congress, the Revolutionary legislature, which body on November 10 appointed Edward Blake Commissary of Stores for the Naval Department. On November 11 the "Defence," 10, manned by her regular complement of seamen, and thirty-five marines taken from the land forces, was detailed to cover a party sent to obstruct certain channels near Charles Town by sinking old schooners. While engaged in this service she exchanged shots with the "Tamar" and "Cherokee" without causing much damage on either side. On November 12, stirred by this encounter, the Provincial Congress voted, though by a narrow majority, to impress, fit out, and arm the ship "Prosper" for the purpose of capturing the British ships in Charles Town harbor; and appointed commissioners to superintend the work.[1]

The Provincial Congress having adjourned on the 29th of November, the Second Council of Safety continued the naval preparations. On December 16 it appointed William Henry Drayton, the well-known Revolutionary agitator and leader, to command the "Prosper" in place of Captain Tufts who had some time before been transferred from the "Defence" to the "Prosper."[2] A third vessel was now obtained, the schooner "Comet," and was placed in charge of Captain Joseph Turpin. Owing to the paucity of seamen in South Carolina, the Council of Safety in December directed Captain Robert Cochran to proceed to Massachussetts and obtain recruits for the navy. When in January, 1776, Cochran was in Philadelphia, the delegates of South Carolina to the Continental Congress called that body's attention to Cochran's mission. In order that no friction should arise between Cochran and the military authorities in Massachusetts over the enlistment of men, Congress recommended to him that he offer to sea-

---

1. Journals of South Carolina Provincial Congress, November 9, 10, 12, 1775.
2. Collections of South Carolina Historical Society, III, Journals of South Carolina Council of Safety, December 16, 1775.

men moderate wages and bounties; that he immediately repair to the camp at Cambridge and take Washington's advice; and that he enlist the seamen in those parts of the country where he would least interfere with the Continental service. The Massachusetts Council agreed to permit Cochran to raise three hundred men.[1] South Carolina also enlisted seamen in Georgia.[2]

On February 15 the Second Provincial Congress, which had met on the 1st, appointed a committee to report on the best means and the expense of building two frigates of thirty-two guns each. It authorized the enlisting, if necessary, of two hundred marines. On March 5 a committee was appointed to prepare "proper Rules and Articles for the better regulation and government of the Navy of this Colony." On the 25th, the report of this committee after amendment was adopted, and on the next day the respective rank of army and navy officers was fixed. On March 14th the Provincial Congress authorized the committee at Georgetown, a port to the north of Charles Town, to purchase and fit out proper armed vessels for the defence of the trade of Georgetown, and on the same day gave

---

1. Force, American Archives, 4th, IV, 1307-08. Journals of Continental Congress, January 16, January 19, 1776.
2. Gibbes, Documentary History of the American Revolution, 1764-1776, 258.

similar orders to a committee of Beaufort, a port to the south of Charles Town. Provision was now made for a Muster-Master General of the Army and Navy.[1] In March the armed schooner "Peggy" was in the service of the state.

On March 26, 1776, a new government under a Constitution went into effect in South Carolina. This provided for a legislature consisting of two houses, a General Assembly and a Legislative Council. The executive of the state was a President, or "President and Commander-in-chief," the title ran, and a Privy Council of seven members. According to the constitution the captains of the navy were to be chosen by a joint ballot of the two houses of the Legislature, and were to be commissioned by the President.[2] Early in April Colonel Pinckney presented in the General Assembly an ordinance to appoint a Commander of the Navy to be subject to the President.[3] On April 9 the Legislature passed an act to prevent the desertion of soldiers and sailors. A hospital for sick and wounded soldiers and sailors was established at Charles Town. On April 11 the Legislature established a Court of Admiralty which was given jurisdiction

---

1. Journals of South Carolina Provincial Congress, February 15, February 22, March 5, 14, 25, 26, 1776.
2. Constitution of South Carolina of 1776.
3. Journals of South Carolina General Assembly, April 10, April 11, 1776.

over all captured ships belonging to "Great Britain, Ireland, the British West Indies, Nova Scotia, East and West Florida." The facts in cases of capture were to be tried by a jury.[1]

On September 21, 1776, President John Rutledge, in a message to the Legislature, recommended the appointment of commissioners to superintend the naval affairs of the state, believing that thereby the navy would be placed upon a better footing. On the same day, in accordance with the President's recommendation, the General Assembly appointed a committee to draft a bill. On October 8 an act was passed which established a Board of Naval Commissioners, consisting of seven men, and empowered "to superintend and direct all matters and things whatsoever to the navy of this state in any wise relating."[2] This act was modelled on the act of Virginia on the same subject. It varies from the Virginia act in a few particulars, and is a little more detailed. The Navy Board was charged with the building, hiring or buying of all naval vessels, and the arming, outfitting and provisioning of the same, and with the construction of

---

1. Journals of South Carolina General Assembly, April 11, 1776; Cooper, Statutes of South Carolina, IV, April 9, April 11, 1776.
2. Journals of South Carolina General Assembly, September 21, 1776; Cooper, Statutes of South Carolina, IV, October 8, 1776.

rope-walks and shipyards. It was authorized to audit the naval accounts, draw warrants on the treasury for necessary expenditures, recommend officers, fill vacancies temporarily with the approval of the President, keep itself informed as to the state of the navy, and report thereon to the Legislature. With the concurrence of the President and the Privy Council the Board could remove or suspend officers for neglect of duty or misbehavior. Soon after the organization of the Board, the question was raised whether it had the power to order the vessels on cruises; the President and Privy Council decided that the Board had no such power, and that the detailing of vessels was a function of their own.[1] In addition to its strictly naval duties the Board directed the procuring and fitting out of trading vessels and transports.

The Navy Board held its first meeting on October 9, 1776, at Charles Town, and organized by electing Edward Blake First Commissioner. On the 12th it chose its clerk.[2] The duty of this officer was to keep a regular journal of the transactions of the Board; and once in three months, or oftener if necessary, to go aboard the vessels and take an

---

1. Force, American Archives, 5th, II, Journals of South Carolina Navy Board, October 25, 1776.
2. Ibid., Journals of South Carolina Navy Board, October 9, 12, 1776.

account of the officers and seamen and pay them their wages. His salary was £1,400 currency, a year. At first a majority of the Board constituted a quorum. When it became difficult to assemble four out of its seven members, two more members were added to the Board, and a quorum was reduced to three men.[1] The act which established the Board was to continue in effect two years. On October 9, 1778, the Board was continued until October 8, 1779, and from thence until the end of the Legislature then in session. The introduction of a bill into the House of Representatives on February 8, 1780, to repeal all previous acts establishing a Board of Naval Commissioners makes it highly probable that the Navy Board was discontinued about this time.[2]

On taking charge of naval affairs the Navy Board found one of its most engrossing duties to be the purchasing of supplies of all sorts—salted beef and pork, bread, pitch, tar, turpentine, tallow, duck, cordage, and spars. On October 17, 1776, it appointed a naval agent at Georgetown to procure and issue supplies to the schooner "Rattlesnake," Captain Stephen Seymour, now in the employ of the state for the pro-

---

1. Cooper, Statutes of South Carolina, IV, August 23, 1777.
2. Journals of South Carolina House of Representatives, February 8, 1780.

tection of this port.¹ The Board continued the building of four galleys, which had been begun by President Rutledge. In April, 1777, it leased Captain Cochran's shipyard at Charles Town, together with five negroes, for the term of five years.² In October, 1778, it bought of Paul Pritchard, shipwright, eighty-five acres on Hobcaw creek, near Charles Town, for a shipyard.³

During 1777 and 1778 the Legislature passed a few ordinances relating to the navy. On January 16, 1777, it fixed the shares of prizes. Officers and seamen were to receive one-half the net proceeds of all captures. This half was then to be divided into sixteen parts and allotted to officers and seamen according to a fixed scale. Captains were given two-sixteenths; seamen and marines, three-sixteenths.⁴ In February the captors' share of vessels of war and privateers was increased to the whole of the prize. In January, 1778, a law of obvious purpose was passed, which freed all seamen who entered into the Continental or state naval service from the obligations of previous con-

---
1. Force, American Archives, 5th, II, Journals of South Carolina Navy Board, October 17, 1776.
2. Journals of South Carolina House of Representatives, September 10, 1779. The contract with Cochran was being dissolved.
3. Notes of Mr. A. S. Salley, Jr., Secretary of the Historical Commission of South Carolina.
4. Cooper, Statutes of South Carolina, IV, January 16, 1777.

tracts made with the owners of private ships. In March, 1778, the appointment of a commodore to command the navy of the state necessitated a new distribution of the proceeds of captures among officers and seamen. The commodore's share was fixed at two-sixteenths.[1] In October, 1778, the Legislature authorized the Navy Board to purchase any "negroes or other slaves for the use of the publick shipyard or rope work," which property was to be vested in the public forever.[2]

During 1776, 1777, and 1778 the Navy Board added a few vessels to the navy. Several galleys were built during this period. In the fall of 1776 the brigantine "Notre Dame" was procured, armed, and sent to France under the command of Captain Robert Cochran on a trading voyage.[3] In 1777 one finds the sloop "Beaufort" in the service of the state, being probably stationed at Beaufort for the defence of the trade of that port. Early in 1779 the Navy Board completed the construction of the brig "Hornet." Now and then the state obtained the

---

1. Cooper, Statutes of South Carolina, IV, February 13, 1777, January 26, March 28, 1778. On February 13, 1777, a new act relating to the Court of Admiralty was passed.
2. Ibid., October 9, 1778.
3. In 1776 the following vessels were employed as merchantmen: schooners, "Polly," "Peggy" and "Little Thomas;" the brigantine "Notre Dame," and the sloop "Margaret."

loan of privateers for short periods. Information concerning South Carolina's privateers is scant. We know, however, that she had a considerable fleet. Between August 17, 1776, and April 16, 1777, President Rutledge granted thirty-seven letters of marque.[1]

Few states exceeded South Carolina in naval expenditures. With the exception of Massachusetts, the vessels of no other state went to sea so often as did those of South Carolina. The navy of South Carolina was smaller than that of Virginia, but much more active. From 1776 to 1779 it captured some thirty-five small prizes, only about half of which, however, reached safe ports.[2] Its principal cruising grounds were off the South Carolina and Florida coasts and in the West Indies. The South Carolina vessels frequently cruised off St. Augustine. This was an important British port during the Revolution, and many privateers and smaller British vessels visited it. The noting of a few captures will show the character of the work of the South Carolina navy. In July, 1777, the "Notre Dame" carried into a South Carolina port the brig "Judith," 12, laden with

1. South Carolina Archives, Miscellaneous Records, A, 18, 19.
2. Files of South Carolina and American General Gazette, and Gazette of State of South Carolina.

dry goods for St. Augustine; and in October the same vessel captured the brig "John," and the schooner "Jemmy and Sally" with cargoes of staves and shingles outward bound from the Mississippi.[1] In the spring of 1779 the "Notre Dame," "Hornet," and "Eagle" made prizes of the sloop "Prince of Wales," 12, and the brig "Royal Charlotte," both bound for Georgia, with West India products.[2]

In December, 1777, President Rutledge and the Privy Council, in opposition to the best military judgment in South Carolina, concerted with Captain Nicholas Biddle, of the Continental frigate "Randolph," 32, an expedition to clear the coasts of the enemy's vessels. South Carolina furnished the "Notre Dame," 16, Captain Hall, and three privateers, which were temporarily taken into the public service. These were the ships "General Moultrie," 18, Captain Sullivan, "Polly," 16, Captain Anthony, and "Fair American," 14, Captain Morgan. One hundred and fifty South Carolina troops were taken on board to serve as marines. Sailing about February 1, 1779, the fleet soon cleared the coast of the enemy, and then proceeded to the West Indies on the lookout for rich West India merchantmen—an object which

---

1. Gazette of State of South Carolina, July 21, November 4, 1777.
2. Ibid., April 7, 1779.

was probably in view from the first. On March 7, when the fleet was to the windward of Barbadoes, the "Randolph" fell in with the British ship of the line "Yarmouth," 64. During a running fight an explosion of tremendous force occurred on board the "Randolph." Burning spars and timbers six feet long, together with an undamaged ensign, fell upon the decks of the "Yarmouth." The "Randolph," with almost her entire crew of 315 men, including Captain Joseph Ioor and fifty South Carolina marines, sank soon after the accident. Five days after the fight the "Yarmouth" picked up four men clinging to the wreckage, the only men rescued. Two of the four South Carolina vessels, the "General Moultrie" and the "Fair American," now returned home, taking on the way a valuable Guineaman. The "Notre Dame" and the "Polly" continued their cruise within the West Indies, the "Notre Dame" reaching as far westward as the Isle of Pines. The two vessels captured eleven small prizes, a number of which, however, were recaptured before reaching safe ports.[1]

The transference of the seat of war from the Northern to the Southern states, in

---

1. Moultrie, Memoirs of American Revolution, I, 193-99; South Carolina and American General Gazette, April 23, May 28, June 4, 1778; Ramsay, Revolution in South Carolina, I, 71; Clowes's Royal Navy, IV, 10.

1779, and the British naval expedition against Charles Town, early in 1780, caused increased naval activity in South Carolina. In August, 1779, the House of Representatives sent to the Senate a bill offering bounties and fixing a new rate of wages for officers and seamen.[1] In September the House passed a bill for building two floating batteries and four galleys.[2] Acting on the recommendations of the Governor, the House in February, 1780, voted that it would be of public utility to employ a number of negroes not to exceed one thousand to act as pioneers and fatigue men in the army and as oarsmen and mariners in the navy.[3] Additional armed vessels were now obtained in different ways. During 1779 the Governor issued commissions to fourteen vessels. A number of small craft, used chiefly as transports, were impressed.[4]

1. Journals of South Carolina House of Representatives, August 31, 1779.
2. Ibid., September 6, 1779. The Senate was not willing to make so large a naval increase.
3. Ibid., February 14, 1780.
4. South Carolina Archives, Miscellaneous Records, A. Among the vessels to which the Governor gave commissions were the following: galleys "Congress," "South Edisto," "Revenge," "Beaufort," "Lee," "Marquis de Bretigny," and "Carolina;" sloop "Count de Kersaint," brigantines "General Lincoln" and "Beaufort," schooner "Eshe," and the vessel "Lovely Julia." The following vessels, a number of which were impressed, were

The "Notre Dame," 16, and the "General Moultrie," 20, were assigned to the defence of Charles Town. The state purchased from France the "Bricole," 44, and the "Truite," 26. The "Bricole" was pierced for sixty guns, and mounted forty-four 24's and 18's. She was the largest vessel owned by any of the states. For the defence of Charles Town France sent "L'Aventure," 26, and "Polacre," 16; and Congress the "Providence," 28, "Boston," 24, "Queen of France," 28, and "Ranger," 18.[1]

The naval defence of Charles Town was intrusted to Captain Abraham Whipple, the senior officer of the four Continental vessels. Whipple advised that a naval defence at the bar on the seacoast, which lay to the eastward of the forts that commanded the entrance to Charles Town harbor, should not be undertaken; and later he gave it as his opinion that it was impracticable for the armed vessels to coöperate with the forts. Such timid counsels prevailed, and no naval defence of Charles Town was made. With the exception of the "Ranger" all the vessels were dismantled and their guns and crews removed to reinforce the land batter-

in the service of the state in 1779 or 1780: galley "Rutledge," schooners "Polly," "Rattlesnake," "Sally," "Anthony," "General Moultrie," "Nancy," "Three Friends," brig "Wasp" and brigantine "Ballony."

1. Almon's Remembrancer, 1780, II, 44-47.

ies and troops in Charles Town. With the fall of the city on May 12, 1780, South Carolina lost her entire navy, with the exception of the frigate "South Carolina," whose fortunes we are about ready to consider. The "Bricole," "Truite," "General Moultrie," and "Notre Dame" were sunk.[1] The "Boston" and "Ranger" were added to the Royal Navy.

In 1781, with the returning tide of the patriot forces a few small vessels were armed at Georgetown.[2] In February, 1783, Governor Guerard recommended the purchase of a ship, which had lately been carried into Wilmington, North Carolina, for the defence of Charles Town harbor. The House was unfavorable to the transaction, because of the lack of means, the difficulty of manning the ship, and the risk of bringing it around.[3] In March, 1783, a committee of the House was appointed to consider what arrangements should be made with respect to the naval officers of the state; and it reported that, by the Articles of Confederation, South Carolina was precluded from

---

1. Previous to the siege of Charles Town, His Majesty's navy had captured the following vessels: February, 1777, "Defence" taken by the "Roebuck" and "Perseus;" December, 1777, "Comet," taken by the "Daphne;" April, 1779, "Hornet," taken by the same.

2. Gibbes, Documentary History of American Revolution, 1776-1782, 181, 183.

3. Journals of South Carolina House of Representatives, February 12, 1780.

having a navy, and that it was therefore of the opinion that the state could not retain in its service its naval officers.[1]

A most interesting episode in the history of the South Carolina navy remains to be told. It properly begins with the commissioning on March 11, 1778, of Alexander Gillon, a prosperous and influential merchant of South Carolina, to be a commodore in the navy with "full and ample power and authority to take the Command, Direction, and Ordering of the said Navy," agreeable to its rules and articles. On the same day John Joyner, William Robertson, and John McQueen received commissions as captains. On March 26 the state decided to raise abroad £500,000 currency, or £71,429 sterling, for the purpose of building or purchasing three frigates. On July 17 Gillon was commissioned to go abroad and undertake the task of securing the loan and procuring the vessels. The exact sum which Gillon was now directed to borrow was less than £500,000 by the sum of the proceeds which he would derive from the sale of certain produce, to be exported from South Carolina to Europe, and consisting chiefly of indigo and rice. Early in the fall of 1778 the "Notre Dame" carried Gillon, his three captains, and other naval officers to Havana, whence they took passage to Europe.

[1]. Journals of South Carolina House of Representatives, March 5, 1783.

On January 31, 1779, Gillon was empowered to borrow, in addition to previous authorizations, £15,000 sterling, which was to be invested in arms, ammunition, and "Indian goods." Of the total sum, £86,429, which he was authorized to obtain, he actually borrowed in Amsterdam, Ghent, Bordeaux and Paris £46,725, and received as the proceeds arising from the sale of exported produce £10,000. It is thus seen that Gillon, in his financial mission, was moderately successful. He was less fortunate in making the proposed naval increase. He succeeded, however, in renting the frigate "Indian" from the Chevalier Luxembourg for one-fourth of her prizes, for a period of three years. The reader recollects that this ship was built at Amsterdam in 1777 by the American Commissioners at Paris, and that owing to lack of money and to complications growing out of the laws of neutrality, they had sold the "Indian" to the French king. Louis XVI. had, in turn, ceded the "Indian" to the Chevalier Luxembourg.[1]

Gillon renamed his frigate the "South Carolina," and mounted her with twenty-eight 32's and twelve 12's. Numerous de-

---

1. South Carolina Archives, Miscellaneous Records, A, 66, 67; Journals of South Carolina House of Representatives, March 10, 1783, report of a committee on certain papers of Commodore Gillon.

lays ensued in getting to sea. Owing to shallow water and the heavy draught of the "South Carolina," she was from July to November, 1780, moving from Amsterdam to the Texel. She spent the winter of 1780–1781 in a small creek near the Texel. These delays caused much expense, and in order to pay off some of his bills, Gillon, in the spring of 1781, sold to Colonel John Laurens for Congress military supplies, which he had recently purchased for South Carolina, to the amount of £10,000. Laurens now engaged Gillon to take these supplies together with others to Philadelphia. Gillon had been given full power to man and officer his vessel, having carried over with him fifteen commissions and thirty warrants in blank. In March, 1781, he wrote that he had about two hundred men on board, and that he expected two hundred and eighty from Dunkirk which the Chevalier Luxembourg had raised for the state.[1]

The "South Carolina" finally got to sea about the first of August, 1781, leaving behind the convoy which had expected to accompany her. Gillon's movements and dealings abroad are not at all points clear. He aroused suspicions as to his honesty, and made a number of enemies. Exactly why he did not at once proceed to Phila-

---

1. South Carolina Historical and Genealogical Magazine, I, 28-32, 136-47, two letters of Gillon.

delphia with the supplies for Congress which he had on board is not certain. On sailing he cruised for a month in the North Sea, and for a time near the English Channel, and then, about the first of October, he put into Coruña, Spain. Gillon said that he had been detained by contrary winds, and had returned for fresh provisions before sailing for America.[1]

On January 12, 1782, Gillon arrived at Havana with five valuable Jamaicamen, loaded with rum and sugar, and said to be worth $150,000. Here he found the Spaniards planning a descent on the Bahama Islands, and he now agreed to take command of the sea-forces consisting of fifty-nine Spanish and American vessels—probably chiefly Spanish. General Cadrigal commanded the troops. The expedition left Havana on April 22, and on May 8 the Bahamas surrendered without firing a shot. Gillon not very modestly attributed the success of the enterprise to the "great attention which the captains and officers of the American vessels of war paid in conveying such a fleet through so difficult and so unfrequented a passage, with a beating wind all the way, whereby we disappointed any plans the enemy might have formed of at-

---

[1]. New York Historical Society Collections, Deane Papers, IV, 450, 468, 478, 519; Wharton, Diplomatic Correspondence, IV, 546-47, note.

tacking us in our way through the gulph of Florida." The island surrendered, not to the joint American and Spanish forces, but to the Spaniards alone.[1] It was reported that the Spaniards and Gillon captured three hundred troops and ninety sail of vessels.[2]

On May 28th the "South Carolina" arrived in Philadelphia, where she was refitting during the summer and fall of 1782. An agent of the Chevalier Luxembourg now removed Gillon from the command of his vessel, which was given to Captain Joyner. The "South Carolina" did not get to sea until December, 1782. Soon after leaving the Capes of the Delaware she was chased by a British squadron, which, after a race of eighteen hours, overhauled her, and at the end of a two hours' fight, forced her to surrender.[3] For the loss of this vessel the Chevalier Luxembourg, in accordance with the terms of his contract, demanded from South Carolina the payment of 300,000 livres. Gillon asserted that Luxembourg had forfeited all right to the money by dis-

---

1. Pennsylvania Packet, March 5, May 31, and June 4, 1782. The issue of June 4 contains a letter of Gillon to Governor Mathewes of South Carolina, dated May 15, 1782, containing an account of the expedition; Gibbes, Documentary History of American Revolution, 1776-1782, 170.
2. Connecticut Gazette, June 14, 1782.
3. Clowes's Royal Navy, IV, 91.

placing him at Philadelphia from his command of the vessel. Further, Gillon declared that the Chevalier had subjected the state to serious losses by sending its marines, in the winter of 1780–1781, on an expedition to the Island of Jersey.[1] One estimate makes the total cost of the frigate to the state more than $200,000, and another puts it at $500,000.[2] The Luxembourg claims remained unsettled until December 21, 1814, when the state made a final payment of $28,894 to the heirs of the Chevalier.[3] South Carolina is still prosecuting her claims against the United States for a reimbursement of the expenses contracted in behalf of the "South Carolina."[4]

---

1. Journals of South Carolina House of Representatives, March 10, 1783.
2. McCrady, South Carolina in Revolution, 1775-1780, 219.
3. Cooper, Statutes of South Carolina, V, December 21, 1814.
4. Conversations with Hon. J. T. Gantt, Secretary of State of South Carolina.

CHAPTER XVI

THE MINOR NAVIES OF THE SOUTHERN STATES

Naval administration in Maryland was vested in the Committee of Safety until March 22, 1777, when it passed to the Governor and Council, the executive under the first state constitution of Maryland. The Committee was given a free hand in its control of the navy. The Provincial Convention empowered it to fix the pay of officers and seamen, and to appoint the commanders of the smaller naval vessels. The Convention, however, established the pay of marines, which was the same as that of the state troops; and it decided that the uniform of the marines should be a blue hunting shirt.[1] The first naval work of the Committee of Safety was the fitting and arming, in February and March, 1776, of the ship "Defence," twenty-two 6-pounders, Captain James Nicholson, the chief vessel in the Maryland navy. In March the schooner "Resolution" was purchased as a

---

1. Force, American Archives, 4th, IV, 744-45; 5th, III, 94.

tender for the "Defence." The Committee of Safety, which held its meetings in Annapolis was early in 1776 assisted in its work at Baltimore, the chief port of the state, by the Baltimore Committee of Observation; and, later in the year, by Jesse Hollingsworth, who was appointed naval agent for Baltimore.

In June and July, 1776, the Provincial Convention ordered the Committee of Safety to build seven row-galleys, and to fit out three small vessels, mounting not more than ten guns each, and a number of armed boats not to exceed six.[1] By the spring of 1777 the Committee of Safety had built, fitted, and officered the galleys "Baltimore," "Conqueror," "Independence," and "Chester," and the armed boat "Plater;" it had in process of construction, ready to launch, the galleys "Johnson" and "Annapolis," and it had purchased the tender "Amelia" and the schooner "Dolphin." During the first years of the war the Committee of Safety hired or purchased several small vessels, which were used chiefly as merchantmen.[2] It is not always easy to distinguish these craft from the naval vessels, which

1. Force, American Archives, 4th, VI, 1487, 1496.
2. The following vessels were employed as trading craft: Sloop "Molly;" schooners "Ninety-Six," "General Smallwood," and "Friendship;" brigs "Sam" and "Friendship," and ship "Lydia."

were now and then sent on trading voyages.
Maryland's most common commercial venture was to ship flour and tobacco to the firm of Harrison and Van Bibber at Martinique, and there laden her vessels for the homeward voyage with munitions of war.[1]

As an inducement to recruits, the Provincial Convention, in October, 1776, offered a bounty of $20 to able seamen, and $10 to landsmen. Officers and seamen who received bounties and wages were given one-third of their prizes, the share granted by the Continental Congress; those who did not receive bounties and wages were given the whole of their prizes.[2] Maryland was unable to meet the competition with privateers for seamen, and her vessels were often forced to remain in port for lack of crews. In December, 1776, the naval agent at Baltimore wrote that he could "load twenty vessels rather than man and sail two. The money paid to captains and sailors is wonderful, and no way to shun it."[3]

Maryland established in her navy the rank of commodore. On June 8, 1778, her Governor commissioned Thomas Grason, who had been appointed commodore on April 21 by the General Assembly.[4] In 1782 a "Commodore Whaley" was in the

---
1. Maryland Archives, XI. XII, XVI, XXI.
2. Force, American Archives, 5th, III, 128.
3. Ibid., 1025.
4. Maryland Archives, XXI, 125.

naval service. Her most prominent captains were James Nicholson, who in 1776 became the senior captain in the Continental navy; and George Cook, who had served seven years in the British navy. Lieutenant John Henry Boucher resigned early in 1776 to enter the Virginia naval service, where he soon rose to the highest rank.

In May, 1776, the Provincial Convention, pursuant to the resolves of the Continental Congress, established a Court of Admiralty, consisting of a judge, marshal, and register. The procedure was to be that usual in such courts; trial by jury was made optional; and the judge was permitted to determine the places of sitting.[1] The privateers of Maryland were generally small craft, mounting on the average eight 4-pounders. They plied their trade chiefly in Chesapeake Bay. From April 1, 1777, to March 14, 1783, a period of almost six years, Maryland issued letters of marque and reprisal to 248 privateers, carrying a total of 1810 guns.[2]

Since a number of her vessels had been for some time idle for lack of crews, Maryland in the first half of 1779 sold all of her naval craft, except the galleys "Conqueror" and "Chester," and the schooner "Dolphin."[3] From 1780 to the

---

1. Force, American Archives, 4th, V, 1596, 1597-98.
2. Scharf, History of Maryland, II, 205.
3. Maryland Archives, XXI, 399.

end of the Revolution the trade in the Chesapeake, and the property of the inhabitants of the Maryland coasts, on both sides of the Bay, suffered severely from the ravages of the British refugee barges, privateers, and small naval craft. These conditions led Maryland to make frequent attempts, during the last years of the war, to provide a naval armament for the defence of the Bay. In 1780 she was moved to renew her naval activities by still other considerations. The success of the British this year in South and North Carolina and on the coasts of Virginia made the outlook for Maryland very threatening. It was also known that Clinton wished to carry the war into Maryland and Virginia.

In October, 1780, Maryland passed her first act for the defence of the Bay. The Governor and Council were ordered to provide, officer, and man four large barges or row-boats, each to carry at least twenty-five men, one galley to be armed with two 18's and two 9's, and one sloop or schooner to carry ten 4's. They were to enlist one hundred marines for three years. The marines were to be paid £2, 5s. a month and a bounty of $40, and the seamen £3 a month and a bounty of $20.[1] During the May session of the legislature in 1781, just after Arnold's invasion into Virginia, this act was

---

1. Statutes of Maryland, October session, 1780, chapter XXXIV.

amended. The Governor and Council were now directed to procure two galleys and a number of barges not to exceed eight.[1]

In passing, mention should be made of the service which Maryland rendered the Continental army in 1781, in transporting troops. When, in the spring of that year, Lafayette and his army were on their way to Virginia to attempt the capture of Arnold, Maryland impressed upwards of one hundred transports, together with three small armed vessels, which she placed under the command of Captain James Nicholson. This fleet carried a large part of Lafayette's troops, stores, guns, and baggage from the head of Elk to Annapolis. In August and September the state rendered similar aid to Washington's army, which was then on its way to Yorktown. Every vessel in the state was pressed into service.[2]

During the last year of the war the British were especially annoying to the trade and coasts of Maryland and Virginia. Fifteen or twenty small craft which made their headquarters on the islands in the Chesapeake were very destructive, and their depredations called forth protective measures not only in Maryland, but in Virginia, as we have seen. In each state private initi-

---

1. Statutes of Maryland, May session, 1781, chapter XXXIV.
2. Scharf, History of Maryland, II, 439-40, 456, 461.

ative did what it could to stop the pillaging, but it was not able to cope with the enemy.

On June 13, 1782, the Maryland legislature appointed William Paca, Walter Tilghman and Robert Goldsborough commissioners to provide for the defence of the Bay. They were ordered to procure four barges and a galley or other vessel of force, to fit them for immediate service against the enemy, and to turn them over to the Governor and Council when ready to be employed. The legislature also appointed William Hanson Harrison, a commissioner to go to Richmond and concert with the Virginia executive or legislature a joint defence of the Bay. A new naval establishment was now effected. The Governor and Council were to raise and officer two hundred and fifty able seamen, watermen, landsmen, and marines, who were to serve until January 1, 1783, or longer. They were to fix the pay and rations of the officers. Officers and seamen who should lose a limb, or be otherwise maimed or hurt, were to receive the same benefits which the state should hereafter give to her soldiers in the Continental army. The naval forces were to be subject to the naval rules and regulations provided by Congress for the Continental navy. A penalty of £50 was prescribed for enticing seamen away from the state service. The expense incurred in providing this naval increase was to be met chiefly from an appropriation of £10,000 and from the sale of the confiscated property of Tories.[1]

Owing to the continuance of the depredations of the British, the legislature in its November session of 1782 passed another act for the defence of the Bay. The Governor and Council were directed to fit out a certain galley or ship, now building for the state, and the barges "Somerset," "Terrible," "Fearnaught," and "Defence," and enlist three hundred and fifty men to serve until January 1, 1784. Two-thirds of the proceeds of captures were now to be given to the captors. The expense of this establishment was to be met by import duties on rum, brandy, and other distilled spirits; on wine, loaf sugar, and coffee; and on all goods and merchandise, with certain exceptions.[2]

The navy of Maryland rendered miscellaneous services. It convoyed merchantmen, imported and distributed arms and provisions, transported troops, watched the fleet of the enemy to report its movements, and defended the trade and coasts of the state. Except when used for commercial purposes, Maryland's vessels rarely passed outside the Capes at the mouth of the Chesapeake. Attempts which were

---

1. Statutes of Maryland, April session, 1782, Chapter III.
2. Statutes of Maryland, November session, 1782, Chapter XXVI.

made to bring about the coöperation of the Maryland and Virginia fleets did not often succeed. A few small prizes were taken, but none of them were of much value. In the fall of 1776 the "Defence," Captain Cook, cruised as far southward as the West Indies, and captured five small prizes, laden with logwood, mahogany, indigo, rum, and sugar.[1] Several sharp encounters between the vessels of Maryland and the enemy took place in the Bay. As early as March, 1776, the "Defence," 22, Captain James Nicholson, checked the advance up the Chesapeake of the British sloop-of-war "Otter," 10, and recaptured several prizes.[2] Now and then attempts were made to dislodge the British from some of the islands in the Bay. So late as the latter part of March, 1783, the state sent a small schooner and two barges against a rendezvous of the British on Devil's Island, one of the Tangiers.[3]

On November 30, 1782, the Battle of the Barges occurred near the Tangier islands. The mortality of the Americans in this engagement was relatively greater than in any other sea fight of the Revolution. In its carnage and in the bravery displayed by the Americans, this fight does not suffer from a comparison with that of Jones off Flamborough Head. The Maryland fleet,

1. Maryland Archives, XII, 500.
2. Ridgely, Annals of Annapolis, 175-77.
3. Scharf, History of Maryland, II, 481-82.

which had been joined by a volunteer Virginia barge, was commanded by Commodore Whaley of the barge "Protector." The British fleet of barges was under the command of Captain Kidd of the "Kidnapper," mounting 18-pounders. For one cause or another the "Protector" was the only American barge which engaged the British fleet. While the "Protector" inflicted much damage on the vessels of her adversary, she naturally was unable to fight long against such tremendous odds. An extract from the simple and pathetic narrative of the fight written by Colonel John Cropper, a volunteer Virginia officer on board the "Protector," possesses interest: "Commodore Whaley was shot down a little before the enemy boarded, acting the part of a cool, intrepid, gallant officer. Captain Joseph Handy fell nigh the same time, nobly fighting with one arm, after the loss of the other. Captain Levin Handy was badly wounded. There went into action in the Protector sixty-five men, twenty-five of them were killed and drowned, twenty-nine were wounded, some of whom are since dead, and eleven only escaped being wounded, most of whom leaped into the water to save themselves from the explosion." Colonel Cropper, to whom, on the death of Whaley, the command of the "Protector" fell, was wounded three times, "and after the surrender knocked down by a four-pound rammer."[1]

During the last years of the war Maryland in her attempts to defend the Chesapeake, obtained as many as ten barges.[2] She had also in the naval service at this time a schooner, the "Flying Fish." The end of her navy may be dated with the statute passed by her legislature in May, 1783, which authorized the Intendant to sell "the galley and the barges."[3]

North Carolina's initial step in procuring a naval armament was taken on December 21, 1775, when her Council of Safety resolved to fit out three armed vessels for the defence of the trade of the state. It ap-

---

1. Southern Literary Messenger, XXIV, (1857), 218, Colonel John Cropper to Colonel Williams Davies, his superior in command in the Continental line.

2. Scharf enumerates the following barges: "Revenge," "Terrible," "Intrepid," "Protector," "Experiment," "Venus," "Defence," "Reformation," "Dolphin," and "Fearnaught." These barges were about forty-two feet long, eight feet wide, and three deep. Each carried about twenty-four oars, from sixteen to thirteen feet long, and mounted two large guns.—Scharf, History of Maryland, II, 204.

3. Statutes of Maryland, April session, 1783, chapter XVI, Votes and Proceedings of Maryland Senate, April session, 1783, 63. For the pay-rolls of the "Flying Fish," "Defence," and several Maryland barges, see Maryland Archives, XVIII, 606-15.

pointed three Boards of Commissioners, each of which was to immediately purchase, arm, man, and victual a vessel. The board for Cape Fear was composed of five men; for Newbern, of eight; and for Edenton, of six.[1] Since it proved difficult to assemble a quorum of the Newbern Board, the Council of Safety in June, 1776, vested its powers in three of its members.[2] In May, 1776, the Provincial Congress fixed the monthly wages of officers, seamen, and marines. Captains were to be paid £10; lieutenants, masters, captains of marines, and doctors, £8 each; marines, £2, 13s., 4d.; "seamen complete," £4; "seamen not complete," £3.[3]

By October, 1776, the Cape Fear Board had fitted out the brigantine "Washington;" the Newbern Board, the brigantine "Pennsylvania Farmer;" and the Edenton Board, the brigantine "King Tammany." The Council of Safety now ordered these three vessels to protect the trade of the state at Ocracoke Bar, and to proceed against the enemy's Jamaicamen homeward bound from the West Indies. "It may be necessary to inform you," it wrote on October 1 to Captain Joshua Hampstead of the "Pennsylvania Farmer," "that the Jamaica fleet will sail for Europe about the middle of this month under the convoy of a twenty-gun

---

1. North Carolina Colonial Records, X, 352.
2. Ibid., 637.
3. Ibid., 584.

ship only, from the best intelligence we can obtain."[1]

For one reason or another these three vessels accomplished very little. For a long time the "Washington," Captain Edward Ingraham, could not obtain a crew. The "Pennsylvania Farmer," Captain Joshua Hampstead, was idle during the summer of 1776, for lack of shot. James Davis, one of the Commissioners for fitting out this vessel, made serious accusations against his fellow Commissioners and the officers and crew of the vessel. As Davis had suffered real or supposed injuries at their hands, his words no doubt must be heavily discounted. In October, 1776, he wrote that the "Pennsylvania Farmer" lay in Newbern "with 110 men on board at the Expence of near Forty Pounds per day, upwards of six months; in the most inglorious, inactive, and dissolute state that perhaps was ever suffered in any Country." The crew of the vessel consisted of "men of all nations and conditions, English, Irish, Scotch, Indians, Men of Wars Men, and the most abandoned sett of wretches ever collected together. Two of the officers broke open the Gun Room, and with a number of the men went off with the Boat, with Intent to join Lord Dunmore's fleet, and actually reached Currituck County. They

---

1. North Carolina Colonial Records, X, 831-32, 848-49, 875-77; North Carolina State Records, XI, 356.

were apprehended, and are still at large on board. They have wasted near 100 pounds of powder in wantonly firing at and bringing to all Boats, Canoes, and Vessels of every sort, even Passengers in the Ferry Boat have been insulted. Capt. Thos. Shine of the Militia, with his Company on board coming up to the General Muster, was fired on and a ball passed within a few inches of his Arm."[1] These are but few of the derelictions contained in Davis's remarkable list. His overstatement of his case causes one to suspect that he was not entirely free from malice.

By December, 1777, the "Washington" was ordered to be sold; and commissioners had been appointed to load the other two vessels and send them on voyages to foreign ports. In April, 1778, the legislature decided to sell the "Pennsylvania Farmer." On May 30 this vessel at a public sale in Edenton "was cried out by John Blackburn on Mr. Joseph Hewes, after which Mr. Hewes denied having bid the sum which she was cried out at."[2]

No other subject of naval interest engaged the attention of North Carolina so much as the defence of Ocracoke Inlet. It is recalled that the waters of Pamlico and

---

1. North Carolina Colonial Records, X, 834-36.
2. North Carolina State Records, XII, 173, 244, 623, 796.

Albemarle Sounds are separated from the
Atlantic by a long sandbar, which is only at
a few points broken by inlets. These connect the waters of the Atlantic with the
waters of the Sound. The most important
inlet at the time of the Revolution was that
of Ocracoke. The protecting and the keeping open of this entrance was a matter of importance not only to North Carolina, but to
Virginia and the Continental Congress, as
well. Most of the foreign trade of Newbern
and Edenton, the two main ports of the
state, passed through this inlet. In a similar way, the trade of Southern Virginia, outward or inward bound, found it convenient
to use this channel. In the first years of the
Revolution, especially in 1778, not a few
goods coming from foreign marts, and destined for the Continental Army, rather than
risk capture off the entrance to the Chesapeake or the Delaware Bay, entered Ocracoke, passed on through Pamlico and Albemarle Sounds into Chowan River, and
thence by the branches of this river to the
town of South Quay, in southern Virginia,
near the confluence of the Nottaway and
Blackwater rivers. From South Quay the
goods were carried by wagons to Suffolk on
the Nansemond, and thence by boat up the
Nansemond into the James. This route
constituted the southern division of the so-called "Inland Navigation." It was along
this road that North Carolina salt pork and

beef, and shoes made by North Carolina Quakers, passed northward on their way to the "Grand Army." In 1778 and 1779 South Quay and Suffolk were important *entrepôts* for Continental goods.

Since the keeping open of communication through Ocracoke Inlet was of importance to both North Carolina and Virginia, the two states concerted a joint naval armament for this purpose. On May 9, 1776, the North Carolina Provincial Congress appointed Allen and Thomas Jones to attend the Provincial Congress of Virginia, "for the purpose of recommending to them the expediency of fitting out two Armed Vessels at the expense of that Colony, to act in conjunction with the armed vessels already fitted out by this Colony for the protection of the trade at Ocracoke."[1] As her part of the joint undertaking, Virginia agreed to construct at South Quay two galleys, to be employed in the defence of the Inlet.

Virginia carried out her promise, and built at the "South Quay ship yard" two ships, the "Caswell" and "Washington."[2] North Carolina ordered her brigantines to defend Ocracoke; and she voted £2,000 towards the equipping of Virginia's ships, and appointed commissioners to invest this money in anchors, guns, rigging, and canvas.[3]

---

1. Force, American Archives, 4th, V, 1357.
2. These vessels were at first called galleys.
3. North Carolina Colónial Records, X, 981.

Finally, as we shall see, she maintained at her expense one of the Virginia ships on the station at Ocracoke for a considerable period. She did not, however, meet Virginia's expectations, which state several times expressed the belief that North Carolina had not done her share in keeping up the joint establishment.[1]

Until 1778 the trade which passed through Ocracoke was rather free from annoyance. It was in January of that year that Joshua Martin, the late Royal Governor of North Carolina, wrote from New York to Lord George Germaine in London: "That the contemptible port of Ocracock has become a great channel of supply to the rebels, while the more considerable ports have been watched by the King's ships. They have received through it considerable importations."[2] On January 1, 1778, there arrived at Newbern a sloop from Martinique, a schooner from St. Eustatius, a schooner with salt from Bermuda, a French schooner from Hispaniola, and two schooners from the Northern states; a French scow was at the same time reported at Ocracoke.[3] A a letter from Edenton, dated June 9, informs us that several foreign vessels were at the Inlet, and that a sloop had recently arrived

---

1. North Carolina State Records, XIV, 19, 126.
2. Ibid., XIII, iii-iv.
3. Ibid., 354.

at Edenton from France, which had on board for the Continental Congress thirteen thousand pairs of shoes, a large quantity of clothing, and a "marble Monument for Genl. Montgomery."[1]

In the spring of 1778 the North Carolina legislature voted to purchase from Virginia the ship "Caswell," stating that it had not been able to keep its agreement with Virginia in providing a joint defence of Ocracoke. The legislature fixed the pay of the officers and seamen on board the "Caswell."[2] In May this ship, under the command of Captain Willis Wilson, with one hundred and seventy men on board, lay off Ocracoke bar. Captain Wilson reported to Governor Caswell on May 20 that the place was not infested with British cruisers, and that a French ship and brig lay outside the Inlet, waiting to come in. In June, however, Wilson wrote that "the enemy (one ship, two sloops, and a brig) take a peep at us every now and then, but are not disposed to venture in."[3] A sloop was now purchased at Beaufort, to act as a tender for the "Caswell," and Rich-

---

1. North Carolina State Records, XIV, 154-55.

2. Ibid., XII, 574-75, 742, 746; XIII, 138-39, 171-72. In June, 1779, Governor Jefferson of Virginia wrote to Governor Caswell offering to sell both the "Caswell" and "Washington." Virginia had found the trade through Ocracoke inconvenient. — North Carolina State Records, XIV, 126, 136.

3. Ibid., XIII, 132, 171.

ard Ellis was appointed agent at Newbern to purchase provisions and naval supplies.[1]

In December, 1778, the "Caswell" was still afloat, but by June, 1779, she had sunk at her station at Ocracoke.[2] With the loss of this vessel North Carolina's naval enterprises came to an end. Her attention was now engrossed by threatening invasions of the enemy from South Carolina.

North Carolina maintained admiralty courts at several ports on the coast. There were such courts at Beaufort, Bath, Roanoke and Currituck. As early as April 25, 1776, a special court of admiralty was appointed to try a prize case.[3] A few of the privateers of this state rendered valuable services. The brig "Bellona," 16, Captain Pendleton, fitted out at Newbern, cruised very successfully.

Georgia's naval armament was small and unimportant. Her Provincial Congress, however, commissioned one of the first armed vessels of the Revolution. In June, 1775, it gave Captains Oliver Bowen and Joseph Habersham command of a 10-gun schooner, and directed them to assist Captains Joyner and Barnwell of South Carolina in capturing a certain British ship, laden with powder, and expected to arrive at Sa-

---

1. North Carolina State Records, XIII, 138-39, 174-75.
2. Ibid., XIV, 136.
3. Force, American Archives, 4th, V, 1339.

vannah. On July 10 the joint forces of the two states captured the ship and obtained thirteen thousand pounds of the highly prized article. Georgia sent five thousand of her share of nine thousand pounds to the Continental Congress at Philadelphia.[1]

On July 5, 1776, the Continental Congress resolved to build four galleys under the direction of the Georgia Provincial Congress.[2] In August the Committee of Safety was building some row-galleys, and also fitting out an armed vessel for which purpose £2,000 were voted. On August 28 the Committee of Safety ordered Captain Bowen to go to Hispaniola to purchase armed vessels to the amount of £3,000, materials for fitting out vessels, and various warlike stores. In October it ordered Captain Pray to go to Cape Francois on a similar errand. Pray was authorized to mount on his vessel carrying his purchases to Georgia as many guns as it would conveniently bear.[3] Whether these two men actually carried out their commissions is not known.

In the spring of 1777 Georgia had three galleys in service, and later she had a fourth. These were named the "Washing-

---

1. Jones, History of Georgia, II, 181.
2. Journals of Continental Congress, July 5, 1776.
3. Collections of Georgia Historical Society, V, part I; Proceedings of Georgia Council of Safety, 96, 101-02, 113.

ton," "Lee," "Bulloch," and "Congress." This little fleet was placed under the command of Commodore Oliver Bowen, and it was employed on the Georgia seacoast chiefly in conjunction with the army. Under orders of President Gwinnett three of the galleys commanded by Commodore Bowen assisted the army in its unsuccessful expedition against East Florida in April and May, 1777.[1] In April, 1778, off Frederica, Georgia, the "Washington," Captain Hardy, "Lee," Captain Braddock, and "Bulloch," Captain Hatcher, with three hundred troops on board, captured His Majesty's brigantine "Hinchinbrooke," 12, the sloop "Rebecca," and a brig.[2]

In the campaign around Savannah early in 1779 all four galleys were lost. In January the "Washington" and "Bulloch" were stranded near Ossabaw Island on the Georgia coast, and were burned by their crews, to prevent their capture. In March, 1779, the "Congress," Captain Campbell, and the "Lee," Captain Milligan, engaged near Yamasee Bluff the British galleys "Comet" and "Hornet." The Americans, after losing three killed, among whom was Captain Campbell, and six wounded, were forced to abandon their galleys. Out of 104 men on

---

1. Jones, History of Georgia, II, 269.
2. McCall, History of Georgia, II, 137-38; Moultrie, Memoirs of American Revolution II, 375.

board the American galleys the British captured but ten.[1] The occupation of Southern Georgia by the enemy from this time until the end of the Revolution stopped further naval endeavors on the part of the Patriot party of the state.

Georgia had a prize court in operation as early as November, 1776. Her constitution of February, 1777, provided for the hearing of prize cases by special county courts, much as in Connecticut.[2]

---

1. McCall, History of Georgia, II, 179. 224-25.
2. Jameson, Essays in Constitutional History of United States, 10.

CHAPTER XVII

THE MINOR NAVIES OF THE NORTHERN STATES

Rhode Island was the first colony to undertake a defence by means of armed vessels. Her initial legislation preceded that of the Continental Congress by almost four months. During 1775 her coasts and trade were annoyed by the vessels of the enemy. In the early summer the conduct of Captain James Wallace, the commander of His Majesty's frigate "Rose," was especially vexatious and insulting. On June 13 Nicholas Cooke, Deputy-Governor of Rhode Island, in accordance with a resolution of the General Assembly, wrote to Wallace demanding the immediate restoration of certain captured vessels, and especially of two packets belonging to citizens of Providence. The acts of Wallace were obviously in the minds of the members of the General Assembly, when, on June 15, it ordered the Committee of Safety to charter and fit out two suitable vessels for the defence of the trade of Rhode Island.

The General Assembly also appointed a committee of three to appraise and hire the two vessels. It ordered the larger vessel to be equipped with eighty men and ten 4-pounders; the smaller vessel was to be manned with not more than thirty men. It appointed Abraham Whipple commander of the larger vessel with the rank and power of commodore over both vessels, and named his lieutenants, master, and quarter-master. Officers were also chosen for the smaller vessel. The establishment of the little fleet was assimilated to that of the land forces of the state. Its cruises were to be determined by the Lieutenant-General, Brigadier-General, and the Committee of Safety.[1]

Two sloops, the "Katy" and "Washington," were at once chartered. Commodore Whipple tells us that on the same day he received his commission, June 15, he captured a tender of the frigate "Rose."[2] This was the first authorized capture of a naval vessel of the enemy. During the summer of 1775 the "Katy" and "Washington" cruised chiefly in Narragansett Bay for the defence of Rhode Island. In August the "Washington" was sent outside of the Bay to warn incoming vessels laden with powder and warlike stores of their danger from British craft. It was at this time that Washington

---

1. Acts and Resolves of Rhode Island, June, 1775.
2. Staples, Annals of Providence, 265.

proposed that one of the sloops should be sent to the Bermudas for powder, which military necessity was much needed by his army.[1] Commodore Whipple, in the "Katy," was dispatched on this errand in September. Arriving at the Bermudas, Whipple found that he had come too late as the powder had already been sent to Philadelphia.

It was while the "Katy" was on this errand that Governor Cooke, on October 10, received orders from the Continental Congress to send his little fleet to the northward to intercept two British transports. The "Washington" was unfit for so large an undertaking. The "Katy," having arrived from the Bermudas, was ordered on November 12, 1775, to cruise between Nantucket Shoals and Halifax. Later her destination was changed, and she was directed to carry to Philadelphia the seamen which Commodore Esek Hopkins had enlisted for the Continental service.[2] On the arrival of the "Katy" in Philadelphia she was taken into the Continental service under the name of the "Providence." About the same time the "Washington" was in all probability returned to her owner, as she had become more or less unseaworthy.

Meantime the General Assembly had or-

---

1. Force, American Archives, 4th, III, 69
2. Ibid., 36-37, 461, 653; Collections of Rhode Island Historical Society, VI, 134-35; see Chapter I, page 55.

dered the construction of two galleys, to carry sixty men, to have fifteen oars on a side, and to mount one 18-pounder in the bow.[1] The work was placed under the direction of a superintendent. In January, 1776, the General Assembly appointed John Grimes commodore of the galleys at a salary of £9 a month. The galleys were named the "Washington" and "Spitfire." They rendered a variety of services in the Bay, cruising in defence of trade, acting as transports, and covering landing parties sent after forage and supplies.[2] In July, 1776, they were ordered to proceed to New York and to assist in the defence of the Hudson.[3] It is probable that this detail was not carried out. By the summer of 1778 they had been captured or destroyed by the enemy.

From June, 1775, until December, 1776, naval administration in Rhode Island during the recess of the General Assembly, was vested in the Committee of Safety, or Recess Committee, as it was sometimes called. This Committee, as constituted by the session of the General Assembly beginning on October 31, 1775, consisted of the Governor

---

1. Acts and Resolves of Rhode Island, August, 1775.
2. Providence Gazette, April 20, April 27, 1776; Acts and Resolves of Rhode Island, November, December, 1776; Arnold, History of Rhode Island, II, 397.
3. Rhode Island Colonial Records, VII, 582.

and eighteen members, together with such members of the General Assembly as happened to be present at the meetings of the Committee. Any seven members constituted a quorum. The composition of the Committee varied slightly at different times. On December 13, 1776, a Council of War was appointed, with whom naval administration was now vested. The Council of War, which included the Governor and Lieutenant-Governor, consisted of nine members, any five of whom formed a quorum. In May, 1778, a Council of War comprising twenty-one members, and representative of the whole state was chosen. The Council of War was virtually the Committee of Safety under a change of name.[1]

In January, 1776, the General Assembly appointed a committee of three to draw up a bill establishing a prize court. On March 18 a bill became a law which established a court of justice for the trying of prize cases. It was to be presided over by a judge, appointed annually. The same act established state privateering. Privateersmen were to enter into bond for £2,000 to observe the provisions of the act and the instructions of the Governor. They were to be commissioned by the Governor. In May, 1776, this act was brought into conformity with the resolutions of Congress on

1. Acts and Resolves of Rhode Island, December, 1776, May, 1778.

the same subject. Captors were given one-half of all armed vessels and one-third of all other prizes.[1] A list containing the names of 193 privateers from Rhode Island has been compiled.[2]

In June, 1777, the General Assembly undertook to add two armed vessels to the naval force of the state, but for some reason its order was not carried out.[3] The same resolution directed the Council of War to procure three merchantmen to be used in importing supplies. The ship "Aurora" and sloop "Diamond" were two of the vessels purchased for commercial purposes.

For a time Rhode Island relied in part for her naval defence upon the two Continental frigates, "Providence" and "Warren," which were built at Providence in 1776, and officered and manned largely with Rhode Island men. The General Assembly and the Council of War furthered the work of the local naval committee which had charge of the construction of the frigates. These two ships left Providence early in 1778. During 1778 and 1779 the state continued to depend upon Continental assistance.

It is recalled that during the summer of 1778 Washington concerted with the French

---

1. Acts and Resolves of Rhode Island, March, May, 1776.
2. W. P. Sheffield, Rhode Island Privateers and Privateersmen.
3. Acts and Resolves of Rhode Island, June, 1777.

fleet a campaign to drive the British from Newport. General Sullivan commanded the land forces of the Americans. On June 25, 1778, Congress directed the Navy Board at Boston to build three galleys, or procure three suitable vessels, for the defence of the Providence, Warren, and Taunton rivers in Rhode Island, if upon advising with the Rhode Island Council of War and General Sullivan, the Navy Board should find such measure expedient. At a conference of the Navy Board, the Council of War, and Sullivan it was decided to procure one large ship. Such a vessel was obtained by Sullivan, but he was compelled soon to return it to its owners.[1] With the consent and recommendation of the Rhode Island authorities, Sullivan, in November, procured the "Pigot" galley, and in the spring of 1779 the sloop "Argo."[2] First the "Pigot," and later the "Argo," was placed under the command of Lieutenant-Colonel Silas Talbot, of the Continental army.

Already Talbot had been twice recommended by Congress for promotion on account of gallant conduct in naval exploits. The Rhode Island General Assembly had

---

1. Publications of Rhode Island Historical Society, VIII, papers of William Vernon and Navy Board, 249, 250.
2. Journals of Rhode Island Council of War, July 17, August 24, November 11, 1781; Acts and Resolves of Rhode Island, February, 1779.

recognized his bravery in capturing the "Pigot" galley off the coast of Rhode Island in October, 1778, by voting him a "genteel silver-hilted sword." As commander of the "Pigot" and later of the "Argo," Talbot was under the orders of Sullivan, and of Gates, Sullivan's successor. During the summer of 1779 Talbot in the "Argo," assisted at times by privateers and the state vessels of Massachusetts, captured fifteen small prizes.[1] As a reward for the conspicuous ability which he showed in this work, Congress made him a captain in the Continental navy. Early in 1780 the "Pigot" and "Argo" closed their services under Continental and state auspices.

Rhode Island's last naval enterprise was made in 1781. In May of that year the General Assembly appointed a committee to "charter a suitable fast sailing Vessel, in order to be fitted out as a Cruiser to clear the Coast of the piratical Boats that infest the same." The committee was voted $5,000, and was ordered to man the vessel, appoint its officers, and send it to sea. It was directed to procure a small vessel of thirty to fifty tons burden, mounting four 3-pounders or 4-pounders. It at once obtained the sloop "Rover," which it placed

---

1. Providence Gazette, August 14, September 25, 1779; Connecticut Gazette, June 24, 1779; Pennsylvania Packet, September 9, 1779.

under the command of Captain Richard Olney. The "Rover" served the state but a short time, and accomplished little.[1]

New York was led to purchase her first armed vessel in order to prevent persons inimical to the liberties of the American Colonies from supplying the Ministerial army and navy with provisions. It was for this purpose that her Provincial Congress on December 20, 1775, appointed a committee of two to buy, arm, and fit out a proper vessel at a cost not to exceed £600. The committee purchased the sloop "General Schuyler," and by March, 1776, had the vessel ready for service. James Smith, who in the summer of 1775 had served as "Commodore on the Lakes," that is, Lakes Champlain and George, was appointed commander of the "General Schuyler." In March the Provincial Congress ordered the sloop "Bishop Landaff" to be fitted out.[2]

On March 11, 1776, the Provincial Congress appointed five of its members, all from New York, a Marine Committee. It empowered this Committee "to take such measures, and give such directions, and employ such persons for the protection or advantage of trade as they may think proper, useful, or necessary." The Marine Com-

---

[1]. Acts and Resolves of Rhode Island, May and October, 1781.
[2]. Journals of New York Provincial Congress, December 20, 1775, March 9, 1776.

mittee was a permanent navy board vested with the management and direction of the naval affairs of the state. Three of its members formed a quorum. Thomas Randall was its chairman. It was authorized to keep secret such matters as it saw fit. It reported to the Provincial Congress, when the Congress was in session, and at other times to the Committee of Safety. It was directed to apply to the Provincial Congress when in need of advice.[1] In March and April it purchased the sloop "Montgomery," and the schooner "General Putnam," and sold the "Bishop Landaff."[2]

On April 17 the New York Committee of Safety issued commissions to Captain William Rodgers of the "Montgomery," Captain James Smith of the "General Schuyler," and Captain Thomas Cregier of the "General Putnam." Rather singularly, these captains executed bonds in favor of John Hancock, President of the Continental Congress, and were given the commissions of Continental privateers. The naval establishment of New York was a mixed one. Her fleet was governed by the Continental naval rules and regulations. The enlisting contract of the "Montgomery" reads at points as if the vessel belonged to the Con-

---

1. Journals of New York Provincial Congress, March 11, 1776.
2. Journals of New York Committee of Safety, April 25, 1776.

tinental Congress: "The said William Rogers, for and in behalf of himself and the said Thirteen Colonies of North America, doth hereby covenant and agree to and with said officers, seamen, and marines" to advance a month's wages. In sharing prizes, in granting bounties to wounded soldiers, and in rewarding exceptional merit, the contract followed the naval regulations of the Continental Congress.[1] On the other hand, the three vessels were owned, fitted out, officered, and manned by New York, which state directed their cruises, and paid their officers and seamen. This mixed establishment may in part be explained by the fact that at first New York's intention was to have Congress take her vessels into the Continental service.[2]

On the evacuation of Boston by the British on March 17, 1776, Washington at once proceeded to New York, whither, it is recollected, the scene of war soon shifted. In April Washington asked for the loan of the New York vessels to assist in the defence of New York city. After some disagreement as to the terms upon which he should receive them, the "General Putnam" and the "General Schuyler" were

[1]. Journals of New York Committee of Safety, April 19, 1776; Fernow, New York in Revolution, 530-33.
[2]. Journals of New York Provincial Congress, January 22, 1776.

turned over to him.¹ Hereafter the state seems not to have had the direction of the "General Schuyler." In October, 1776, a mutiny having occurred on board the "General Putnam," the New York Committee of Safety ordered this vessel to be sold.²

New York's fleet captured some eight or ten prizes. It cruised chiefly in the waters surrounding Long Island. The "Montgomery" had best success. On April 19, 1776, the Marine Committee reported to the Committee of Safety a draft of instructions for Captain Rodgers. He was ordered to cruise between Sandy Hook and Cape May, or from Sandy Hook to the east end of Long Island, and he was cautioned to always keep "some inlet under your lee, so that you may secure a retreat from a superior force."³ Prizes were to be sent to some place of safety in the United Colonies. The "Montgomery" cruised in this general region until June, 1777; in July she was sold for £3,550. She captured several merchantmen, which were libeled in the admiralty courts of Rhode Island, Connecticut, and Maryland. In the condemning and selling of these prizes, New York's interests were attended to by agents appointed for the purpose. The

---

1. Journals of New York Committee of Safety, April 24, May 10, 1776.
2. Ibid., September 21, September 24, October 7, 1776.
3. Ibid., April 19, 1776.

"Montgomery's" most valuable prize was the schooner "Hannah," libeled in Baltimore, which, with her cargo of clothing, cloths, and provisions, sold for £11,281. Another prize, the "Minerva," with a cargo of salt, was tried by the court at the same time with the "Hannah," and was freed; whereupon, Francis Lewis, a delegate of New York to the Continental Congress, which was then in session in Baltimore, appealed the case of the "Minerva" to Congress.[1]

In August, 1776, the Secret Committee, which was assisting in the defence of the Hudson, was fitting out two small armed sloops, the "Camden" and "Hudson."[2] As late as January, 1777, the Committee of Safety was planning for a naval armament; orders were then given for cutting the timbers for a 74-gun ship.[3] The permanent occupation of New York city by the British stopped New York's naval enterprises on state account. She continued, however, to grant a few privateering commissions, until the end of the war. In passing, one should mention that in 1776 New York contributed officers, seamen, and naval supplies to Arnold's campaign on lakes Champlain and

1. Journals of New York Committee of Safety, February 13, 1777; Journals of New York Provincial Congress, April 1, 1777.
2. Journals of New York Provincial Congress, August 16, 1776.
3. Journals of New York Committee of Safety, January 15, 1777.

George. By the terms of New York's Constitution of 1777 the Governor was "commander-in-chief of all the militia and admiral of the navy of this state." The Constitution implied that there was to be a Court of Admiralty, although it did not make definite provision for such court.[1]

New Hampshire's only naval undertaking was her participation, at the suggestion of Massachusetts, in the Penobscot expedition of July, 1779. She contributed to the ill-starred fleet the "Hampden," 22, Captain Titus Salter, which vessel was captured by the British.[2] On July 3, 1776, New Hampshire passed an act "to encourage the fixing out of Armed Vessels to defend the seacoast of America, and to cruise on the enemies of the United Colonies, as also for erecting a court to try and condemn all Ships and other Vessels." This act was modeled on similar acts of Massachusetts. It established state privateering. A "Court Maritime," consisting of one judge, was erected at Portsmouth to try cases of capture. Salvage was prescribed in accordance

---

1. New York Constitution of 1777. See Carson, Supreme Court of United States, p. 45, for further references to the admiralty legislation of New York.
2. New Hampshire Archives, VIII, 106, 186, 195. In March, 1776, the New Hampshire House of Representatives appointed a committee of three to look out for an armed vessel to guard the coast. It is believed that no vessel was procured.

with the proportions fixed by the Continental Congress. In cases of prizes captured by a Continental vessel, appeals lay from the Court Maritime to the Continental Congress.[1]

In July, 1776, a Committee of Newark, New Jersey, requested the New Jersey Provincial Congress to build four "gondolas," or row-galleys, to be mounted with cannon, and to ply between the mouths of the Passaic and Hackensack rivers and the town of Perth Amboy. The Provincial Congress referred the proposition to a committee of four. It finally ended the business by referring the report of this committee to the Continental Congress.[2]

Until October 5, 1776, when New Jersey passed an act establishing an admiralty court, her Provincial Congress decided prize cases. So early as February 15, 1776, a committee of the Provincial Congress, which had been appointed to draft an ordinance for erecting a Court of Admiralty, reported that it had consulted William Livingston, one of the New Jersey delegates to the Continental Congress, on the subject, and had proposed to him, whether it would not be of manifest advantage to the Colonies if "Con-

---

1. Force, American Archives, 5th, I, 90-96.
2. Minutes of Provincial Congress and Council of Safety of New Jersey, 1775-1776, 510, 520, 525, 528.

gress should, by one general ordinance, institute the powers and mode of erecting a Court of Admiralty to be adopted by all the Colonies." Livingston agreed to take the first opportunity for proposing the matter to Congress.[1] Nothing came of the recommendation.

---

1. Minutes of Provincial Congress and Council of Safety of New Jersey, 1775-1776 370-71, 396, 479.

APPENDICES

APPENDIX A

A BIBLIOGRAPHY

THE CONTINENTAL NAVY

MANUSCRIPT SOURCES

Adams, John. Letters for 1775 and 1776, deposited for the present by Charles Francis Adams with the Massachusetts Historical Society, Boston.
    A few letters are valuable for the early history of the Continental Navy.

Continental Congress. Manuscript Journals. Supplements and corrects the printed journals.

Continental Congress. Records and Papers, formerly found in the Bureau of Rolls and Library, Department of State, Washington; but now in most part in the Library of Congress, Division of Manuscripts. There are many volumes of these documents. Most of the material relating to the navy is found in the following volumes:
    No. 28, 1 vol., Reports of committees of Congress on naval affairs, 1776–1786.
    No. 37, 1 vol., Reports of Marine Committee and Board of Admiralty, 1776–1780.

No. 50, 1 vol., Letters of Oliver Pollock, Commercial Agent at New Orleans, to President and to committees of Congress, 1776–1782.

No. 58, 1 vol., Letters and Papers of John Hancock.

No. 78, 24 vols., Letters to President of Congress.

No. 90, 1 vol., Letters of the commercial agents at Martinique to President of Congress.

No. 137, 3 vols., Letters and Reports of Robert Morris, Agent of Marine.

No. 138, 3 vols., Reports of the Board of Treasury, 1784–1789.

Nos. 82–96, 132, 168, and 193.
> The Records and Papers of the Continental Congress are especially valuable for the years from 1780 to 1783. They contain many important letters of John Paul Jones. The letters of Pollock give a full account of his services at New Orleans.

Deane, Silas. Papers in the library of the Connecticut Historical Society, Hartford.
> A few of these papers relate to the navy.

Force Transcripts. These are copies of many of the Records and Papers of the Continental Congress, made by Peter Force, and now in the possession of the Library of Congress, Division of Manuscripts.
> The copying is accurately done. The pagination often differs from that of the originals.

Hopkins, Esek. Letters and papers, in the library of the Rhode Island Historical Society, Providence.
> Quite valuable for 1775, 1776, and 1777. The best of them have been printed in Edward Field's Esek Hopkins.

Jones, John Paul. Manuscripts, in the Division of Manuscripts, Library of Congress. Have been excellently catalogued by C. H. Lincoln in Calendar of John Paul Jones Manuscripts.

> An important original source for the naval history of the Revolution. A number of the most important manuscripts, however, have been published, notably in Sands's Life and Correspondence of John Paul Jones.

Marine Committee Letter Book. Letters of the Marine Committee and the Board of Admiralty, in the Division of Manuscripts, Library of Congress.

> Quite the most important manuscript source for the history of the Continental navy from 1776 to 1780. Contains 217 pages, folio, and 505 letters. They are copies of the originals. Of these letters, 371 were written by the Marine Committee between August 22, 1776, and November 20, 1779; and 134 by the Board of Admiralty between December 10, 1779, and September 19, 1780. Eighty-six letters are addressed to the Navy Board at Boston. Hitherto the Marine Committee Letter Book has been little used.

Tucker, Samuel. Papers, in the Harvard Library, Cambridge. Valuable for the career of Samuel Tucker, a captain in the Continental navy. The best of the papers have been published by J. H. Sheppard in his Life of Samuel Tucker, 1868. (See entry under Sheppard.)

Miscellaneous Manuscripts, Division of Manuscripts, Library of Congress

> Of noteworthy importance is a list of commissioned officers in the Continental navy, far more complete than any yet published.

PRINTED SOURCES

Adams, John. Works, 10 vols. Boston, 1856.
> Almost the only source for the debates in Congress on naval affairs in the fall of 1775. His Notes on Debates are more reliable than his Autobiography.

Appleton. Cyclopedia of American Biography. 7 vols. New York, 1898–1900.
> Contains a little information of interest to students of naval history.

Annual Register for 1775–1783. London.
> Of slight value for naval history.

Bancroft, George. History of the United States. 6 vols New York, 1884–85.
> A few references to naval history.

Barney, Mary. Memoirs of Commodore Joshua Barney. Boston, 1832.
> Not satisfactory.

Beatson, Robert. Naval and Military Memoirs of Great Britain, 1727–1783. London, 1804.
> Contains accounts of some of the important naval engagements of the Revolution.

Bigelow, John. Works of Benjamin Franklin. 10 vols. New York, 1887–88.
> Contains valuable original material for Franklin's naval services in Paris.

Bolton, C. K. Private Soldier under Washington, New York, 1902.
> A few references to the navy.

Boston Gazette for 1775–1783. Boston.
> Of great value for a history of the movements of the Continental vessels. In its advertisements of libeled prizes, one of the very best sources for the work of the Massachusetts privateers.

British Marine Encyclopedia, in Hogg's Naval Magazine for 1801. London.

Excellent for definitions of naval terms used in the British navy.

Buell, A. C. Paul Jones, Founder of the American Navy. 2 vols. New York, 1900.
> Very interesting; attractive style. Contains many inaccuracies. Chapter II, Volume I, entitled, Founding of the American Navy, is in no small part fiction.

Canadian Archives, report on, for 1895. Ottawa.
> Under the subject Prince Edward Island, will be found references to Broughton and Selman's expedition in 1775.

Carson, H. L. Supreme Court of the United States. Philadelphia, 1902.
> Contains a brief account of the prize courts of the Revolution.

Caulkins, Frances M. History of New London, Connecticut. New London, 1852.
> A few valuable references to the Continental navy.

Clark, Thomas. Naval History of the United States. Philadelphia, 1814.
> The earliest history of the United States navy. Has considerable merit. Gives sources of his information. His interviews with naval officers constitute original material.

Clowes, W. L. Royal Navy. 7 vols. Boston and London, 1897–1903.
> Chapter XXXI, Volume III, and Chapter I, Volume IV, are important sources for the engagements of Continental vessels with vessels of the Royal Navy. Scientific treatment. Some sources have been used which are not accessible in America. The most important contribution to the history of the Continental navy since Cooper's naval history, written in 1839.

Connecticut Colonial Records for 1775–1776; Connecticut State Records for 1776–1780. Hartford, 1890, 1894–95.

> Contain references to the Continental vessels built in Connecticut.

Connecticut Gazette for 1775–1783. New London.
> Contains important bits of information relating to the movements of the Continental vessels.

Connecticut Historical Society Collections, vol. VIII. Hartford, 1901.
> Contains rolls of the Connecticut companies who served in the navy on Lake Champlain.

Continental Congress, Journals of, for 1775–1788. 13 vols. Philadelphia, 1777–88.
> The most valuable and extensive source for the history of naval legislation and administration during the Revolution. The edition of W. C. Ford, now being published by the Library of Congress, supersedes previous editions.

Continental Congress, Secret Journals, for 1775–1788. 4 vols. Boston, 1821.
> Contributes some information on the work of naval agents abroad.

Continental Journal and Weekly Advertiser for 1776–1783. Boston.
> Supplements the information found in the Boston Gazette.

Cooper, James Fenimore. History of the Navy of the United States of America. London, 1839.
> Several editions of this work have been issued. The first part treats of the Continental navy. This varies little in the different editions. Clear and interesting style. The most satisfactory account of the engagements of the Continental navy. Treats of its fights with merchantmen and privateers, as well as with the vessels of the Royal Navy. More complete than Clowes, but not so scientific.

Bibliography 487

Deane Papers. Collections of the New York Historical Society. 5 vols. New York, 1886–90.
    Valuable for the naval services of Silas Deane in France.

Emmons, Lieutenant G. F. Navy of the United States. Washington, 1853.
    Names of the Continental vessels and their prizes arranged in tables. Treatment statistical. Valuable, but far from complete. Privateers of the Revolution similarly treated.

Field, Edward. Esek Hopkins. Providence, 1898.
    Valuable. Prints many important Hopkins papers.

Field, Edward. State of Rhode Island and Providence Plantations. 3 vols. Boston and Syracuse.
    Contains some additional information relating to the early life of Esek Hopkins.

Force, Peter. American Archives. 9 vols. Folio. Washington, 1837–53.
    A source of very great value for naval history during 1775 and 1776. Prints the chief public records for these years, together with important letters and miscellaneous papers.

Ford, W. C. Writings of George Washington. 14 vols. New York and London, 1889–93.
    One of the chief sources for the history of Washington's fleets.

Ford, W. C. Letters of William Lee. 3 vols. Brooklyn, 1891.
    Valuable for the work of the commercial agents in France.

Goldsborough's Naval Chronicle. Washington, 1824.

Griffin, M. I. J. Commodore John Barry. Philadelphia, 1903.
    Especially valuable for the numerous documents which are printed.

Hale, Edward Everett and Edward Everett, jr.
 Franklin in France. 2 vols. Boston, 1887.
  Prints many documents. Chapter XI, American Prisoners, Chapter XVI, Privateers form Dunkirk, and Chapter XVII, Captain Landais, Volume I, are of special interest to students of naval history.

Hamersly, L. R. Naval Encyclopedia. Philadelphia, 1881.
  Suggestive.

Hamilton, J. C. Works of Alexander Hamilton. 7 vols. New York, 1850–51.
  Contains Hamilton's views on single-headed executives.

Hatch, L. C. Administration of the American Revolutionary Army, Harvard Historical Studies, X. New York and London, 1904.
  Suggestive for the Continental navy.

Independent Chronicle and Universal Advertiser for 1775–1783, Boston.
  Supplements the Boston Gazette.

Ingraham, E. D. Papers relating to Silas Deane. Philadelphia, 1855–57.
  Relate to his controversy with Congress.

Jameson, J. F. Essays in the Constitutional History of the United States. Baltimore, 1886.
  Chapter I gives a good account of the Continental prize courts. Chapter II treats of the administrative organs of the Continental Congress. Scientific.

Johnston's Correspondence and Public Papers of John Jay. 4 vols. New York, 1890–93.
  Volume I contains a valuable letter of Jay's relating to naval administration.

Jones, C. H. Gustavus Conyngham. Philadelphia, 1903.
  A brief, but good account.

King's Regulations and Admiralty Instructions for 1772. London.

Gives the rules and regulations of the Royal Navy at the opening of the Revolution.

Lincoln, C. H.   Calendar, John Paul Jones Manuscripts   Washington, 1903.
Excellent catalogue and digest of the Jones manuscripts in the Library of Congress.   Dr. Lincoln's purpose is to enlarge his calendar so as to include the additional Jones material which is found in the Records and Papers of the Continental Congress.

Lossing, B. J.   Field-Book of the American Revolution.   2 vols.   New York, 1851–52.
Slight naval information.

Maclay, E. S.   History of the United States Navy.   2 vols.   New York, 1894.
Narrative of the Continental navy somewhat popular.

Massachusetts Historical Society Collections. Boston, 1806– .
Brief references to the Continental navy.

New England Historical and Genealogical Register for 1865.   Boston.
Contains a list of prisoners confined at Mill prison, Plymouth, during the Revolution.

New Hampshire Gazette for 1775–1783.   Portsmouth.
Contains information concerning the Continental vessels which were built in New Hampshire, or which arrived at Portsmouth.

New London County Historical Society, Records and Papers.   Volume I.   New London, 1890–94.
Gives a most excellent account of the fight between the Continental frigate "Trumbull" and the Liverpool privateer "Watt."

Outlook, January 3, 1903.   Tragedy of the Lost Commission by James Barnes.

A brief, but excellent, account of the exploits of Captain Gustavus Conyngham.

Pennsylvania Archives, 1st Ser. 12 vols. Philadelphia, 1852–56.
Of special value for the movements of the Continental vessels in the Delaware river and bay.

Pennsylvania Packet for 1775–1783. Philadelphia.
Valuable for the movements of the Continental vessels and the Pennsylvania privateers. The prizes which were sent into Philadelphia are advertised in its columns.

Providence Gazette for 1775–1783. Providence.
Valuable for Continental vessels in 1775 and 1776. Contains names of prizes.

Rhode Island Historical Society Publications, VIII. Providence, 1900. Papers of William Vernon and the Navy Board.
A valuable source of information for the work of the Navy Board at Boston. A number of important letters and documents are printed.

Root, M. P. Chapter Sketches of Connecticut Daughters of the American Revolution. New Haven, 1901.
Contains the best account of the life of Nathaniel Shaw, jr., naval agent at New London.

Royal Navy, List of. New York, 1782.

Sands, R. Life and Correspondence of John Paul Jones. New York, 1830.
Valuable reprints.

Scribner's Magazine for 1898. New York. John Paul Jones in the American Revolution, by Captain A. T. Mahan.
Contains a technical account of the fight between the "Bon Homme Richard" and the "Serapis."

Sheppard, J. H. Commodore Samuel Tucker. Boston, 1868.
> A good account of Tucker's life. Reprints the best of the Tucker papers found in the Harvard Library.

Sherburne, J. H. Life of John Paul Jones. New York, 1825, 1851.
> A fair account.

Sparks, Jared. American Biography, 2nd Ser. Vol. IX. Gammell's Life of Samuel Ward. Boston, 1846.
> Contains a bit of important information with reference to the founding of the navy.

Sparks, Jared. Gouverneur Morris. 3 vols. Boston, 1832.
> Volume I contains Morris's description of an ideal secretary of the navy.

Spears, J. R. History of Our Navy. 5 vols. New York, 1897–99.
> The account of the Continental navy is somewhat popular.

Staples, W. R. Annals of Providence. Providence, 1843.
> Of some value for 1775 and 1776.

Stevens's Facsimiles. 24 portfolios. London, 1889–95.
> Valuable for the diplomatic relations between England and France for 1776 and 1777, and for the movements of American vessels in European waters during these years.

Sumner, W. G. Financier and Finances of the American Revolution. 2 vols. New York, 1891.
> Gives a few facts about Morris's career as Agent of Marine.

Town, Ithiel. Some Details of the American Revolution. New York, 1835.
> Of slight value for naval history.

Waite, H. E. Origin of the American Navy. Boston, 1890.

Contains letters written by John Adams, Elbridge Gerry, and John Langton in 1813. These relate chiefly to the services of Washington's fleet at Boston.

Wells, W. V. Life and Public Services of Samuel Adams. 3 vols. Boston, 1865.

Adds to our knowledge of Samuel Adams as member of the Marine Committee.

Wharton, Francis. Revolutionary Diplomatic Correspondence, 1775–1783. 6 vols. Washington, 1889.

Of primary importance for the history of the naval services of American representatives in foreign countries.

Williams, Gomer. Liverpool Privateers. Liverpool, 1897.

Valuable for the sea fights of the Liverpool privateers.

Winsor, Justin. Narrative and Critical History of the United States. 8 vols. Boston and New York, 1884–89.

Volume VI contains a history of the Revolutionary navy by E. E. Hale.

Brief and suggestive.

THE STATE NAVIES

THE NAVY OF MASSACHUSETTS

Amory's James Sullivan. 2 vols. Boston, 1859.
>Throws some light upon Massachusetts's prize courts.

Austin's Elbridge Gerry. 2 vols. Boston, 1828–29.
>Contains information in respect to prize courts.

Boston Gazette for 1775–1783. Boston.
>Of the highest value for the cruises, engagements, and prizes of the Massachusetts navy.

Clowes. W. L. Royal Navy. 7 vols. Boston and London, 1897–1903.
>Volume IV contains an account of the naval battle at the mouth of the Penobscot.

Continental Journal and Weekly Advertiser for 1775–1783. Boston.
>Supplements the Boston Gazette.

Goodell, Acts and Resolves of Massachusetts. 5 vols. 1869–86.
>Volume V contains the legislation of Massachusetts with reference to prize courts. The notes to the laws are a valuable guide to the sources of the events which led to the passage of the laws.

Maclay, E. S. History of American Privateering. New York, 1899.
>Of value for the Revolutionary privateers of Massachusetts.

Massachusetts Historical Society Collections.
   67 vols. Boston, 1792–1894.
      Contains references to the Penobscot ex
      pedition.
Massachusetts Historical Society Proceedings.
   30 vols. Boston, 1859–94.
      Contains information upon the Penobscot
      expedition.
Massachusetts, Journals of the House of Representatives for 1775–1783.
      Contemporaneous print. Incomplete.
      The journals found in the state library
      may be supplemented by those found in
      the library of the Boston Athenaeum.
Massachusetts, Records of the Council for
   1775–1776.
      Are printed in part in Force's American
      Archives.
Massachusetts, Journals of the Third Provin-
   cial Convention, 1775.
      Are printed in Force's American Arch-
      ives. The chief sources for the early civil
      history of the Massachusetts navy are
      the Journals of the Third Provincial Con-
      vention, Journals of the House, Records
      of the Council, and the Resolves of the
      General Court.
Massachusetts, Records of the General Court
   for 1775–1783. MSS.
      Supplements the Journals and the Re-
      solves.
Massachusetts Resolves, for 1775–1783.
      Contemporaneous print. A most valu-
      able source. Most of the naval legisla-
      tion of Massachusetts was passed in the
      form of Resolves, and not Laws.
Massachusetts Revolutionary Archives, MSS.
      A very extensive and valuable source.
      Many volumes contain material relating
      to the navy. Volumes XXXIX, XL, and
      XLIV have the greatest value. They con-
      tain the rolls of naval vessels, letters of of-

ficers, and miscellaneous papers. Volume CXLV has many documents relating to the Penobscot expedition. The Archives are rich in material relating to privateers. The Board of War Letters, Board of War Minutes, and Board of War Orders contain much naval material. An Index compiled by Justin Winsor affords a valuable key to the Archives.

Pickering and Upham's Timothy Pickering. 4 vols. Boston, 1867, 1874.
Of value for the work of the Massachusetts prize courts.

Virginia Gazette for 1779. Williamsburg.
Prints a valuable letter about Massachusetts privateers.

Weymouth Historical Society Publications. 2 vols. Boston, 1881–85.
Volume I gives the best account of the Penobscot expedition, and prints the original Journal of General Solomon Lovell kept on the expedition.

Winsor, Justin. Narrative and Critical History of the United States. 8 vols. Boston and New York, 1884–89.
Article on the Revolutionary navy by E. E. Hale, in Volume VI, contains information on the Massachusetts navy. Valuable bibliography.

Works of John Adams. 10 vols. Boston, 1856.
Gives John Adams's opinion of the Massachusetts statute establishing privateering.

THE NAVY OF CONNECTICUT

Caulkins, Frances M. History of Norwich. Norwich, 1845.
Contains information relative to the naval part which Norwich and Norwich men played in the Revolution.

Bibliography

Connecticut Revolutionary Archives. MSS.
: Contains much miscellaneous information relating to the Connecticut navy. Volumes VIII and IX contain valuable material concerning the prizes captured by Connecticut vessels.

Connecticut Colonial Records for 1775–1776. Hartford, 1890.
: Valuable for the beginnings of the Connecticut navy.

Connecticut Gazette for 1775–1779. New London.
: The best newspaper for naval news in the state. Captured prizes are advertised in its columns.

Connecticut Historical Society Collections. 8 vols. Hartford, 1860–1901.
: Volume II contains a description of Bushnell's submarine boat.

Connecticut in the Revolution. Hartford, 1889.
: Of slight naval value.

Connecticut Journal for 1775–1779. New Haven.
: Supplements the Connecticut Gazette in a few particulars, but contains much less news.

Connecticut State Records, 1776–1779. 2 vols. Hartford, 1894–95.
: Of great value for the years covered.

Force, Peter. American Archives. 9 vols. Folio. Washington, 1837–53.
: Contains miscellaneous information relating to the Connecticut navy.

Ford, W. C. Writings of George Washington. 14 vols. New York and London, 1889–93.
: Volume X contains Washington's account of Bushnell's submarine boat.

Hartford Courant for 1775–1779. Hartford.
: For naval news, the newspaper in the state next in importance to the Connecticut Gazette.

New London County Historical Society. Records and Papers. Volume I. New London, 1890–94.
> Valuable. Contains a fair account of the Connecticut navy, and a list of Connecticut privateers.

Wharton, Francis. Revolutionary Diplomatic Correspondence. 6 vols. Washington, 1889.
> Volume II has a reference to the voyage of the "Spy" to France in 1778.

THE NAVY OF PENNSYLVANIA

Almon's Remembrancer for 1778. London.
> Valuable for an account of the British raid to the north of Philadelphia in May, 1778.

Bioren, Laws of Pennsylvania. 4 vols. Philadelphia, 1810.
> Contains statutes relating to the establishment of prize courts.

Barney, Mary. Memoirs of Commodore Barney. Boston, 1832.
> Of value for a history of the "Hyder Ally."

Jameson, J. F. Essays in the Constitutional History of the United States. Baltimore, 1886.
> Chapter I, Predecessor of the Supreme Court, gives an excellent account of the capture of the sloop "Active" by the brig "Convention."

Pennsylvania Archives. 1st and 2nd Ser. 31 vols. Philadelphia and Harrisburg, 1852-90.
> The most important source after the Colonial records. Volume I of the second series contains the minutes of the Pennsylvania Navy Board, a brief historical account of the navy, and a list of Pennsylvania privateers.

Pennsylvania Colonial Records. 16 vols. Philadelphia, 1852-53.
> A source of great value for the history of the Pennsylvania navy.

Pennsylvania Journal and Weekly Advertiser for 1775-1783. Philadelphia.
> Supplements the Pennsylvania Packet.

Pennsylvania Packet for 1775-1783. Philadelphia.
> Valuable for the prizes captured by Pennsylvania naval vessels and by privateers. Not printed while the British occupied Philadelphia.

Scharf and Westcott. History of Pennsylvania. 3 vols. Philadelphia, 1884.
> Contains bits of naval information.

Wallace, J. W. Colonel William Bradford. Philadelphia, 1884.
> Valuable for the naval campaigns around Philadelphia.

THE NAVY OF VIRGINIA

Almon's Remembrancer for 1779 and 1781. London.
> Contains original material for the raids into Virginia of Matthews and Collier, and of Arnold and Phillips.

Calendar of Virginia State Papers. 10 vols. Richmond, 1875-92.
> Volumes I-III throw light upon the years 1780-1783. Volume VIII, pages 75-240, prints the Journals of the Committee of Safety of Virginia, February 7 to July 5, 1776.

Force, Peter. American Archives. 9 vols Folio. Washington, 1837-53.
> Prints important state records.

Ford, W. C. Writings of Jefferson. 10 vols. New York and London, 1892-99.
> Of value for Jefferson's naval services while governor of Virginia.

Hening's Statutes of Virginia. 13 vols. Philadelphia and New York, 1823.
> A most important source for naval legislation and administration in Virginia.

Lull, E. P. History of the United States Navy yard at Gosport, Virginia. Washington, 1874.
> Gives the early history of the navy yard at Norfolk.

Maryland Archives, 21 vols. Baltimore, 1883–1901.
> Contains information about Commodore Boucher of the Virginia navy.

North Carolina Records. 18 vols. Raleigh, 1886–1900.
> Contains information upon the raid of Matthews and Collier.

Rowland, K. M. George Mason. 2 vols. New York, 1892.
> Volume I is valuable for Virginia's "Potomac river fleet."

Southern Literary Messenger for 1857. Richmond.
> Contains a series of valuable articles entitled the "Virginia Navy of the Revolution." A good account of the Virginia navy. Somewhat extravagant in tone. Popular rather than scientific.

Virginia Archives, Richmond. Letter Book of Governor Thomas Jefferson; Letter Book of Governor Benjamin Harrison. MSS.
> Contain bits of naval information.

Virginia Archives, Richmond. Journals of the Virginia Navy Board. MSS.
> A valuable source for both the civil and military history of the navy.

Virginia Archives, Richmond. Virginia State Navy Papers. 2 vols. MSS.
> An important original source. Contains much information relative to the different vessels of the navy.

Virginia Gazette for 1775–1779. Williamsburg.
> Not complete files. Those in the Library of the Virginia Historical Society may be supplemented by those in the Virginia State Library. Of some value for the cruises of the Virginia fleet.

Virginia Historical Register. 6 vols. Richmond, 1848–53.
> Contains some important bits of naval information.

THE NAVY OF SOUTH CAROLINA

Almon's Remembrancer for 1780. London.
> Valuable for the naval defence of Charleston, 1779–1780.

Clowes, W. L. Royal Navy. 7 vols. Boston and London, 1897–1903.
> Gives good accounts of the cruise of the "Randolph" in 1778, and the capture of the "South Carolina" in 1782.

Connecticut Gazette for 1782, New London.
> Reports the capture of the Bahamas by the Spaniards and Commodore Gillon.

Cooper's Statutes of South Carolina. 10 vols. Columbia, 1836–41.
> Valuable for naval legislation.

Deane Papers. Collections of the New York Historical Society. 5 vols. New York, 1886–90.
> Serviceable for Gillon's movements in Europe.

Drayton, W. H. Memoirs of the American Revolution. 2 vols. Charleston, 1821.
> Throws light on the naval history of 1775.

Force, Peter. American Archives. 9 vols. Folio. Washington, 1837–53.
> Prints important South Carolina official records, notably the early journals of the South Carolina Navy Board. The manu-

script journals of the South Carolina Navy Board are in the New York State Library at Albany.

Gazette of State of South Carolina for 1776–1779. Charleston.
>Files for part of the period at Charleston. Valuable for the cruises of the naval vessels.

Gibbes, R. W. Documentary History of the American Revolution. 3 vols. New York, 1853–57.
>Contains some naval information.

McCrady, Edward, History of South Carolina in the Revolution. 2 vols. New York and London, 1901–02.
>Of value for 1775 and for a history of the "South Carolina."

Moultrie, William. Memoirs of the American Revolution. 2 vols. New York, 1802.
>Of little value for naval history.

Poore's Constitutions. Washington, 1877.
>Contains the constitution of South Carolina of 1776.

Pennsylvania Packet for 1782. Philadelphia.
>Contains valuable material for the movements of the "South Carolina" during 1782.

Ramsay, David. Revolution of South Carolina, Trenton, 1785.
>Of slight value for naval history.

South Carolina and American General Gazette for 1776–1779. Charleston.
>Files for part of the period at Charleston. Valuable for the cruises of the naval vessels.

South Carolina Archives, Columbia. Journals of General Assembly for 1776. MSS.
>Of value for the civil history of the navy.

South Carolina Archives, Columbia. Journals of the House of Representatives for 1779–1780. MSS.

Throws light upon the naval history for 1779–1780.

South Carolina Archives, Columbia. Journals of the House of Representatives for 1783. MSS.
    Valuable for the naval services of Commodore Gillon.

South Carolina Archives, Columbia. Miscellaneous Records A. MSS.
    Contains some important naval records.

South Carolina Historical Society Collections. 3 vols. Charleston, 1857–59.
    Reprints a part of the Journals of the South Carolina Committee of Safety.

South Carolina Historical and Genealogical Magazine. 2 vols. Charleston, 1900–01.
    Prints two important letters of Commodore Gillon.

Wharton, Francis. Revolutionary Diplomatic Correspondence. 6 vols. Washington, 1889.
    Contains a note upon Commodore Gillon.

THE MINOR NAVIES OF THE SOUTHERN STATES

Force, Peter. American Archives. 9 vols. Folio. Washington, 1837–53.
    Prints official records. Of considerable value for the navies of Maryland, North Carolina, and Georgia.

Georgia Historical Society Collections. 5 vols. Savannah, 1840–1902.
    Prints a part of the proceedings of the Georgia Council of Safety. Contains a few naval items of importance.

Jones, C. C., jr. History of Georgia. 2 vols. Boston, 1883.
    Contains a few references to the work of the Georgia galleys.

Maryland Archives. 21 vols. Baltimore, 1883–1901.

Contains much information concerning the Maryland navy. This may be found by consulting the index for the names of the vessels.

Maryland Statutes. Kilty, 2 vols. Annapolis, 1799–1800.

Kilty is best. Hanson supplements Kilty.

McCall, Hugh. History of Georgia. 2 vols. Savannah, 1811–16.

Volume II gives some information in respect to the Georgia galleys.

North Carolina Records. 18 vols. Raleigh, 1886–1900.

The most valuable source for the history of the North Carolina navy.

Ridgely, David. Annals of Annapolis. Baltimore, 1841.

Narrates an important event or two in the history of the Maryland navy.

Scharf, J. T. History of Maryland. 3 vols. Baltimore, 1879.

Volume II contains naval information of considerable value.

Southern Literary Messenger for 1857. Richmond.

Contains an excellent account of the Battle of the Barges.

THE MINOR NAVIES OF THE NORTHERN STATES

Arnold, Samuel G. History of Rhode Island, 2 vols. New York, 1859.

Volume II contains a few items of naval information.

Carson, H. L. Supreme Court of the United States. Philadelphia, 1902.

Contains references to the admiralty legislation of New York.

Connecticut Gazette for 1779. New London.

Gives a good account of the achievements of Captain Talbot.

Fernow's New York in the Revolution. Albany, 1887.
> Contains the rolls of several New York vessels.

Force, Peter. American Archives. 9 vols. Folio. Washington, 1837-53.
> Prints important records for Rhode Island, New Hampshire, and New York.

New Hampshire Archives. MSS. Concord.
> References to the "Hampden."

New Jersey, Minutes of the Provincial Congress and Council of Safety, 1775-1776. Trenton, 1879.
> Of some value for the prize legislation in New Jersey.

New York, Journals of New York Provincial Convention, etc. 2 vols. Albany, 1842.
> Valuable for the history of the New York navy.

Providence Gazette for 1775-1779. Providence.
> Valuable for the movements and prizes of Rhode Island vessels.

Pennsylvania Packet for 1779. Philadelphia.
> Contains original material for the cruises of Captain Talbot.

Poore's Constitutions. Washington, 1877.
> Contains the constitution of New York for 1777.

Rhode Island, Acts and Resolves for 1775-1783.
> Contemporaneous prints. A valuable source for the history of the Rhode Island navy.

Rhode Island Colonial Records. 10 vols. Providence, 1856-65.
> Supplements the information contained in the Acts and Resolves.

Rhode Island Historical Collections. 8 vols. Providence, 1827-92.
> Contains letters which are valuable for the naval history of 1775.

Rhode Island Historical Society Publications
VIII. Providence, 1900.
    Important for the naval history of Rhode Island for 1778.
Rhode Island. Journals of the Council of War. MSS. Providence.
    Of some value for the years 1779–1781.
Staples, W. R. Annals of Providence. Providence, 1843.
    Contains a brief account of the Rhode Island navy.
Sheffield, W. P. Rhode Island Privateers and Privateersmen. Newport, 1883.
    A fairly good account.

APPENDIX B

A LIST OF COMMISSIONED OFFICERS WHO SERVED IN THE NAVY AND MARINE CORPS OF THE UNITED STATES DURING THE AMERICAN REVOLUTION[1]

NAVY

COMMANDER-IN-CHIEF

1. Esek Hopkins.

CAPTAINS

1. Joseph Nicholson.
2. John Manly.
3. Hector McNeil.
4. Dudley Saltonstall.
5. Nicholas Biddle.

---

1. This list is compiled from two lists of naval officers which are now found in the Division of Manuscripts of the Library of Congress. One of these was prepared by the Naval Department in 1781, the other by the Auditor's Office of the Treasury Department in 1794. A complete roster of the naval officers of the Revolution does not exist. The list now printed is almost complete. It may contain a few inaccuracies. The names are arranged alphabetically, with the exception of those of the first twenty-four naval captains, which are arranged according to rank.

List of Officers

6. Thomas Thompson.
7. John Barry.
8. Thomas Read.
9. Thomas Grennel.
10. Charles Alexander.
11. Lambert Wickes.
12. Abraham Whipple.
13. John B. Hopkins.
14. John Hodge.
15. William Hallock.
16. Hoysted Hacker.
17. Isaiah Robinson.
18. John Paul Jones.
19. James Josiah.
20. Elisha Hinman.
21. Joseph Olney.
22. James Robinson.
23. John Young.
24. Elisha Warner.
25. John Ayres.
26. Peter Brewster.
27. William Burke.
28. Samuel Chew.
29. Gustavus Conyngham.
30. Benjamin Dunn.
31. John Green.
32. Seth Harding.
33. John Hazard.
34. Henry Johnson.
35. Peter Landais.
36. John Nicholson.
37. Samuel Nicholson.
38. William Pickles.
39. John P. Rathburn.
40. Thomas Simpson.
41. John Skimmer.
42. William Stone
43. Silas Talbot.
44. Samuel Tucker
45. Daniel Waters.

LIEUTENANTS

1. Robert Adamson.
2. Joseph Adams.
3. Thomas Albertson.
4. Blaney Allison.
5. John Angus.
6. James Armitage.
7. Rhodes Arnold.
8. Josiah Audibert.
9. John Baldwin.
10. William Barnes.
11. Joshua Barney.
12. Benjamin Barron.
13. William Barron.
14. Benjamin Bates.
15. George Batson.
16. Daniel Bears.
17. John Bellenger.
18. Elijah Bowen.
19. Christopher Bradley.
20. Jacob Brooks.
21. John Brown.
22. Philip Brown.
23. Isaac Buck.
24. Charles Bulkley.
25. Edward Burke.
26. Ezekiel Burroughs.
27. Samuel Cardal.
28. George Champlin.
29. John Channing.
30. Seth Clarke.
31. David Cullam.
32. Richard Dale.
33. James Degge.
34. William Dennis.
35. Peter Deville.
36. Silas Devol.
37. Arthur Dillaway.
38. Joseph Doble.
39. Marie Sevel Dorie.

40. William Dunlap.
41. William Dupar.
42. John Fanning.
43. Joshua Fanning.
44. Wilford Fisher.
45. Patrick Fletcher.
46. Robert French.
47. William Gamble.
48. Nicholas E. Gardner.
49. Joseph Greenway.
50. Stephen Gregory.
51. William Grinnell.
52. James Grinwell.
53. Simon Gross.
54. Elijah Hall.
55. William Ham.
56. Benjamin Handy.
57. James Handy.
58. Robert Harris.
59. Abraham Hawkins.
60. John Hennesey.
61. Stephen Hill.
62. Christopher Hopkins.
63. Esek Hopkins, jr.
64. William Hopkins.
65. George House.
66. Robert Hume.
67. Aquilla Johns.
68. John Kemp.
69. John Kerr.
70. Michael Knies.
71. Benjamin Knight.
72. William Leeds.
73. Edward Leger.
74. John Lewis.
75. Muscoe Livingston.
76. George Lovie.
77. Cutting Lunt.
78. Henry Lunt.
79. John McDougal.
80. John McIvers.

81. Jonathan Maltbie.
82. John Margisson.
83. Robert Martin.
84. Richard Marvin.
85. Luke Mathewman.
86. William Mollison.
87. John Moran.
88. William Moran.
89. William Morrison.
90. Alexander Murray.
91. Isaac Olney.
92. Benjamin Page.
93. David Phipps.
94. James Pine.
95. Jonathan Pitcher.
96. Robert Pomeroy.
97. David Porter.
98. William Potts.
99. Jonathan Pritchard.
100. Benjamin Reed.
101. Peter Richards.
102. John Rodez.
103. James Robertson.
104. John Robinson.
105. Peter Rosseau.
106. Robert Saunders.
107. John Scott.
108. Robert Scott.
109. John Scranton.
110. Nicholas Scull.
111. Benjamin Seabury.
112. James Sellers.
113. Josiah Shackford.
114. Peter Shores.
115. John Sleymaker.
116. Daniel Starr.
117. James Stephens.
118. John Stevens.
119. Adam W. Thaxter.
120. Mathew Tibbs.
121. Daniel Vaughan.

List of Officers

122. Thomas Vaughan.
123. Joseph Vesey.
124. Thomas Weaver.
125. David Welch.
126. Hezekiah Welch.
127. John Wheelwright.
128. Jacob White.
129. Jacob White (?).
130. Richard Wickes.
131. James Wilson.
132. Robert Wilson.
133. Hopley Yeaton.
134. Samuel York.

MARINE CORPS

MAJOR

1. Samuel Nichols.

CAPTAINS

1. Edward Arrowsmith.
2. Seth Baxter.
3. Abraham Boyce.
4. Isaac Craig.
5. Benjamin Dean.
6. James Disney.
7. John Elliott.
8. Robert Elliott.
9. Joseph Hardy.
10. John Hazard.
11. William Holton.
12. William Jones.
13. Dennis Leary.
14. William Mathewman.
15. William Morris.
16. Robert Mullen.
17. William Nicholson.
18. George Jerry Osborn.
19. Richard Palmes.
20. Matthew Parke.
21. Miles Pennington.
22. Andrew Porter.
23. —— Rice.
24. Gilbert Saltonstall.
25. Samuel Shaw.
26. Joseph Shoemaker

27. —— Spence.
28. John Stewart.
29. John Trevitt.
30. Elihu Trowbridge.
31. John Welch.

LIEUTENANTS

1. William Barney.
2. William Barney (?).
3. Henry Becker.
4. Peter Bedford.
5. David Bill.
6. Gurdon Bill.
7. Abraham Boyce.
8. Peregrine Brown.
9. Benjamin Catlin.
10. Seth Chapin.
11. John Chilton.
12. James Clark.
13. James Cokely.
14. James Connolly.
15. William Cooper.
16. David Cullam.
17. Robert Cummings.
18. Henry Dayton.
19. Robert Davis.
20. Panatier De la Falconier.
21. Lewis De la Valette.
22. John Dimsdell.
23. Stephen Earl.
24. Thomas Elting.
25. Thomas Elwood.
26. Zebadiah Farnham.
27. William Fielding.
28. Thomas Fitzgerald.
29. John Fitzpatrick.
30. Samuel Gamage.
31. William Gilmore.
32. Peter Green.
33. John Guignace.
34. Roger Haddock.

List of Officers

35. James Hamilton
36. Jonas Hamilton.
37. William Hamilton.
38. John Harris.
39. John Harris (?).
40. Richard Harrison.
41. Samuel Hempsted.
42. Daniel Henderson.
43. Samuel Holt.
44. Benjamin Huddle.
45. William Huddle.
46. Robert Hunter.
47. William Jennison.
48. —— Kelly.
49. Hugh Kirkpatrick.
50. Daniel Longstreet.
51. David Love.
52. Eugene McCarthy.
53. James McClure.
54. Richard McClure.
55. Charles McHarron.
56. Robert McNeal.
57. Peter Manifold.
58. Stephen Meade.
59. Jonathan Mix.
60. Hugh Montgomery.
61. Abel Morgan.
62. William Morris.
63. Alexander Neilson.
64. Avery Parker.
65. Samuel Powars.
66. Thomas Pownal.
67. Samuel Prichard.
68. Thomas Plunkett.
69. William Radford.
70. Franklin Reed.
71. Jerry Reed.
72. Nathaniel Richards.
73. Alpheus Rice.
74. Jabez Smith.
75. Walter Spooner.

List of Officers

76. Edmund Stack.
77. Daniel Starr.
78. J. M. Strobach.
79. Benjamin Thompson.
80. George Trumbull.
81. Thomas Turner.
82. Nathaniel Twing.
83. Abraham Vandyke.
84. Zebulon Varnam.
85. ——— Wadsworth.
86. Samuel Wallingsworth.
87. James Warren.
88. James Warren (?).
89. William Waterman.
90. Jacob White.
91. James H. Wilson.
92. Jonathan Woodworth.

APPENDIX C

A LIST OF ARMED VESSELS IN THE SERVICE OF THE UNITED STATES DURING THE AMERICAN REVOLUTION[1]

PRINCIPAL FLEET OF THE CONTINENTAL CONGRESS

	Rig.	Name.	No. of guns.	Period of Service.
1	ship	Alfred	24	1775–1778
2	ship	Columbus	20	1775–1778
3	brig	Andrew Doria	14	1775–1777
4	brig	Cabot	14	1775–1777
5	sloop	Providence	14	1775–1779
6	sloop	Hornet	10	1775–1777
7	schooner	Wasp	8	1775–1777
8	schooner	Fly	8	1775–1777
9	brig	Lexington	16	1776–1777
10	brig	Reprisal	16	1776–1777
11	brig	Hampden	14	1776–1777
12	sloop	Independence	10	1776–1778
13	sloop	Sachem	10	1776–1777
14	sloop	Mosquito	4	1776–1777
15	frigate	Raleigh	32	1777–1778
16	frigate	Hancock	32	1777
17	frigate	Warren	32	1777–1779

1. The term "Period of Service" is used in a somewhat general sense. The dates are close approximations. Among the vessels used by the Naval Department as packets, merchantmen, or scout-ships are the following: "Despatch," "Georgia Packet," "Phœnix," "Mercury," "Baltimore," "Enterprise," and "Fame."

List of Armed Vessels

18	frigate	Washington	32	1777–1778
19	frigate	Randolph	32	1777–1778
20	frigate	Providence	28	1777–1780
21	frigate	Trumbull	28	1777–1781
22	frigate	Congress	28	1777
23	frigate	Virginia	28	1777–1778
24	frigate	Effingham	28	1777–1778
25	frigate	Boston	24	1777–1780
26	frigate	Montgomery	24	1777
27	frigate	Delaware	24	1777
28	ship	Ranger	18	1777–1780
29	brigantine	Resistance	10	1777–1778
30	sloop	Surprise	....	1777
31	frigate	Alliance	32	1778–1785
32	ship	General Gates	18	1778–1779
33	brigantine	Retaliation	....	1778
34	galley	Pigot	8	1778
35	frigate	Confederacy	32	1779–1781
36	sloop	Argo	12	1779
37	brig	Diligent	12	1779
38	ship	Saratoga	18	1780–1781
39	ship of the line	America	74	1782
40	ship	Washington	20	1782–1784
41	ship	Duc de Lauzun	20	1782–1783
42	frigate	Bourbon	36	1783

FLEET FITTED OUT IN FRANCE

1	ship	Bon Homme Richard	42	1779
2	ship	Indian	40	1777
3	frigate	Deane or Hague	32	1777–1783
4	frigate	Queen of France	28	1777–1780
5	ship	Pallas	30	1779
6	ship	Ariel	20	1780–1781
7	cutter	Cerf	18	1779
8	cutter	Revenge	14	1777–1779
9	brig	Vengeance	12	1779
10	cutter	Dolphin	10	1777
11	lugger	Surprise	10	1777

518   List of Armed Vessels

POLLOCK'S FLEET

1	ship	Morris	24	1778–1779
2	sloop	West Florida	....	1779–1780
3	schooner	....	....	1779

WASHINGTON'S FLEET

1	schooner	Hannah	....	1775
2	schooner	Lynch	....	1775–1776
3	schooner	Franklin	....	1775–1776
4	schooner	Lee	4	1775–1776
5	schooner	Harrison	....	1775–1776
6	schooner	Warren	....	1775–1776
7	brigantine	Washington	10	1775–1776
8	schooner	Hancock	....	1776
9	sloop	Gen'l Schuyler	....	1776
10	sloop	Gen'l Mifflin	....	1776
11	galley	Lady Washington		1776–1777

ARNOLD'S FLEET[1]

1	sloop	Enterprise	12	1776
2	schooner	Royal Savage	12	1776
3	schooner	Revenge	8	1776
4	schooner	Liberty	8	1776
5	gondola	New Haven	3	1776
6	gondola	Providence	3	1776
7	gondola	Boston	3	1776
8	gondola	Spitfire	3	1776
9	gondola	Philadelphia	3	1776
10	gondola	Connecticut	3	1776
11	gondola	Jersey	3	1776
12	gondola	New York	3	1776
13	galley	Lee	6	1776
14	galley	Trumbull	8	1776
15	galley	Congress	8	1776
16	galley	Washington	8	1776
17	galley	Gates	8	1776

1. Several of Arnold's vessels were employed on the Lakes in 1775.

INDEX

ABACO, Island of, 58.
Abercrombie, Lieutenant-Colonel, 414.
"Accomac," the, 406, 411.
Accounts, Naval, settling of, 70, 196, 225, 227-228, 246-247, 303-304, 440.
"Active," the, 335 and note, 349, 352.
Adams, John, early naval services, 32, 36-41, 46, 48, 51, 82-83, 86, 97, 98 and note, 135; in France, 161, 254-255, 257, 276, 292; and Massachusetts naval affairs, 321, 324.
Adams, Samuel, naval services, 83, 86, 89 and note; administrative views, 186, 211, 215, 225; and Penobscot expedition, 349.
"Admiral Duff," the, 345.
"Admiral Keppel," the, 369.
Admiralty Courts, of Continental Congress, 48-49, 67-68, 203, 233, 478; of Massachusetts, 68, 148, 322-323, 327-328; of Connecticut, 365, 474; of Pennsylvania, 148, 391-392; in France, 266-267, 282-283; of Virginia, 403-405; of South Carolina, 423-424; of Maryland, 444, 474; of North Carolina, 459; of Georgia, 462; of Rhode Island, 467-468, 474; of New York, 476; of New Hampshire, 476-477; of New Jersey, 477-478.
"Adventure," the brig, 397, 406.
"Adventure," the schooner, 397.
Africa, 173, 176, 279-280.
Agent of Marine, appointment of, 218-226; office of, 226-228; legislation under, 228-235; movement of fleet under, 235-240; recommendations of, 240-244; last work of, 244-250; 257, 302, 394.

"Albany," the, 350.
Alexander, Charles, 123.
"Alfred," the, 52, 55, 57, 59, 97, 133, 158, 175, 281.
"Alliance," the, 122, 204, 206, 220, 231, 235, 236-238, 248-250, 295-300, 302.
"Amelia," the, 442.
"America," the, 111, 122, 145, 204, 219-220, 235, 247.
"American Congress," the, 398.
"American Turtle," the, 364.
Amsterdam, 264, 311, 436-437.
"Andrew Doria," the, 52, 57, 59.
Annapolis, 442, 446.
"Annapolis," the, 442.
Antigua, 306-307, 344.
Appeals in prize cases, 49, 68, 327, 365-366, 391, 404-405, 475, 477.
Appointments, in Continental navy, 52-55, 105-107, 108-109, 119, 124-125, 160, 257-260, 309.
"Ariadne," the, 408.
"Ariel," the, 300.
"Argo," the, 469-470.
Arnold, Benedict, 73-78, 414, 415, 446.
"Arnold," the, 376, 379, 385.
Arnold and Phillips, raid of, 408, 413-415, 446.
Arnold's fleet, 71-78, 475.
Articles of Confederation, 197, 200-202, 417, 434-435.
"Atalanta," the, 206.
"Augusta," the, 385.
"Aurora," the, 468.
Aylett, William, 405.
Azores, the, 368.

BAGADUCE, Maine, 348-351.
Bahamas, the, 58, 328, 438.
"Baille," the, 236.
Baltimore, 51, 56, 57, 93, 99, 102, 168, 249, 331, 442, 443, 475.

"Baltimore," the, 442.
Baltimore Committee of Observation, 93, 442.
Barbadoes, the, 176, 431.
Barclay, Thomas, 302-303.
Barney, Joshua, 248-249, 394.
Barnwell, John, 418, 459.
Barron, James, 397, 402, 407, 416.
Barron, Richard, 397, 407.
Barry, John, 109 note, 206, 236-238, 802.
Bartlett, Josiah, 86.
"Batchelor," the, 169.
Battle of the Barges, 449-451.
Beaufort, S. C., 423, 428.
"Beaufort," the, 428.
Belfast, 293.
"Bellona," the, 459.
Bergen, 304.
"Berkenbosch," the, 273.
Bermudas, the, 156, 167, 171, 173, 180, 206, 236, 328, 342, 457, 465.
"Betsey," the, 419.
Beverly, Mass., 63.
Bilbao, 256, 331.
Biddle, Nicholas, 54, 57, 120, 123, 430.
Biddle, Owen, 373.
Bingham, William, 266, 305-306.
"Bishop Landaff," the, 471-472.
Blackburn, John, 454.
"Black Duck," the, 389.
"Black Prince," the privateer, 260-261.
"Black Prince," the ship, 52.
"Black Princess," the, 260-261.
Blake, Edward, 420, 425.
Bland, Theodoric, 222, 223.
Blewer, Joseph, 382.
"Blonde," the, 350.
Board of Admiralty, appointment, 181-188; duties, 188-189; pay, 189-190; selection, 190-194; legislative work, 194-203; movement of fleet under, 203-208; discontinuance, 208-209, 219-222, 227-229.

Board of Treasury, Continental, 184, 188, 205, 247, 249, 250.
Board of War, Continental, 184, 187.
Board of War, Massachusetts, 329-332, 335-337, 343, 345, 348, 351.
"Bolton," the, 59.
"Bon Homme Richard," the, 163, 258, 295-298.
Bordeaux, 256, 276, 292, 436.
Bordentown, 97, 99, 102, 387.
Boston, 63, 93, 94, 113, 114, 139, 140, 148, 154, 168, 172, 203, 206, 247, 248, 328, 352, 353, 361.
"Boston," the, 91, 158, 204, 207, 292, 344, 390, 433, 434.
Boston Bay, 156.
Boucher, John Henry, 402, 444.
Boulogne, 262.
Bounties, 46, 128, 146, 198, 403, 410, 411, 432, 443.
"Bourbon," the, 92, 122, 204, 235, 240.
Bowen, Oliver, 459, 460, 461.
Boys, Captain, 395.
Braddock, Captain, of Georgia navy, 461.
Bradford, John, 69, 94, 95.
Bradford, William, 382, 387.
Brest, 256.
"Bricole," the, 433, 434.
"Britannia," the, 357.
British fleet on Lake Champlain, 76.
Brooke, Walter, 402.
Broughton, Nicholson, 33, 61-63, 66.
Brown, John, 227, 231.
Bryan, George, 190.
"Bulloch," the, 461.
Burdon, George, 293.
Burgoyne, General, 77, 384.
Bushnell, David, 363-364.
Buzzard's Bay, 339.

"Cabot," the, 52, 57, 58, 59, 158, 175.
Cadiz, 261.

Cadrigal, General, 438.
Caldwell, Thomas, 378.
Calvert, Captain, 308.
Canada, 72, 151, 173.
"Camden," the, 475.
"Camilla," the, 350.
Campbell, Captain, 461.
Campbell, Lord William, 419-420.
Cape Cod, 279.
Cape Fear, 156, 165, 452.
Cape Francois, 207, 237, 305, 331, 460.
Captures, Continental, legislation concerning, 49-50, 126-127, 200-201, 232-234. See Prizes.
Carleton, Sir Guy, 76, 77.
Carmichael, William, 260.
Castine, Maine, 348.
Caswell, Governor, 458.
"Caswell," the, 406, 456, 458, 459.
Catherine II. of Russia, 274.
Champlain, Lake, 72-78, 475.
Champlin, George, 165.
"Chance," the, 169.
Charleston, S. C., 154, 156, 166, 167. 369, 419-423, 425, 427, 432-434.
Chase, Samuel, 51, 82, 86.
Chatham, Conn., 92, 204.
"Chatham," the, 390.
Chaumont, Ray de, 296.
"Cherokee," the, 419, 420.
"Chester," the, 442, 444.
Chew, Samuel, 165.
Chickahominy shipyard, 400, 401. 413. 414.
Clinton, General Henry, 408, 445.
Clouston, John, 332, 343.
Cochran, Robert, 421-422, 427.
Coit, William, 359, 368 note.
Collier, Sir George, 350.
"Columbus," the, 52, 57, 59, 133, 175.
"Comet," the galley, 461.
"Comet," the schooner, 421.

"Commerce," the, 419.
Commerce, American, 241.
Commercial agents of Congress, 105, 253, 256-257, 305-311.
Commercial Committee of Congress, 160, 162, 257, 307.
Commissary-General of Issues, 204.
Commissary-General of Prisoners, 96, 116, 209, 222.
Commissary-General of Purchases, 116.
Commissioners at Paris, 105, 116, 254; work of, 255-294.
Commissions for Continental Navy, 50, 109, 188, 197, 199-200, 258; for privateers, 127, 200, 260-261, 321; for Massachusetts navy, 201; for Pennsylvania navy, 374.
Committee of Foreign Affairs, 160, 162, 255, 277-280.
Committee of Secret Correspondence, 162, 255, 258, 260, 276, 283, 305.
"Confederacy," the, 112, 122, 204, 207-208, 306, 390.
"Confederate," the, 208.
"Congress," the frigate, 92.
"Congress," the galley, 461.
Connecticut Council, 354, 355, 366.
Connecticut Council of Safety, 75, 95, 354-363, 369, 371.
Connecticut Gazette, 359, 362.
Connecticut General Assembly, 354, 355, 358, 360, 361, 363-367, 371-372.
Connecticut, Governor of, 75, 92, 95, 354-364, 369, 371.
Connecticut House of Representatives, 354, 366.
Connecticut Journal, 362.
Connecticut Navy, 315; beginning of, 355-360; administration of, 360-363; regulations of, 361, 366-367; vessels, 355-360, 367-370; end of, 369-370.
Connecticut, warfare of armed boats, 370-372.

"Conoueror," the, 442, 444.
Consuiar bureau, 139-140.
Continental agents, 95, 103, 105, 257, 305, 307.
Continental Congress, movement for a navy in, 34-38, 81-84; legislation respecting navy, 37-38, 41-51, 84-85, 105-107, 109, 119-133, 145-146, 154, 196-203, 228-235, 245-250, 259, 261-263; legislation respecting Naval Department, 37-38, 86-88, 93-94, 96-98, 101-103, 109, 113, 187-193, 195-196, 208-209, 216-224, 301-304; prepares a fleet on Lakes, 71-73; and prize courts, 48-50, 67-69, 203, 327, 365, 391, 404, 467, 477-478; action respecting Esek Hopkins, 133-138; action respecting consuls, 140; ignorance of navy, 182-183; establishes administrative boards, 184, 212; factions of, 186; 210-216; refuses to increase navy, 240-244; ends navy, 245; relations with Oliver Pollock, 307-311; 315, 322, 333, 357, 385, 392, 402, 405, 409, 412, 417, 418, 421, 437, 438, 443, 447, 460, 465, 469, 472, 473, 475.
Continental Navy, movements for a, 32-42, 80-85; executive organs of, 38-41, 60, 86-90, 93-103, 187-196, 216-218, 223-228, 252-257, 302-307; rules of, 43-48; legislation respecting, 42-51, 85-86, 121-133, 196-201, 228-230, 232-234; vessels of, 51-52, 90-93, 110-112, 114, 121-123, 156-158, 203-205, 219-220, 235, 247-249, 261-266, 281, 306, 315, 344, 349, 388, 394, 433, 434, 465, 469-470; officers of, 51-55, 105-110, 117, 123-126, 128-129, 133-139, 158-160, 165, 258-260; expeditions of, 55-60, 168-169, 171-173, 205-208, 236-239, 283-284, 286-300, 302, 308-311; uniform of, 117-118; conditions of, 141-160; general movements of, 161-180, 276-280; recommendations for increase of, 239-243; end of, 244-251; breaches of neutrality by, 273-274, 284-292; 375, 427, 444, 447.

Contraband, 200, 232.
"Convention," the, 377, 385, 388, 389.
Conyngham, Gustavus, 173, 179, 258, 260, 268, 273, 287, 290.
Cook, Captain James, 258, 275 note.
Cook, George, 444, 449.
Cooke, Nicholas, 463, 465.
"Cormorant," the, 244, 415-416.
Cornwallis, surrender of, 239, 240.
Coromandel Coast, 170, 279.
Coruña, 256, 438.
Cottineau, Captain, 297.
Coulthard, Captain, 206.
"Countess of Scarborough," the, 164, 296-297.
Courts-martial and courts of inquiry, in Continental navy, 44-45, 109, 131-139, 198-199, 228-232, 298-299, 300; in Connecticut navy, 366; in Pennsylvania navy, 375, 386-387.
Court of appeals for trial of prize cases, 203.
Crane, Stephen, 84.
"Crane," the, 360, 369.
Crawford, John, 231.
Cregier, Thomas, 472.
Cropper, John, 450.
Cross, Stephen, 336.
Cushing, Nathan, 323.
Cushing, Thomas, 328

DALE, Richard, 258.
Dalton, John, 398.
Danish government, 304.
Dartmouth, Mass., 325, 339.
Davidson, Samuel, 378-379.
Davis, Caleb, 337, 338.
Davis, James, 453-454.
Dawson, George, 238.
Deane, Silas, 37, 38, 51-52, 54, 82, 86, 148, 154; in France, 254, 258-260, 266, 276-278, 282, 292.
"Deane," the, 171, 203, 220, 231, 232, 235, 236, 262, 263, 306, 344, 352, 390.

"Defence," the barge, 448.
"Defence," the schooner, 420, 421.
"Defence," the ship, of the Connecticut navy, 359, 368, 369, 370.
"Defence," the ship, of the Maryland navy, 441, 442, 449.
"Defence," the sloop, 339.
Delaware, 315.
"Delaware," the frigate, 93.
"Delaware," the schooner, 377, 385.
Deshon, John, 98, 99, 113, 196, 355, 357.
D'Estaing, Count, 116, 139, 167.
Devil's Island, 449.
Dewey, Admiral, 179.
"Diamond," the, 468.
"Dickinson," the, 386, 387.
"Diligence," the, 406, 411.
"Diligent," the brig, 349.
"Diligent," the schooner, 320.
"Dolphin," the cutter, 262, 281, 287, 289.
"Dolphin," the schooner, 442, 444.
Douglass, William, 72.
Dover, England, 262.
"Dragon," the, 406, 411.
"Drake," the, 164, 293.
Drayton, William Henry, 421.
Duane, James, 223.
"Duc de Lauzun," the, 235, 237, 248, 303.
Dunkirk, 256, 260, 287, 290, 437.
Dunmore, Lord, 56, 396, 453.
"Duras," the, 295.
Dutch government, 273.
Dyer, Eliphalet, 82.

"Eagle," the British ship, 364.
"Eagle," the, of the South Carolina navy, 430.
Eastern Coast, the, 320, 338, 339, 343, 344, 353.
East Haddam, Conn., 360.
Edenton, N. C., 93, 452, 455, 458.
"Effingham," the frigate, 92, 388.
"Effingham," the galley, 386.

Ellery, William, 90, 182, 191-194, 196, 208.
Elliot, Samuel, 361, 362 and note.
Ellis, Richard, 458-459.
Ellsworth, Oliver, 222, 355.
"Enterprise," the ship, 76.
"Enterprise," the sloop, 72.
Executive Departments of Congress, 107.
Executive system, defects of, 210-214.

FACTIONS, in Congress, 186, 210-216.
"Fair American," the, 430.
"Falcon," the, 339.
Falconer, Nathaniel, 101.
"Fame," the, 306-307.
"Fearnaught," the, 448.
Ferrol, 291.
Fisk, John, 328, 332, 343.
Flags, 55, 120, 275-276, 327, 377.
Florida, 167, 173, 175, 461.
Floyd, William, 191.
"Fly," the, of Continental navy, 56, 57, 158.
"Fly," the, of Virginia navy, 416.
"Flying Fish," the, 451.
Forbes, James, 191, 192.
Ford, Samuel, 386.
Foreign Office of Congress, 160, 255.
Fort Mercer, 385.
Fort Mifflin, 385.
Forton prison, 267, 270.
"Fowey," the, 396.
"Fox," the, 163.
Franklin, Benjamin, 83, 378; in France, 254-256, 261, 262, 265-274, 282-284, 295, 296, 298-303.
"Franklin," the galley, 54, 390.
"Franklin," the schooner, 63, 64.
"Freedom," the, 325, 332, 343, 352.
French fleet, 139, 166-167, 205, 207, 242, 247-248, 263, 276, 294, 344, 371, 389, 413.
French government, 263, 265, 273, 282-289, 294, 295, 298.

GADSDEN, Christopher, 38, 39, 82, 83, 86.
"Gallatea," the, 350.
Galvez, governor of Louisiana, 307-311.
Gates, General Horatio, 74, 470.
"General Gates," the, 122, 165, 173, 306.
"General Greene," the, 390-391.
"General Mifflin," the, 70.
"General Monk," the, 393, 394.
"General Moultrie," the, 430, 431, 433, 434.
"General Putnam," the, 70, 472, 473, 474.
"General Schuyler," the, 70, 472, 473, 474.
Genoa, State of, 260.
Georgetown, S. C., 422, 426, 434.
Georgia Committee of Safety, 460.
Georgia Navy, 315, 459-462.
Georgia Provincial Congress, 459, 460.
Gerard, French minister to United States, 119, 140, 161, 166.
Germaine, Lord George, 457.
Gerry, Elbridge, 321, 323.
Ghent, 436.
Gibraltar, 268.
Gillon, Alexander, 435-440.
Glasgow, 276, 278.
"Glasgow," the, 59, 133, 186.
"Gloucester," the, 265.
Glover, John, 62, 63.
Goldsborough, Robert, 447.
"Good Intent," the, 274.
Gosport navy-yard, 93, 400, 408.
Goodrich, a Tory privateersman, 165.
Grannis, John, 136.
Grason, Thomas, 443.
Great Bridge, Va., 396.
Green, John, 258, 263.
"Greyhound," the, 350.
Grimes, John, 466.
Griswold, William, 356.
Groton, Conn., 371.
Guadaloupe, 331.
Guerard, Benjamin, 434.

"Guilford," the, 367, 370.
Gwinnett, Button, 461.

HABERSHAM, Joseph, 459.
"Hague," the, 236, 248.
Halifax, 156, 167, 465.
Hall, Captain, 430.
Hall, Giles, 355, 357.
Hallet, Allen, 345.
Hamilton, Alexander, 211, 213, 217-218.
"Hampden," the brig, 175.
"Hampden," the ship, 349, 476.
Hampstead, Joshua, 452, 453.
Hampton, Va., 396, 402, 412.
Hancock, John, 86, 89, 353, 472.
"Hancock," the frigate, 91, 158, 239, 344.
"Hancock," the galley, 390.
"Hancock," the schooner, 63.
Handy, Joseph, 450.
Handy, Levin, 450.
"Hannah," the, a merchantman, 475.
"Hannah," the, of Washintgon's fleet, 33, 61, 62.
Haraden, Jonathan, 343.
Harding, Seth, 207, 359.
Hardy, Captain, 461.
Harris, Captain, 407.
Harrison, Benjamin, 413.
Harrison, William Hanson, 447.
"Harrison," the, of Virginia navy, 416.
"Harrison," the, of Washington's fleet, 63, 65.
Harrison and Van Bibber, 443.
Hartford, Conn., 355.
Hartford Courant, 362.
Hartley, David, 269.
Hatcher, Captain, 461.
Havana, 237, 305, 309, 311, 435, 438.
"Hawk," the, 59.
Hayden, Uriah, 359.
"Hazard," the, 335, 342, 349, 352.
Hazelwood, John, 376, 380, 384, 385, 386, 388.
Heath, General, 116.

Henry, Patrick, 211.
"Henry," the, 411.
Hewes, Joseph, 38, 41, 86, 90, 454.
"Hibernia," the, 168, 169.
Hill, Whitmill, 193.
"Hinchinbrooke," the, 461.
Hispaniola, 175, 305, 457, 460.
Hodge, William, 262, 291.
Holker, John, 140, 205.
"Holker," the, 391.
Hollingsworth, Jesse, 442.
"Honor," the, 368.
Hopkins, Daniel, 208.
Hopkins, Esek, 53-60, 91, 105, 116, 125, 133-139, 185, 419.
Hopkins, J. B., 53, 54, 168.
Hopkins, Stephen, 38, 39-40, 53, 81, 82, 86, 90, 91, 92, 119.
Hopkinson, Francis, 96-97.
"Hornet," the brig, 428.
"Hornet," the galley, 461.
"Hornet," the sloop, 55, 56, 57.
Hosmer, Titus, 203.
Houston, John, 86.
Howe, General William, 77, 384.
Howe, Lord Richard, 120.
Howe, Tyringham, 59.
"Hudson," the, 475.
Huntington, Benjamin, 356, 359.
Huntington, Daniel, 193.
"Hussar," the, 353.
"Hyder Ally," the, 394, 395.

IMPRESSMENT of seamen, 146.
"Independence," the brigantine, 325, 352.
"Independence," the galley, 442.
"Independence," the sloop, 281.
"Indian," the, 264, 304, 436.
"Industry," the, 389.
Ingraham, Edward, 453.
Ioor, Joseph, 431.
Ipswich, Mass., 322, 328.

"Iris," the, 238.
Isle of Pines, 431.

"JACKALL," the, 236.
Jamaica, 156, 175, 345.
"Jane," the, 407.
"Jason," the, 169, 171.
Jay, John, 185, 186, 211, 219, 261.
Jefferson, Thomas, 303, 405, 409, 413.
"Jefferson," the, 407, 411, 414.
"Jemmy and Sallie," the, 430.
Jenifer, Daniel of St. Thomas, 193, 221.
Jersey, island of, 440.
"John," the, 169.
"John," the, 430.
"Johnson," the, 442.
Jones, John Paul, 54, 55, 106, 125, 164, 173-176, 179, 183, 207; in Europe, 258, 270-271, 273, 292-300, 303, 304, 449.
Josiah, James, 120, 123.
Joyner, John, 418, 435, 439, 459
"Judith," the, 429.

"KATY," the, 55, 464, 465.
Kidd, Captain, commander of a British vessel, 450.
Kingston, Mass., 325.
"King Tammany," the, 452.
Knox, Henry, 53.

"LADY WASHINGTON," the, 71.
Lafayette, 161, 295, 446.
Lake Champlain, battle of, 77.
Landais, Peter, 199, 258, 259, 294-300.
Langdon, John, 37, 38, 91, 95, 106.
Langdon, Timothy, 323.
Laurens, Henry, 89, 311
Laurens, John, 437.
"L'Aventure," 433.
Lawrence, John, 387.
Lebanon, Conn., 355.
Ledyard, William, 371.

Lee, Arthur, 186, 211, 254, 280, 282, 300.
Lee, R. H., 38, 83, 86, 89, 93, 186, 211, 215, 256.
Lee, William, 186, 211, 256.
"Lee," the galley, 461.
"Lee," the schooner, 63, 65.
Leghorn, 277.
Lemprière, Clement, 419.
Lewis, Francis, 86, 90, 191-194, 196, 208, 475.
"Lexington," the, 281, 287, 289, 291.
"Liberty," the armed boat, 397, 415, 416, 417.
"Liberty," the brig, 397, 407.
Lilly, Thomas, 397.
Little, George, 353.
Liverpool, 206, 278.
"Liverpool," the, 384.
Livingston, Musco, 119.
Livingston, William, 119, 477-478.
Logie, Commander, 236.
Long Island, 70, 368, 370, 474.
L'Orient, 237, 256, 286, 299, 300, 302.
Louis XVI., 202, 294, 436.
Lovell, Solomon, 350.
"Loyalist," the, 415, 416.
Loyalists, 338, 348, 370, 448.
Luxembourg, Chevalier, 436, 439-440.
Luzerne, French minister to United States, 248.
"Lydia," the, 389.
"Lynch," the, 63, 64.
Lyon, Samuel, 386.

McClehany, William, 231.
McDougall, Alexander, 213, 217-218, 224.
McKean, Thomas, 222.
Macpherson, John, 119.
McQueen, John, 435.
Machias, Maine, 320, 339.
"Machias Liberty," the, 320.
Madeira, 237.
Madison, James, 192.
"Magnifique," the, 247.
Mahan, A. T., 78, 143.

Manchac, 309.
Manly, John, 64, 65, 123, 163, 236.
Marblehead, Mass., 62, 63, 149.
"Margaretta," the, 339.
"Maria," the, 169.
Marine Committee, appointment of, 80-87; offices of, 87; chairmen, 88-90; agents of, 90-103, 105-115; work of, 105-140; conditions of the naval service under, 141-160; general movements of its fleet, 161-180; defects of, 181-186; superseded, 187; 69, 70, 247, 279, 349.
Marines, Continental, 43 and note, 51, 58, 117-118, 123, 129, 131, 136, 158-159, 197, 207, 229-230; of Massachusetts, 326; of Connecticut, 357, 358; of Pennsylvania, 376, 377, 392; of Virginia, 397, 398, 410, 411; of South Carolina, 420, 422, 427, 430, 440; of Maryland, 441, 445, 447; of North Carolina, 452.
"Mars," the, 201, 273, 338, 343, 344.
Martha's Vineyard, 339.
Martin, Joshua, 457.
Martinique, 204, 266, 305, 331, 353, 407, 443, 457.
Maryland commissioners for defense of Chesapeake bay, 447.
Maryland Committee of Safety, 441, 442.
Maryland, Governor of, 443.
Maryland Governor and Council, 441, 445, 446, 447, 448.
Maryland Legislature, 445, 447, 448, 451.
Maryland Navy, 122, 315, 402, 415, 441-451.
Maryland Provincial Convention, 441, 442, 443, 444.
Mason, George, 398.
"Massachusetts," the, 325, 332, 343.
Massachusetts Agent of the Commonwealth, 337, 338.
Massachusetts admiralty courts, 68, 69, 322-323, 327.

Massachusetts Board of War, 329-332, 335, 336, 337, 343, 345, 348, 351.
Massachusetts Commissary-General, 338, 353.
Massachusetts Committee of Foreign Affairs, 343.
Massachusetts Committee of Safety, 319.
Massachusetts Constitution, 337.
Massachusetts Council, 37, 319, 320, 322, 323, 324, 341, 347, 351, 422.
Massachusetts General Court, 319, 321, 323-326, 329, 332-336, 338, 339, 341.
Massachusetts, Governor of, 337, 338, 353.
Massachusetts House of Representatives, 319, 321, 324, 347, 351.
Massachusetts Navy, 151, 201, 275, 315-353, 470; beginnings of, 318-328; documents respecting, 328-329, 332-333; 334-337, 345-347; administration of, 329-332, 337-338; regulations respecting, 325-327, 333-335; vessels of, 325, 331, 335-339, 341-344, 352-353; expeditions of, 332-333, 341-353; end of, 353.
Massachusetts Provincial Congress, 318, 319.
Massachusetts trading vessels, 330-331.
Matthews and Collier, raid of, 408.
Mauritius, 179, 279.
Maxwell, James, 401, 409, 413.
"Medea," the, 352.
"Mercury," the, 311.
"Merlin," the, 385.
Middletown, Conn., 355, 359.
Mifflin, Samuel, 380.
Mifflin, Thomas, 192.
"Mifflin," the, 367.
"Milford," the cartel-ship, 270.
"Milford," the frigate, 344.
Milligan, Captain, 461.
Mill prison, 267, 268, 270.
"Minerva," the merchantman, 475.
"Minerva," the, of the Connecticut navy, 356, 357, 358.

Mississippi, the, 175, 307-311, 430.
Mobile, expedition against, 166, 311.
"Molly," the, 122.
"Montague," the, 120, 165.
Montgomery, General, 458.
Montgomery, James, 390.
"Montgomery," the frigate, 92.
"Montgomery," the ship, 71, 472-475.
"Montgomery," the sloop, 376, 379, 380, 385, 386.
Moore, Lieutenant, 339.
Moravian mission, 274.
Morgan, Captain, 430
Morris, Gouverneur, 211, 214.
Morris, Robert, 86, 90, 173-176, 182 and note, 211; agent of marine, 218-251, 256, 257, 302, 394; and the Pennsylvania navy, 376, 378, 394.
Morris, Thomas, 256.
"Morris," the, 308-309.
"Mosquito," the, 407.
Moylan, Stephen, 62, 63.
Mud Island, 384.

'NANCY," the, 65, 236.
Nantes, 256, 262, 266, 284, 286, 331, 369.
Nantucket, 279, 328, 342, 465.
Nassau, New Providence, 58, 173, 419.
'Nautilus," the, 350.
Naval administration in the states, in general, 315-318.
Naval Agents, of Washington, 62-63, 69-70; of Congress, 90-96, 103, 105-107, 110, 116, 117, 150, 189, 195, 196, 221, 227, 247, 256-257, 263-264, 266, 303-311; of Massachusetts, 327, 329; of Connecticut, 361-363; of Virginia, 401; of South Carolina, 426; of Maryland, 442-443; of North Carolina, 458-459.
Naval Committee, appointment of, 35-39; quarters of, 39; description of, 39-40; active life of, 40-41; legislative work, 42-51;

prepares a fleet, 51-56; appoints officers, 52-55; orders of, 56; summary of work, 60; its successor, 87; settling of its accounts, 246-247.
Naval Office at Paris, origin of, 252-253; duties and work, 253-254, 257-304; personnel of, 254-255; headquarters of, 255; agents of, 256-257; movements of the fleet under, 286-300.
Naval operations, 161-180.
Naval stations, Continental, 154-155; British, 155-156.
Navy Board at Boston, origin of, 97-103; duties of, 105-116, 164-165; abolition of, 221, 223, 227; 145, 168, 171, 176, 178, 182, 189, 191, 195, 196, 197, 247, 349, 469.
Navy Board at Philadelphia, origin of, 96-97, 99-103; duties of, 105-116; abolition of, 221, 223, 227; 145, 189, 195, 196, 197, 247.
Navy of the American Revolution. See Continental Navy, Massachusetts Navy, Connecticut Navy, etc.
Nesbit, J. M., 95.
Neutral rights, 200, 253, 266, 271-274, 281-292.
New Bedford, Mass., 339.
Newbern, N. C., 93, 452, 453, 455, 457, 459.
Newburyport, Mass., 62, 91, 320, 328, 336.
Newfoundland, 164, 167, 169; Grand Banks of, 166, 170, 236; fisheries of, 180, 276, 291-292.
New Hampshire Navy, 315, 349, 476-477.
New Haven, Conn., 73, 355, 360, 362.
New Jersey, 315, 477-478.
New Jersey Provincial Congress, 477.
New London, Conn., 92, 93, 95, 116, 165, 196, 236, 355, 357, 359, 362, 363, 371.
New Orleans, 160, 307-309.
New Providence Expedition, 55-60, 133.
New York, city of, 52, 69, 70, 75, 93, 154, 155, 206, 207, 239, 247, 364, 368, 471, 473.

Newport, R. I., 99, 194, 371.
New York Committee of Safety, 70, 472, 474, 475.
New York Convention, 96.
New York, Governor of, 476.
New York Marine Committee, 471, 472.
New York Navy, 70-71, 315, 471-476.
New York Provincial Congress, 71, 72, 471, 472.
New York Secret Committee, 475.
Nichols, Samuel, 58, 123.
Nicholson, James, 123, 124, 125 note, 206, 238-239, 441, 444, 446, 449.
Nicholson, Samuel, 236, 258, 262, 263.
Niles, Robert, 357, 370.
Niles, Samuel, 356, 357.
Nixon, John, 52, 95, 96, 97, 376, 378.
"Noble," the, 407.
"North," the, 350.
North Carolina Council of Safety, 451, 452.
North Carolina Naval Commissioners, 451-454.
North Carolina Navy, 315, 451-459.
North Carolina Provincial Congress, 452, 456.
North Yarmouth, Maine, 322.
Norwich, Conn., 92, 355, 356, 359, 360, 372.
"Notre Dame," the, 428-431, 433, 434, 435.

O'Brian, Jeremiah, 320.
Ocracoke Inlet, 155, 400, 406, 452, 454-459.
Officers, in Continental navy, 45-46, 50, 109, 123; in Massachusetts navy, 333; in Connecticut navy, 357; in Pennsylvania navy, 374; in Virginia navy, 397, 401; in North Carolina navy, 452; in Rhode Island navy, 464.
"Oliver Cromwell," the, of the Connecticut navy, 359, 368-370.
"Oliver Cromwell," the, of the Virginia navy, 415.
Olney, Joseph, 168.
Olney, Richard, 471.
"Orpheus," the, 208.

Osbornes, Va., engagement at, 414.
Ossabaw Island, 461.
"Otter," the, 350, 449.
"Oxford," the, 265.
PACA, William, 203, 447.
Paine, R. T., 82.
Palfrey, William, 302.
"Pallas," the, 296.
Palmer, Joseph, 324.
Parsons, Alston and Company, 305.
"Patriot," the armed boat, 397.
"Patriot," the schooner, 416.
Pay, in Continental navy, 46, 50-51, 128, 145-146, 198; in Massachusetts navy, 325-326, 333; in Connecticut navy, 357, 361, 366-367; in Pennsylvania navy, 380-381; in Virginia navy, 397, 403, 411, 416; in South Carolina navy, 422, 432; in Maryland navy, 441, 443, 445; in North Carolina navy, 452.
"Peggy," the, 423.
Pendleton, Captain, 459.
Pennell, Joseph, 227, 246, 247, 250.
Pennsylvania commissioners for defense of the Delaware, 393-395.
Pennsylvania Committee of Safety, 373-381, 391.
Pennsylvania Council of Safety, 378-381.
Pennsylvania Convention, 378.
Pennsylvania General Assembly, 389, 391-394.
Pennsylvania Navy, 123, 315, 373-395; beginnings of, 373-380; rules and regulations, 375; commodores, 378-379; pay, 380-381; navy board, 381-383; in 1777 and 1778, 383-389; in 1779, 390-391; prize courts, 391-392; in 1782, 393-395.
Pennsylvania Navy Board, 377, 381-383, 385, 387-389.
Pennsylvania Provincial Conference of Committees, 379.
Pennsylvania Supreme Executive Council, 378, 382, 383, 387-392, 394, 395.

"Pennsylvania Farmer," the, 452-454.
Penobscot Expedition, 337, 347-352, 476.
Pensacola, 175, 308, 311.
Pensions, 46, 129-131, 366, 381, 392, 410, 447.
Philadelphia, 39, 73, 92, 93, 94, 99, 102, 115, 140, 154, 166, 171, 196, 235, 238, 247, 311, 360, 373, 383, 384, 385, 389, 393, 413, 437-440, 465.
"Phoenix," the, 408.
Pickering, Timothy, 323.
Pickles, William, 309-311.
Piercy, Thomas, 297.
"Pigot," the, 469, 470.
Pinckney, Colonel, 423.
"Plater," the, 442.
Plymouth, Mass., 63, 64, 98, 322.
"Polacre," the, 433.
Pollock, Oliver, 160, 307-310.
"Polly," the, 430, 431.
Pontchartrain, Lake, 309, 310.
Porto Rico, 237.
Portsmouth, N. H., 64, 91, 93 106, 111, 116, 122, 169, 196, 204, 476.
Portsmouth, Va., 400.
Portuguese government, 273.
Poughkeepsie, N. Y., 92, 96, 166.
Pray, Captain, 460.
President of the Continental Congress, 89, 118, 188, 257, 301.
Prince Edward Island, 66.
"Prince Frederick," the, 169.
"Prince of Wales," the, 430.
Prisons, naval, 150-151, 267.
Prisoners, naval, 151, 188, 209, 222, 227, 245, 261, 267-272, 281, 341.
Privateers and Privateering, Continental, 49-50, 112, 119, 127-128, 136, 146-148, 201, 306, 308; in Europe, 260-261, 281; English, 151, 164, 165, 345-347, 411, 429, 445, 446, 449-451; Massachusetts, 148-149, 320-323, 327, 339-341, 344-347, 349; Connecticut,

148, 364-365; Pennsylvania, 148, 382, 390, 392-393; Virginia, 148, 405; South Carolina, 427, 428, 429; Maryland, 148, 443, 444; North Carolina, 459; Rhode Island, 146, 148, 467-468; New York, 475; New Hampshire, 476.
Prize Agents, Continental, 93-95, 103, 110, 195-196, 226-227, 247, 303-304; of Massachusetts navy, 327; of Connecticut navy, 363; of New York navy, 474.
Prizes of Continental navy, 59, 163-164, 165, 168-169, 172-173, 177-178, 206, 236, 237, 267, 273, 281-288, 293, 296-297, 308, 311; of Washington's fleet, 62, 64-71; of Massachusetts navy, 332-333, 335, 343-347, 353; of Connecticut navy, 357, 361, 368-369; of Pennsylvania navy, 385, 391, 394; of Virginia navy, 407; of South Carolina navy, 418-419, 429-430, 431, 438-439; of Maryland navy, 449; of Georgia navy, 461; of Rhode Island navy, 464; of New York navy, 474.
Prizes, sharing of, in Continental navy, 43, 46, 49-50, 51, 127, 129-130, 232-234; in Washington's fleet, 62; in Massachusetts navy, 326, 333; in Connecticut navy, 361, 366; in Pennsylvania navy, 381; in South Carolina navy, 427-428, 436, 439-440; in Maryland navy, 443, 448; in Rhode Island navy, 468; in New York navy, 473.
Pritchard, Paul, 427.
Promotions in the Continental navy, 123-125.
"Prosper," the, 421.
"Protector," the barge, 450.
"Protector," the ship, of the Massachusetts navy, 201, 336, 344, 345, 353.
"Protector," the ship, of the Virginia navy, 406.
Providence, R. I., 91, 93, 95, 98, 113, 135, 136, 148, 360, 468.
"Providence," the frigate, 91, 172, 204, 207, 292, 433, 468.

"Providence," the sloop, 55, 57, 59, 173, 175, 349, 465.
Prussian government, 177.
"Putnam," the, 377, 385.
"QUEEN OF FRANCE," the, 169, 171, 172, 204, 207, 263, 433.
Quincy, Joseph, 32.
"RAISONNABLE," the, 350.
"Raleigh," the brig, 408.
"Raleigh," the frigate, 91, 281.
Randall, Thomas, 472.
Randolph, Peyton, 82, 119.
"Randolph," the, 92, 430.
"Ranger," the galley, 387.
"Ranger," the ship, 106, 168, 169, 171, 172, 292-293, 433, 434.
Rank, naval, 123-126, 197, 257-258, 422.
Rathburn, John P., 172.
Rations in Continental navy, 128-129; in Massachusetts navy, 333; in Maryland navy, 447.
"Rattlesnake," the, 426.
Read, George, 86.
Read, James, 101, 196, 226, 250.
Read, Thomas, 123, 374, 376, 378.
"Rebecca," the, a merchantman, 308.
"Rebecca," the sloop, 461.
Recaptures, 50, 232, 322-323.
Red Bank, 373, 384.
Reed, Joseph, 391.
"Renown," the, 414.
"Reprisal," the, a privateer, 308.
"Reprisal," the sloop, 262, 269, 281, 283, 284, 286, 287, 291.
"Republic," the, 325, 331.
"Resistance," the, 165.
"Resolution," the, 442.
"Revenge," the brig, 345.
"Revenge," the cutter, 262, 281, 290, 291.
Revere, Paul, 350.

Rhode Island Committee of Safety, 463, 464, 466, 467.
Rhode Island Council of War, 138-139, 467, 468, 469.
Rhode Island General Assembly, 80, 463-470.
Rhode Island, Governor of, 465-467.
Rhode Island Inferior Court of Common Pleas, 138.
Rhode Island instructions to the Continental Congress, 33, 80-85.
Rhode Island Navy, 80, 315, 463-471.
"Richmond," the, 416.
Richmond, Va., 401, 414, 447.
"Rising Empire," the, 325, 338.
Roach, John, 106, 107.
Robertson, William, 435.
Rodgers, William, 472, 473.
"Roebuck," the, 208, 352, 384.
Rogers, Josias, 394.
"Rose," the, 80, 463, 464.
Ross, Elizabeth, 377.
Ross, John, 256.
"Rover," the, 470, 471.
"Royal Charlotte," the, 430.
Rules and Regulations, of Continental navy, 43-48, 109, 110, 202-203, 231; of British navy, 47-48, 202; of Massachusetts navy, 333-335; of Connecticut navy, 361, 366; of Pennsylvania navy, 374, 375, 391; of South Carolina navy, 422; of Maryland navy, 447; of New York navy, 472.
Rush, Benjamin, 374.
Russian navy, 304.
Rutledge, Edward, 36.
Rutledge, John, 82, 119, 424, 429, 430.

St. Augustine, Fla., 156, 419, 429, 430
St. Christopher, island of, 175.
St. Eustatius, island of, 237, 305, 306, 331, 457.
St. Mary's Isle, 293.
St. Thomas, island of, 335.

544 Index

Salem, Mass., 62, 149, 320, 328.
Salisbury, Mass., 91, 325.
"Sally," the, 389.
Salter, Titus, 476.
Saltonstall, Dudley, 54, 57, 133, 350, 352.
Saltonstall, Gilbert, 206.
Saltonstall, Gurdon, 154.
Salvage, 50, 201, 232, 323.
Samson, Simeon, 343.
Sandy Hook, 370, 390, 474.
"Saratoga," the, 122, 204, 208.
Sartine, French minister of marine, 274, 278, 296.
Savage, P. H., 330.
Savannah, 156, 167, 418, 459.
Saybrook, Conn., 74, 359.
Schuyler, General, 71-74, 116, 213.
"Schuyler," the, 367.
Schweighauser, a commercial agent in France, 256.
Seal of the Naval Department, 199, 209, 222.
Seamen in Continental navy, difficulties of enlistment, 144-147; numbers, 158-159.
Searle, James, 101.
Sears, Isaac, 358.
Secretary of Congress, 140, 209, 222.
Secretary of Foreign Affairs, 214, 255.
Secretary of Marine, 208-209, 214-218, 221, 224, 229.
Secretary of War, 216.
Secret Committee of Congress, 162.
Selkirk, Earl of, 293.
Selman, John, 63, 66.
"Serapis," the, 163, 164, 296, 297.
Seymour, Stephen, 426.
Seymour, Thomas, 380.
"Shark," the, 360, 369.
Shaw, Jr., Nathaniel, 95, 355, 362-363.
Sheridan, Patrick, 231.
Sherman, Roger, 221, 355.
"Sibylle," the, 237.

Simpson, Thomas, 168, 172.
Skimmer, John, 120, 165.
Smith, James, 72, 471, 472.
Smith, Meriwether, 220, 221.
Smith, William, 101.
"Somerset," the, 448.
"South Carolina," the, 436-440.
South Carolina Council of Safety, 418-421.
South Carolina, Governor of, 432, 434.
South Carolina House of Representatives, 432, 434.
South Carolina Legislature, 423-428.
South Carolina Navy, 173, 275, 315, 418-440; beginnings of, 418-424; operations of, 418-421, 428-434, 437-440; navy board, 424-428; ordinances of 1777 and 1778, 427-428; privateers, 428-429; Gillon and the "South Carolina," 435-440.
South Carolina Navy Board, 424-428.
South Carolina, President of, 423-425, 427, 429, 430.
South Carolina Privy Council, 423, 425, 430.
South Carolina Provincial Congress, 420-422.
South Quay, Va., 400, 406, 455, 456.
Spanish-American War, 179.
Spanish fleet, 166, 173, 242.
Spanish government, 219, 273, 282, 308.
"Speedwell," the, 389.
"Spitfire," the, 466.
"Spy," the, 356, 357, 368, 370.
State Navies, 152-153, 160; in general, 315-318; in particular, 318-478. See Massachusetts navy, Connecticut navy, etc.
Stonington, Conn., 357.
Stormont, Lord, 269-270, 284-289.
Stranger, Captain, 345.
Submarine invention, 363-364.
Subsistence money, 128, 198.
Suffolk, Va., 455-456.
Sullivan, Captain, 430.
Sullivan, General, 469, 470.

Sullivan, James, 321, 323.
Superintendant of Finance, 216, 219, 224, 227.
"Surprise," the, 262, 281, 287
Swanzey, Mass., 325.
Swedish Court, 273.
"Sylph," the, 309.

TALBOT, Silas, 469-470.
"Tamar," the, 419-420.
"Tartar," the, of the Massachusetts navy, 339, 353.
"Tartar," the, of the Virginia navy, 406.
Taylor, Richard, 397, 407.
"Tempest," the, 406-407, 411, 414
Ternay, Chevalier de, 207.
"Terrible," the, 448.
Texel, the, Holland, 204, 271, 297-298, 437.
"Thetis," the, 407, 411.
Thompson, Thomas, 133.
Tilghman, Walter, 447.
Tillinghast, Daniel, 95.
Tories, 338, 348, 370, 448
Travis, Edward, 397.
"Trepassey," the, 206.
"Trimmer," the, 393.
"Truite," the, 433, 434.
Trumbull, Jonathan, 92, 95, 354, 355.
"Trumbull," the, 92, 113, 204, 206, 220, 235, 238-239.
Tucker, Samuel, 292.
Tufts, Simon, 420-421.
Turner, George, 227.
Turpin, Joseph, 421.
"Tyrannicide," the, 325, 328, 342, 343, 345, 349, 352.

UNIFORMS, of Continental navy, 117-118; of Massachusetts navy, 327; of Pennsylvania marines, 377; of Maryland marines, 441.

VARNUM, J. M., 223.
Vergennes, French minister, 261, 284, 285, 289, 291.
Vernon, William, 98-99, 113, 182.
"Victory," the, 87.
"Virginia," the frigate, 93, 124.
"Virginia," the ship, of the Royal navy, 350.
"Virginia," the ship, of the Virginia navy, 407.
Virginia Board of Trade, 409.
Virginia Board of War, 409.
Virginia commissioners for defence of Chesapeake bay, 415-416.
Virginia Commissioner of Navy, 409, 415.
Virginia Committee of Safety, 396-398.
Virginia General Assembly, 401-404, 408-411, 415.
Virginia Governor and Council, 399, 401, 403, 411.
Virginia Naval Commissioner, 409.
Virginia naval magazines, 401.
Virginia Navy, 152, 315, 396-417, 429, 446-447, 449, 450, 456-458; beginnings of, 396-403; navy board, 398-403; admiralty courts, 403-405; vessels, 397-398, 405-408, 414-417; raids, 408, 413-415; later legislation, 408-413, 415-416; end of navy, 416-417.
Virginia Navy Board, 398-403, 405, 408, 409, 424.
Virginia navy-yards, 400, 408, 414.
Virginia Provincial Convention, 396, 398, 403.

WALLACE, James, 463.
Ward, Artemas, 69, 351.
Ward, Samuel, 81, 83.
Waring, Thomas, 190-191.
Warner, Seth, 74.
Warren, James, 51, 98, 112, 330.
"Warren," the frigate, 92, 119, 136, 168, 171, 349, 468.
"Warren," the schooner, 63.
Warwick, Va., 401, 414.

Washington, George, 33, 37, 42, 48, 73, 116, 154, 166, 167, 204, 211, 362, 388, 422, 446, 468, 473; fleets of, 61-71; on failure of navy, 184-186; on committees of Congress, 213.
"Washington," the, of the Continental navy (frigate), 92, 388.
"Washington," the, of the Continental navy (ship), 235, 248-249, 393-396.
"Washington," the, of the Georgia navy, 460-461.
"Washington," the, of the North Carolina navy, 452-454.
"Washington," the, of the Rhode Island navy (galley), 466.
"Washington," the, of the Rhode Island navy (sloop), 464, 465.
"Washington," the, of the Virginia navy, 406, 456.
"Washington," the, of Washington's fleet, 63, 65.
"Wasp," the, 55, 57, 158.
Waterford, Conn., 370.
Waterbury, David, 77, 358.
"Watt," the, 206-207.
Weaver, Lieutenant, 58.
Webb, William, 377.
"West Florida," the, 310-311.
West Indies, the, 80, 151, 161, 165, 167, 169, 173, 175, 179, 207, 236, 237, 242, 283, 305-307, 335, 342, 358, 368-369, 406, 424, 429, 430, 449, 452.
Wethersfield, Conn., 355, 356.
"Weymouth," the, 368.
Whaley, Commodore, 450.
Whaling fleets, 151, 170, 268, 278-279.
Wharton, John, 96, 97, 101, 196, 374, 387.
Whipple, Abraham, 54-55, 57, 80, 133, 172, 433, 464-465.
Whipple, William, 89, 90, 105-106, 190, 211.
White, Robert, 373.
"Whiting," the, 360, 369.

Whiting, Thomas, 260.
Wickes, Lambert, 173, 179, 262, 269, 287-291.
Williams, Jonathan, 256.
Williams, J. F., 345.
Williamsburg, Va., 93, 398.
Willing, Captain, 308.
Wilson, Willis, 458.
Wilmington, N. C., 93, 434.
Winder, William, 101, 196.
"Winthrop," the, 339, 353.
"Wolodimer," the, 304.
Woodford, Thomas, 193.
Wynkoop, Jacobus, 72, 74.
Wythe, George, 203.

"Yarmouth," the, 431.
"York," the, 416.
Yorktown, siege of, 415, 446
Young, John, 208.

Zubly, John J., 82.